Distributed Programming

A. Udaya Shankar

Distributed Programming

Theory and Practice

 Springer

A. Udaya Shankar
Department of Computer Science
University of Maryland
Paint Branch Dr
College Park, MD
USA

ISBN 978-1-4899-9593-3   ISBN 978-1-4614-4881-5 (eBook)
DOI 10.1007/978-1-4614-4881-5
Springer New York Heidelberg Dordrecht London

In memory of my parents, Ajjampur Ananthapadmanabha Rau and Vishalakshi.

To Carol and Naveen.

Preface

This book presents a practical and rigorous method to write correct distributed programs. A *distributed* program, also called a *concurrent* or *multi-threaded* program, is executed simultaneously by multiple interacting threads that may be spread over more than one computer. An example is a distributed web program in which a thread executing a browser program interacts with a thread executing a server program. In contrast, a *single-threaded* program is executed by a single thread; it interacts with the environment only at the start and at the end.

Distributed programs, originally present only in operating systems, are now everywhere. Practically every interactive digital system, from a digital camera to a computer network, is a realization of a distributed program. Most programming languages now support distributed programming, providing constructs to create threads to execute functions and constructs to synchronize threads (e.g., semaphores, locks, and condition variables).

Writing *correct* distributed programs is not easy because, in addition to the difficulties of single-threaded programming, one has to account for all possible variations in the execution speeds of threads (i.e., race conditions). This book uses the well-established discipline of *assertional reasoning* for this purpose. It is worth noting that for a single-threaded program, assertional reasoning reduces to annotating the program with pre- and postconditions and loop invariants, a discipline usually covered in introductory programming courses.

A related difficulty is in achieving *compositionality*. A program is usually a collection of interacting component programs. Consider a program B that interacts with a program A. In order to write B without delving into the internals of A (regardless of whether or not A's source code is available), one needs a definition of the intended external behavior of A. We refer to this as the *service* of A. The service of A plays two roles: (1) it is used instead of A when writing B and (2) it defines the conditions that A, or any program that *implements* the service, must satisfy. If A is single-threaded, its service simply defines A's outputs in terms of its inputs. But if A is multi-threaded, it is not so simple. The service must define all possible outputs of A for every possible sequence of past inputs and outputs, and do this in a way that is usable for the two roles mentioned above.

In this book, services are defined by *service programs*, which are programs with special structure and powerful synchronization constructs. These features make a service program easy to understand. Because it is a regular program, it can be directly used as a component when writing other programs. We show how to prove that a program implements a service.

Most books on distributed programming focus on a particular distributed programming language. They describe how to write distributed programs in that language, but not how to ensure that the programs are correct regardless of variations in thread speeds. They also do not give a way to define services. In particular, they characterize the external behavior of a program A by a so-called interface, which states the signatures of A's public functions. But this is not adequate as a service: the signature of a function does not relate its outputs to inputs, nor does it define all the situations when the function can be called.

There are books that rigorously address both difficulties mentioned above. They have methods to account for all possible variations in thread speeds, and they have methods to define services. However, they typically use a programming notation that hides threads. A program is written as a collection of atomic actions any of which can be executed at any time (perhaps constrained by a boolean guard). Thread creation and thread synchronization are not explicit. As a result, their programs and proofs are very elegant, but translating the programs into a real programming language is not straightforward. Perhaps this is why these methods are not commonly used by programmers.

The purpose of this book is to explain a practical method to write services of distributed programs and to write correct distributed programs that can make use of services. The method, called SESF (for "Systems and Services Framework"), uses a realistic programming notation, so that whatever is practiced in the book can also be done easily with real-life distributed programming languages (such as C, C++, Java, Python).

This book presents numerous applications of SESF to problems in distributed computing and networking. It consists of three parts. The first part introduces SESF by examples of gradually increasing complexity: simple locks, bounded buffers, channels, and sliding window protocols. The second part presents the theory underlying SESF. The third part consists entirely of applications to classical problems in distributed computing, including locks, termination detection, object transfer, shared memory, network sockets, and transport protocols. There are exercises throughout, some straightforward and some quite sophisticated. Solutions are available on the book's website.

An undergraduate course can easily cover the first part, preferably accompanied by coding the examples in a real language, say Python. A graduate course can cover most, if not all, of the book. Professional programmers can use the book to learn an effective way to think about distributed programs.

Acknowledgments

This book has suffered a long and torturous gestation, involving at least one re-incarnation. As such, there are many people who have influenced the book, directly or indirectly. There are some I would like to thank specifically.

Simon Lam and Jayadev Misra got me started in this area long ago and supported me in my efforts over the years. Simon was my Ph.D. advisor; he introduced me to computer networking protocols and their compositional verification. Jayadev introduced me to distributed programming and assertional reasoning. They have had a profound, albeit indirect, influence on this book.

Tamer El-Sharnouby, a former Ph.D. student, showed me how to bring SESF into the context of real programming languages. He wrote service programs in Java for several network protocols. He developed a distributed harness for testing a protocol implementation against its service program, and used it in an undergraduate computer networks course. His work convinced me to make threads explicit, which resulted in a new incarnation of SESF.

Kirsten Stephen and Jeff Stuckman provided valuable feedback when they were students in a graduate class in which I used an earlier draft of this book. Kirsten combed the material like a crime scene, exposing loose ends and dubious accounts. Jeff taught me a devious property about distributed timestamps that I had never suspected.

Bobby Bhattacharjee has provided keen insights and advice at various points during the writing of this book. He also suggested the title of the book, a drastic improvement over the title I originally had in mind. Hanan Samet has been a source of inspiration and support throughout my years at UMD, especially in difficult times. Larry Davis has kindly spared me from certain administrative and teaching tasks during the book's interminable "almost finished" state. Ashok Agrawala has generously made me a co-conspirator in many of his endeavors over the years, expanding my horizons in unsuspecting ways.

Carol Whitney, my wife, has given me ample emotional and intellectual support. Early on, she read *several* drafts, giving crucial advice on what worked and what did not. Near the end, she exhorted me to put the book out of its misery before I get further behind. Throughout, she has taken me to beautiful places with elegant birds.

Maryland, USA   A. Udaya Shankar

Contents

Chapter 1
Introduction

1.1 Objective

In the computer world, active entities are called **threads** and they execute **programs**, analogous to cooks executing recipes. (Threads are also known as "processes".) A program is said to be **single-threaded** if at most one thread is executing it at any time. The thread starts when the environment calls the program and ends by returning an output to the environment. In contrast, a **distributed** program, also known as a **multi-threaded** program, can have multiple threads executing it simultaneously, interacting with each other while executing. A distributed program is often made up of multiple programs, perhaps spread over different computers. Distributed programs are everywhere, in the hardware level of processors and IO devices, in operating systems, in computer networks, and in distributed applications.

Writing correct distributed programs is not easy. The fundamental difficulty, not present in single-threaded programming, is in ensuring that the program works correctly regardless of variations in the execution speeds of threads. Because program code usually effects non-linear transformations, practically every multi-threaded program has the following characteristic: *small variations in the execution speeds of its threads result in widely differing evolutions.* Consequently a multi-threaded program has many possible evolutions, and any particular behavior is not easily reproducible. This is why debugging a distributed program is so infuriating.

Our objective is to design programs so that *every* possible evolution does what it is supposed to do. Such programs would work correctly in any environment, regardless of variations in the speeds of their threads. A related objective is **compositionality**, which allows one to write a program that makes use of other programs without delving into the internals of the other programs. This is essential

A.U. Shankar, *Distributed Programming: Theory and Practice*,
DOI 10.1007/978-1-4614-4881-5__1,
© Springer Science+Business Media New York 2013

if the source code of the other programs is not available; even if it is, one may not able to keep track of all the details. To achieve these objectives, the following are needed:

- A method to express the *desired external behavior* of a program. We refer to this description as the **service** of the program. (In software engineering, this is often called the *specification* of the program.) Because the service, unlike the program, is not constrained by implementation and efficiency issues, it is usually much easier to understand than the program. The service B of a program A is used instead of A when *writing* a program C that has A as a component. When C is *executed*, B is replaced by A or by any other program that implements B.
- A definition of "program **implements** service" such that, in any program C that makes use of a service B, if B is replaced by any program A that implements B, then program C continues to satisfy *all* the properties that it previously did.
- A method to establish whether a given program implements its intended service. The fundamental obstacle for any such method is to account for *all* the possible evolutions of the program. Practically any program with parameters and unbounded data structures would have a large, typically unbounded, set of evolutions.

Compositional design of single-threaded programs is a standard discipline. It is usually covered in introductory programming courses, using pre- and post-conditions for services and program annotation for proofs. Handling multi-threaded programs is not standard, and that is the subject of this book. Our approach, distilled to its essence, is as follows. Services are expressed as programs with special structure, referred to as **service programs**. Consequently, when designing a program C that makes use of a service B, the latter can be inserted just like a regular component program. Another consequence is that the definition of "program A implements service B" reduces to correctness properties of a hypothetical program of A and a modified B. The hypothetical program can be analyzed using any program analysis method, and our choice is **assertional reasoning**. The remainder of this chapter gives a more leisurely introduction to distributed programs, assertional reasoning, and our approach to compositional design and implementation.

1.2 Programs and Services

A program is made up of **instructions**, organized into **main code** and **functions**. A program comes to life when it is *instantiated*, at which point an instance of the program, referred to as a **system**, is set up (in computer memory) and a thread starts executing the system's main code. The thread leaves the system when it reaches the end of the main code, but the system remains in existence until it is explicitly terminated. While the system exists, threads in the environment can call its functions. In addition to defining and updating variables, instructions of the system can do three things with respect to threads and systems. First, they can create new

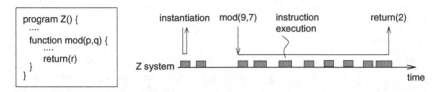

Fig. 1.1 Program Z and an evolution of its system

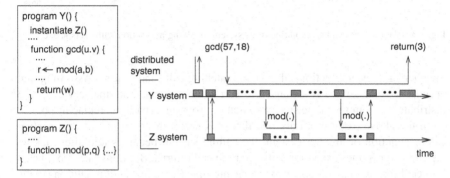

Fig. 1.2 An evolution of the distributed system of Y and Z

threads and start them executing functions of the system. Second, instructions can call functions of *other* systems, causing threads to start executing the functions in the called systems. This is how systems interact. A thread terminates when it completes executing its function. Thus in general, a system has zero or more threads, each executing some function of the system. Third, instructions can instantiate programs, thereby creating a collection of systems executing concurrently, perhaps on different computers.

Figure 1.1 illustrates a program, named Z, that has a function, named mod, that takes two integer parameters, p and q, and returns the remainder of p divided by q. Also shown is an evolution of a Z system. The program's inputs are its instantiation and mod(p,q) calls, and its outputs are the returns of these calls. Assuming that at most one call of mod is supposed to be ongoing at any time, the *service* of Z would define as acceptable any sequence of alternating calls and returns such that (1) the value returned after a mod(p,q) call equals the remainder of p divided by q, and (2) every call is eventually followed by a return. Note that the service places constraints on both Z and its environment. The environment is constrained to call function mod only when no other call is ongoing and only with integer parameters. Z is constrained to eventually return every call of mod with the proper value.

Figure 1.2 illustrates a program Y that has a function gcd that takes two integer parameters and returns their greatest common denominator. Program Y makes use of program Z to help in this task; specifically, Y instantiates Z, and gcd repeatedly calls the Z system's mod function. Also shown is an evolution of the distributed system of Y and Z. It consists of a Y system evolution and a Z system evolution "stitched

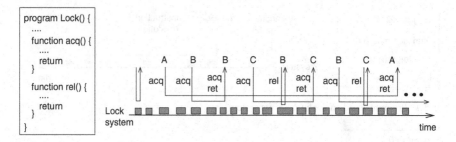

Fig. 1.3 Program Lock and an evolution of its system involving interaction with users A, B, C

together" at their interactions, that is, at matching calls and returns. Assuming that at most one call of gcd is supposed to be ongoing at any time, the service of the distributed system would be similar to that of program Z (with gcd replacing mod).

In the above examples, only one thread is *active* at any time: when a system calls a function of another system, the calling system becomes idle after making the call and resumes execution only after the call returns. But things need not be so limited. Programs can be designed to have multiple (incoming and/or outgoing) calls ongoing at the same time. For example, consider a program Lock that implements a *lock*, which is a popular building block of distributed systems. Lock has two functions that other systems, which we refer to as "users", can call: acq, to acquire the lock; and rel, to release the lock. Different users can call acq concurrently. A user requests the lock when it calls acq and acquires the lock when the call returns; Lock returns the call only when the lock is not currently held by a user. Such a call is said to be **blocking**. In contrast, a release call is **non-blocking**; Lock can return it immediately. Figure 1.3 illustrates the program and an evolution of its system. Lock's inputs are its instantiation, acq calls and rel calls. Its outputs are the instantiation return, acq returns and rel returns. Its service would define as acceptable any sequence of instantiation call and instantiation return followed by acq calls, acq returns, rel calls, and rel returns such that:

1. For every user u, the interactions with u cycle through acq call, acq return, rel call, and rel return. (Thus only a user without the lock can request the lock, and only a user with the lock can release it.)
2. Between every two acq returns, there is a rel call. (Thus at most one user has the lock at any time.)
3. Every rel call is followed eventually (i.e., not necessarily immediately) by its return.
4. If every acq return is followed eventually by a rel call, then every acq call is followed eventually by its return. (Thus if no user holds the lock indefinitely, then every acquire request is satisfied.)

Figure 1.4 illustrates a program ProdCons that starts three other systems, namely, instantiations of programs Producer, Consumer, and Lock. Producer puts items into Consumer, and they both make use of Lock to synchronize their activities, for example,

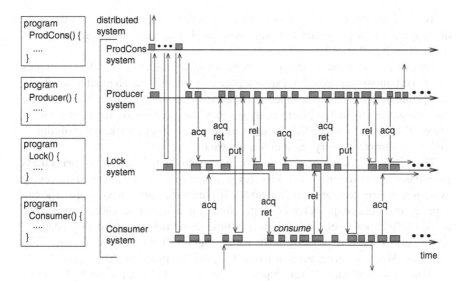

Fig. 1.4   An evolution of the distributed system of ProdCons, Producer, Lock, and Consumer

to ensure that Consumer does not try to consume an item while it is being put in by Producer. Also shown is an evolution of the distributed system of all four systems. Clearly, small changes in the speeds of the component systems can result in very different evolutions of the distributed system, unlike in the case of programs Y and Z. In Fig. 1.4 for example, if the Consumer system is faster, it may obtain the lock several times before finding items to consume. Indeed, the program has a serious flaw: if the Producer system is much faster than the ProdCons system, it will attempt to acquire the lock *before* the lock system has been created, resulting in a fault. The figure also shows that a system need not remain idle between issuing a call and getting the return; Producer is idle while its first lock acquire is pending, but not while its second lock acquire is pending.

1.3   Correctness Properties and Assertional Reasoning

Our objective is to design programs such that every possible evolution satisfies desired properties. Evolutions have been illustrated in the preceding figures. We now make the notion precise. An **evolution** of a program is a sequence of alternating states and transitions of the program. Each transition is the execution of a statement; it takes the program from the preceding state to the succeeding state and perhaps involves an input or output. An evolution always starts with an initial state (a value assignment to any program parameters). It can be finite, in which case it ends in a state, or infinite. Given an evolution, every prefix ending in a state is an evolution. The **state** of a program, if it does not start another system, is defined by the values of its variables and the location (i.e., next instruction to execute) of each thread in the program. If the program starts other systems, then its state would include a state for each such system.

Invariably, one is interested in the behavior of a program only when its inputs satisfy certain assumptions. For example, one may assume that an input is an integer or a prime number, or that a function is called by at most one thread at any time. These assumptions should be explicitly stated in the program. An input is said to be **allowed** in a state if it satisfies the input assumptions in that state. An evolution is said to be **allowed** if every input in it is allowed.

The class of properties that we are interested in are so-called **correctness properties**. A correctness property for a program is a statement about every evolution of the program. For all practical purposes, correctness properties can express any desired property of a program (including invariance, termination, deadlock-freedom, livelock-freedom, real-time properties, sample-path probabilistic properties, etc.). A property holds for a program iff it holds for *every allowed* evolution. When the program is instantiated in another program, the property would hold for the instantiation *if* every input it gets is allowed; if not, one has to do a fresh analysis of the evolutions of the instantiation.

There are fundamentally two kinds of correctness properties, **safety properties** and **progress properties** (also called *liveness* properties). Roughly speaking, a safety property states that "nothing bad" happens, whereas a progress property states that "something good" eventually happens. Consider program Lock of Fig. 1.3, for example. A desired safety property would be "at most one user has the lock". A desired progress property may be "every acquire call eventually returns". But in fact the latter is not realizable; one has to settle for the weaker progress property that "every acquire call eventually returns provided no user holds the lock indefinitely".

We need a convenient method to state and prove correctness properties of a program. Our choice is **assertional reasoning**. Here, correctness properties are expressed by temporal logic formulas, or **assertions** for short. Assertions consist of *predicates*, which are boolean-valued expressions in the program state, and *temporal operators*, which apply the predicates to sequences of program states. We use four temporal operators: **invariant** and **unless** for safety properties, and **leads-to** and **fairness** for progress properties. An invariant assertion has the form $Inv\,P$, where P is a predicate; it means that P always holds. Formally, it is satisfied by an evolution if every non-initial state of the evolution satisfies P. A leads-to assertion has the form P *leads-to* Q, where P and Q are predicates; it says that if P holds at some point then eventually Q holds. Formally, it is satisfied by an evolution if, for every non-initial state of the evolution that satisfies P, that state or some later state in the evolution satisfies Q. Unless and fairness assertions are described later. Finally, an evolution with an undefined transition (division by zero, out-of-bound array reference, etc.) does not satisfy *any* assertion.

To illustrate, consider the trivial program U in Fig. 1.5. It has an integer parameter N and integer variables x, na and nr initialized to zero. It has two functions callable by the environment, add and rmv. The former increments x and na if $x < N$ holds.

```
program U(int N) {
    // input assumption: at most one thread
    // is in the program at any time

    x ← 0; na ← 0; nr ← 0;

    function add() {
        if (x < N)
            {x ← x+1; na ← na+1;}
    }

    function rmv() {
        if (x > 0)
            {x ← x-1; nr ← nr+1;}
    }
}
```

Fig. 1.5 Program U

The latter decrements x and increments nr if x > 0 holds. Its input assumption states that there can be at most one thread in the program at any time, i.e., at most one call to U (to either add or rmv) is ongoing at any time.

Here are two assertions about the program. The first says that nr never exceeds na. The second says that nr eventually attains any value attained by na.

- *Inv* $nr \leq na$
- forall($k: na = k$ *leads-to* $nr = k$)

Having expressed desired correctness properties of a program by assertions, one is faced with the task of proving that the program satisfies the assertions. In assertional reasoning, this is done by developing a sequence of *intermediate* assertions leading to the desired assertions such that each assertion in the sequence follows from the program and previous assertions via a straightforward proof. The intermediate assertions are usually developed in *reverse* order, starting from the desired assertions. In each step, one takes an existing assertion and identifies additional conditions that, together with the program, imply the assertion; these additional conditions then become new intermediate assertions. It is worth noting that for a single-threaded program that interacts with the environment only at the start and the end, assertional reasoning reduces to the familiar method of "annotating" the program with predicates such that each statement satisfies its pre- and post-conditions (i.e., executing the statement with the preceding predicate holding results in the following predicate holding).

Whether the sequence of intermediate assertions is generated in forward order or reverse order, each step consists, in general, of proving that the program satisfies a given assertion assuming that it satisfies other assertions. There are two fundamentally different ways of doing this: operational and assertional. An **operational proof** considers an arbitrary evolution of the program and reasons about it in natural language, with statements like "if B holds now then C must have held at some earlier point" and so on. Here is an operational proof that program U (Fig. 1.5) satisfies assertion $Inv\, nr \leq na$.

> *Proof.* Variable nr can be incremented only if x can be decremented. The latter can happen only if x has already been incremented, in which case na has already been incremented. Thus nr can be incremented only if na has already been incremented. Hence $Inv\, nr \leq na$ holds.   □

Operational proofs come naturally to humans. They can give insight but they are error-prone. Their accuracy and readability depend entirely on the analyst's maturity and clarity of expression. For example, program U would not satisfy $Inv\, nr \leq na$ if x were initially positive, say 1. Yet the above operational proof does not mention the initial value of x.

An **assertional proof**, on the other hand, establishes an assertion by applying a "proof rule" to the program and assumed assertions. Here are two proof rules for program U (Fig. 1.5), where P, Q and R are any predicates in U's variables:

Proof rule 1. Program U satisfies $Inv\, P$ if

- P holds after the initial step (initialization of x, na, nr).
- Functions add and rmv each *unconditionally* preserves P. (This means that executing the function assuming *only* that P holds prior to the execution results in P holding after the execution.)

Proof rule 2. Program U satisfies $Inv\, R$ if

- $(P \text{ and } Q) \Rightarrow R$ holds
- U satisfies $Inv\, P$ and $Inv\, Q$.

Note that predicate $nr \leq na$ does not satisfy proof rule 1 because function rmv does not unconditionally preserve the predicate. (If nr equals na prior to its execution, then $nr \leq na$ does not hold after the execution.) Here is an assertional proof that program U satisfies assertion $Inv\, nr \leq na$. It is based on the observation that $nr+x$ equals na and that x is never negative.

> *Proof.* Predicate $nr+x = na$ satisfies proof rule 1. (Specifically, x, na and nr are initialized to zero; add increases both x and na; and rmv decreases x and increases na.) Thus U satisfies $Inv\, nr+x = na$. Predicate $x \geq 0$ also satisfies proof rule 1. Thus U satisfies $Inv\, x \geq 0$. Predicates $nr+x = na$ and $x \geq 0$ imply $nr \leq na$. Hence U satisfies $Inv\, nr \leq na$ by proof rule 2.   □

Assertional proofs involve a different way of thinking from operational proofs. They can give wonderful insight, especially for multi-threaded programs. Furthermore, an assertional proof can be *checked* without understanding the program, which makes it free from hidden (and potentially false) assumptions about the program. In fact, it can be mechanically checked by a first-order theorem prover (e.g., [24, 26, 27, 75, 93, 106]), but this is an arduous undertaking.

In summary, assertional reasoning on a program involves developing a sequence of assertions such that each assertion follows from the program and earlier assertions via an operational or assertional proof. Both operational and assertional proofs have their merits. Sometimes only an assertional proof can provide clarity and rigor. Sometimes an operational proof is adequate and much shorter. Overall, assertional reasoning can achieve rigor without excessive formalism.

It is worth emphasizing that the analysis of programs is, in general, *not* a mechanical procedure. Although an assertional proof can be mechanically checked, developing the proof requires invention. For instance, in the above assertional proof of program U, formulating the key predicate, $nr+x = na$, required invention. There are methods, such as model checking (e.g., [21, 22]), that can automatically analyze *finite-state* programs, i.e., programs whose variables range over an adequately small set of values. They do this, roughly speaking, by generating the states of the program reachable from the initial state and evaluating them against the desired properties. These methods are used successfully on program models of digital hardware, which have the desired finite-state characteristics. But *most* programs are not finite-state programs. They use unbounded variables (e.g., integers, sequences) in ways such that their range of values cannot be provably abstracted by small sets. Also, methods like model checking cannot handle parameterized properties; for example, they can analyze program U for particular values of N (e.g., $N = 1, \cdots, 100$) but not for N uninstantiated (except in very special cases, e.g., [46, 53]).

1.4   Services and Systems Framework (SESF)

Given the above background on programs and assertional reasoning, we are now in a position to describe our approach to compositional design and implementation. The approach, called SESF (for "Services and Systems Framework"), is characterized by the following features, which are expanded upon in the rest of this chapter.

- **Programs:** Programs are written in a generic programming syntax (along the lines of Java and Python). Functions callable from the environment are referred to as "input" functions. The program can create threads and start them executing functions, call input functions of other systems, and instantiate programs. The program makes explicit the atomicity and progress assumed of the underlying execution platform, which eliminates a common source of ambiguity in distributed programs and is essential for any meaningful analysis. Programs whose assumptions are satisfied by typical platforms are referred to as "implementation" programs.
- **Service programs:** A service is expressed by a service program, which is a program with special structure. It has input functions and "output" functions.

The former do not call other systems, and the latter always call other systems. Every atomic step involves an input or an output. The program can start threads at any time but only to execute output functions. It does not start any system. Because of its structure, a service program describes external behavior without any internal implementation constraints. Service programs, unlike implementation programs, can assume unrealistic atomicity and progress of their platforms.

- **Implements relation:**   Program A implements program B if (1) A can accept any input that is valid with respect to B, (2) any output A does is valid with respect to B, and (3) A satisfies the progress assumption of B. For the case where B is a service program, these conditions are cast as correctness properties of a hypothetical distributed program of A and a modified B, which can be analyzed using any program analysis method and can be mechanically tested by executing it. If A implements B, then A can replace B in any program C without disturbing any correctness properties of C.

- **Assertional reasoning:**   As described earlier, the program analysis method we choose is assertional reasoning based on temporal logic, because it can achieve rigor without excessive formalism. Assertions are a convenient way to codify the intermediate steps of an analysis. They can be proved by operational arguments or by proof rule applications, and they can be mechanically checked in testing.

Programming conventions   Our programs look like Java programs in overall structure, e.g., code blocks, variable definitions, and function definitions. For brevity, we make extensive use of untyped variables and container structures (sets, sequences, maps), where we use Python-like syntax. The intent is not to develop a new programming language but to have a convenient notation that can be readily translated to existing languages.

One difference from Java and Python is in the operators for assignment and equality. Assignment is denoted by "$\leftarrow$" and not "=", as in "x$\leftarrow$4". Equality is denoted by "=" and not "= =", as in "3+1 = 4". We do this to avoid saying "3+1 equals equals 4". Another difference is that the name of a container structure (e.g., a set), when used in an expression, stands for the value of the structure rather than a pointer to the structure. Thus if x and y are two sets, then "x = y" means that the two sets have the same contents and not that they point to the same structure. (In Java, this would be written like "x.equals(y)".)

1.5   Programs in SESF

A **program** has main code and functions. Functions of the program callable from the environment are referred to as **input functions**. A program is instantiated when a thread in the environment executes a "start-system" instruction with the program name as a parameter. At this point a system, referred to as a **basic system**, is created, and the instantiating thread executes its main code and returns upon encountering a "return" instruction. Calling an input function of a system is similar:

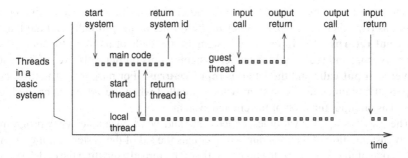

Fig. 1.6 Evolution of threads in a basic system

the calling thread executes the function body and returns upon encountering a "return" instruction. (Actually, if the called system and the calling thread are in different address spaces, a "proxy" thread is created in the called system to execute code on behalf of the calling thread. But we can treat the two threads as the same *for purposes of analysis* because the calling thread waits for the proxy thread to complete.)

There is another way in which threads can start executing within a basic system. A thread in the system can create a new thread and start it executing a (non-input) function of the system. We refer to such threads as **local threads** of the system. We refer to threads that have entered the system by calling its input functions or main code as **guest threads**.

Every system gets a unique **system id**, or **sid** for short. The sid is either chosen arbitrarily at creation time or chosen earlier and passed as a parameter at instantiation. The sid is needed for calling an input function of the system. Typically, it is returned by the main code. If the main code has created additional systems, it may also return their sids.

Every thread gets a unique **thread id**, or **tid** for short, either chosen arbitrarily at creation time or chosen earlier and passed as a parameter. When a local thread is created, its tid is returned to the creating thread. Figure 1.6 illustrates an evolution of the threads in a basic system.

A thread is terminated when it reaches the end of the function it was started to execute. A system is terminated when an "end-system" instruction has been executed in the system and the system is in a so-called **endable** state, which means that (1) there are no guest threads in the system and (2) no local thread of the system is in a call to another system's function. Upon system termination, all local threads are terminated and the system's state is cleaned up. Waiting for the system to be endable ensures that a thread is not left in limbo. The wait should be finite.

A call of an input function of a system has the form x.f(p), where f is the name of the function, p are the parameters (if any) of the function, and x is the sid of the called system. The call itself is an output of the calling system and an input to the called system. The return, on the other hand, is an input to the calling system and an output of the called system. Thus the **outputs** of a system are the calls it does to input functions (of other systems) and the returns it does to calls of its input functions (by other systems); we refer to the former as **output calls** and the latter as **output returns**. The **inputs** to a system are the calls of its input functions (by other systems) and the returns (by other systems) to its output calls; we refer to the former as **input calls** and the latter as **input returns**. For purposes of inputs and outputs, the main code of a system, which is called when the system is created, is treated as an input function of the created system.

There are two special variables, called mysid and mytid, available in any program. In any instantiation of the program, mysid equals the sid of the system. At any point in the code of the system, mytid equals the tid of the thread executing the code. These variables cannot be modified by the program.

Finally, a basic system is said to become **faulty** if it executes an undefined operation (division by zero, out-of-bound array reference, dereferencing a null pointer, etc.). Once a system becomes faulty, it may crash, execute abnormally, whatever; in particular, it would not satisfy any correctness assertion. We do not care what a system does after it becomes faulty.

1.5.1 Input Assumptions

Recall that analyzing a program invariably involves making assumptions about the inputs it can receive from the environment. These assumptions are explicitly stated in the program. Every input function of a program has an attribute called the **input assumption**, which is a predicate in the function's parameters and the program's variables that is *assumed* to hold when the function is called. Similarly, an output call has an input assumption associated with its return, stating what is assumed to hold when the call returns. Similarly, the main code has an input assumption stating what is assumed of the parameters of the program.

Type constraints on an input are part of the input assumption. But input assumptions can also express more complex constraints, for example, the constraint that a parameter is a prime number, or the constraint that a lock's rel is called by the same thread whose acq call was the last to return. For our purposes, *input assumptions are for analysis only*. The program need not check them, but it may do so, say, for error reporting or efficient implementation.

1.5.2 Platforms

Every program executes on some underlying **platform**. Platforms range from the primitive, such as that provided by bare computer hardware, to the sophisticated, such as that provided by an operating system (which is itself a multi-threaded program executing over bare hardware). A platform can be limited to a single computer or span a network of computers (perhaps on one chip). Whatever the platform, every multi-threaded program makes assumptions about the atomicity and progress provided by the platform. We explain below the nature of these assumptions, why one cannot analyze the program without identifying them, and what the typical platform provides. Programs whose assumptions are satisfied by typical platforms are referred to as **implementation programs**. In contrast, service programs assume unrealistically powerful atomicity and progress.

1.5.3 Atomicity Assumptions About the Platform and Effective Atomicity

The **atomicity assumption** of a program identifies the chunks of the program that the underlying platform is assumed to execute "atomically", that is, as *indivisible units whose intermediate states are not influenced or observed by the environment.* (This is made precise when we explain effective atomicity below.) The issue of atomicity arises when two instructions of the program are executed simultaneously (by different threads) and one of them writes into a variable accessed by the other. The two instructions are said to **conflict**. For example, suppose a memory location x is simultaneously updated by two threads, one updating it to 12 and the other to 34, as shown in Fig. 1.7. If writes to x are atomic, then x ends up being either 12 or 34. If only writes of individual digits of x are atomic, then x ends up being 12, 34, 14 or 32, depending on how the digit updates were interleaved. If only each bit of x is atomically updated, then x ends up being any one of the possible merges of the bit string of 12 and the bit string of 34. If atomicity is not present at any granularity, then x may end up being any a bit pattern or, worse yet, the system may become faulty. Fundamentally, without any atomicity, a multi-threaded program cannot be viewed as a discrete-event system.

Bare computer hardware invariably provides atomic reads and atomic writes of individual memory words. It may also provide a limited set of atomic read-modify-write operations on a memory word, such as a test-and-set instruction. An operating system platform usually provides more powerful atomicity constructs, such as locks, condition variables, semaphores, and message sends and receives.

Not every statement of a multi-threaded program needs to be covered by the atomicity assumption. It need not cover a statement R if no conflicting statement can be executed simultaneously with R. (The program may have no conflicting statement, or it may not have threads that execute them simultaneously, or it may use a lock to prevent their simultaneous execution.) Furthermore, such an R can be treated as part of an adjacent atomic statement. More generally, a code chunk can be treated

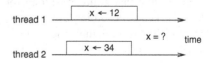

Fig. 1.7 Conflict: simultaneous execution of statements with write overlap

as atomic *for purposes of analysis* if it contains at most one statement that conflicts with code executed by other threads and that statement (if present) is atomic. Such a code chunk is "effectively" atomic. Formally, code chunk S is **effectively atomic** if for every evolution x of the program in which S is executed, there is an evolution y in which (1) S is executed *without* intervening executions of non-S statements, and (2) y has the same sequence of inputs and outputs as does x.

The analysis of a multi-threaded program becomes easier as its atomicity becomes coarser. Hence the first step in the analysis is invariably to identify effectively-atomic code chunks, making use of any of various sufficient conditions that have been developed, e.g., [23, 25, 39, 70, 72, 74, 91].

1.5.4   Progress Assumptions About the Platform

The **progress assumption** of a program identifies the progress expected of the underlying platform in executing the threads of the program. Implementation programs typically assume **weak fairness** for threads, which just means that every once in a while every thread gets some processor cycles; in other words, the thread executes with non-zero speed. This ensures that if a thread is at a nonblocking statement, then it *eventually* executes that statement. The same is true if the thread is at a blocking statement (e.g., a lock acquire) *and* the statement is *continuously* unblocked (i.e., the lock is continuously available). Formally, weak fairness of a thread is satisfied by an evolution if either the evolution is finite and the thread is blocked in the last state of the evolution, or the evolution is infinite and the thread eventually takes a step if it is continuously unblocked.

One may also assume **strong fairness** for a thread at certain blocking statements, which means that if the thread is at such a statement and the statement is either unblocked continuously or unblocked intermittently but *infinitely often*, then the thread eventually executes the statement. (Weak fairness cannot ensure this because the thread may get processor cycles only when the statement is blocked.) Formally, strong fairness of a thread is satisfied by an evolution if either the evolution is finite and the thread is blocked in the last state of the evolution, or the evolution is infinite and the thread takes an infinite number of steps if it is infinitely often unblocked.

Practically any decent platform provides weak-fairness for the threads executing on it. In a bare hardware platform, for example, the threads are (CPU and IO) processors and the bus arbiter ensures that each processor gets regular access to memory. A decent operating system platform would ensure that every thread gets regular access to processor cycles and memory pages. Some platforms also provide strong fairness in specific situations. For example, a decent lock implementation would ensure that a thread waiting for the lock eventually gets the lock provided the lock keeps becoming available (i.e., provided a user does not hold the lock forever). In any case, the underlying platform must provide *some* level of progress. Otherwise, the platform can choose to never execute anything, and one cannot claim any progress properties for a program executing on it.

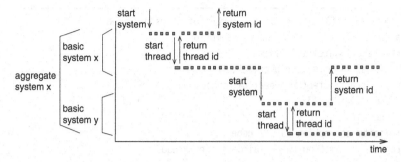

Fig. 1.8 One basic system creating another basic system; the created system returns its sid to the creating thread

1.5.5 Aggregate Systems

Given a basic system x, we define the **aggregate system** x to be the basic system x together with all the basic systems created directly or indirectly by x; i.e., basic system x and all its descendant systems, where y is a descendant of x if y was created by x or by a descendant of x. This is illustrated in Fig. 1.8. For any program Y, define the **aggregate system** Y to be the aggregate system obtained by instantiating Y without renaming or constraining its parameters. *The evolutions and properties of program Y are those of aggregate system Y.*

The inputs of an aggregate system are simply the union of the inputs of its component systems, unless some of these inputs are explicitly hidden from the environment. The outputs of an aggregate system are the union of the outputs of its component systems that are directed to the environment of the aggregate system; i.e., an output of a component system that matches an input of another component system is not an output of the aggregate system.

1.5.6 Composite Systems

It is often convenient to treat an arbitrary collection of basic systems as a system; we refer to such a collection as a **composite system**. An aggregate system is a composite system, but the converse is not necessarily true. When we say "system" without qualifying it as basic or aggregate or composite (either explicitly or from context), then it usually doesn't matter.

```
program ProdCons(J) {    // J: max number of items produced
    ia {J ≥ 1}            // input assumption
    lck ← startSystem(Lock());
    cons ← startSystem(Consumer(lck, J));
    prod ← startSystem(Producer(lck, cons, J));
    return [prod, cons];
    // end main
    atomicity assumption {}  // none
    progress assumption {weak fairness for thread}
}
```

Fig. 1.9 Producer-consumer program

1.5.7   Producer-Consumer-Lock Example

Figure 1.9 outlines a program called ProdCons, based on the producer-consumer-lock example from Fig. 1.4. The program has a parameter J and consists only of main code. The construct ia{...} states the input assumption of the program. When the program is instantiated, a basic system is created and the main code is executed by the instantiating thread. It starts three basic systems, a Lock system, a Consumer system, and a Producer system, recording their (dynamically chosen) sids in variables lck, cons, and prod, respectively. Each sid is passed to subsequent systems at instantiation, so that the consumer can call the lock and the producer can call the lock and the consumer. Finally, it returns the sids of the producer and consumer systems to the instantiating thread. (It could also have returned mysid and/or lck.) Program ProdCons has no atomicity assumption because only one thread executes in it (because it starts no local thread and has no input function). The progress assumption is that this thread executes with weak fairness.

Aggregate system ProdCons involves four basic systems, namely, lck, cons, prod, and the instantiation of ProdCons. Nothing is said about the "physical" distance between the systems. They may be on the same computer, perhaps even threads of a single operating-system-level process. Or they may be on different computers connected by a network. ProdCons may be a real program executed by a computer. Or it may be a virtual program executed by three humans typing at separate computers and interacting (say, over telephone) to ensure that the systems are started in the specified order. What is important about a program is what it does, not who or what executes it.

Figures 1.10–1.12 outline programs Lock, Producer and Consumer, focusing on the inputs, outputs, sids and threads. Lock's main code defines some variables and returns its sid. Lock has three functions: mysid.acq() and mysid.rel(), for acquiring and releasing the lock; and mysid.end(), for initiating termination of the lock system. Each is an input function and returns no value (as indicated by void). Because Lock starts no local threads, at any time after its main code ends the lock system has as many threads executing in it as the number of ongoing input function calls.

```
program Lock() {
    ia {...}
    define variables;
    return mysid;
    // end main

    input void mysid.acq() {
        ia {...}
        ...
        return;
    }

    input void mysid.rel() {
        ia {...}
        ...
        return;
    }

    input void mysid.end() {
        ia {...}
        endSystem();
        return;
    }

    atomicity assumption {...}
    progress assumption {...}
}
```

Fig. 1.10 Lock program

Producer's main code defines some variables and starts a local thread executing function produce. Because Producer has no input function, this is the only thread in the system after the main code ends. The thread repeatedly produces an item, acquires the lock, puts the item into the consumer, and releases the lock. After putting the Jth item into the consumer, the thread executes endSystem, initiating termination of the producer system. The system is endable at this point and so can be terminated immediately.

Consumer's main code defines some variables and starts a local thread executing function consume. Consumer has an input function, mysid.put(.), so at any time after its main code ends it can have guest threads in addition to the local thread. The local thread repeatedly acquires the lock, consumes any items, and releases the lock. When consume gets the Jth item, it initiates termination of the lock system (lck.end) and then of its own system (endSystem). Both systems are endable at this point (because consume gets the final item only after the producer has finished its interactions with the consumer and the lock), and so they can be terminated immediately.

```
program Producer(lck, cons, J) {          program Consumer(lck, J) {
   ia {...}                                  ia {...}
   define variables;                         define variables;
   t ← startThread(produce());               t ← startThread(consume());
   return mysid;                             return mysid;
   // end main                               // end main

   function void produce() {                 function void consume() {
     for (i in 1..J) {                         for (i in 1..J) {
       produce item;                             lck.acq();
       lck.acq();                                consume item;
       cons.put(item);                           lck.rel();
       lck.rel();                              }
     }                                       lck.end();
     endSystem();                            endSystem();
   }                                       }

   atomicity assumption {...}               input void mysid.put(item) {
   progress assumption {...}                   ia {...}
}                                              ...
                                               return;
```
                                            }

Fig. 1.11 Producer program

```
                                            atomicity assumption {...}
                                            progress assumption {...}
                                         }
```

Fig. 1.12 Consumer program

Finally, note that each input function (in Lock and Consumer) has a header of the form mysid.f(p), where f is the function name and p is the function's arguments. Although the prefix mysid is redundant here, we include it because we will soon encounter input functions where the sid prefix is not equal to mysid.

1.6   Service Programs

A **service program** is a program with special structure. Its code has three parts: main code, input functions, and so-called "output" functions. It does not start any new system. It starts a local thread only at the beginning of an output function, as explained below. Atomicity is maximized: the main code is atomically executed, and each subsequent atomic step always involves an input or an output.

An input function of a service program consists of an **input part** followed by an **output part**. The input part consists of an **input condition** followed by code. The input condition, expressed by the construct ic{...}, is a predicate like an input assumption *except that it is checked*. The input part is executed atomically when the input function is called if the input condition holds. If the input condition does not hold when the function is called, *the program becomes faulty*. The output part consists of an **output condition** followed by code. The output condition, expressed by the construct oc{...}, is a predicate like the input condition. The output part is executed atomically only if (but not necessarily if) the output condition holds, and its execution ends by doing the return of the input function call.

An **output function** is like an input function in reverse. It consists of an output part followed by an input part. The output part has an output condition followed by code. The output part is executed atomically by a local thread only if the output condition holds. *The local thread is created at the beginning of the output part.* The output part ends with an output call, i.e., a call to an input function of another system. The input part consists of an input condition followed by code. When the call issued by the output part returns, the input part is executed atomically if the input condition holds. *The local thread is terminated at the end of the input part.* If the input condition does not hold when the call returns, the program becomes faulty.

All the calls that the program makes to a particular input function are grouped together in one output function, instead of being spread over different functions.

The atomicity assumption of a service program is always the same: input parts and output parts are atomic. The progress assumption of a service program defines conditions under which output parts (in input and output functions) are eventually executed. It is expressed in terms of leads-to assertions. Fairness assertions are avoided (because they complicate obtaining the service inverse).

Service programs typically do not use the endSystem instruction, even though programs that implement services would typically use it. This is because neither termination of a system nor the initiation of termination is relevant to the system's input-output behavior, which is what a service program deals with. Informing the system's environment that the system will no longer interact with the environment *is* part of the system's service. But beyond that, the service is not concerned with whether the system no longer exists or still exists but is not interacting. In particular, a service should not rule out implementations that do not terminate.

Figure 1.13 outlines a service program, called LockService, that defines the service of program Lock. It has no output function (because Lock does no output call). It has three input functions, acq, rel and end, just like Lock. Each of them can be called only if end has not yet been called. Note that the output part of function acq checks and updates the status of the lock in one atomic step. Function end does not have an endSystem instruction (but we could have added it in the input or output part). The service allows users to be served in any order, as long as no user is made to wait indefinitely while the lock becomes available repeatedly. Any practical implementation will be able to realize only a small subset of the possible evolutions.

A typical service program cannot be executed on a typical platform. Its atomicity and progress assumptions would be usually too demanding for a typical platform (as illustrated by LockService's acq's return). Its input and output parts would often have

```
service LockService() {
    ic {true}
    define variables to track status of users;
    ending ← false;                        // termination initiated
    return mysid;
    // end main

    input void mysid.acq() {               // input part
        ic {not ending and                 // input part
            thread mytid does not have lock}  //     "     "
        add mytid to requesting users;     //     "     "
        oc {no user has lock}              // output part
        update status of mytid;            //     "     "
        return;                            //     "     "
    }

    input void mysid.rel() {               // input part
        ic {not ending and                 // input part
            thread mytid has lock}         //     "     "
        remove mytid from requesting users;  //   "     "
        oc {true}                          // output part
        return;                            //     "     "
    }

    input void mysid.end() {               // input part
        ic {not ending}                    // input part
        ending ← true;                     //     "     "
        oc {true}                          // output part
        return;                            //     "     "
    }
    atomicity assumption {input parts and output parts}

    progress assumption {
        forall(thread u: (u in rel) leads-to (not u in rel));

        forall(thread u: (u holds lock) leads-to (u in rel))
        ⇒ forall(user u: (u in acq) leads-to (not u in acq));

        forall(thread u: (u in end) leads-to (not u in end));
    }
}
```

Fig. 1.13 Lock service program

unreasonable computational and memory requirements, such as reads and writes of
global history variables. This is not a problem because a service program is intended
not for execution but to provide an easily understandable definition of the service.
*It is precisely this freedom from "physical-world" constraints that makes a service
program easier to understand than a program that implements the service.*

1.6.1 Distributed Services

Thus far, input function headers have the form mysid.f(.), and hence calls to them have the form x.f(.) where x is the sid of the called system. A bit more flexibility is needed to specify the service of a distributed system that consists of multiple basic systems. Consider a distributed system that provides a message-passing service from a location a1 to another location a2, as shown in Fig. 1.14. The distributed system may have many basic systems, but the users interact with only two of them, namely, x1 at a1 and x2 at a2. Specifically, a user at a1 calls x1.tx(msg) to send a message msg, and a user at a2 calls x2.rx() to receive a message. (The latter is a blocking call whose return delivers the message.)

Now consider a service program MsgService that defines the message-passing service. Its input functions would be accessed by users calling x1.tx and x2.rx. So if we want the input function headers to be mysid.tx and mysid.rx, respectively, the service program would need to start two basic systems with sids x1 and x2, as shown in Fig. 1.15. But it does not make sense to burden the service program with the system-level structure of the composite system. For example, we may want the service to have a variable indicating the messages in transit from x1 to x2; this variable would be read and updated by both x1 and x2, and it is meaningless to put this variable inside either x1 or x2.

A more sensible approach is to have the service program define a single basic system that has input functions with headers x1.tx and x2.tx, as shown in Fig. 1.16. The corresponding service program is outlined in Fig. 1.17. The construct sid() in the main code returns an sid but does not create a system. Thus the main code obtains two sids, stores them in x1 and x2, and returns them. The program uses x1 and x2 as the sid prefixes of input functions tx and rx, respectively. Note that the neither x1 nor x2 is the sid of the instantiated service program (i.e., the value of its mysid). This is why we explicitly state the sid prefix in input function headers. (The service program returns [x1,x2] in one atomic step. An implementation of the service would typically return x1 and x2 separately, but the two returns together would be effectively atomic.)

1.7 Implements Definition

We have described programs and service programs. We now describe what it means for a program A to implement a program B, i.e., for aggregate system A to implement aggregate system B. For now, we do not restrict A or B to be a service program. The definition of A implements B has two parts, safety and progress. The safety part, roughly speaking, is that whenever A and B have undergone the same input-output history, A can accept any input that B can accept and any output A can do is an output that B can do. The progress part is that A satisfies the progress assumption of B.

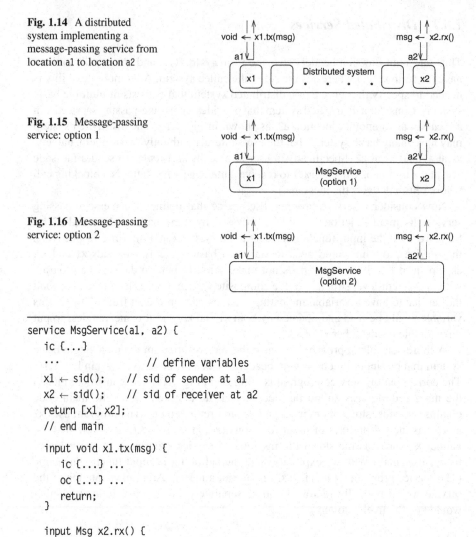

Fig. 1.14 A distributed system implementing a message-passing service from location a1 to location a2

Fig. 1.15 Message-passing service: option 1

Fig. 1.16 Message-passing service: option 2

```
service MsgService(a1, a2) {
   ic {...}
   ...                    // define variables
   x1 ← sid();    // sid of sender at a1
   x2 ← sid();    // sid of receiver at a2
   return [x1, x2];
   // end main

   input void x1.tx(msg) {
      ic {...} ...
      oc {...} ...
      return;
   }

   input Msg x2.rx() {
      ic {...} ...
      oc {...} ...
      return msg;
   }

   atomicity assumption {...}
   progress assumption {...}
}
```

Fig. 1.17 Service program of distributed message-passing system (option 2)

We now express this more precisely. We say a system can **accept** an input at a point in an evolution if the system can receive the input at that point without becoming faulty. For any evolution x of a system, let $ext(x)$ denote the sequence of inputs and outputs in x. We say x is **safe** with respect to B, abbreviated "safe wrt" B, if x is fault-free and $ext(x)$ can be generated by a fault-free evolution y of B, i.e., $ext(y)$ equals $ext(x)$. We say x is **complete** with respect to B, abbreviated "complete wrt" B, if x is fault-free and $ext(x)$ can be generated by an evolution of B that satisfies B's progress assumption.

Then A **implements** B if:

- Safety condition: For every finite evolution x of A that is safe wrt B:

  - Input: For every input e of B, if extending x with e is safe wrt B then A can accept e at the end of x.
  - Output: Any step that A can do at the end of x is fault-free, and if that step does an output f, then extending x with f is safe wrt B.

- Progress condition: For every evolution x of A that is safe wrt B: If x satisfies A's progress assumption then x is complete wrt B.

It turns out that the above definition achieves compositionality; that is, if A implements B, then in any program C that has an instantiation of B as a component, B can be replaced by A without invalidating any property of C (except, of course, internal properties of the instantiation of B). But the definition can be difficult to apply in practice because its conditions are stated in terms of the evolutions of A and B.

It is preferable to express the safety and progress conditions in terms of programs A and B. To achieve this, the key idea is to modify program B to a program, say $\bar{B}$, such that $\bar{B}$ has the same evolutions as B except that outputs become inputs and inputs become outputs. We refer to $\bar{B}$ as the **inverse** of B. Obtaining it is not easy in general, but it is straightforward if B is a service program. One treats the main code's return value as a parameter, and massages input functions into output functions and vice versa. The progress assumption is now referred to as a progress condition; it is no longer an assumption about the platform.

Figure 1.18 shows the inverse of the lock service program and indicates how it is obtained from the lock service program. It has only output functions (because the lock service has only input functions). Recall that an output function is executed by a local thread that is created at the start of the function and terminated at the end. The creation of the local thread is not explicitly stated; it is implicit in the output condition of an output function.

The next step is to define a distributed program, say Z, that simply instantiates programs A and $\bar{B}$, say as systems sA and s$\bar{B}$, and has them interact solely with each other (i.e., aggregate system Z has no external inputs or outputs). In any evolution of Z, if w is the input-output sequence that aggregate system sA has undergone thus far and w is safe wrt B, then the following hold: (1) s$\bar{B}$ can send an input e to sA iff extending w with e is safe wrt B; and (2) for any output f generated by sA, extending w with f is safe wrt B iff s$\bar{B}$'s input condition for f holds.

```
service LockService() {
program LockServiceInverse(lck) {   // lck: lock system
  ic {true}
  define variables to track status of users;
  ending ← false;
  return mysid;
  // end main

  input void mysid.acq() {
  output doAcq() {                   // mysid.acq() inverse
    ic oc {not ending and
           thread mytid does not have lock}
    add mytid to requesting users;
    lck.acq();                       // add call
    oe ic {no user has lock}
    update status of mytid;
    return;
  }

  input void mysid.rel() {
  output doRel() {                   // mysid.rel() inverse
    ic oc {not ending and
           thread mytid has lock}
    remove mytid from requesting users;
    lck.rel();                       // add call
    oe ic {true}
    return;
  }

  input void mysid.end() {
  output doEnd() {                   // mysid.end() inverse
    ic oc {not ending}
    ending ← true;
    lck.end();                       // add call
    ic {true}
    return;
  }

  atomicity assumption {...}              // as before

  progress assumption condition {....} // as before
}
```

Fig. 1.18 Lock service inverse program, obtained from lock service program after deletions and additions (*underlined*)

```
program Z() {
  ia {LockService.ic}
  inputs();    // aggregate Z has no inputs
  outputs();   // aggregate Z has no outputs
  lck ← startSystem(Lock());
  lsi ← startSystem(LockServiceInverse(lck));
  return mysid;

  atomicity assumption {}

  progress assumption {weak fairness}
}
```

Fig. 1.19 Program Z of lock and lock service inverse

* *Inv* (thread t at lsi.doAcq().ic) ⇒ lsi.(no user has lock)
* lsi.(progress condition)

Fig. 1.20 Assertions to be satisfied by program Z in order for Lock to implement LockService

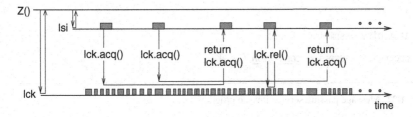

Fig. 1.21 An evolution of aggregate system Z; threads within lck and lsi are not shown

Consequently, it turns out that A implements B iff program Z satisfies the following assertions.

* For every input condition ic{P} in $\bar{\text{B}}$:
    Inv ((thread at s$\bar{\text{B}}$.ic{P}) ⇒ s$\bar{\text{B}}$.P)   (safety condition)
* s$\bar{\text{B}}$.(progress condition)   (progress condition)

We have achieved our objective of expressing "A implements B" in terms of programs A and B.

Figure 1.19 shows program Z for the lock and lock service inverse programs, instantiated as systems lck and lsi, respectively. Figure 1.21 shows an evolution of Z. Figure 1.20 shows the assertions that Z must satisfy for lock to implement service. There is only one assertion for the safety condition, dealing with the return of an acq call (thread at lsi.doAcq.ic). No assertion is needed for the return of a rel call because lsi.doRel's input condition is vacuous. The same holds for the return of an end call.

```
service MsgService(a1, a2) {
program MsgServiceInverse(a1, a2, [x1,x2]) {
    ic {...}
    define variables;
    x1 ← sid();
    x2 ← sid();
    return [x1,x2] mysid;

    output doTx(msg) {
        ie oc {...} ...
        x1.tx(msg);
        oe ic {...} ...
        return;
    }

    output doRx() {
        ie oc {...} ...
        msg ← x2.rx();
        oe ic {...} ...
        return msg;
    }

    atomicity assumption {...}

    progress assumption condition {...}
}
```

Fig. 1.22 Message passing service inverse program

```
program Z(a1,a2) {
    ia {MsgService.ic}
    inputs(); outputs();
    [x1,x2] ← startSystem(MsgImp(a1,a2));
    si ← startSystem(MsgServiceInverse(a1,a2, [x1,x2]));
    return mysid;

    atomicity assumption {}

    progress assumption {weak fairness}
}
```

Fig. 1.23 Program Z of candidate implementation MsgImp and message passing service inverse

Figures 1.22–1.24 illustrate the same steps for the message passing service, MsgService(a1,a2), and a candidate implementation, MsgImp(a1,a2). Figure 1.22 shows the message passing service inverse. Figure 1.23 shows program Z for the candidate implementation and service inverse. Figure 1.24 shows the assertions to be satisfied by Z.

- *Inv* (thread t at si.doRx().ic)
      ⇒ si.doRx().ic
- si.(progress condition)

Fig. 1.24 Assertions to be satisfied by program Z in order for MsgImp to implement MsgService

```
program ProdCons1(J) {
    ia {...}           // input assumption
    lck ← startSystem(Lock() LockService());
    cons ← startSystem(Consumer(lck,J));
    prod ← startSystem(Producer(lck,cons,J));
    return mysid;
    // end main
    atomicity assumption {}  // none
    progress assumption {weak fairness for thread}
}
```

Fig. 1.25 Producer-consumer program using lock service

- *Inv* (thread t at lck.acq.ic) ⇒ lck.(not ending and t does not have lock)
- *Inv* (thread t at lck.rel.ic) ⇒ lck.(not ending and t has lock)

Fig. 1.26 Assertions to be satisfied by program ProdCons1 for proper use of LockService

1.8 Using Services to Design Programs

We have seen how to define the service B of a program A and how to establish that A implements B. The fundamental reason for doing all this is so that B can be used instead of A when designing a program C that uses A. This makes the design and analysis of C easier because B is invariably simpler than A. Any correctness properties established for C would still hold when B is replaced by A, or any program that implements B.

For example, consider the distributed system of producer, consumer and lock defined by programs ProdCons, Lock, Consumer and Producer (Figs. 1.9–1.11). To establish correctness properties of this distributed system, we should analyze program ProdCons with Lock replaced by LockService, that is, the program ProdCons1 shown in Fig. 1.25. As part of this analysis, we would have to show that every call to lck satisfies its input condition, i.e., that ProdCons1 satisfies the assertions in Fig. 1.26. Otherwise, lck would become faulty. More to the point, one cannot say anything about the properties of program ProdCons1 after the lock service is replaced by a lock implementation.

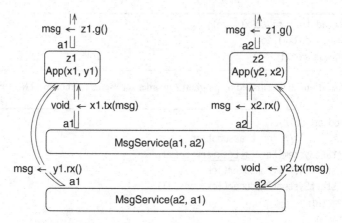

Fig. 1.27 A distributed system of two App systems interacting via two message-passing services

```
program DistApp(a1, a2) {
    ia {...}          // input assumption
    [x1,x2] ← startSystem(MsgService(a1,a2));   // sender x1; receiver x2
    [y2,y1] ← startSystem(MsgService(a2,a1));   // sender y2; receiver y1
    z1 ← startSystem(App(x1,y1,a1,a2));
    z2 ← startSystem(App(y2,x2,a2,a1));
    return [z1,z2];
    // end main
    atomicity assumption {} // none
    progress assumption {weak fairness for thread}
}
```

Fig. 1.28 Distributed application program using two message-passing services

For another example, consider a distributed system in which two instantiations of a program App, which has an input function g(), interact using two instantiations of the message passing service, MsgService, as illustrated in Fig. 1.27. The program of the distributed system is shown in Fig. 1.28. Here, z1 and z2 are the sids of the two App systems; x1 and x2 are the sids of the sender and receiver systems in the message passing service from a1 to a2; and y2 and y1 are sids of the sender and receiver systems in the message passing service from a2 to a1. Clearly, it is far easier to analyze program DistApp than one where the message-passing-service programs are replaced by their distributed implementation programs (illustrated in Fig. 1.14).

We can repeat the exercise with program DistApp, by defining a service program, say DistAppService, that captures the desired external behavior of DistApp. The service program, called DistAppService, is outlined in Fig. 1.29. When designing a program that makes use of DistApp, one would use DistAppService instead of DistApp.

```
service DistAppService(a1, a2) {
    ...
    z1 ← sid(); z2 ← sid();
    return [z1,z2];
    // end main

    input Msg z1.g() {...}

    input Msg z2.g() {...}

    atomicity assumption {...}
    progress assumption {...}
}
```

Fig. 1.29 Service of program DistApp

This paradigm of defining services and using them to design programs that implement further services is repeatedly demonstrated in this book. In particular, program ProdCons1 (Fig. 1.25) is analyzed in Chap. 2, using real programs for Producer, Consumer and LockService (instead of the outlines in Figs. 1.11–1.13). A distributed program with the structure of program DistApp (Figs. 1.27 and 1.28) is developed in Chap. 5; the program has two systems that use an unreliable message-passing service to implement a reliable message-passing service. Programs using and implementing more complex services, including sequentially-consistent shared memory and TCP-like transport service, are developed in later chapters.

1.9 Background to SESF

This completes the informal introduction to SESF. To reiterate, programs are written in a generic syntax, with explicit instantiations of programs and threads. The atomicity and progress assumed of the underlying platform is explicitly stated. Implementation programs have assumptions that are satisfied by typical platforms. Services are expressed by service programs; they have a special structure and can assume unrealistic atomicity and progress. If program A implements service B, then replacing B by A in any program C preserves all the properties of C. The conditions for "A implements B" are expressed as correctness properties of the hypothetical program of A and B-inverse. The program can be analyzed using any program analysis method, and our choice is assertional reasoning. The program can also be mechanically tested by executing it on an appropriate platform [44, 45].

SESF is one of many formalizations of compositionality based on assertional reasoning (e.g., [1, 2, 9–11, 13, 18, 19, 62, 67, 69, 71, 78, 80, 104, 109]. They all share the basic notions of services and implements, However, the formalizations can differ in technical specifics. One difference is whether the interaction between systems is in the form of function calls or reads and writes of shared variables [94]. The two approaches are equivalent in expressive power, although they differ in technical development and, of course, syntax. The function call approach has become dominant in programming paradigms, and is the one followed in this book. Another difference concerns how concurrent activity is specified in programs. In our approach, as in many programming languages, concurrent activity is initiated by explicit thread creation constructs. One consequence is that implementation programs look rather different from service programs. Whereas in most other approaches, threads are implicit: a program is written as a bag of atomic steps with blocking conditions, any of which can be executed when it is unblocked. In such an approach, implementation programs have the same structure as service programs, and compositionality and proof rules are syntactically cleaner.

Assertional reasoning was introduced by Floyd [48] for single-threaded programs that interact with the environment only at the start and at the end. Here, assertional reasoning reduces to annotating the program with predicates (pre- and post-conditions and loop invariants). Hoare formalized this into a program logic, namely, Hoare-logic [6, 56], in which properties are expressed by triples of the form ⟨precondition, code, postcondition⟩ and proved by applications of inference rules. Dijkstra introduced the concept of weakest preconditions and developed a program calculus for single-threaded programs with nondeterministic guarded commands [31, 36].

Assertional reasoning for multi-threaded programs involves some extensions. Because the threads of a program interact (and interfere) with each other, it is necessary to assume some level of atomicity in their interaction [30, 37]. Assertional proofs of safety properties of multi-threaded programs were investigated by Ashcroft [7] and by Owicki and Gries [90, 91]. Handling progress (or liveness) properties of multi-threaded programs requires reasoning about infinite evolutions and fairness of threads [97]. Pnueli introduced the use of temporal logic for reasoning formally about the progress properties of multi-threaded systems [97, 98]. Since then, various assertional formalisms based on temporal logic have been proposed, for example, [1, 2, 5, 9, 10, 14, 17–19, 61, 67, 69, 71, 73, 78–84, 92]. There is a large body of experience indicating that assertional reasoning is an effective method for analyzing multi-threaded programs (for example, [3–5, 8–13, 15–20, 32–36, 38–40, 42, 43, 47, 49–52, 54, 55, 57–60, 64, 66, 68, 77, 85–90, 99–103, 105, 107, 109, 112–114]).

1.10   Organization of This Book

The remainder of this book is organized in three parts. The first part (Chaps. 2–5) introduces SESF by way of examples. The second part (Chaps. 6–8) presents the theory of SESF. The third part (Chap. 9 onwards) consists of applications of SESF. Each chapter here defines either a service or a program that implements a service; it can be read independently of earlier chapters except for those whose services it uses. A more detailed overview of the three parts is given below. Conventions and program constructs are introduced incrementally in the book; for reference, they are collected together in Appendix A.

1.10.1   Introducing SESF by Examples (Chaps. 2–5)

Chapter 2 fleshes out the producer-consumer-lock example outlined in this chapter. A simple lock program that requires only a bare hardware platform, i.e., atomic reads and writes of memory words and weak fairness of threads, is presented. Its desired external behavior is defined by a lock service program. The lock program is shown to implement the service program, illustrating both operational and assertional proofs. The lock service is then used in a producer-consumer program to achieve desired properties; naturally, the lock service can be replaced by the lock program without disturbing any of the desired properties.

Chapter 3 defines a bounded-buffer service and several programs that implement the service. The service program illustrates the modeling of input functions that return non-void values. The programs implementing the service illustrate the use of thread synchronization constructs available in operating system platforms, namely, locks, condition variables, and semaphores, as well as a more convenient synchronization construct, namely the "await". Programs using awaits are easier to write and analyze than those using the standard synchronization constructs, and can be mechanically transformed to use the latter. The programs also illustrate how to reduce unnecessary blocking, thereby increasing parallelism.

Chapter 4 defines several kinds of message-passing services, or "channels" for short. A channel has a set of addresses at which users can send and receive messages (e.g., as in the IP layer of a computer network [28, 96]). Three kinds of "connection-less" channels are defined: reliable channels, which behave as fifo (first-in-first-out) buffers; lossy channels, which can lose messages; and LRD channels, which can lose, reorder, and duplicate messages. In the context of computer networking, lossy channels correspond to single-hop physical links and LRD channels correspond to multi-hop (IP) links. A simple "connection-oriented" channel is also defined.

Chapter 5 presents a distributed program, called a data transfer protocol, that implements a fifo channel between two addresses given an unreliable (either lossy or LRD) channel connecting the two addresses. The protocol consists of two systems, one at each end-point. Fifo data transfer is achieved using the popular sliding-window algorithm, in which data blocks are tagged with cyclic sequence numbers and retransmitted until they are acked. Achieving this over LRD channels involves real-time constraints (specifically, upper bounds on message lifetime and transmission rate). This is a fairly complex example, illustrating practically all aspects of SESF in depth.

1.10.2   Theory of SESF (Chaps. 6–8)

Chapter 6 covers the structure and semantics (i.e., mathematical model) of programs, service programs, and correctness assertions. The notion of effective atomicity is formalized. Proof rules for correctness assertions are given.

Chapter 7 presents the core of the SESF theory. The notion of "program A implements program B" is formalized in terms of the evolutions of A and B. Compositionality is established: if A implements B, then replacing an instantiation of B in any program C by an instantiation of A preserves the properties of program C. Finally, "program A implements service B" is expressed in terms of correctness properties of the program of A and B inverse.

Chapter 8 extends the theory of SESF to time-constrained programs, that is, programs whose statements are subject to time constraints. A time-constrained program A is shown to be equivalent to a regular (non-time-constrained) program A′ obtained by mechanical modifications to A. Thus the theory of Chaps. 6 and 7 can be applied with minimal modifications to time-constrained programs.

1.10.3   More Applications of SESF (Chap. 9 Onwards)

Chapters 9 and 10 present two centralized lock implementations, the former based on Peterson's algorithm [95] and the latter on the bakery algorithm [63, 111]. Each implementation assumes a bare hardware platform. Each is shown to implement the lock service defined in Chap. 2.

Chapter 11 presents a lock service appropriate for a distributed environment. Here users at different locations can access the lock by interacting with a local lock access system. Chapter 12 presents a distributed program that implements the distributed lock service. The program makes use of a fifo channel connecting the lock access systems and employs logical timestamps [65] to achieve a consistent ordering of conflicting requests.

Chapter 13 defines a termination-detection service for a distributed environment. It is often the case in a distributed computation that we want a thread of the computation to determine, without disturbing the computation, when and if the computation has terminated, i.e., all threads are inactive and no messages are in transit. This chapter formalizes this requirement in the form of a "termination-detection channel", i.e., a fifo channel augmented with termination detection service. Chapter 14 presents a distributed program that implements the termination detection channel for the case when only one user is active initially. The program makes use of a regular fifo channel and employs a diffusing computation algorithm [38].

Chapter 15 defines a distributed "object-transfer" service that allows users at different locations to share objects, each object being characterized by an id and a mutable value. Users can acquire objects (to read or write), release objects, and receive requests for objects they hold. Chapter 16 presents an implementation of the object-transfer service. The component systems of the implementation communicate via a fifo channel and employ a distributed "path-reversal" algorithm [76, 110, 115] to track the current location of an object. This algorithm is very efficient and has some rather complicated evolutions.

Chapter 17 defines a distributed shared-memory service with sequential consistency [72]. Distributed shared memory provides a common memory address space to users on different computers. Sequential consistency means that the sequence of reads and writes can be reordered to a sequence that is consistent with traditional (atomic) shared memory and preserves each user's sequence of reads and writes. Distributed programs running on such memory can be analyzed as if they were running on traditional memory (which is not realizable in a distributed environment).

Chapter 18 presents a program that implements the distributed shared memory service of Chap. 17. The memory address space is divided into pages which are dispersed among the computers, and moved to different locations as and when they are needed. The program makes use of the object-transfer service (from Chap. 15) to move pages.

Chapter 19 presents another program that implements the distributed shared memory service of Chap. 17. It improves the performance of the first implementation (in Chap. 18) by allowing additional "read-only" copies of a page, which are invalidated prior to a write. The program makes use of the object-transfer service (Chap. 15) for moving pages and the fifo channel (Chap. 4) for doing invalidation. If the object-transfer service is replaced by its path-reversal implementation (Chap. 16), the resulting program corresponds to a popular implementation (Algorithm 2 in [76]).

Chapter 20 presents a reliable transport-layer service, corresponding to (the TCP part of) Internet sockets [29, 41, 96, 108]. Users can request connections (as clients) to users at other socket addresses, accept or reject incoming connection requests (as servers), exchange data over established connections, and close or abort connections. Data sent in one connection is not delivered in a later connection between the same pair of socket addresses. (The latter is not an idle concern when implementing the service over channels that can duplicate and reorder messages.)

Chapter 21 presents a distributed program, called a transport protocol, that implements the transport service in Chap. 20. The transport protocol makes use of a LRD (loss, reorder, duplication) channel (Chap. 4) and is roughly equivalent to TCP [29, 96, 108]. Like TCP, each end-point identifies connection attempts with cyclic sequence numbers, and stores information about a connection's remote end-point only for the duration of the connection. Unlike TCP, there is a clean separation between the connection management mechanism and the data transfer mechanism within each connection. The connection management provides each connection with a dedicated *virtual* channel and starts a data-transfer end-point system at each end. Thus any data transfer protocol can be run in a connection, for example, the one from Chap. 5.

References

1. M. Abadi, L. Lamport, The existence of refinement mappings. Theor. Comput. Sci. **82**(2), 253–284 (1991). doi:10.1016/0304-3975(91)90224-P. http://dx.doi.org/10.1016/0304-3975(91)90224-P

2. M. Abadi, L. Lamport, Composing specifications. ACM Trans. Program. Lang. Syst. **15**(1), 73–132 (1993). doi:10.1145/151646.151649. http://doi.acm.org/10.1145/151646.151649. Also in Stepwise Refinement of Distributed Systems, LNCS 430, Springer, 1990

3. C. Alaettinoglu, A.U. Shankar, Stepwise assertional design of distance-vector routing algorithms. in *Protocol Specification, Testing and Verification XII*, ed. by R.J. Linn Jr., M.M. Uyar. Proceedings of the IFIP TC6/WG6.1 Twelth International Symposium on Protocol Specification, Testing and Verification, Lake Buena Vista, Florida, USA, 22–25 June 1992. IFIP Transactions, vol. C-8 (North-Holland, New York, 1992), pp. 399–413

4. G.R. Andrews, A method for solving synchronization problems. Sci. Comput. Program. **13**(4), 1–21 (1989)

5. G.R. Andrews, F.B. Schneider, Concepts and notations for concurrent programming. ACM Comput. Surv. **15**(1), 3–43 (1983). doi:10.1145/356901.356903. http://doi.acm.org/10.1145/356901.356903

6. K.R. Apt, Ten years of hoare's logic: a survey-part i. ACM TOPLAS **3**, 431–483 (1981)

7. E.A. Ashcroft, Proving assertions about parallel programs. J. Comput. Syst. Sci. **10**(1), 110–135 (1975). doi:10.1016/S0022-0000(75)80018-3. http://dx.doi.org/10.1016/S0022-0000(75)80018-3

8. R.J. Back, Invariant based programming: basic approach and teaching experiences. Form. Aspects Comput. **21**, 227–244 (2009). doi:10.1007/s00165-008-0070-y

9. R.J.R. Back, R. Kurki-Suonio, Decentralization of process nets with centralized control, in *Proceedings of the Second Annual ACM Symposium on Principles of Distributed Computing, PODC '83* (ACM, New York, 1983), pp. 131–142. doi:10.1145/800221.806716. http://doi.acm.org/10.1145/800221.806716

10. R.J.R. Back, F. Kurki-Suonio, Distributed cooperation with action systems. ACM Trans. Program. Lang. Syst. **10**(4), 513–554 (1988). doi:10.1145/48022.48023. http://doi.acm.org/10.1145/48022.48023

11. R.J.R. Back, K. Sere, Stepwise refinement of parallel algorithms. Sci. Comput. Program. **13**(2–3), 133–180 (1990). doi10.1016/0167-6423(90)90069-P. http://dx.doi.org/10.1016/0167-6423(90)90069-P

12. R.J. Back, K. Sere, Stepwise refinement of action systems. Software **12**, 17–30 (1991)

13. R.J. Back, J.V. Wright, Contracts, games, and refinement. Inf. Comput. Control **156**, 25–45 (2000). doi:10.1006/inco.1999.2820

14. R.J. Back, J.V. Wright, Compositional action system refinement. Form. Aspects Comput. **15**, 103–117 (2003). doi:10.1007/s00165-003-0005-6

15. M. Ben-Ari, *The Art of Multiprocessor Programming*, 2nd edn. (Addison-Wesley, San Francisco, 2006)

16. J.A. Carruth, J. Misra, Proof of a real-time mutual-exclusion algorithm. Parallel Process. Lett. **6**(2), 251–257 (1996)

17. K.M. Chandy, J. Misra, The drinking philosophers problem. ACM Trans. Program. Lang. Syst. **6**(4), 632–646 (1984). doi:10.1145/1780.1804. http://doi.acm.org/10.1145/1780.1804

18. K.M. Chandy, J. Misra, An example of stepwise refinement of distributed programs: quiescence detection. ACM Trans. Program. Lang. Syst. **8**(3), 326–343 (1986). doi:10.1145/5956.5958. http://doi.acm.org/10.1145/5956.5958

19. K.M. Chandy, J. Misra, *Parallel Program Design: A Foundation* (Addison-Wesley, Boston, 1989)

20. K.M. Chandy, J. Misra, Proof of distributed algorithms: an exercise, in: *Developments in Concurrency and Communication*, ed. by C.A.R. Hoare (Addison-Wesley Longman, Boston, 1990), pp. 305–332. http://dl.acm.org/citation.cfm?id=107155.107171

21. E.M. Clarke, E.A. Emerson, A.P. Sistla, Automatic verification of finite-state concurrent systems using temporal logic specifications. ACM Trans. Program. Lang. Syst. **8**(2), 244–263 (1986). doi:10.1145/5397.5399. http://doi.acm.org/10.1145/5397.5399

22. E.M. Clarke Jr., O. Grumberg, D.A. Peled, *Model Checking* (MIT, Cambridge MA, 1999)

23. E. Cohen, *Modular Progress Proofs of Asynchronous Programs*, Ph.D. thesis, University of Texas, Austin, 1993. UMI Order No. GAX93-23370

24. E. Cohen, Validating the microsoft hypervisor, in: *FM 2006: Formal Methods*, ed. by J. Misra, T. Nipkow, E. Sekerinski. 14th International Symposium on Formal Methods. Lecture Notes in Computer Science, vol. 4085 (Springer, New York, 2006), pp. 81–81

25. E. Cohen, L. Lamport, Reduction in tla, in *Proceedings of the 9th International Conference on Concurrency Theory, CONCUR '98* (Springer, London, 1998), pp. 317–331. http://dl.acm.org/citation.cfm?id=646733.701301

26. E. Cohen, M. Dahlweid, M. Hillebrand, D. Leinenbach, M. Moskal, T. Santen, W. Schulte, S. Tobies, Vcc: a practical system for verifying Concurrent c, in *Proceedings of the 22nd International Conference on Theorem Proving in Higher Order Logics, TPHOLs '09* (Springer, Berlin/Heidelberg 2009), pp. 23–42. doi:10.1007/978-3-642-03359-9_2. http://dx.doi.org/10.1007/978-3-642-03359-9_2

27. E. Cohen, M. Moskal, W. Schulte, S. Tobies, Local verification of global invariants in concurrent programs, in *Proceedings of the 22nd International Conference on Computer Aided Verification, CAV'10* (Springer, Berlin/Heidelberg, 2010), pp. 480–494. doi:10.1007/978-3-642-14295-6_42. http://dx.doi.org/10.1007/978-3-642-14295-6_42

28. D. Comer, *Internetworking with TCP/IP*, 4th edn. Vol 1: Principles, Protocols, and Architectures (Prentice-Hall, Upper Saddle River, 2000)

29. D.E. Comer, D.L. Stevens, *Internetworking with TCP/IP*, 1st edn. Vol. 3: Client-Server Programming and Applications, Linux/Posix Sockets Version (Prentice Hall, Upper Saddle River, 2000)

30. E.W. Dijkstra, Cooperating sequential processes. Technical report, Burroughs, Nuenen, 1965. EWD-123

31. E.W. Dijkstra, Guarded commands, nondeterminacy and formal derivation of programs. Commun. ACM **18**(8), 453–457 (1975). doi:10.1145/360933.360975. http://doi.acm.org/10.1145/360933.360975

32. E.W. Dijkstra, A correctness proof for communicating processes – a small exercise. Technical report, Burroughs, Nuenen, 1977. EWD-607

33. E.W. Dijkstra, Two starvation-free solutions of a general exclusion problem. Technical report, Nuenen, 1978. EWD-625

34. E.W. Dijkstra, Finding the correctness proof of a concurrent program, in *Program Construction, International Summer Schoo* (Springer, London, 1979), pp. 24–34. http://dl.acm.org/citation.cfm?id=647639.733356

35. E.W. Dijkstra, The distributed snapshot of k.m. chandy and l. lamport, in *Proceedings of the NATO Advanced Study Institute on Control flow and Data Flow: Concepts Of Distributed Programming* (Springer, New York, 1986), pp. 513–517. http://dl.acm.org/citation.cfm?id=22086.22099. Also EWD-864a

36. E.W. Dijkstra, *A Discipline of Programming*, 1st edn. (Prentice Hall, Upper Saddle River, 1997)

37. E.W. Dijkstra, Cooperating sequential processes, in *The Origin of Concurrent Programming*, ed. P.B. Hansen (Springer, New York, 2002), pp. 65–138. http://dl.acm.org/citation.cfm?id=762971.762974

38. E.W. Dijkstra, C.S. Scholten, Termination detection for diffusing computations. Inf. Process. Lett. **11**(1), 1–4 (1980)

39. E.W. Dijkstra, L. Lamport, A.J. Martin, C.S. Scholten, E.F.M. Steffens, On-the-fly garbage collection: an exercise in cooperation. Commun. ACM **21**(11), 966–975 (1978). doi:10.1145/359642.359655. http://doi.acm.org/10.1145/359642.359655

40. E.W. Dijkstra, W.H.J. Feijen, A.J.M. van Gasteren, Derivation of a termination detection algorithm for distributed computations. Inf. Process. Lett. **16**(5), 217–219 (1983). Also EWD 840

41. M.J. Donahoo, K. Calvert, *TCP/IP Sockets in C, Practical Guide for Programmers*, 2nd edn. (Morgan Kaufmann, Burlington, 2009)
42. N.J. Drost, J.V. Leeuwen, *Assertional Verification of a Majority Consensus Algorithm for Concurrency Control in Multiple Copy Databases* (Springer, New York, 1988). doi:10.1007/3-540-50403-6_48
43. M.R. Drost, A.A. Schoone, Assertional verification of a reset algorithm. Technical report, DSpace at Utrecht University, Netherlands, 1988 [http://dspace.library.uu.nl:8080/dspace-oai/request]. http://igitur-archive.library.uu.nl/math/2006-1214-201542/UUindex.html
44. T. Elsharnouby, A.U. Shankar, SeSFJava harness: service and assertion checking for protocol implementations. IEEE J. Sel. Areas Commun. **22**(10), 2035–2047 (2004). doi:10.1109/JSAC.2004.836012
45. T. Elsharnouby, A.U. Shankar, Using SeSFJava in teaching introductory network courses, in *Proceedings of the 36th SIGCSE Technical Symposium on Computer Science Education, SIGCSE '05* (ACM, New York, 2005), pp. 67–71. doi:10.1145/1047344.1047381. http://doi.acm.org/10.1145/1047344.1047381
46. E.A. Emerson, V. Kahlon, Rapid parameterized model checking of snoopy cache coherence protocols, in *TACAS 2003*, vol. 2619, ed. by H. Garavel, J. Hatcliff. Lecture Notes in Computer Science (Springer, New York, 2003), pp. 144–159
47. W.H.J. Feijen, A.J.M. van Gasteren, *On a Method of Multiprogramming* (Springer, New York, 1999)
48. R.W. Floyd, Assigning meanings to programs, in *Proceedings of a Symposium on Applied Mathematics*, vol. 19, ed. by J.T. Schwartz. Mathematical Aspects of Computer Science (American Mathematical Society, Providence, 1967), pp. 19–31. http://www.eecs.berkeley.edu/~necula/Papers/FloydMeaning.pdf
49. D. Ginat, *Adaptive Ordering of Contending Processes in Distributed Systems*. Ph.D. thesis, University of Maryland, Computer Science Department, College Park, 1989. CSTR-2335
50. D. Ginat, A.U. Shankar, An assertional proof of correctness and serializability of a distributed mutual exclusion algorithm based on path reversal. Technical report, University of Maryland, Computer Science Department, 1988. CSTR-2104
51. D. Ginat, A.U. Shankar, A.K. Agrawala, An efficient solution to the drinking philosophers problem and its extensions, in *Distributed Algorithms*, vol. 392, ed. by J.C. Bermond, M. Raynal. Lecture Notes in Computer Science (Springer, Berlin/Heidelberg, 1989), pp. 83–93. http://dx.doi.org/10.1007/3-540-51687-5_34. doi:10.1007/3-540-51687-5_34
52. D. Gries, An exercise in proving parallel programs correct. Commun. ACM **20**(12), 921–930 (1977). doi:10.1145/359897.359903. http://doi.acm.org/10.1145/359897.359903
53. R. Guerraoui, T.A. Henzinger, B. Jobstmann, V. Singh, Model checking transactional memories, in *Proceedings of the 2008 ACM SIGPLAN Conference on programming Language Design and Implementation, PLDI '08* (ACM, New York, 2008), pp. 372–382. doi:10.1145/1375581.1375626. http://doi.acm.org/10.1145/1375581.1375626
54. B. Hailpern, S. Owicki, Modular verification of computer communication protocols. IEEE Trans. Commun. **31**(1), 56–68 (1983). doi:10.1109/TCOM.1983.1095720
55. M. Herlihy, N. Shavit, *The Art of Multiprocessor Programming* (Morgan Kaufmann, San Francisco, 2008)
56. C.A.R. Hoare, An axiomatic basis for computer programming. Commun. ACM **12**(10), 576–580 (1969). doi:10.1145/363235.363259. http://doi.acm.org/10.1145/363235.363259
57. E. Knapp, An exercise in the formal derivation of parallel programs: maximum flows in graphs. ACM Trans. Program. Lang. Syst. **12**(2), 203–223 (1990). doi:10.1145/78942.78945. http://doi.acm.org/10.1145/78942.78945
58. D.E. Knuth: Verification of link-level protocols. BIT **21**(1), 31–36 (1981)
59. R.A. Krzysztof, E.R. Olderog, *Verification of Sequential and Concurrent Programs* (Springer, New York, 1991)
60. P. Ladkin, L. Lamport, B. Olivier, D. Roegel, Lazy caching in tla. Distrib. Comput. **12**(2–3), 151–174 (1999). doi:10.1007/s004460050063. http://dx.doi.org/10.1007/s004460050063

61. S.S. Lam, A.U. Shankar, A relational notation for state transition systems. IEEE Trans. Softw. Eng. **16**(7), 755–775 (1990). doi:10.1109/32.56101. http://dx.doi.org/10.1109/32.56101

62. S.S. Lam, A.U. Shankar, Specifying modules to satisfy interfaces: a state transition system approach. Distrib. Comput. **6**(1), 39–63 (1992). doi:10.1007/BF02276640. http://dx.doi.org/10.1007/BF02276640

63. L. Lamport, A new solution of dijkstra's concurrent programming problem. Commun. ACM **17**(8), 453–455 (1974). doi:10.1145/361082.361093. http://doi.acm.org/10.1145/361082.361093

64. L. Lamport, Proving the correctness of multiprocess programs. IEEE Trans. Softw. Eng. **3**(2), 125–143 (1977)

65. L. Lamport, Time, clocks, and the ordering of events in a distributed system. Commun. ACM **21**(7), 558–565 (1978). doi:10.1145/359545.359563. http://doi.acm.org/10.1145/359545.359563

66. L. Lamport, An assertional correctness proof of a distributed algorithm. Sci. Comput. Program. **2**(3), 175–206 (1982)

67. L. Lamport, Specifying concurrent program modules. ACM Trans. Program. Lang. Syst. **5**(2), 190–222 (1983). doi:10.1145/69624.357207. http://doi.acm.org/10.1145/69624.357207

68. L. Lamport, A fast mutual exclusion algorithm. ACM Trans. Comput. Syst. **5**(1), 1–11 (1987). doi:10.1145/7351.7352. http://doi.acm.org/10.1145/7351.7352

69. L. Lamport, A simple approach to specifying concurrent systems. Commun. ACM **32**(1), 32–45 (1989). doi:10.1145/63238.63240. http://doi.acm.org/10.1145/63238.63240

70. L. Lamport, A theorem on atomicity in distributed algorithms. Distrib. Comput. **4**, 59–68 (1990). http://dx.doi.org/10.1007/BF01786631. doi:10.1007/BF01786631

71. L. Lamport, The temporal logic of actions. ACM Trans. Program. Lang. Syst. **16**(3), 872–923 (1994). doi:10.1145/177492.177726. http://doi.acm.org/10.1145/177492.177726

72. L. Lamport, How to make a correct multiprocess program execute correctly on a multiprocessor. IEEE Trans. Comput. **46**(7), 779–782 (1997). doi:10.1109/12.599898. http://dx.doi.org/10.1109/12.599898

73. L. Lamport, *Specifying Systems: The TLA+ Language and Tools for Hardware and Software Engineers* (Addison-Wesley Longman, Boston, 2002)

74. L. Lamport, F.B. Schneider, Pretending atomicity. Technical report, Cornell University, Ithaca, 1989

75. D. Leinenbach, T. Santen, Verifying the microsoft hyper-v hypervisor with vcc, in: *Proceedings of the 2nd World Congress on Formal Methods, FM '09* (Springer, Berlin/Heidelberg, 2009), pp. 806–809. doi:10.1007/978-3-642-05089-3_51. http://dx.doi.org/10.1007/978-3-642-05089-3_51

76. K. Li, P. Hudak, Memory coherence in shared virtual memory systems. ACM Trans. Comput. Syst. **7**(4), 321–359 (1989). doi:http://doi.acm.org/10.1145/75104.75105

77. N.A. Lynch, *Distributed Algorithms* (Morgan Kaufmann, San Francisco, 1996)

78. N.A. Lynch, M.R. Tuttle, Hierarchical correctness proofs for distributed algorithms, in *Proceedings of the Sixth Annual ACM Symposium on Principles of Distributed Computing, PODC '87* (ACM, New York, 1987), pp. 137–151. doi:10.1145/41840.41852. http://doi.acm.org/10.1145/41840.41852

79. N.A. Lynch, M.R. Tuttle, An introduction to input/output automata. Technical report, MIT/LCS/TM-373 (1988). Also CWI-Quarterly, September 1989 Massachusetts Institute of Technology, Laboratory for Computer Science, **2**(3), 219–246,

80. Z. Manna, A. Pnueli, Adequate proof principles for invariance and liveness properties of concurrent programs. Sci. Comput. Program. **4**(3), 257–289 (1984). doi:10.1016/0167-6423(84)90003-0. http://dx.doi.org/10.1016/0167-6423(84)90003-0

81. Z. Manna, A. Pnueli, *The Temporal Logic of Reactive and Concurrent Systems* (Springer, New York, 1992)

82. Z. Manna, A. Pnueli, *Temporal Verification of Reactive Systems: Safety* (Springer, New York, 1995)

83. J. Misra, A discipline of multiprogramming. ACM Comput. Surv. **28**(4es) (1996). doi:10.1145/242224.242286. http://doi.acm.org/10.1145/242224.242286

84. J. Misra, *A Discipline of Multiprogramming: Programming Theory for Distributed Applications* (Springer, Secaucus, 2001)

85. S.L. Murphy, A.U. Shankar, A note on the drinking philosophers. ACM TOPLAS **10**(1), 178–188 (1988)

86. S.L. Murphy, A.U. Shankar, Connection management for the transport layer: service specification and protocol verification. IEEE Trans. Commun. **39**(12), 1762–1775 (1991). doi:10.1109/26.120163. Earlier version in Proceedings ACM SIGCOMM '87 Workshop, Stowe, Vermont, Aug 1987

87. A.L. Oláh, *Design and Analysis of Transport Protocols for Reliable High-Speed Communications*. Ph.D. thesis, University of Twente, Enschede, 1997. http://doc.utwente.nl/13676/

88. A.L. Oláh, S.M.H.d. Groot, Assertional verification of a connection management protocol, in *Proceedings of the IFIP TC6 Eighth International Conference on Formal Description Techniques VIII* (Chapman and Hall, London, 1996), pp. 401–416. http://dl.acm.org/citation.cfm?id=646214.681518

89. A.L. Oláh, S.M. Heemstra de Groot, Alternative specification and verification of a periodic state exchange protocol. IEEE/ACM Trans. Netw. **5**(4), 525–529 (1997). doi:10.1109/90.649467. http://dx.doi.org/10.1109/90.649467

90. S. Owicki, D. Gries, An axiomatic proof technique for parallel programs – i. Acta Inform. **6**, 319–340 (1976)

91. S. Owicki, D. Gries, Verifying properties of parallel programs: an axiomatic approach. Commun. ACM **19**(5), 279–285 (1976). doi:http://doi.acm.org/10.1145/360051.360224

92. S. Owicki, L. Lamport, Proving liveness properties of concurrent programs. ACM Trans. Program. Lang. Syst. **4**(3), 455–495 (1982). doi:10.1145/357172.357178. http://doi.acm.org/10.1145/357172.357178

93. S. Owre, N. Shankar, A brief overview of pvs, in *TPHOLs '08: Proceedings of the 21st International Conference on Theorem Proving in Higher Order Logics* (Springer, Berlin/Heidelberg, 2008), pp. 22–27. doi:http://dx.doi.org/10.1007/978-3-540-71067-7_5

94. D.L. Parnas, A technique for software module specification with examples. Commun. ACM **15**(5), 330–336 (1972). doi:10.1145/355602.361309. http://doi.acm.org/10.1145/355602.361309

95. G.L. Peterson, Myths about the mutual exclusion problem. Inf. Process. Lett. **12**(3), 115–116 (1981)

96. L.L. Peterson, B.S. Davie, *Computer Networks: A Systems Approach*, 3rd edn. (Morgan Kaufmann, San Francisco, 2003)

97. A. Pnueli, The temporal logic of programs, in: *Proceedings of the 18th Annual Symposium on Foundations of Computer Science, SFCS '77* (IEEE Computer Society, Washington DC, 1977), pp. 46–57. doi:10.1109/SFCS.1977.32. http://dx.doi.org/10.1109/SFCS.1977.32

98. A. Pnueli, The temporal semantics of concurrent programs. in *Proceedings of the International Sympoisum on Semantics of Concurrent Computation* (Springer, London, 1979), pp. 1–20. http://dl.acm.org/citation.cfm?id=647172.716123

99. A.A. Schoone, Verification of connection-management protocols. Technical report, DSpace at Utrecht University, Netherlands, 1987 [http://dspace.library.uu.nl:8080/dspace-oai/request]. http://igitur-archive.library.uu.nl/math/2006-1214-201341/UUindex.html

100. A.U. Shankar, Verified data transfer protocols with variable flow control. ACM Trans. Comput. Syst. **7**(3), 281–316 (1989). doi:10.1145/65000.65003. http://doi.acm.org/10.1145/65000.65003

101. A.U. Shankar, An introduction to assertional reasoning for concurrent systems. ACM Comput. Surv. **25**(3), 225–262 (1993). doi:10.1145/158439.158441. http://doi.acm.org/10.1145/158439.158441

102. A.U. Shankar, S.S. Lam, An HDLC protocol specification and its verification using image protocols. ACM Trans. Comput. Syst. **1**(4), 331–368 (1983). doi:10.1145/357377.357384. http://doi.acm.org/10.1145/357377.357384

103. A.U. Shankar, S.S. Lam, Time-dependent distributed systems: proving safety, liveness and real-time properties. Distrib. Comput. **2**, 61–79 (1987). http://dx.doi.org/10.1007/ BF01667079. doi:10.1007/BF01667079

104. A.U. Shankar, S.S. Lam, A stepwise refinement heuristic for protocol construction. ACM Trans. Program. Lang. Syst. **14**(3), 417–461 (1992). doi:10.1145/129393.129394. http:// doi.acm.org/10.1145/129393.129394. Earlier version appeared in Stepwise Refinement of Distributed Systems, LNCS 430, Springer, 1990

105. A.U. Shankar, D. Lee, Minimum-latency transport protocols with modulo-n incarnation numbers. IEEE/ACM Trans. Netw. **3**(3), 255–268 (1995). doi:10.1109/90.392385. http://dx. doi.org/10.1109/90.392385

106. K. Slind, M. Norrish: A brief overview of hol4, in: *TPHOLs '08: Proceedings of the 21st International Conference on Theorem Proving in Higher Order Logics* (Springer, Berlin/Heidelberg, 2008), pp. 28–32. doi:http://dx.doi.org/10.1007/978-3-540-71067-7_6

107. M.G. Staskauskas, The formal specification and design of a distributed electronic funds-transfer system. IEEE Trans. Comput. **37**(12), 1515–1528 (1988). doi:10.1109/12.9730. http://dx.doi.org/10.1109/12.9730

108. W.R. Stevens, *UNIX Network Programming*, vol 1. Second Edition: Networking APIs: Sockets and XTI. (Prentice-Hall, Englewood Cliffs, 1998). Chapter 4, ISBN 0-13-490012-X

109. K. Suonio, *A Practical Theory of Reactive Systems: Incremental Modeling of Dynamic Behaviors* (Springer, Secaucus, 2005). (Texts in Theoretical Computer Science. An EATCS Series)

110. R.E. Tarjan, J. van Leeuwen, Worst-case analysis of set union algorithms. J. ACM **31**(2), 245–281 (1984). doi:10.1145/62.2160. http://doi.acm.org/10.1145/62.2160

111. G. Taubenfeld, The black-white bakery algorithm and related bounded-space, adaptive, local-spinning and fifo algorithms, in *DISC*, ACM (Association for Computing Machinery), New York, pp. 56–70 (2004)

112. G. Tel, Assertional verification of a timer-based protocol. Technical report, DSpace at Utrecht University, Netherlands, 1987 [http://dspace.library.uu.nl:8080/dspace-oai/request]. http://igitur-archive.library.uu.nl/math/2006-1214-201352/UUindex.html

113. G. Tel, F. Mattern, The derivation of distributed termination detection algorithms from garbage collection schemes. sACM Trans. Program. Lang. Syst. **15**(1), 1–35 (1993). doi:10.1145/151646.151647. http://doi.acm.org/10.1145/151646.151647

114. G. Tel, R.B. Tan, J. van Leeuwen, The derivation of graph marking algorithms from distributed termination detection protocols. Sci. Comput. Program. **10**(2), 107–137 (1988). doi:10.1016/0167-6423(88)90024-X. http://dx.doi.org/10.1016/0167-6423(88)90024-X

115. M. Trehel, M. Naimi, A distributed algorithm for mutual exclusion based on data structures and fault tolerance, in: *6th Annual International Phoenix Conference on Computers and Communication* (Scottsdale, Arizona, 1987), pp. 35–39

Chapter 2
Simple Lock

2.1 Introduction

This chapter fleshes out a simplified version of the producer-consumer-lock example outlined in the previous chapter. Section 2.2 presents a "simple lock" program that implements a lock assuming a platform with minimal atomicity, namely, atomic reads and writes of memory words, and minimal progress, namely, weak fairness of threads. Section 2.3 presents a service program that defines the desired external behavior of the simple lock program. Section 2.4 states the conditions for the simple lock to implement the simple lock service. Section 2.5 proves that the conditions hold. This section also illustrates assertional proofs. Section 2.6 presents a program in which a producer and a consumer make use of the simple lock service.

To keep things simple, the lock users are restricted to have thread ids $0, 1, \cdots, N-1$, where N is a parameter of the program. This allows the lock program to track its users with an array. (Tids of general structure complicates the handling of simultaneous lock requests.) Also for simplicity, the simple lock program has a local thread that continuously checks for user requests. (Implementations without local threads are presented in Chaps. 9 and 10.)

2.1.1 Conventions

Assignment is denoted by "←" and equality by "=". Conjunction is denoted by "and", disjunction by "or", and implication by "⇒". These operators are "short-circuit" evaluated from left to right; e.g., when evaluating "A and B", first A is evaluated and then B is evaluated iff A is true. For an implication "A ⇒ B", we refer to A as the "lhs" (left-hand side) and to B as the "rhs" (right-hand side). Likewise, a leads-to assertion "A *leads-to* B" has lhs A and rhs B.

A.U. Shankar, *Distributed Programming: Theory and Practice*,
DOI 10.1007/978-1-4614-4881-5__2,
© Springer Science+Business Media New York 2013

The construct j..k, where j and k are integers, is the sequence of integers j, j+1, ···, k; it is empty if j exceeds k. The construct mod(j,N) stands for j modulo-N, the non-negative remainder of j divided by N.

The type Sid denotes sids (system ids); they are pointers to systems. A non-null sid z is said to be "alive" iff it points to a system; i.e., a system with sid z has been created and not yet terminated. The construct sid() returns a non-null sid that is not alive; a system can be created later with that sid. The construct sid(z), where z is an integer or character string, returns a non-null non-alive sid with value z if sid z is not currently allocated; otherwise it returns null.

The type Tid denotes tids (thread ids); they are pointers to threads. A non-null tid z is said to be "alive" iff it points to a thread. The constructs tid() and tid(z) are analogous to the corresponding constructs for sids.

The following predicates are available for stating properties of programs. The predicate "thread t in S", where S is a statement or code chunk, is true iff thread (with tid) t is inside S. The predicate "thread in S" is true iff some thread is in S. The predicate "not thread in S" is true iff there is no thread in S. In these predicates, "in" can be replaced by "at" to mean that the thread is at the start of S, and by "on" to mean that the thread is at or in S.

For a non-null sid (or tid) z, the predicate "z.alive" is true iff z is alive. For notational convenience, we assume that the state of a system z is available for writing assertions even after z has been terminated; this allows us, for example, to shorten "z.alive and (thread in z.f)" to "thread in z.f".

Given an atomic step e and predicates P and Q, we say e **unconditionally establishes** Q **from** P to mean that Q holds after an execution of e assuming *only* that P and any input assumption of e hold prior to the execution. If P is vacuous (i.e., true), we say e **unconditionally establishes** Q. If P and Q are the same, we say e **unconditionally preserves** P.

End of conventions

2.2   Lock Program

The simple lock program is shown in Fig. 2.1 (ignore the "•"s for now). The program, called SimpleLock, has one parameter, N, indicating the number of possible users; their tids would be 0, ..., N-1. The program input assumption requires N to be at least 1. The main code first defines some variables. Boolean array xreq has its ith entry true if user i has a request pending. Boolean xacq is true if a user has the lock. Integer xp is an index into xreq. The main code then starts a thread to execute function serve and stores its tid in variable t. The main code ends by returning its sid. (Tid t may coincidentally be in 0..N-1, but it doesn't matter.)

In function serve, thread t repeatedly cycles through xreq. When it finds that the user corresponding to xp is waiting, it sets xacq to true, sets xreq[xp] to false (freeing thread xp to return from its acq call), and busy waits until xacq becomes false (which happens when the thread releases the lock).

```
program SimpleLock(int N) {        // Implements lock for users 0, ... , N-1
  ia [N ≥ 1]                        // program input assump; for analysis only
  boolean[N] xreq ← false;          // xreq[i] true if user i has requested lock
  boolean xacq ← false;             // true if a user has acquired the lock
  int xp ← 0;                        // index into xreq
  Tid t ← startThread(serve());     // start thread t executing function serve()
  return mysid;
  // end main

  function void serve() {
    while (true) {
a0:   if • (xreq[xp]) {
a1:     • xacq ← true;
a2:     • xreq[xp] ← false;
a3:       while • (xacq) skip;
        }
a4:   xp ← mod(xp+1,N);
    }
  }

  input void mysid.acq() {
    ia [mytid in 0..N-1]   // for analysis only
a5: xreq[mytid] ← true;
a6: while • (xreq[mytid]) skip;
    return;
  }

  input void mysid.rel() {
    ia [mytid in 0..N-1]          // for analysis only
a7: xacq ← false;
    return;
  }

  input void mysid.end() {
    ia [true]                      // for analysis only
    endSystem();
  }

  atomicity assumption {                          // for analysis only
    reads and writes of xacq, xreq[0], ..., xreq[N-1]
  }

  progress assumption {weak fairness for threads}  // for analysis only
}
```

Fig. 2.1 Simple lock program; statement labels a0, ..., a7 are used in analysis; "•"s are atomicity breakpoints

There are three input functions: acq and rel to acquire and release the lock; and end to initiate termination of the lock system. In acq and rel, the input assumption requires the calling thread's tid, mytid, to be in 0..N-1. When thread i calls acq, it sets xreq[i] to true, busy waits until xreq[i] becomes false (due to thread t executing a2 with xp equal to i), and returns. When thread i calls rel, it sets xacq to false (which frees thread t from waiting on a3) and returns. Function end can be called by any thread (its tid need not be in 0..N-1). It executes endSystem, initiating termination of the lock system. Termination occurs if and when the system has no guest threads. So it may may never occur, or it may occur when the lock is with a user.

The atomicity assumption requires the underlying platform to atomically execute reads and writes of the boolean variables xacq, xreq[0], $\cdots$, xreq[N-1]. These variables are subject to simultaneous conflicting accesses by the local thread t and the guest threads 0, $\cdots$, N-1 (executing input functions). Specifically, variable xacq is accessed by thread t and any thread calling rel, and variable xreq[i] is accessed by threads i and t.

The progress assumption requires that thread t and the guest threads are run with weak fairness by the underlying platform, i.e., no thread enters a state where it gets no further processor cycles. The atomicity and progress assumptions are very conservative, and would be provided by practically any bare hardware platform.

Note that mysid.acq's input assumption allows the calling thread to already have the lock. Similarly, mysid.rel's input assumption allows the calling thread to not have the lock. These requirements, which will be imposed later in the lock service, are omitted here *purely to illustrate* that an implementation can assume that users obey the service. While these particular requirements can be easily checked in the input function bodies, in general, the check may be expensive. They would also be redundant if the callers can be trusted. We could have even set the input assumptions to simply true, but then the program would not satisfy the fault-freedom and effective-atomicity proved below.

Each evolution of SimpleLock is a sequence of transitions, each transition being an execution of a statement in the main code or in a function of the program. Each transition takes the program from one state to another, starting from the initial state defined by a value for N. Many evolutions are possible because requests and releases can occur at arbitrary times.

2.2.1 Fault-Freedom and Effective Atomicity

We now prove two properties of program SimpleLock, that is, properties satisfied by every *allowed* evolution (i.e., assuming inputs satisfy their input assumptions). The first property is that program SimpleLock is fault-free. There only two ways that the program can become faulty. The first way is if xreq is defined with negative N; this is ruled out by the program's input assumption. The second way is an out-of-bound reference to xreq in functions mysid.acq or serve. The former is not possible because of mysid.acq's input assumption. The latter is not possible because xp is initially in 0..N-1 and is changed only by a4, which keeps xp in this range. Thus the following holds.

A_0 : SimpleLock is fault-free

It's worth noting that SimpleLock has allowed evolutions that are undesirable. For example, if a user calls rel when it does not have the lock, two users may end up having the lock at the same time (how?).

The second property is a partition of its code into effectively-atomic steps. We denote the partition by selecting a subset of control points. The selected control points, which we refer to as **atomicity breakpoints**, are indicated in Fig. 2.1 by the "•"s. *The sequence of instructions that a thread executes from one atomicity breakpoint until the next atomicity breakpoint is effectively atomic.* In particular, each such sequence has at most one atomic instruction that conflicts with code executed by other threads. Details follow:

- Initial step: The main code (which has no internal atomicity breakpoints) together with function serve upto its first atomicity breakpoint (at a0) is effectively atomic. It conflicts only in return mysid (after which input functions can be called).
- Function serve: Each of a0, a1, a2, and a3's iteration is atomic (from the program's atomicity assumption). Each conflicts with code of other threads, so no two of them can be grouped together. Statement a4 does not conflict, so it can be grouped with the preceding atomic step; i.e., a4 can be executed atomically with a0 when xreq[xp] is false and with a3 when xacq is false. (Thread t may be terminated, along with the system, after partially executing a4, but this is equivalent to not having started executing a4.)
- Function mysid.acq: From the start of the function to the atomicity breakpoint at a6 is effectively atomic; its only conflict is in the atomic write in a5. From the atomicity breakpoint at a6 to the next atomicity breakpoint at a6 (or to the return) is effectively atomic; its only conflict is the atomic read in a6.
- Function mysid.rel: The entire body is effectively atomic; its only conflict is the atomic write in a7.
- Function mysid.end: The entire body is effectively atomic.

2.3 Lock Service Program

The lock service program, called SimpleLockService, is shown in Fig. 2.2. The program parameters and program input condition are as in SimpleLock. It has three input functions, acq, rel and end, and no output functions. The main code defines an array acqd that indicates the user (if any) that has acquired the lock, and a boolean ending that indicates whether end has been called. The program is fault-free. Faulty initialization of acqd is precluded by the program input assumption. Out-of-

```
service SimpleLockService(int N)  { // lock service for users 0, ..., N-1
   ic {N ≥ 1}
   boolean[N] acqd ← false;      // acqd[i] is true iff i has lock
   ending ← false;               // termination initiated
   return mysid;
   // end main
   }

   input void mysid.acq() {
      ic {not ending and (mytid in 0..N-1)
          and not acqd[mytid]}
      oc {forall(j in 0..N-1: not acqd[j])}
      acqd[mytid] ← true;
      return;
   }

   input void mysid.rel() {
      ic {not ending and (mytid in 0..N-1)
          and acqd[mytid]}
      acqd[mytid] ← false;
      oc {true}
      return;
   }

   input void mysid.end() {
      ic {not ending}
      ending ← true;
      oc {true}
      return;
   }

   atomicity assumption {input parts and output parts}

   progress assumption {
      // rel call returns
      forall(Tid i: (thread i in mysid.rel) leads-to (not i in mysid.rel));

      // if no one holds the lock forever then acq call returns
      forall(i in 0..N-1: acqd[i] leads-to not acqd[i])
         ⇒ forall(Tid i: (thread i in mysid.acq) leads-to (not i in mysid.rel));

      // end call returns
      forall(Tid i: (thread i in mysid.end) leads-to (not i in mysid.end));
   }
}
```

Fig. 2.2 Simple lock service program

bound reference to acqd is precluded by the conjunct "mysid in 0..N-1" in the input conditions of acq and rel. (A faulty service program is useless as a standard for implementation.)

A_1 : SimpleLockService is fault-free

The input condition of function acq is more constraining than in the simple lock. In addition to requiring the calling thread's tid to be in 0..N-1, it requires that end has not been called and that the calling thread does not have the lock. The output condition of acq requires that the return be executed only if no user has the lock. The input condition of function rel is more constraining than in the simple lock, requiring also that end has not been called and that the calling thread have the lock. Its output condition is vacuous, so it is non-blocking. The input condition of function end requires that end has not been called. Its output condition is vacuous, so it is non-blocking.

A program that implements this service can assume that its input functions will be called only when their service input conditions hold; it need not check for them. As with any service program, the input and output parts are to be executed atomically by the platform. The powerful (read-modify-write) atomicity of acq's return is not a problem because the lock service program is intended for analysis and not for execution. The progress assumption is expressed with "leads-to" assertions rather than fairness assertions.

Each allowed evolution of the service program consists of an atomic execution of the main code followed by a sequence of atomic executions of input parts and output parts. At any time, any input (or output) part can be executed as long as the input (or output) condition holds and a thread exists or can arrive from the environment. Thus the program defines *all* evolutions such that: (1) each user i cycles through acq call, acq return, rel call, and rel return; (2) between any two successive acq returns, there is a rel call by the user of the first acq return; (3) no calls can be made after an end call; (4) every rel call eventually returns; (5) every end call eventually returns; and (6) every acq call eventually returns provided no user holds the lock indefinitely. The last three conditions come from the progress assumption.

This lock service is more general than the simple lock because it allows requests to be served in any order, only requiring that no request is indefinitely delayed. Thus it represents many possible implementations, including the simple lock given earlier.

2.4 Implements Conditions

We now state the conditions that must hold for SimpleLock(N) (or any other program) to implement SimpleLockService(N). The conditions are proved in the next section. There is a safety condition and a progress condition. Roughly speaking, the safety condition is that whenever the lock and the service have undergone the same input-output history, the lock can accept any input that the service can accept, and any output the lock does is an output that the service can do. The progress condition is that the lock satisfies the service's progress assumption. These conditions can be formalized in terms of the evolutions of the lock and the service (as shown in Sect. 1.7). But it is better formalized in terms of the lock and service programs, and we proceed with that now.

The first step is to "invert" the service program, i.e., interchange its inputs and outputs, resulting in a program that provides the most general environment that the lock can expect. This program, called SimpleLockServiceInverse, is shown in Figs. 2.3 and 2.4. It has an additional parameter, lck, matching the return value of the service program's main code; it will be set to the sid of the lock implementation to be tested. Input parts become output parts, output parts become input parts, and mysid becomes lck. For example, input function mysid.acq becomes an output function that does an output call lck.acq. The progress assumption is now a condition to be satisfied. For example, the first progress assertion, where mysid.rel has become lck.rel, requires system lck to eventually return lck.rel calls.

The next step is to define a program, say Z, that executes the lock and service inverse concurrently. The program is shown in Fig. 2.5. It has the same parameter and input condition as the service program. It starts a lock system, lck, and a service inverse system, lsi, which interact solely with each other (because aggregate system Z is "closed"). It needs no atomicity assumptions because its basic system has only thread.

The final step is to write down the assertions that aggregate system Z must satisfy in order for lock to implement service. They are shown in Fig. 2.6. B_0 is a safety assertion stating that lck returns an acq call only if the corresponding input conditions in lsi holds. No assertion is needed for lck's return of a rel call because lsi.doRel's input condition is vacuous. The same is true for lck's return of an end call. $B_1 - B_3$ are simply the assertions in lsi's progress condition. (We can write "thread i in lck.rel" without preceding it by "lck.alive" because of our convention that lck's state is available for writing assertions even after its termination.)

2.5 Proving the Implements Conditions

The goal is to prove that aggregate system Z satisfies assertions $B_0 - B_3$. For ease of reference, the simple lock and service inverse programs are shown together in Fig. 2.7. The service inverse has an atomicity breakpoint (marked by "●") at each output condition; this is the case for any service or service inverse program. Together with the atomicity breakpoints of SimpleLock, they define the following steps to be effectively atomic:

- Z's initial step: consisting of Z's main, lck's initial step, and lsi's main.
- Step lsi.doAcq call: from lsi.doAcq's output condition to the atomicity breakpoint in lck.a6.

```
service SimpleLockService(int N) {
program SimpleLockServiceInverse(int N, Sid lck) {
    // lck: lock system being tested
    ic {N ≥ 1}
    boolean[N] acqd ← false;
    ending ← false;
    return mysid;
    // end main

    input void mysid.acq() {
    output doAcq() {
        ie oc {not ending and (mytid in 0..N-1)
              and not acqd[mytid]}
        lck.acq();                                    // added call
        oe ic {forall(j in 0..N-1: not acqd[j])}
        acqd[mytid] ← true;
        return;
    }

    input void mysid.rel() {
    output doRel() {
        ie oc {not ending and (mytid in 0..N-1)
              and acqd[mytid]}
        acqd[mytid] ← false;
        lck.rel();                                    // added call
        oe ic {true}
        return;
    }

    input void mysid.end() {
    output doEnd() {
        ie oc {not ending}
        ending ← true;
        lck.end();                                    // added call
        oe ic {true}
        return;
    }

// continued
```

Fig. 2.3 Part 1: SimpleLockServiceInverse, obtained from SimpleLockService after deletions and additions (*underlined*)

```
// SimpleLockServiceInverse continued

   atomicity assumption {input parts and output parts}

   progress assumption condition {
      forall(Tid i: (thread i in mysid lck.rel) leads-to (not i inmysid lck.rel));

      forall(i in 0..N-1: acqd[i] leads-to not acqd[i])
        ⇒ forall(Tid i: (thread i in mysid lck.acq)
                         leads-to (not i in mysid lck.acq));

      forall(Tid i: (thread i in mysid lck.end) leads-to (not i in mysid lck.end));
   }
}
```

Fig. 2.4 Part 2: SimpleLockServiceInverse, obtained from SimpleLockService after deletions and additions (*underlined*)

```
program Z(int N) {
  ic {N ≥ 1}
  inputs(); outputs();                        // aggregate system Z is closed
  Sid lck ← startSystem(SimpleLock(N));        // lock
  Sid lsi ← startSystem(SimpleLockServiceInverse(N, lck)); // service inverse
  return mysid;

  atomicity assumption {}
  progress assumption {weak fairness}
}
```

Fig. 2.5 Program of lock and inverse lock service; main body is effectively atomic

---

B_0 : *Inv* (thread i at lsi.doAcq.ic) ⇒ forall(j in 0..N-1: not acqd[j])
B_1 : forall(Tid i: (thread i in lck.rel) *leads-to* (not i in lck.rel))
B_2 : forall(i in 0..N-1: acqd[i] *leads-to* not acqd[i])
          ⇒ forall(Tid i: (thread i in lck.acq) *leads-to* (not i in lck.acq))
B_3 : forall(Tid i: (thread i in lck.end) *leads-to* (not i in lck.end))

Fig. 2.6 Assertions to be satisfied by program Z in order for SimpleLock to implement SimpleLock-Service

- Step lck.acq return: from the atomicity breakpoint in lck.a6 to the end of lsi.doAcq.
- Step lsi.doRel: from lsi.doRel's output condition to the end of lsi.doRel, including lck.rel's body.

```
program SimpleLock(int N) {           program SimpleLockServiceInverse
   ia {N ≥ 1}                                       (int N, Sid lck) {
   boolean[N] xreq← false;             ic {N ≥ 1}
   boolean xacq ← false;              boolean[N] acqd ← false;
   int xp ← 0;                        ending ← false;
   Tid t ← startThread(serve());      return mysid;
   return mysid;
                                      output doAcq() {
   function void serve() {            • oc {not ending
     while (true) {                          and (mytid in 0..N-1)
a0:    if • (xreq[xp]) {                      and not acqd[mytid]}
a1:      • xacq ← true;                   lck.acq();
a2:      • xreq[xp] ← false;              ic {forall(j in 0..N-1: not acqd[j])}
a3:        while • (xacq) skip;           acqd[mytid] ← true;
       }                                  return;
a4:    xp ← mod(xp+1,N);               }
     }
   }                                   output doRel() {
                                       • oc {not ending
   input void mysid.acq() {                  and (mytid in 0..N-1)
     ia {mytid in 0..N-1}                     and acqd[mytid]}
a5:  xreq[mytid] ← true;                   acqd[mytid] ← false;
a6:  while • (xreq[mytid]) skip;           lck.rel();
     return;                               ic {true}
   }                                       return;
                                       }
   input void mysid.rel() {
     ia {mytid in 0..N-1}             output doEnd() {
a7:  xacq ← false;                     • oc {not ending}
     return;                               lck.end();
   }                                       ic {true}
                                           return;
   input void mysid.end() {            }
     ia {true}
     endSystem();                      atomicity assumption {...}
   }
                                       progress condition {...}
   atomicity assumption {...}        }
   progress assumption {...}
}
```

Fig. 2.7 Component programs of Z(N); "•"s are atomicity breakpoints

- Step lsi.doEnd: from lsi.doEnd's output condition to the end of lsi.doEnd, including lck.end's body.
- The steps inside lck defined by the internal atomicity breakpoints at a0, a1, a2 and a3. (The input condition of lsi and the output conditions of lsi.doAcq, lsi.doRel and lsi.doEnd ensure that every input to lck is allowed. Hence the atomicity breakpoints established for SimpleLock also hold for instantiation lck.)

2.5.1 Proving the Safety Condition: B_0

We now prove that Z satisfies B_0. Given Z's effective atomicity, thread i comes to lsi.doAcq.ic iff it was on statement lck.a6 and lck.xreq[i] was false. Thus B_0 is equivalent to $Inv\,C_0$, where C_0 is as follows. (Note that C_0 is the predicate of invariant assertion $Inv\,C_0$, whereas B_0 is an invariant assertion.)

C_0 : ((thread i on lck.a6) and not lck.xreq[i])
$\Rightarrow$ forall(j in 0..N-1: not lsi.acqd[j])

It suffices to prove that Z satisfies $Inv\,C_0$. Henceforth we omit the lck and lsi prefixes when there is no ambiguity, and we sometimes shorten "thread t on S" to "t on S". Let's take a closer look at the evolution of Z assuming that lck remains alive. After Z's initial step, xacq and the entries of xreq and acqd are false, and thread t starts repeatedly executing a0 and a4. When a thread i executes step doAcq call, it sets xreq[i] to true and waits on a6. When thread t finds xreq[xp] true (in a0), it executes a1 and a2 and waits on a3. Until t executes a2, every acqd entry is false. Thread xp, which would be waiting on a6, finds xreq[xp] false and executes step lck.acq return, which sets acqd[xp] to true (in doAcq's input part). Thread t remains on a3 until thread xp executes step doRel, setting xacq and acqd[xp] to false. At this point, t executes a3 and a4 and returns to a0.

So when thread t is not on a3 (and lck is alive), nobody has the lock. When thread t is on a3 (which also implies that lck is alive), thread xp has the lock or is about to get it, and nobody else has the lock. In terms of assertions, we have established $Inv\,C_1$ and $Inv\,C_2$, where:

C_1 : (lck.alive and not (thread t on a3))
$\Rightarrow$ forall(j in 0..N-1: not acqd[j])
C_2 : (thread t on a3)
$\Rightarrow$ ((acqd[xp]
or (not acqd[xp] and (thread xp on a6) and not xreq[xp]))
and forall(j in 0..N-1, j $\neq$ xp: not acqd[j]))

Given that $Inv\,C_1$ and $Inv\,C_2$ hold, it's easy to prove $Inv\,C_0$. Assume that lck is alive, otherwise C_0 holds vacuously. Initially C_0 holds (vacuously, because thread i is not on a6). Thread i comes to a6 by executing step doAcq call; this sets xreq[i] to true and hence preserves C_0 vacuously. Variable xreq[i] becomes false when t executes a2 with xp equal to i; at this point no one has the lock (because C_1 holds non-vacuously before this step) and hence C_0's rhs holds. While thread i remains on a6, no other thread can set its acqd entry to true (because that would violate $Inv\,C_2$). When thread i leaves a6, C_0 holds vacuously. So $Inv\,C_0$ holds and we are done.

2.5.2   Proving the Progress Condition: $B_1 - B_3$

We now prove that Z satisfies assertions $B_1 - B_3$. B_1 says that every lck.rel call returns. It holds because the body of step lck.rel has no loops and is executed with weak fairness (from lck's progress assumption). B_3 says that every lck.end call eventually returns. It holds in the same way as B_1. B_2 says that every lck.acq call returns if the lock is not acquired indefinitely. It is has the form $D_0 \Rightarrow D_1$, where

D_0 : forall(i in 0..N-1: acqd[i] *leads-to* not acqd[i])
D_1 : forall(i in 0..N-1: (thread i in lck.acq) *leads-to* (not i in lck.acq))

What remains is to establish that Z satisfies D_1 assuming D_0. Because step doAcq call is atomic, "thread j in lck.acq" is equivalent to "thread j at a6". Suppose thread t is at a0 with xp = j and xreq[j] true. At this point, thread j is waiting on a6 and xreq[j] stays true (because only t can make it false). Thus t eventually executes statements a0..a2 (because of weak fairness), setting xreq[j] to false and xacq to true, and starts waiting on a3. Hence thread j, which is still on a6, eventually executes step lck.acq return, at which point acqd[j] becomes true. Thus the following holds:

D_2 : ((thread t on a0) and xp = j and xreq[j])
          leads-to ((t on a3) and xp = j and acqd[j])

If D_2's rhs holds, then thread j eventually executes doRel (because of assumption D_0), making xacq false. It stays false (because only t can make it true), and so t eventually leaves a3. Thus the following holds. (Recall that a4's execution is combined with a3's.)

D_3 : ((thread t on a3) and xp = j and acqd[j])
          leads-to ((t on a0) and xp = mod(j+1,N))

D_2 and D_3 imply the following:

D_4 : ((thread t on a0) and xp = j) *leads-to* ((t on a0) and xp = mod(j+1,N))

Thus xp keeps increasing modulo-N. Hence for every thread j such that j on a6, thread lck eventually comes to a0 with xp = j, where it finds xreq[j] to be true, and so eventually acqd[j] becomes true (from D_2). This establishes D_1, and we are done.

2.5.3   Assertional Proof of Inv C_1

The previous analysis illustrated assertional reasoning with operational proofs. We now illustrate an assertional proof for $InvC_1$, that is, a proof consisting of applications of proof rules. We use only one proof rule.

> **Invariance induction rule**: Z satisfies $InvC_1$ if there is a predicate D satisfying the following:
>
> 1. Z's initial atomic step unconditionally establishes D.
> 2. Every non-initial atomic step of Z unconditionally preserves D.
> 3. $D \Rightarrow C_1$ holds.

Given a predicate D, it is easy to check whether the conditions of the rule hold. Finding a suitable D may not be easy. The natural way to do this is to consider atomic steps that do not preserve C_1, and then identify what more needs to hold so that they preserve C_1.

Note that if we don't want acqd[j] to hold in a situation, then we also don't want thread j to be about to get the lock, i.e., "thread j on a6 and not xreq[j]" to hold. Otherwise thread j can execute the lck.acq return, making acqd[j] true. Let z(j) denote that j has the lock or is about to get it. Formally,

z(j): acqd[j] or ((thread j on a6) and not xreq[j])

We will establish the invariance of the following stronger version of C_1:

E_0 : (lck.alive and not (thread t on a3)) $\Rightarrow$ forall(j in 0..N-1: not z(j))

In order for E_0 to hold when t leaves a3, the following should be invariant:

E_1 : ((t on a3) and not xacq) $\Rightarrow$ forall(j in 0..N-1: not z[j])

When t is on a3 and xacq is true, we expect that thread xp, and no one else, has the lock or is about to get it.

E_2 : ((t on a3) and xacq) $\Rightarrow$ (z(xp) and forall(j in 0..N-1, j $\neq$ xp: not z(j)))

Conversely, when thread i has the lock or is about to get it, we expect thread t to be waiting on a3 for i:

E_3 : z(i) $\Rightarrow$ ((t on a3) and xp = i and xacq)

The following are also needed (e.g., E_4 is needed to preserve E_3 after t does a2):

E_4 : (t on a2) $\Rightarrow$ xacq
E_5 : (t on a1..a2) $\Rightarrow$ (xreq[xp] and (xp on a6))
E_6 : forall(j in 0..N-1: xreq[j] $\Rightarrow$ (j on a6))

It's easy to check that the conjunction of $E_0 - E_6$ is a suitable predicate D for the invariance induction rule. Consider the initial step: it establishes the rhs of E_0 and E_1, and falsifies the lhs of the others. Consider step a0 by t: it preserves E_0 (i.e., E_0 before the step ensures that E_0 holds after the step); it preserves E_3 and E_6; it establishes E_1, E_2, E_4 vacuously; it establishes E_5 (from E_6 holding prior to the step). Each of the remaining atomic steps can be similarly shown to preserve $E_0 - E_6$. Note that one can *check* this without having any global understanding of program Z. All that is needed is to understand the individual constructs of program Z and predicate D.

2.5.4 Assertional Proof of D_2

We now illustrate an assertional proof for the progress assertion D_2. The following proof rules are used:

Leads-to via thread t rule: Z satisfies P *leads-to* Q if the following hold:

1. Every non-initial atomic step of Z unconditionally establishes P or Q from P and not Q.
2. Every non-initial atomic step of thread t in Z unconditionally establishes Q from P and not Q.

Leads-to closure rules:

- P *leads-to* Q holds if P *leads-to* R and R *leads-to* Q hold.
- P *leads-to* Q holds if $Inv\,(P \Rightarrow Q)$ holds.

The following lines establish that Z satisfies D_2. Each line below states an assertion (at the left) and a proof rule application (at right) that establishes the assertion. D_2 follows from the closure of F_0 through F_5.

F_0 : ((t on a0) and xp = j and xreq[j])
         leads-to ((t on a1) and xp = j and xreq[j])   [via t]

F_1 : ((t on a1) and xp = j and xreq[j])
         leads-to ((t on a2) and xp = j and xreq[j])   [via t]

F_2 : ((t on a2) and xp = j and xreq[j])
         leads-to ((t on a2) and xp = j and xreq[j]
                and xacq and (j on a6))   [F_1, $Inv\,E_4$, $Inv\,E_6$, closure]

F_3 : ((t on a2) and xp = j and xreq[j]
        and xacq and (j on a6))
            leads-to ((t on a3) and xp = j and not xreq[j]
                    and xacq and (j on a6))   [via t]

F_4 : ((t on a3) and xp = j and not xreq[j]
        and xacq and (j on a6))
            leads-to ((t on a3) and xp = j and not xreq[j]
                    and xacq and (j on a6)
                    and forall(i in 0..N−1, i ≠ j: not acqd[j]))   [$Inv E_2$]

F_5 : ((t on a3) and xp = j and not xreq[j]
        and xacq and (j on a6)
        and forall(i in 0..N−1, i ≠ j: not acqd[j]))
            leads-to ((t on a3) and xp = j and acqd[j])   [via j]

2.6 Producer and Consumer Using Lock Service

So far we have seen one role of the lock service program, that is, as the standard
that any lock implementation must satisfy. We now illustrate the other role of the
lock service, that is, to serve as a lock in the design of a larger program that
makes use of locks. Figure 2.8 shows a program ProdCons1 in which a producer
and consumer make use of the lock service. (This corresponds to the program of the
same name in Chap. 1.) Using the service instead of a lock implementation makes

```
program ProdCons1(int J) {
    ia [J ≥ 0]      // J: number of items produced in total
    inputs();       // no external inputs; hides lck.end

    Tid tP ← tid(0);
    Tid tC ← tid(1);
    if (tP = null or tC = null)
        return [−1, mysid];

    // tids available; start lock, consumer, producer
    Sid lck ← startSystem(SimpleLockService(2));
    Sid cons ← startSystem(Consumer(lck, tC, J));
    Sid prod ← startSystem(Producer(lck, cons, tP, J));
    return [0, mysid];


    atomicity assumption {} // none
    progress assumption {weak fairness}
}
```

Fig. 2.8 Producer-consumer program

ProdCons1 easier to analyze because the service program is simpler. Any correctness property of ProdCons1 is preserved when the service program is replaced by any valid implementation, including the simple lock program.

Because the lock service restricts user tids to 0 and 1, program ProdCons1 first attempts to obtain these tids (via tid(0) and tid(1)). If the tids are not available, ProdCons1 gives up and returns the tuple [-1, mysid], where -1 indicates failure. Otherwise it instantiates the lock service (Fig. 2.9), consumer (Fig. 2.11), and producer (Fig. 2.10), passes tids 0 and 1 to the producer and consumer, and returns the tuple [0, mysid], where 0 indicates success.

The producer repeatedly produces an item and gives it to the consumer by calling the consumer's input function put. (This function should have an item parameter, but it's omitted for simplicity.) After producing J items, the producer terminates itself. The consumer repeatedly empties its cache of items and consumes them. The producer and consumer use the lock service to ensure that an item is not put in the cache while the cache is being consumed. After consuming J items, the consumer terminates the lock system and then itself.

We start our analysis of aggregate system ProdCons1 by showing that it is fault-free. System lck is instantiated first; it has no local thread so it makes no calls. System cons is instantiated next; it has a local thread whose only calls are to lck, which already exists. System prod is instantiated next; it has a local thread whose only calls are to lck and cons, both of which already exist. Systems prod and cons use the lock service correctly, i.e., lck is called only by a thread with tid 0 or 1, and that each thread cycles through lck.acq and lck.rel. (If this did not hold, the lock implementation, which would replace the lock service at run time, can do anything, and nothing could be claimed about aggregate ProdCons1.) Thus aggregate system ProdCons1 is fault-free.

Next we partition the code of aggregate system ProdCons1 into effectively atomic steps. It turns out that a single atomicity breakpoint, at lck.acq.oc, is all that is needed. Thus the following steps are effectively atomic:

- ProdCons1 initial step: consisting of ProdCons1 main, lck main, cons main, prod main, consume initial step (start to atomicity breakpoint), and produce initial step (start to atomicity breakpoint).

   Except for the consume and produce initial steps, this step is executed by a single thread. System lck's main has no conflict with lck's input functions because those functions are called only after prod and cons become alive, which happens only after lck's main returns. Similarly, cons's main has no conflict with cons's input function because the latter is called only after prod becomes alive, which happens only after cons main returns. The initial steps of produce and consume, executed by threads tP and tC, have no conflict because np and nc are accessed by only one thread.

- Step produce iteration: thread tP executing from atomicity breakpoint back to the atomicity breakpoint or to producer termination (if np equals J). In particular, the calls to cons.put, lck.rel and endSystem are nonblocking.

```
service SimpleLockService(int N) {
  ic {N ≥ 1}    // N: # lock users
  ...
  return mysid;

  input void mysid.acq() {
    ic {...}
    • oc {...}
  }

  input void mysid.rel() {...}

  input void mysid.end() {...}

  atomicity assumption {...}
  progress assumption {...}
}
```

Fig. 2.9 Lock service; "•" is atomicity breakpoint

```
program Producer(Sid lck, Sid cons,
                 Tid tP, int J) {
  ia {true}
  int np ← 0; // # items produced
  startThread(tP, produce());
  return mysid;

  function void produce() {
    while (np < J) {
      np ← np+1; // produce item
      lck.acq();  // acquire lock
      cons.put(); // item to cons
      lck.rel();  // release lock
    }
    endSystem();
  }

  // none: only one thread
  atomicity assumption { }

  progress assumption {weak fairness}
}
```

Fig. 2.10 Producer program

```
program Consumer
            (Sid lck, Tid tC, int J) {
  ia {true}
  int nc ← 0;    // # items consumed
  int cache ← 0; // # items in cache
  startThread(tC, consume());
  return mysid;

  function void consume() {
    while (nc < J) {
      lck.acq();  // acquire lock
      // consume cache
      nc ← nc+cache;
      cache ← 0;
      lck.rel();  // release lock
    }
    lck.end();
    endSystem();
  }

  input void mysid.put() {
    ia {true}
    cache ← cache+1;
    return;
  }

  // none: uses lck instead
  atomicity assumption { }

  progress assumption {weak fairness}
}
```

Fig. 2.11 Consumer program

- Step consume iteration: thread tC executing from atomicity breakpoint back to the atomicity breakpoint or to consumer termination (if nc equals J).

  In particular, consume's accesses to cache do not conflict with put's access to cache because the lock service prevents them from being executed at the same time. (If this observation is not obvious, one can prove it by treating the statements involving cache as null statements and proving that the resulting program allows at most one thread at any of the null statements at any time.)

Any further analysis can now be conveniently done. Here are some desired properties, whose proof is left as an exercise. G_0 says that only produced items are consumed. G_1 says that J items are consumed eventually. G_2 says that the producer, consumer, and lock systems are eventually terminated.

G_0 : *Inv* cons.nc $\leq$ prod.np
G_1 : true *leads-to* cons.nc $= $ J
G_2 : true *leads-to* not (lck.alive or prod.alive or cons.alive)

2.7 Concluding Remarks

This chapter has illustrated all the main pieces of SESF. We presented a simple lock that assumes a platform with only read-write atomicity and weak fairness. We defined its intended lock service. We defined the conditions for the simple lock to implement the lock service, and showed that they hold. We then used the lock service in a producer-consumer program.

To keep the example simple, our lock service constrains user ids to be from 0..N-1 where N is fixed at lock creation. Whereas the lock service usually provided in a programming language does not have this constraint. Also for simplicity, the lock implementation here has a local thread that constantly checks for a request, which is wasteful. Of course, there are algorithms that assume the same platform and avoid local threads, e.g., [1–4]. We will see such lock implementations in Chaps. 9 and 10.

The implementation here also makes users do busy waiting; i.e., when a user thread requests the lock, it busy waits until it acquires the lock. This is unavoidable given an underlying platform without any built-in synchronization constructs (i.e., a bare hardware platform). Most programming languages that provide locks execute on platforms that provide non-busy waiting (i.e., without consuming processor cycles), and their lock implementation would, of course, exploit that. These languages also usually provide synchronization constructs that allow threads to sleep and be awakened. We will see such constructs in Chap. 3.

Exercises

2.1. Change the order of a1 and a2 in SimpleLock, that is, put "xacq ← true" after "xreq[xp] ← false". Does this revised program implement the simple lock service. If you answer no, give a counter-example evolution.

2.2. Show that aggregate program ProdCons1 (in Fig. 2.8) satisfies the assertions G_0–G_2 (in Sect. 2.6). Here are some intermediate assertions you may want to prove:

- (prod.np $\geq$ k and k < J) *leads-to* prod.np $\geq$ k+1
- prod.np $\geq$ k *leads-to* cons.nc $\geq$ k
- true *leads-to* lck.endable
- true *leads-to* cons.endable
- true *leads-to* prod.endable

2.3. Write a service program for program Producer (in Fig. 2.10). The program would have no input functions and three output functions (calling lck.acq, lck.rel and cons.put).

2.4. Write a service program for program Consumer (in Fig. 2.11). The program would have one input function (mysid.put) and two output functions (calling lck.acq and lck.rel).

2.5. Program ProdCons2 is like ProdCons1 except that system lck can be instantiated to handle more than two users, and threads in the environment of aggregate system ProdCons2 can call lck.acq and lck.rel.

```
program ProdCons2(int J, int N) {
    ia {J ≥ 0 and N > 2}
    // lck.acq() and lck.rel() callable by threads outside aggregate ProdCons2
    inputs(lck.acq(), lck.rel());

    Tid tP ← tid(0);
    Tid tC ← tid(1);
    if (tP = null or tC = null)          // if tid 0 or 1 not available, exit
        return [-1, mysid];

    Sid lck ← startSystem(SimpleLockService(N));  // lock service for N users
    Sid cons ← startSystem(Consumer(lck, tC));       // local thread tC
    Sid prod ← startSystem(Producer(lck, cons, tP)); // local thread tP
    return [0, mysid];

    atomicity assumption {} // none
    progress assumption {weak fairness}
}
```

Thus threads with tids from 2..N-1 in the environment of aggregate system ProdCons2 can acquire and release the lock.

(a) Under what conditions will any safety property of aggregate ProdCons1 also hold in aggregate ProdCons2?
(b) Under what conditions will any progress property of aggregate ProdCons1 also hold in aggregate ProdCons2?

2.6. Modify the simple lock service so as to allow a user to request the lock even if it already has it and to release the lock even if it does not have it. The lock service should ignore invalid requests and otherwise provide the usual lock service.

2.7. Modify the simple lock service so that the service can inform a user to release the lock. Specifically, add a new "release indication" input function, say relInd(), which a user can call when it has the lock. The service returns the call either to tell the user to release the lock or after the user releases the lock.

(Such a lock service would be relevant in situations where conflicts between users are settled by aborting one or more users. Consider a database of objects, each with its own lock. A transaction updates a sequence of objects, obtaining their locks as needed. If two transactions conflict, i.e., both are half-way and each has done updates inconsistent with the other's, then at least one has to be aborted, in which case it has to be told to give up the locks it currently owns.)

2.8. Exercise 2.7 defined a lock service in which the service can tell a user to give up the lock. Another way to achieve such as service is as follows: (1) add a parameter, say sys, to the lock request input by which the user provides a sid when it requests the lock; (2) add an output function that does a "release request" output s.relReq(lck), where s is the sys provided by the user with the lock; and (3) make all the modifications you think necessary. Compare this service with that obtained in Exercise 2.7. Which do you prefer and why?

2.9. Obtain the inverse program of the lock service from Exercise 2.7.

2.10. Obtain a lock that implements the lock service in Exercise 2.7. Your lock program should assume the same platform as program SimpleLock.

2.11. Obtain the inverse program of the lock service from Exercise 2.8.

2.12. Obtain a lock that implements the lock service in Exercise 2.8. Your lock program should assume the same platform as program SimpleLock.

References

1. E.W. Dijkstra, Solution of a problem in concurrent programming control. Commun. ACM **8**(9), 569– (1965). doi:10.1145/365559.365617. http://doi.acm.org/10.1145/365559.365617
2. L. Lamport, A new solution of dijkstra's concurrent programming problem. Commun. ACM **17**(8), 453–455 (1974). doi:10.1145/361082.361093. http://doi.acm.org/10.1145/361082.361093
3. G.L. Peterson, Myths about the mutual exclusion problem. Inf. Process. Lett. **12**(3), 115–116 (1981)
4. G. Taubenfeld, The black-white bakery algorithm and related bounded-space, adaptive, local-spinning and fifo algorithms. In: *DISC* ACM, New York, (2004), pp. 56–70

Chapter 3
Bounded Buffer

3.1 Introduction

This chapter presents a bounded-buffer service and several implementations, using them to introduce several aspects of programs. First, the service illustrates how input functions that return (non-void) values are defined in service programs. Second, the programs that implement services illustrate the use of standard thread synchronization constructs available in concurrent programming languages, namely, locks, condition variables, and semaphores. (The lock program in Chap. 2 uses only read-write atomicity of memory words.) Third, a more powerful and more convenient synchronization construct, namely "awaits", is introduced. Programs using awaits are easier to write and analyze than those using the standard synchronization constructs, and can be mechanically transformed to use the latter. Fourth, the programs illustrate how to use synchronization constructs without unnecessarily blocking threads, thereby increasing parallelism in programs (and hence their performance). Fifth, the programs illustrate how blocked input calls can be canceled, thereby allowing a user that is no longer interested in such a call to retrieve its thread from the call.

Section 3.2 defines the bounded-buffer service and its inverse. Section 3.3 introduces the await construct and gives a program that implements the bounded-buffer service using awaits. Section 3.4 shows how to transform a program using awaits into one using locks and condition variables, and illustrates with the bounded-buffer implementation from Sect. 3.3. Section 3.5 shows how to transform a program using awaits into one using semaphores, and illustrates with the bounded-buffer implementation from Sect. 3.3. Section 3.6 shows how to use synchronization constructs to achieve desired atomicity without overly restricting the extent of parallelism. Section 3.7 defines a "cancelable" version of the bounded-buffer service, one that allows the environment to cancel a blocked put or get call.

A.U. Shankar, *Distributed Programming: Theory and Practice*,
DOI 10.1007/978-1-4614-4881-5__3,
© Springer Science+Business Media New York 2013

3.1.1   Conventions

The programs here make use of sequences and untyped variables. The construct "Val x" defines x to be a variable that takes values of any type. An enumerated list within square brackets denotes a sequence; e.g., [2,3,1] is a sequence with 2 at the head and 1 at the tail. The construct [] denotes the empty sequence. The construct "Seq y" defines y to be a sequence. The number of items in y is given by y.size. The jth entry in y is referenced by y[j], with y[0] being the head entry. The construct y.append(x) appends x to the tail of y. The construct y.remove() removes the entry at the head of y if y is not empty, and otherwise has no effect.

End of conventions

3.2   Bounded-Buffer Service

Figures 3.1 and 3.2 defines a bounded-buffer service. It has a parameter N denoting the size of the buffer. It has three input functions: put(x), to append item x to the buffer; get(), to remove an item from the buffer and return it; and end(), to stop further calls of put and end. (In an implementation, function end would typically execute endSystem.) Variable buff is the buffer; it is a sequence that is empty initially. Variable ending is true if end has been called. Variable putBusy (getBusy) is true iff a put (get) call is ongoing.

Function put(x) can be called whenever end has not been called and no put call is ongoing. Its output part appends x to buff and returns only if buff has space for x; otherwise it waits. Function get() can be called whenever end has not been called and no get call is ongoing. Its output part removes the item from the head of buff and returns it only if buff is not empty; otherwise it waits. Function end() can be called only if it has not been called already. The atomicity assumption is the usual: input parts and output parts are atomic. The progress assumption is equivalent to weak fairness for all threads.

Let's take a closer look at input function get(). The return value, x, is defined as a parameter of the output part, and it appears in the output condition and body. This means that *the output part is executed with any value of x that satisfies the output condition*. In effect, the output condition "assigns" a value to the parameter x; in this case, the value is the item at the head of buff.

Instead of introducing x as a parameter of the output part, we could have introduced it as a regular variable in the body of the output part and updated it there. The output part of get would then be as follows.

```
oc {buff.size > 0}
Val x ← buff[0];
buff.remove();
return x;
```

```
service BoundedBuffer(int N) {        // bounded buffer of size N
   ic {N ≥ 1}
   Seq buff ← seq();                  // buffer; initially empty
   boolean ending ← false;            // true iff end has been called
   boolean putBusy ← false;           // true iff thread in put
   boolean getBusy ← false;           // true iff thread in get
   return mysid;

   input void mysid.put(Val x) {
      ic {not ending and not putBusy}
      putBusy ← true;
      oc {buff.size < N}              // return only if buffer has space
      buff.append(x);                 // add item to buffer
      putBusy ← false;
      return;
   }

   input Val mysid.get() {
      ic {not ending and not getBusy}
      getBusy ← true;
      output(Val x) {                 // output parameter; return value
         oc {buff.size > 0            // return only if buffer not empty
            and x = buff[0]}          //    with item at head of buffer
         buff.remove();               // remove item from buffer
         getBusy ← false;
         return x;
      }
   }

   input void mysid.end() {
      ic {not ending}
      ending ← true;
      oc {true}
      return;
   }

// continued
```

Fig. 3.1 Part 1: bounded-buffer service program

But we don't do this in a service program for two reasons. First, updating the return value in the output part's body can make it difficult to invert the function (though not in this particular case). Second, in many services, the value to be returned can

---

```
// BoundedBuffer continued

    atomicity assumption {input and output parts}

    progress assumption {
        // thread in put returns if buffer has space for item
        (putBusy and buff.size < N) leads-to not putBusy;

        // thread in get returns if buffer has an item
        (getBusy and buff.size > 0) leads-to not getBusy;

        // thread in end returns
        (thread u in mysid.end) leads-to (not u in mysid.end);
    }
}
```

Fig. 3.2 Part 2: bounded-buffer service program

be any one of a set of possibilities (see Sect. 3.7). It is simpler to define this set in the output condition than in the body (where multiple threads or non-deterministic choice operators would be needed).

3.2.1   Bounded-Buffer Service Inverse

The inverse of service BoundedBuffer is shown in Fig. 3.3. It is obtained from the service program in the usual way. An additional parameter, bb, is introduced, matching the service's main code's return value; it points to the bounded-buffer implementation to be tested. Input function mysid.put(x) in the service program becomes an output function doPut(x) in the service inverse. It calls bb.put(x) and requires that the buffer not be full when the call returns. Input function mysid.get() in the service program becomes an output function doGet(x) in the service inverse. It calls bb.get() and requires that the returned value is in fifo order. Input function mysid.end() in the service program becomes an output function doEnd() in the service inverse. It calls bb.end(). The only progress assertion to be modified is the last one, where mysid is changed to bb.

3.3   Awaits

An **await** construct has the form "await (B) S", where B is a predicate and S is non-blocking code. A thread at the construct executes S only if B holds, with the test and execution done atomically. The thread is blocked if B does not hold. Thus

```
service BoundedBuffer(int N) {
program BoundedBufferInverse(int N, Sid bb) {
    ic {N ≥ 1}
    Seq buff ← seq();
    boolean ending ← false;
    boolean putBusy ← false;
    boolean getBusy ← false;
    return mysid;

    input void mysid.put(Val x) {
    output doPut(Val x) {
        ie oc {not ending and not putBusy}
        putBusy ← true;
        bb.put(x);
        oe ic {buff.size < N}
        buff.append(x);
        putBusy ← false;
        return;
    }

    input Val mysid.get() {
    output doGet() {
        ie oc {not ending and not getBusy}
        getBusy ← true;
        output(Val x) {
        Val x ← bb.get(x);
        oe ic {buff.size > 0 and x = buff[0]}
        buff.remove();
        getBusy ← false;
        return →x;
        }
    }

    input void mysid.end() {
    output doEnd() {
        ie oc {not ending}
        ending ← true;
        lck.end();
        oe ic {true}
        return;
    }

    atomicity assumption {...}
    progress assumption condition {...mysid bb...}
}
```

Fig. 3.3 Bounded-buffer service inverse program

"await (B) S" is similar to an output part "oc [B] S" in a service program, only more powerful because S can include calls to non-blocking input functions of other systems. S can end with a return, in which case the effect of the await ends with the return. The special case "await (true) S" just executes S atomically; we often shorten it to "atomic [S]".

Programs written with awaits are easier to understand and analyze than equivalent programs written with standard synchronization constructs. Programming languages do not usually provide the await construct. However, a program with awaits can be mechanically transformed to one that uses standard synchronization constructs if the program satisfies the following restrictions. First, the program must not use any other synchronization construct. Second, any statement not within an await construct must not conflict with code executed by other threads (including code in await constructs). We refer to such programs as **await-structured** programs, and we use them extensively in this book.

3.3.1   Bounded-Buffer Implementation Using Awaits

Figure 3.4 shows an await-structured program, called BBuffAwait, that implements the bounded-buffer service. Because awaits are similar to output parts of service programs, the program is almost identical to the bounded-buffer service program. Variable buff is the buffer. The atomicity assumption reminds us that the platform must execute the awaits with the expected atomicity. The progress assumption implies that it suffices if the awaits are executed with weak fairness. The atomicity breakpoints are indicated by "•"s as usual; they partition the program into effectively atomic steps.

Proving that BBuffAwait implements BoundedBuffer is straightforward. Figure 3.5 shows a program Z that concurrently executes an implementation system bb and a service inverse system si. Figure 3.6 gives the assertions that Z must satisfy. B_0 says that when bb returns put, the corresponding input condition in si holds. B_1 says that when bb returns get with value x, the corresponding input condition (which involves x) in si holds. B_2–B_4 are just the assertions in si's progress condition.

The atomicity breakpoints in Z are the two at bb's awaits and one at each output condition of si. Thus B_0's predicate can be replaced by C_0 below, and B_1's by C_1 below.

C_0 : ((thread at bb.put.await) and bb.buff.size < N) $\Rightarrow$ si.buff.size < N
C_1 : ((thread at bb.get.await) and bb.buff.size > 0)
$\quad\quad\quad \Rightarrow$ (si.buff.size > 0 and bb.buff[0] = si.buff[0])

C_0 and C_1 are invariant because bb.buff tracks si.buff. Formally, let

C_2 : bb.buff = si.buff

```
program BBuffAwait(int N) { // bounded buffer implementation using awaits
    ia [N ≥ 1]
    Seq buff ← seq();                // buffer; initially empty
    return mysid;

    input void mysid.put(Val x) {
    • await (buff.size < N)          // wait for non-full buffer
          buff.append(item);         // add item to buffer
      return;
    }

    input Val mysid.get() {
    • await (buff.size > 0) {        // wait for non-empty buffer
          Val x ← buff[0];           // get item from buffer and assign to x
          buff.remove();
          return x;
      }
    }

    input void mysid.end() {
      endSystem();
        return;
    }

    atomicity assumption [awaits]

    progress assumption [weak fairness for threads]
}
```

Fig. 3.4 Bounded-buffer implementation using awaits; "•"s indicate atomicity breakpoints

```
program Z(int N) {
    ic [N ≥ 1]
    inputs(); outputs();
    bb ← startSystem(BBuffAwait(N));
    si ← startSystem(BoundedBufferInverse(N,bb));
    return mysid;

    atomicity assumption []
    progress assumption [weak fairness]
}
```

Fig. 3.5 Program of bounded-buffer implementation and service inverse

---

B_0 : Inv (thread at si.doPut.ic) $\Rightarrow$ si.buff.size < N
B_1 : Inv (thread at si.doGet.ic)
          $\Rightarrow$ (si.buff.size > 0 and x = si.buff[0])
B_2 :   (si.putBusy and si.buff.size < N)
          $leads$-to not si.putBusy
B_3 :   (getBusy and buff.size > 0)
          $leads$-to not getBusy
B_4 :   (thread u in bb.end) $leads$-to (not u in bb.end)

Fig. 3.6 Assertions to be satisfied by program Z in order for BBuffAwait to implement BoundedBuffer

C_2 holds initially and is unconditionally preserved by each atomic step of Z. Thus $Inv\,C_2$ holds. C_2 implies C_0 and C_1. Thus $Inv\,C_0$ and $Inv\,C_1$ hold. Thus B_0 and B_1 hold.

Now for B_2–B_4. The first conjunct in B_2's lhs implies that a thread is at bb.put's await. The second conjunct in B_2's lhs, together with C_2, implies that bb.buff.size < N; the latter cannot be falsified by another thread (because at most one thread can be in put). Hence weak fairness (from bb's progress assumption) implies that the thread at bb.put's await eventually returns, establishing B_2's rhs. Thus B_2 holds. B_3 holds in the same way. B_4 holds directly from weak fairness. This completes the proof that BBuffAwait(N) implements BoundedBuffer(N).

3.4   Locks and Condition Variables

Leaving aside programming languages for "bare" hardware, most programming languages provide locks and condition variables. The typical lock provided by a programming language is a bit different from what was presented in Chap. 2. It is a regular variable of a system, not a separate system. A lock lck is introduced in a program with the construct "Lock lck" (rather than "lck ← startSystem(Lock())"). It is accessible only to threads in the system in which it is defined. Otherwise, there is no difference: a thread without lock lck acquires it via lck.acq; a thread holding lock lck releases it via lck.rel. *Henceforth, we will use locks according to these conventions* (rather than the conventions in Chap. 2).

Locks can ensure that a variable is updated by at most one thread at any time: simply introduce a lock and surround each update to the variable with lock acquire and lock release. But if an update is subject to a blocking condition involving the variable, e.g., "await (z=4) z←z+1", the solution requires busy waiting: i.e., acquire the lock, if z is not 4 then release the lock and retry. Condition variables allow us to solve this without busy waiting.

A **condition variable** is a variable that is associated with a lock. The construct "Condition(lck) cv" in a program introduces cv as a condition variable associated with (a previously defined) lock lck. Condition variable cv can be accessed only by a thread that holds lck, and in only two ways. A thread can do a **wait** on cv, denoted by cv.wait(). This makes the thread atomically release lck and start "waiting on" cv. A thread can do a **signal** on cv, denoted by cv.signal(). This chooses an arbitrary thread (if any) waiting on cv and changes its state to waiting to acquire lck. When the chosen thread acquires the lock, it gets past its cv.wait. As with any blocking construct, cv.wait can be executed with weak or strong fairness.

Now "await($z=4$) $z \leftarrow z{+}1$" can be implemented with a lock and an associated condition variable. When a thread attempting the update finds $z=4$ false, it waits on the condition variable. When another thread does an update that makes $z=4$ true, it signals the condition variable. When the thread waiting on the condition variable is awakened, it checks whether $z=4$ is true; if so it executes $z \leftarrow z{+}1$ and if not it waits again on the condition variable. It has to check $z=4$ after waking up because *another thread may have acquired the lock after the signal and falsified* $z=4$. This check can be omitted if $z=4$ can be falsified only by a thread waiting on the condition variable. Any await-structured program can be implemented using locks and condition variables as follows.

Theorem 3.1 (implementing awaits with locks and condition variables). *Let* P *be an await-structured program with await statements* await(B_i) S_i *for* $i = 1, 2, \cdots$, *where* B_i *can be* true. *Let* Q *be* P *transformed as follows:*

- *Introduce a lock, say* lck.
- *For every distinct non-*true B_i, *introduce a condition variable, say* cvB$_i$, *associated with* lck.
- *Replace* await(B_i) S_i *by*
  ```
  lck.acq();
  while (not Bᵢ)    // absent if Bᵢ is true
      cvBᵢ.wait();  //  "   "   "   "   "
  Sᵢ;
  for every cvB_k
      if (B_k)
          cvB_k.signal();
  lck.rel();
  ```
- *Let* cvB$_i$.wait() *have the same fairness as the corresponding await.*
- *Let* lck.acq() *have strong fairness if any await has strong fairness, and weak fairness otherwise.*

Then Q *implements* P. □

Proof. In program Q, statement S_i is executed only if the executing thread holds lck and finds B_i true. Any statement in Q that conflicts with S_i would be in some S_j (because P is an await-structured program). Thus S_i is executed atomically and is executed only if B_i holds. Thus program Q implements the safety part of await(B_i) S_i. It implements the progress part because of the fairness assumptions on lck and cvB$_i$. □

3.4.1   Bounded-Buffer Implementation Using Locks
and Condition Variables

Applying the transformation in Theorem 3.1 to the await-structured program
BBuffAwait (in Fig. 3.4) results in the program BBuffLockCv shown in Fig. 3.7. There
are two condition variables, cvSpace and cvItem. Condition variable cvSpace blocks
a thread in put if the buffer is full. It is signaled when get removes an item from
the buffer. Condition variable cvItem blocks a thread in get if the buffer is empty. It
is signaled when put adds an item to the buffer. The atomicity assumption reminds
us that the platform must execute operations on lck, cvItem and cvSpace with the
expected atomicity. The progress assumption implies that it suffices if lck.acq,
cvItem.wait and cvSpace.wait are executed with weak fairness. Two atomicity
breakpoints (the "●"s) suffice. There is no atomicity breakpoint at lck.acq because
any blocking here is indistinguishable from a temporary delay (while the thread that
holds lck releases it either explicitly or by doing a wait).

Theorem 3.1 assures us that program BBuffLockCv implements program BBuffAwait. Hence BBuffLockCv implements service BoundedBuffer (because BBuffAwait
implements BoundedBuffer). One could establish directly that program BBuffLockCv
implements service BoundedBuffer, just we did for program BBuffAwait. The proof
would be essentially the same.

3.5   Semaphores

Most programming languages that provide locks and condition variables also
provide another synchronization construct, namely semaphores. There are two kinds
of semaphores, "binary" and "counting". A **counting semaphore** is a variable that
is initialized to a non-negative integer value and is accessed via so-called P() and
V() operations. A P() on a counting semaphore atomically decrements it by 1 if
it is positive and blocks if it is zero. A V() on a counting semaphore atomically
increments it by 1. A thread can do P's and V's on a semaphore any number of times
and in any order (unlike acquires and releases on a lock). A **binary semaphore** is
like a counting semaphore except that its value is limited to 0 and 1. So regardless
of its value, a P() on a binary semaphore sets it to 0, and a V() sets it to 1.

Semaphores can subsume locks and condition variables. A semaphore initialized
to 1 can be used as a lock, with P() corresponding to acquire and V() to release.
A semaphore initialized to 0 can be used as a condition variable, with P()
corresponding to wait and V() to signal. The following theorem formalizes this.

Theorem 3.2 (implementing locks and condition variables with semaphores).
Let P *be a program that uses locks and condition variables. Let* Q *be* P *transformed
as follows:*

```
program BBuffLockCv(int N) {    // N is size of buffer
   ia [N ≥ 1]
   Seq buff ← seq();            // buffer; initially empty
   Lock lck;                    // protects buffer
   Condition(lck) cvItem;       // signaled when buffer not empty
   Condition(lck) cvSpace;      // signaled when buffer not full
   return mysid;

   input void mysid.put(Val x) {
      lck.acq();                // acquire lock. Note: no '•'
      while (buff.size = N)      // while buffer full
       • cvSpace.wait();        //   wait for space
      buff.append(x);           // add x to buffer
      cvItem.signal();          // signal that buffer not empty
      lck.rel();                // release lock
      return;
   }

   input Val mysid.get() {
      lck.acq();                // acquire lock. Note: no '•'
      while (buff.size = 0)      // if buffer empty
       • cvItem.wait();         //   then wait for item
      Val x ← buff[0];          // remove item from buffer and assign to x
      buff.remove();
      cvSpace.signal();         // signal that buffer not full
      lck.rel();                // release lock
      return x;
   }

   input void mysid.end() {
      endSystem();
      return;
   }

   atomicity assumption {lck, cvItem, cvSpace}

   progress assumption {weak fairness for threads}
}
```

Fig. 3.7 Bounded-buffer implementation using locks and condition variables

- *For every lock* lck:

  - *Introduce a binary semaphore, say* lckSem, *initialized to* 1.
  - *Replace every* lck.acq() *by* lckSem.P(), *with the same fairness as* lck.acq.
  - *Replace every* lck.rel() *by* lckSem.V().

- *For every condition variable* cv *associated with lock* lck:

  - *Introduce a binary semaphore, say* cvSem, *initialized to* 0.
  - *Replace every* cv.wait() *by*
        lckSem.V();cvSem.P();lckSem.P(),
    with cvSem.P *having the same fairness as* cv.wait.
  - *Replace every* cv.signal() *by* cvSem.V().

Then Q *implements* P.   □

Thus any program that uses locks and condition variables can be transformed into one that uses only binary semaphores. From this and Theorem 3.2, any await-structured program can be transformed into one that uses only binary semaphores. Would Theorem 3.2 hold if the binary semaphores were replaced by counting semaphores?

3.5.1 *Bounded-Buffer Implementation Using Semaphores*

A semaphore-based program that implements the bounded-buffer service can be obtained by applying the transformation in Theorem 3.2 to program BBuffLockCv. We now describe another solution that uses counting semaphores in an interesting way. The program, called BBuffSemaphore, is shown in Fig. 3.8. There are three semaphores: mutex, nItem and nSpace. Semaphore mutex, which can be binary or counting, is used like a lock so that at most one thread accesses the buffer at any time. It is initially 1; each thread does a P before accessing the buffer, and a V after.

Semaphore nItem is a counting semaphore that tracks the number of items in the buffer *and* blocks the consumer if the buffer is empty. It is initially 0, the consumer does a P before removing an item from the buffer, and the producer does a V after adding an item to the buffer. Note that one thread does P and another does V.

Semaphore nSpace is a counting semaphore that plays a similar role as nItem. It tracks the number of spaces in the buffer *and* blocks the producer if the buffer is full. It is initially N, the producer does a P before adding an item to the buffer, and the consumer does a V after removing an item from the buffer.

Two atomicity breakpoints suffice. As in program BBuffLockCv, there is no atomicity breakpoint at mutex.P. Proving that program BBuffSemaphore implements service BoundedBuffer is left as an exercise; it would be very similar to the analysis of program BBuffAwait. In functions put and get, can the P operations be done in reverse order? Can the V operations be done in reverse order?

```
program BBuffSemaphore(int N) { // N is size of buffer
    ia {N ≥ 1}
    Seq buff ← seq();              // buffer; initially empty
    BinarySemaphore(1) mutex;      // protects buffer; initially 1
    // tracks number of items in buffer; initially 0
    CountingSemaphore(0) nItem;
    // tracks number of spaces in buffer; initially N
    CountingSemaphore(N) nSpace;
    return mysid;

    input void mysid.put(Val x) {
    • nSpace.P();                 // wait if buffer is full
      mutex.P();                  // acquire buffer. Note: no '•'
      buff.append(x);             // add x to buffer
      mutex.V();                  // release buffer
      nItem.V();                  // increase number of items
      return;
    }

    input Val mysid.get() {
    • nItem.P();                  // wait if buffer is empty
      mutex.P();                  // acquire buffer. Note: no '•'
      Val x ← buff[0];            // remove item from buffer and assign to x
      buff.remove();
      mutex.V();                  // release buffer
      nSpace.V();                 // increase number of items
      return x;
    }

    input void mysid.end() {
      endSystem();
      return;
    }

    atomicity assumption {mutex, nItem, nSpace}

    progress assumption {weak fairness for threads}
}
```

Fig. 3.8 Bounded-buffer implementation using counting semaphores

3.6   Increasing Parallelism

When designing a program to implement a service, one typically uses synchronization constructs to protect larger-than-needed chunks of code, because it simplifies
the design. As a result, the program would have unnecessary blocking. That is,
it would block threads from executing code chunks in parallel even though such
execution would not have conflicts. Let's refer to such code chunks as **strongly
nonconflicting**. Once the program is developed, it is worth the effort to reduce
unnecessary blocking so that more threads can execute in parallel. This would
improve performance (assuming the platform can accommodate the increased load).
Two techniques are applicable: (1) identify strongly-nonconflicting code chunks and
relax the synchronization constraints to allow threads to execute them in parallel;
and (2) modify the underlying code so as to increase the extent of strongly-
nonconflicting code, prior to applying the first technique.

3.6.1   Technique 1

Regarding the first technique, consider an await-structured program with N await
statements, say await 1, ..., await N, where await i is short for "await (B_i) S_i"; for
notational simplicity, assume that every B_i is distinct and not vacuous. Figure 3.9
shows the awaits implemented using locks and condition variables according to
theorem 3.1; there is a single lock, lck, and N associated condition variables, cvB_1,
$\cdots$, cvB_N. Because every await implementation acquires lck, at most one await
implementation can be executing at any time.

Locks and condition variables
```
Lock lck;
Condition(lck) cvB₁, ⋯, cvBₙ;
```

Implementation of await (B_i) S_i for $i = 1,...,N$
```
lck.acq();
while (not Bᵢ)
   cvBᵢ.wait();
Sᵢ;
for (j in 1..N)
   if (Bⱼ)
      cvBⱼ.signal();
lck.rel();
```

Fig. 3.9 Implementing a program with awaits $1, \cdots, N$ using locks and condition variables

Locks and condition variables

```
Lock lck_i.j;              for i·j in KK
Condition(lck_i.j) cvB_i;   for i in 1..N and j = min(K_i)
```

Implementation of await i

```
for (increasing j in K_i)        // acquire i's locks in order
    lck_i.j.acq();

while (not B_i) {
    for (j in K_i, j ≠ min(K_i))     // release all but lowest lock
        lck_i.j.rel();

    cvB_i.wait();                    // release/wait/reacquire lowest lock
    for (increasing j in K_i, j ≠ min(K_i))
        lck_i.j.acq();               // acquire all but lowest lock in order
}

S_i;

for (j in K_i) {
    if (B_j) cvB_j.signal();
    lck_i.j.rel();                   // release i's locks
}
```

Fig. 3.10 An implementation of a program with awaits $1, \cdots, N$ such that await pairs not in KK are strongly nonconflicting

More parallelism can be achieved if some await pairs are strongly nonconflicting. For a trivial example, suppose that for a subset, say K, of the awaits, any await in K and any await not in K are strongly nonconflicting. Then the implementation of the awaits in K can use a separate lock and their condition variables would be associated with this lock. This would allow an await in K to be executed in parallel with an await not in K.

For a more interesting example, let KK be the set of *unordered* pairs of await indices such that await i and await j are strongly nonconflicting if the pair of i and j is not in KK. We denote the unordered pair of i and j by $i·j$; i.e., $i·j$ and $j·i$ are the same. (Note that KK would contain $i·i$ if two threads can execute await i simultaneously and they conflict.) An implementation that allows await pairs not in KK to be executed in parallel can be obtained as follows. For every $i·j$ in KK, introduce a lock, say $lck_{i.j}$. We refer to the locks involving i as the locks of await i. The implementation of await i acquires all its locks at the start and releases them at the end.

Deadlock can result if the locks are acquired in arbitrary order (e.g., await 1 acquires $lck_{1.2}$, await 2 acquires $lck_{2.3}$, and await 3 acquires $lck_{3.1}$). One way to prevent deadlock is to have await i acquire its locks in increasing order, where $lck_{i.j}$ is less than $lck_{i.k}$ if j is less than k. (So await i's lowest lock is $lck_{i.j}$ where j is the lowest index such that $i \cdot j$ is in KK.) This order must be maintained after waking up from cvB_i.wait. Hence cvB_i is associated with await i's lowest lock. Await i releases all but its lowest lock before waiting on cvB_i, and acquires all but its lowest lock in order after waking up. Figure 3.10 shows this implementation, where K_i denotes the set of await indices j such that $i \cdot j$ is in KK, and $\min(K_i)$ is the lowest entry in K_i.

3.6.2 Technique 2

We now consider the second technique mentioned above, i.e., modifying the underlying code so as to increase the amount of strongly nonconflicting of code chunks. Conceptually, one looks for variables subject to high contention by threads, and re-organizes them into separate memory addresses so that they can be accessed in parallel. Of course, this is not a mechanical procedure.

We illustrate the technique with an example. Consider program BBuffLockCv. It allows only one thread to access buff at any time. If buff were implemented so that accesses to *different* indices of buff do not conflict with each other, then put and get could execute in parallel as long as they do not access the same location. This would improve performance significantly if the append and remove operations take considerable time, which would be the case if the items are large.

One way to achieve such an implementation of buff is with a "circular" array, defined as follows. Let buffA be an array of size N, where each entry can hold an item (or, more realistically, a pointer to an item buffer). Let integer in indicate the position in buffA where the next item is put. Let integer out indicate the position in buffA from where to get the next item. Let cnt indicate the number of items in the buffer. An item is put in buffA[in] only if cnt < N holds, after which cnt is incremented and in is incremented modulo-N. An item is removed from buffA[out] only if cnt > 0 holds, after which cnt is decremented and out is incremented modulo-N.

The resulting program, called BBuffParallelized, is shown in Figs. 3.11 and 3.12. Note that lck protects only cnt directly. In particular, it does not directly protect statements p2 and g2. So threads can be accessing buffA[in] and buffA[out] at the same time, which, of course, is intended. However, we do not want threads to access these two statements at the same time if in equals out; then there would be a conflict resulting in a fault (because the entries of buff are not covered by the atomicity assumption). We don't expect this to happen, but it's not obvious that it does not (as it would be, for example, if statements p2 and g2 were directly protected by lck). So as part of any analysis of the program, we need to *prove* that statements p2 and g2 do not conflict. We can do this by treating the statements p2 and g2 as vacuous and proving that threads are not at p2 and g2 simultaneously when in equals out.

Formally, let X *be the program* BBuffParallelized *with atomicity breakpoints* p1, p2, g1, g2, *and each of statements* p2 *and* g2 *replaced by the* skip *statement.* It suffices to prove that program X satisfies *Inv* D_0, where

D_0 : (thread at p2) and (thread at g2) $\Rightarrow$ in $\neq$ out

```
program BBuffParallelized(int N) { // N is size of buffer
    ia {N ≥ 1}
    Val[N] buffA;               // buffer
    int in ← 0;                 // next put into buffA[in]
    int out ← 0;                // next remove from buffA[out]
    int cnt ← 0;                // number of items in buffA
    Lock lck;                   // protects cnt
    Condition(lck) cvItem;      // signaled when cnt > 0
    Condition(lck) cvSpace;     // signaled when cnt < N
    return mysid;

    input void mysid.put(Val x) {
        ia {not (thread in put)}
        lck.acq();              // acquire lock
        while (cnt = N)         // wait for buffA not full
p1:       • cvSpace.wait();
        lck.rel();             // release lock
p2: •   buffA[in] ← x;         // add x; not protected by lck
        lck.acq();             // acquire lock
        cnt ← cnt+1;
        cvItem.signal();       // signal buffA not empty
        lck.rel();             // release lock
        in ← mod(in+1, N);
        return;
    }

// continued
```

Fig. 3.11 Part 1: modified BBuffLockCv allowing parallel put and get. Atomicity breakpoints at p2 and g2 can be dropped

Program X would not satisfy *Inv D₀* if two get calls or two put calls can be ongoing simultaneously. (For example: put executes, put thread comes to p2, two get threads come to g2, one get completes; at this point, in, out, and cnt are all 1 and threads are at p2 and g2.) This is not a concern because the bounded-buffer service, which is the goal of the program, precludes two ongoing put (or get) calls. But it does mean that if program X is to satisfy *Inv D₀* then this restriction must be incorporated in X. This explains the input assumptions for the put and get functions. (Alternatively, we could have kept the input assumptions vacuous and proved *Inv D₀* when analyzing the composite program of X and the service inverse.)

Four atomicity breakpoints, at p1, p2, g1, g2, suffice for program X, yielding the following effectively-atomic steps:

- Initial step: From start of main to end of main. (Input functions are called only after main returns.)

```
// BBuffParallelized continued

    input Val mysid.get() {
        ia [not (thread in get)]
        lck.acq();                      // acquire lock
        while (cnt = 0)                 // wait for buffA not empty
g1:         • cvItem.wait();
        lck.rel();                      // release lock
g2: • Val x ← buffA[out];              // remove item; not protected by lck
        lck.acq();                      // acquire lock
        cnt ← cnt - 1;
        cvSpace.signal();              // signal buffer not full
        lck.rel();                      // release lock
        out ← mod(out+1, N);
        return x;
    }

    input void mysid.end() {
        endSystem();
        return;
    }

    atomicity assumption [lck, cvItem, cvSpace]
    progress assumption [weak fairness for threads]
}
```

Fig. 3.12 Modified BBuffLockCv allowing parallel put and get. Atomicity breakpoints at p2 and g2 can be dropped

- Step put call: From start of function put to p1 (if cnt equals N) or to p2 (otherwise). (The only conflict is the read of cnt. The wait at lck.acq is indistinguishable from a temporary delay.)
- Step p1: From p1 to p1 (if cnt equals N) or to p2 (otherwise). (The only conflict is the read of cnt.)
- Step p2: From p2 to end of function put. (The only conflict is the lck-protected update to cnt; p2 is now a skip.)
- Step get call: From the start of function get to g1 (if cnt equals 0) or g2 (otherwise). (Same as step put call.)
- Step g1: From g1 to g1 (if cnt equals 0) or g2 (otherwise). (Same as step p1.)
- Step g2: From g2 to the end of function get. (Same as step p2.)

We now give an assertional proof that X satisfies $Inv D_0$. Define the following predicates.

D_1 : (at most one thread in put)
D_2 : (at most one thread in get)
D_3 : (thread on p2) $\Rightarrow$ cnt < N
D_4 : (thread at g2) $\Rightarrow$ cnt > 0
D_5 : cnt = mod(in − out, N)

The conjunction of predicates D_1–D_5 is unconditionally established by the initial step and unconditionally preserved by every other step of X. Details follow:

- Initial step establishes D_1–D_5 because it lets no thread enter put or get, and it sets in, out and cnt to zero.
- Step put call preserves D_1 because of put's input assumption. If the thread goes to p2, then D_3 holds non-vacuously, otherwise D_3 holds vacuously. The other D_i's are not affected.
- Step p1 does not affect D_1–D_5 if the thread returns to p1. Otherwise it establishes D_3 and does not affect the other D_i's.
- Step p2 leaves put with no thread (from D_1 prior to the step), thus establishing D_1 and D_3. It preserves D_5 because it increments in and cnt by 1 and because cnt is less than N prior to this (from D_3).
- Step get call preserves D_1–D_5. (Analogous to step put call.)
- Step g1 preserves D_1–D_5. (Analogous to step p1.)
- Step g2 preserves D_1–D_5. (Analogous to step p2.)

Thus program X satisfies $Inv\,(D_1$–$D_5)$. Predicates D_3–D_5 imply D_0. (D_0's lhs and D_3–D_4 imply cnt in 1..N-1, which together with D_5 implies in $\neq$ out.) Hence program X satisfies $Inv\,D_0$. Hence the atomicity breakpoints at p2 and g2 can be dropped in program X and also in program BBuffParallelized. Additional analysis can now be conveniently done. In particular, showing that program BBuffParallelized implements BoundedBuffer is left to the reader (see Exercise 3.5).

3.7 Bounded-Buffer Service with Cancelable Put and Get

The service defined by BoundedBuffer (Figs. 3.1 and 3.2) does not allow a user to cancel a put or get call. A thread blocked in put (because the buffer is full) remains blocked until another thread calls get and makes space. Similarly, a thread blocked in get (because the buffer is empty) remains blocked until another thread calls put and adds an item. We now modify the service so that a user can cancel a put or get call. The ability to cancel a blocking input call is useful in many situations. For example, the system whose thread, say t, is blocked in a put call may be asked (via another thread) to terminate itself, which would require the system to retrieve its thread t. Or the bounded-buffer service may need to be terminated while a put or get call is blocked.

The bounded-buffer service is modified as follows. Two new input functions are introduced: cancelPut, to cancel an ongoing put call, and cancelGet, to cancel an ongoing get call. Function end now cancels any ongoing put and get calls (thereby allowing an implementation to become endable). Function put now returns the sequence [-1] when canceled and the sequence [0] when completed successfully. Function get returns [-1] when canceled and [0,x] when completed successfully, where x is the returned item.

The modified service is shown in Figs. 3.13 and 3.14. There are two new variables, putCancel and getCancel, indicating whether a put call or get call, respectively, is to be canceled. The output condition in function put has a new construct, OR, denoting disjunction that is *not* short-circuited. So if both buff.size < N and putCancel hold, the service allows function put to *non-deterministically* either cancel or complete successfully. Function cancelPut can be called even when a put call is not ongoing. This flexibility is necessary because it is entirely possible that cancelPut is called just as a put call is returning. Functions get and getCancel have similar characteristics; e.g., get has the freedom to non-deterministically cancel or complete successfully when both buff.size > 0 and getCancel hold. The progress assumptions are equivalent to weak fairness of threads. Implementations of this service are developed in Exercises 3.6 and 3.7.

3.8   Concluding Remarks

This chapter illustrated service programs in which input functions can return non-void values and can non-deterministically choose the value. It presented implementations of services that illustrated the standard synchronization constructs (locks, condition variables, semaphores) as well as the await synchronization construct. It also illustrated how to go about reducing unnecessary blocking, thereby increasing the parallelism and hence performance. A key ingredient here is the use of data structures that allow fine-grained concurrent access. Such structures are available in many programming languages (e.g., ConcurrentMap in Java and in C++).

Semaphores were invented by Dijkstra, and are the earliest of the standard synchronization constructs [2–4]. Locks and condition variables were introduced by Brinch Hansen [5] and by Hoare [6]. Brinch Hansen's formulation is the one covered in this chapter and what most programming languages provide. In Hoare's formulation, a thread releases the associated lock immediately after doing a signal and a waiting thread (if any) is chosen and immediately resumed; hence a thread waiting on a condition variable does not need to re-check the condition upon awakening. Awaits were introduced by Owicki and Gries [7,8], as a synchronization construct that is more convenient for analysis of multi-threaded programs (including the formulation of proof rules).

A thread waiting on a condition variable is stuck forever if nobody signals the condition variable. In some situations we want the wait to be limited in time; e.g., because the signaling thread may have terminated. For this purpose, programming languages typically provide a "timed" variant of the wait construct, say timedWait(D), where D is a time duration. When a thread executes this on a

```
service BoundedBufferCancelable(int N) {        // Bounded buffer of size N
   ic {N ≥ 1}
   Seq buff ← seq();                            // buffer; initially empty
   boolean ending ← false;                      // true if being terminated
   boolean putBusy ← false;                     // true if thread in put
   boolean getBusy ← false;                     // true if thread in get
   boolean putCancel ← false;                   // true if put to be canceled
   boolean getCancel ← false;                   // true if get to be canceled
   return mysid;

   input Seq mysid.put(Val x) {
      ic {not ending and not putBusy}
      putBusy ← true;
      output(Seq r) {                           // return value
         oc {(buff.size < N and r = [0])        // success: return [0]
             OR (putCancel and r = [-1])}       // cancel: return [-1]
         if (r = [0])
            buff.append(x);
         putCancel ← putBusy ← false;
         return r;
   } }

   input void mysid.cancelPut() {
      ic {true}
      putCancel ← true;
      oc {true}
      return;
   }

   input Seq mysid.get() {
      ic {not ending and not getBusy}
      getBusy ← true;
      output(Seq r) {                           // return value
         oc {(buff.size > 0 and r = [0, buff[0]]) // success: return [0,item]
             OR (getCancel and r = [-1])}        // cancel: return [-1]
         if (r[0] = 0)
            buff.remove();
         getCancel ← getBusy ← false;
         return r;
   } }
}

// continued
```

Fig. 3.13 Part 1: bounded-buffer with cancelable put and get

```
// BoundedBufferCancelable continued

    input void mysid.cancelGet() {
        ic {true}
        getCancel ← true;
        oc {true}
        return;
    }

    input void mysid.end() {
        ic {not ending}
        ending ← true;
        putCancel ← true;
        getCancel ← true;
        oc {not putBusy and not getBusy}
        endSystem();
        return;
    }

    atomicity assumption {input and output parts}

    progress assumption {
        // thread in put returns if buffer has space or put is canceled
        (putBusy and (buff.size < N or putCancel)) leads-to not putBusy;

        // thread in get returns if buffer has item or get is canceled
        (getBusy and (buff.size > 0 or getCancel)) leads-to not getBusy;

        // thread in cancelPut returns
        (thread t in cancelPut) leads-to (not t in cancelPut);

        // thread in cancelGet returns
        (thread t in cancelGet) leads-to (not t in cancelGet);

        // thread in end returns
        (thread t in end) leads-to (not t in end);
    }
}
```

Fig. 3.14 Part 2: bounded-buffer with cancelable put and get

condition variable, it stops waiting on the condition variable (and starts waiting on the associated lock) after D seconds have elapsed, if this has not already happened earlier (due to a signal).

Exercises

3.1. In the bounded-buffer implementation using locks and condition variables (Fig. 3.7), the cvSpace.wait is done in a while loop; i.e., after a thread is awakened from this wait, it checks buff.size again. Can the "while" be changed to an "if"?

3.2. In program BoundedBuffer (Figs. 3.1 and 3.2), introduce the following two variables: np, to record the sequence of items added to the buffer, and nc, to record the sequence of items removed from the buffer. Formally, initialize np and nc to the empty sequence in main, add np.append(x) in put's output part, and add nc.append(x) in get's output part. (Such variables, which record information but do not influence the evolution of the program, are known as "auxiliary" variables [7] or "history" variables [1].)

Does the program satisfy the following assertions:

(a) *Inv* (nc prefixOf np)
(b) *Inv* (np.size − N ≤ nc.size ≤ np.size)

For each assertion, if you answer no, supply a counter-example evolution, i.e., an evolution that ends in a state where the assertion's predicate does not hold. If you answer yes, supply a predicate, say P, that satisfies the invariance induction rule, i.e., (1) P implies the assertion's predicate, (2) the initial atomic step of the program unconditionally establishes P, and (3) every non-initial atomic step of the program unconditionally preserves P.

(Hint: Look at the analysis in Sect. 1.3.)

3.3. Repeat Exercise 3.2 for the bounded-buffer implementation using locks and condition variables (Fig. 3.7). Can you make use of the analysis in Exercise 3.2?

3.4. Repeat Exercise 3.2 for the bounded-buffer program using semaphores (Fig. 3.8). Can you make use of the analysis in Exercise 3.2?

3.5. Show that program BBuffParallelized (Figs. 3.11 and 3.12) implements BoundedBuffer (Figs. 3.1 and 3.2).

(Hint: Formulate a predicate that maps the implementation's buffA to the service's buff (like C_2 in Sect. 3.3), and establish its invariance.)

3.6. Obtain an await-structured program that implements the cancelable bounded-buffer service (Fig. 3.13).

(Hint: The easiest approach is to replace each non-vacuous output condition in the service by an await. Regarding the progress assumptions, weak fairness suffices.)

3.7. Implement the program in Exercise 3.6 using locks and condition variables.

(Hint: Introduce two condition variables, say cvSpaceCancel and cvItemCancel. The former cvSpaceEnd is signaled when variable putCancel is set to true and when get returns (with success or cancellation). Condition cvItemEnd is signaled when variable getCancel is set to true and when put returns (with success or cancellation).

3.8. Implement semaphores using awaits. Specifically, supply a code chunk for each of the constructs

- Semaphore(N) sem
- sem.P()
- sem.V()

such that in any program P that uses semaphores, replacing the constructs with your code chunks results in a program Q that implements P.

(Hint: The code chunk for Semaphore(N) sem can introduce an integer variable, say sem.value. The code chunks for sem.P and sem.V can use awaits so that sem.value tracks the value of sem.)

3.9. Implement locks using awaits. Specifically, supply a code chunk for each of the constructs

- Lock lck
- lck.acq()
- lck.rel()

such that in any program P that uses locks (and no condition variables), replacing the constructs with your code chunks results in a program Q that implements P.

(Hint: The code chunk for Lock lck can introduce a tid pointer, say lck.acqd. The code chunks for lck.acq and lck.rel can use awaits so that lck.acqd is null if the lock is available and otherwise equal the tid of the thread holding the lock. Don't forget to capture the (weak or strong) fairness of lck.acq.)

3.10. Repeat Exercise 3.9 for condition variables. Specifically, assume that locks are implemented with awaits as per your solution to Exercise 3.9. Now supply a code chunk for each of the constructs

- Condition(lck) cv
- cv.wait()
- cv.signal()

such that in any program P that uses locks and condition variables, replacing the constructs with your code chunks results in a program Q that implements P.

(Hint: The code chunk for Condition(lck) cv can introduce a set variable, say cv.waiting. The code chunks for cv.wait() and cv.signal() can use awaits so that cv.waiting contains the tids of all threads waiting on cv. Don't forget to capture the (weak or strong) fairness of cv.wait().)

3.11. Write a program that uses an instance of BoundedBuffer(N1) and an instance of BoundedBuffer(N2) to implement BoundedBuffer(N1+N2).

3.12. Write a program that uses one BoundedBufferCancelable(N1) instance and one BoundedBufferCancelable(N2) instance to implement BoundedBufferCancelable(N1+N2).

3.13. Implement the timedWait construct assuming a platform that provides locks, condition variables with regular waits and signals, and a sleep(D) construct that makes the executing thread sleep for D time units.

3.14. Define an "N-user lock" to be a lock that handles at most N users; that is, the number of threads that are either waiting for the lock or have acquired the lock is at most N. Obtain a N-user lock by using multiple instances of 2-user locks.

(Hint: Consider a binary tree with N leaves, and associate a 2-user lock with every node of the tree. Each user is associated with a leaf node. The user acquires the N-user lock by acquiring all the 2-user locks on the path from its leaf node to the root of the tree.)

References

1. M. Abadi, L. Lamport, The existence of refinement mappings. Theor. Comput. Sci. **82**(2), 253–284 (1991). doi:10.1016/0304-3975(91)90224-P. http://dx.doi.org/10.1016/0304-3975(91)90224-P
2. E.W. Dijkstra, Cooperating sequential processes. Technical report, Burroughs, Nuenen (1965). EWD-123
3. E.W. Dijkstra, The structure of the the-multiprogramming system. Commun. ACM **11**, 341–346 (1968). doi:http://doi.acm.org/10.1145/363095.363143. http://doi.acm.org/10.1145/363095.363143
4. E.W. Dijkstra, Cooperating sequential processes, in *The Origin of Concurrent Programming*, ed. by P.B. Hansen (Springer, New York, 2002), pp. 65–138. http://dl.acm.org/citation.cfm?id=762971.762974
5. P.B. Hansen, Structured multiprogramming. Commun. ACM **15**(7), 574–578 (1972). doi:10.1145/361454.361473. http://doi.acm.org/10.1145/361454.361473
6. C.A.R. Hoare, Monitors: an operating system structuring concept. Commun. ACM **17**(10), 549–557 (1974). doi:10.1145/355620.361161. http://doi.acm.org/10.1145/355620.361161
7. S. Owicki, D. Gries, An axiomatic proof technique for parallel programs – i. Acta Inform. **6**, 319–340 (1976)
8. S. Owicki, D. Gries, Verifying properties of parallel programs: an axiomatic approach. Commun. ACM **19**(5), 279–285 (1976). doi:http://doi.acm.org/10.1145/360051.360224

Chapter 4
Message-Passing Services

4.1 Introduction

This chapter presents several message-passing services, or **channels** for short. A channel allows a user at one location to transmit a message to be received by a user at another location. Because a channel is a service that is spread over different locations, users access the service via multiple systems, one at each location (unlike the previous lock service and bounded-buffer service). Specifically, a channel has a set of **addresses**, each identifying a location. (MAC addresses, IP addresses, and URLs are examples of addresses.) At each address there is a system within the channel, referred to as an **access system**, with which users interact. Figure 4.1 illustrates a channel where each access system provides functions tx(k,msg), to transmit message msg to address k, and rx(), to receive a message. Messages are sequences. We require channels to have at least one address. Although a channel with one address doesn't do anything, it can be convenient for writing programs that use the channel.

In the context of computer networking, a channel can be "connection-less" or "connection-oriented". With a **connection-less** channel, a user can send and receive messages without any prior intimation to the service. Connectionless channels typically do not guarantee any level of service, e.g., an arbitrary fraction of the messages sent by a user may be lost. With a **connection-oriented** channel, a user can send and receive messages to a remote user *only after* a "connection" to the

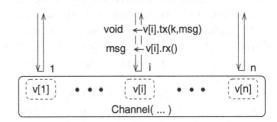

Fig. 4.1 A channel with addresses 1, ..., n, and access system v[i] at address i

A.U. Shankar, *Distributed Programming: Theory and Practice*,
DOI 10.1007/978-1-4614-4881-5__4,
© Springer Science+Business Media New York 2013

remote user is established, which amounts to asking and getting permission from the service to talk to the remote user. Here, each access system has functions to open and close connections, in addition to the transmit and receive functions. Connection-oriented channels typically guarantee some level of service, e.g., bounds on loss and delay. (Their implementations use the connection establishment phase to allocate appropriate resources, delaying, or even rejecting, connect requests if adequate resources are not available.)

This chapter presents several connection-less channels, a connection-oriented channel, and a distributed program that multiplexes ports onto a connection-less channel (similar to UDP over IP [5,9]). Three kinds of connection-less channels are defined: fifo, lossy and LRD. A **fifo** (first-in-first-out) channel transfers messages in order without loss between any two addresses; this is the message-passing service assumed in most descriptions of distributed algorithms (e.g., [3, 4, 7]). A **lossy** channel can lose messages in transit (as in a single-hop physical link where noise can clobber messages [5,6,9,11]). An **LRD** channel can lose, reorder, and duplicate messages in transit (as in a multi-hop IP link [5, 9, 10]). The connection-oriented channel defined here provides a very basic form of connection establishment and termination. A more realistic connection-oriented channel, equivalent to that provided by TCP sockets, is covered in Chap. 20.

The channel programs in this chapter are used as building blocks in distributed programs throughout the book. In particular, the next chapter shows a distributed program that uses a lossy or LRD channel to implement a fifo channel between two addresses.

One interesting feature of these channel programs is that they have **internal nondeterminism**, which means that a program can have different evolutions with the same input-output sequence. It turns out that this is helpful, though not necessary, to capture the property that messages sent from two or more addresses to the same destination can be received in any merged order. Obtaining the inverse of such a service program involves a twist. We also show how to avoid internal nondeterminism, usually at the cost of making the service program harder to understand.

4.1.1   Conventions

Our programs make extensive use of sets, bags, sequences, tuples and maps. **Sets** are collections of entries where duplicate values are not distinguished. The construct "Set x" defines variable x to be a set of entries of any type. The construct "Set<U> x" defines x to be a set of entries of type U. For a set x: x.size is the number of entries in x; x.add(m) adds m to x; and x.remove(m) removes m from x if m is in x and otherwise has no affect.

There is a set(...) construct for defining sets. In its simplest usage, the argument just enumerates the set; thus set() is the empty set, and set(0,4,2) is the set with entries 0, 4 and 2, as is set(0,4,4,2,0). More generally, set(e: x in Z; P), where Z is a set or a sequence, x is a parameter, P is a predicate in x, and e is an expression in x, denotes the set of values of e for x ranging over the elements of Z such that P holds. Thus, set(2*i: i in 0..4; mod(i,2) = 0) is the set [0,4,8].

Bags are collections of entries where duplicate values are distinguished. The constructs for bags are the same as for sets, with "set" replaced by "bag", for example, "Bag x", "Bag<U> x" and "bag(e: x in Z; P)".

Sequences were introduced in the previous chapter, and we now give more conventions about them. Recall that an enumerated list within square brackets is a sequence, e.g., [2,3,1] is a sequence with 2 at the head and 1 at the tail. The empty sequence is []. The construct "Seq x" defines x to be a sequence of entries of any type. The construct "Seq<U> x" defines x to be a sequence of entries of type U.

For a sequence x: x.size is the number of items in x; x[j] is the jth entry in x, with x[0] being the head; x.last is the last entry in x (i.e., x[x.size-1]); and x.keys is the sequence of indices of x (i.e., the sequence 0..x.size-1). The construct x.append(m) appends m to the tail of x. The construct x.remove() removes the entry at the head of x; it has no effect if x is empty. The construct x.remove(k) removes the entry x[k]; it has no effect if k is not in x.keys. (Thus x.remove(0) is the same as x.remove().)

The operator "∘" denotes sequence concatenation; e.g., [a]∘[b,c] is the sequence [a,b,c], as are [a,b]∘[c] and [a,b,c]∘[]. Logical operators prefixOf, suffixOf, and subsequenceOf have the usual meaning; for example, "[a,b] prefixOf [a,b,d,c]" is true. For a set S of sequences, mergeOf(S) is the set of all merges of the sequences in S.

There is a [...] construct analogous to the set(...) construct. Specifically, [e: x in Z; P], where Z is a sequence, x is a parameter, P is a predicate in x, and e is an expression in x, denotes the sequence of values of e for x ranging (in order) over the sequence Z such that P holds. For example, [2*i: i in 0..4; mod(i,2) = 0] equals [0,4,8].

We let int also denote the sequence of integers in increasing order.

Sets and sequences as types: Sets and sequences can be treated as types for defining variables; e.g., "X y", where X is a set or a sequence, defines y to be a variable that takes values from X. Similarly, types can be treated as sets for membership predicates; e.g., "y in X", where X is a type and y a value, is true iff y is of type X. This can also be written as X(y).

Tuples are sets of sequences of the same length. The construct Tuple<...> defines a set of tuples where the argument indicates the number of elements and, optionally, their type. For example, Tuple<,,> defines the set of sequences of length 2, and Tuple<U,V> defines the set of [u,v] sequences where u is from U and v is from V.

Maps are collections of two-tuples where the first element is a key and the second is a value, the keys are distinct, and map entries can be indexed by the key. The construct "Map x" defines variable x to be a map. The construct "Map<U,V> x" defines variable x to be a map with keys from U and values from V.

For a map x: x.size is the number of tuples in the map, x.keys is the sequence of its keys, and x.vals is the sequence of its values. If j is in x.keys, then x[j] refers to the value associated with j, i.e., x has the tuple [j,x[j]]. The construct x.add(j,v) adds the tuple [j,v] to x, replacing any prior tuple with key j; this can also be written as x[j] ← v. The construct x.remove(j) removes the tuple with key j; it has no effect if j is not in x.keys.

There is a map(...) construct analogous to the set(...) construct. For example, map([2,100], [3,200]) is the map with entries [2,100] and [3,200]; and map([2*i,10*i]: i in 0..4; mod(i,2) = 0) is the map with entries [0,0], [4,20], and [8,40].

Don't-care value "." We use "." as a "don't-care" value to abbreviate the writing of predicates. Let predicate P contain a "." and let R denote the smallest predicate in P containing the ".". Then P is equivalent to P with with R replaced by forsome(x: R). For example, "thread in f(.)", where f(.) is a function with parameters, is equivalent to "forsome(x: thread in f(x))". For another example, "not (thread in f(.))", is equivalent to "not forsome(x: thread in f(x))" (and not "forsome(x: not thread in f(x))" because quantification is over the smallest predicate enclosing the ".").

Finally, define ongoing(S) as an abbreviation for (thread in S).

End of conventions

4.2 Connection-less Fifo Channels

The service program for a connection-less fifo channel is given in Fig. 4.2. The program has one parameter, ADDR, the set of addresses. Its input condition states that there is at least one address. The main code defines two maps, txh and rxh, indexed by address pairs, for recording the transmit and receive histories. Entry txh[[j,k]] is the sequence of messages transmitted at address j to address k. Entry rxh[[j,k]] is the sequence of messages received at address k from address j. Thus the sequence of messages in transit from j to k is the last txh[[j,k]].size − rxh[[j,k]].size messages in txh[[j,k]].

The main code also defines a map v, indexed by addresses, where v[j] stores the sid of the access system at address j. The main code ends by returning map v. In the service program, map v is returned in one atomic step. Whereas in an implementation of the channel, each v[j] would be returned separately by the component system at address j. This is fine because the returns together would be effectively atomic. (A user cannot distinguish between the situation where v[j] does not yet exist and the situation where v[j] exists but the user is slow to learn that.)

At each address j, the program has two input functions. Function v[j].tx(k,msg) transmits message msg to address k. Address k cannot equal j, and at most one v[j].tx(.) call can be on going at any time. (Thus txh[[j,j]] and rxh[[j,j]] are always empty.) Function v[j].rx() receives an incoming message. It blocks until it returns a received message, and at most one v[j].rx() call can be on going at any time. Functions to terminate the service are added later.

The output part of function v[j].rx() has two parameters: msg, the message returned by the function; and k, the originating address of the message. This means

```
service FifoChannel(Set ADDR) {      // Fifo channel. ADDR: addresses
   ic {ADDR.size ≥ 1}

   // txh[[j,k]]: sequence of messages sent at j to k
   Map txh ← map([[j,k], []]: j,k in ADDR);
   // rxh[[j,k]]: sequence of messages received at k from j
   Map rxh ← map([[j,k], []]: j,k in ADDR);
   // v[j]: sid of access system at j
   Map v ← map([j, sid()]: j in ADDR);
   return v;

   input void v[ADDR j].tx(ADDR k, Seq msg) { // at j transmit msg to k
      ic {j ≠ k and not ongoing(v[j].tx(.))}
      txh[[j,k]].append(msg);
      oc {true}
      return;
   }

   input Seq v[ADDR j].rx() { // at j receive msg
      ic {not ongoing(v[j].rx())}
      output (Seq msg, ADDR k) {
      // msg is the received message. k is the originating address of msg
      // k is completely determined by j if ADDR.size ≤ 2
         oc {(rxh[[k,j]] ∘ [msg]) prefixOf txh[[k,j]]}
         rxh[[k,j]].append(msg);
         return msg;
      }
   }

   atomicity assumption {input parts and output parts}

   progress assumption {
      forall(j in ADDR: ongoing(v[j].tx) leads-to not ongoing(v[j].tx));

      // if there is an incoming message from address k to j,
      // it is eventually delivered provided a user is receiving at j
      forall(j,k in ADDR, i in int:
            txh[[k,j]].size ≥ i
                  leads-to  (rxh[[k,j]].size ≥ i or not ongoing(v[j].rx)));
   }
}    // FifoChannel
```

Fig. 4.2 Connection-less fifo channel program

(as explained in Sect. 3.2) that the output part is executed with any values of msg and k that satisfy the output condition. In particular, k is any address such that rxh[[k,j]] with msg appended to it remains a prefix of txh[[k,j]], thereby ensuring fifo delivery of messages from k to j.

Parameter msg is the return value and hence is externally visible; we refer to it as an **external parameter**. Parameter k, on the other hand, is not externally visible; we refer to it as an **internal parameter**. For ADDR.size equal to 2, parameter k is uniquely determined by j; it is simply the address other than j. But for ADDR.size greater than 2, parameter k is not uniquely determined by j; hence it allows the program to have internal nondeterminism, that is, different evolutions with the same input-output sequence. For example, starting from an empty channel, if two addresses each send the same message m to j and subsequently v[j].rx returns m, then the user at j does not know which m was received. (It may find out later on in its evolution.)

Avoiding internal nondeterminism: Can the service can be specified without internal nondeterminism for ADDR.size greater than 2? Yes, by letting a message be receivable at j only if the received message sequence at j remains a prefix of *some* merge of the message sequences one sent by the different users to j. However, the resulting service program may be harder to understand. (See Exercise 4.19.)

4.2.1 Weaker Progress Assumption

The progress assumption of the channel program may be a bit too strong. An implementation may ensure that if messages are in transit to address j then one of them is eventually delivered provided a user is waiting to receive at j, but it may not ensure fairness between the senders. For example, a user at address j may never get messages from address i because another user at address k keeps sending messages to j and the channel delivers only these messages. To specify this weaker property, one would change the progress assumption to the following. (Below, sum(.) returns the sum of the terms in its argument.)

```
forall(j,k in ADDR, i in int:
    sum(txh[k,j].size: k in ADDR) ≥ i  leads-to
    (sum(rxh[k,j].size: k in ADDR) ≥ i or not ongoing(v[j].rx)))
```

4.2.2 Termination and Rx Cancellation

In the interest of brevity, the service program has been defined without providing a way for users to terminate the service. This can be easily added.

- One option is to provide at each address j an input function, say v[j].endLocal(), that shuts down address j without affecting any other address. For example, allow

v[j].endLocal() to be called at any time, and after that disallow v[j].tx(.) and
v[j].rx() from being called.
- Another option is to provide at a special address, say j0, an input function,
  say v[j0].endGlobal(), that shuts down all addresses. (Presumably the user at
  j0 would inform other users before calling this function.)

In either option, if address j is shut down when a v[j].rx call is ongoing and
no message is in transit to j, then it would be blocked permanently. One could
also augment v[j].end so that it cancels any ongoing v[j].rx call (just as in the
cancelable bounded-buffer service in Sect. 3.7). Augmenting the service program to
handle these options is left to the reader. (See Exercises 4.3–4.6.)

4.2.3 Fifo Channel Inverse

The inverse of program FifoChannel is obtained, as usual, by adding the sid map
v as a parameter and changing the input functions of FifoChannel into output
functions. Input function v[j].tx(k,msg) is changed to an output function, say
doTx(j,k,msg), which calls v[j].tx(k,msg). Input function v[j].rx() is changed to
an output function, say doRx(j), which calls v[j].rx() and checks that the message
returned is in fifo order.

But accounting for the internal parameter k in function v[j].rx *involves a twist.*
To see why, consider the aggregate system of the service inverse and a candidate
implementation of the fifo channel, say X. Suppose at some point in an evolution
of the aggregate system, output function doRx(j) calls v[j].rx of X and the latter
returns a message, say msg, sent from address k. Then the input part of doRx(j) should
check that $F(k)$ holds, where $F(k)$ is "rxh[[k,j]]∘[msg] prefixOf txh[[k,j]]", and
it should append msg to rxh[[k,j]].

But how does doRx(j) obtain k? If $F(i)$ does not hold for any address i, then X is
not a valid implementation. If $F(i)$ holds for exactly one address i, then k equals i.
But if $F(i)$ holds for more than one i, then doRx(j) cannot identify which rxh[[i,j]]
variable to update. The choice is important because it would, in general, affect which
future receptions from these senders are safe. Only X can correctly identify msg's
sender, and X has to convey this to the service inverse. A natural way to do this is
to pass the sender address k along with the delivered message in the return of the
v[j].rx() call. That is, *for purposes of testing against the service inverse*, the input
function v[j].rx() in X is modified to return a message *and a sender address*. The
service inverse program is given in Fig. 4.3. Note that v[j].rx (in doRx(j)'s body) is
assumed to return a tuple [msg,k], where k is msg sender's address.

```
service FifoChannel(Set ADDR) {
program FifoChannelInverse(Set ADDR, Map<ADDR,Sid> v) {

    ic {ADDR.size ≥ 1}
    Map txh ← map([[j,k], []]: j,k in ADDR);
    Map rxh ← map([[j,k], []]: j,k in ADDR);
    Map v ← map([j,sid()]: j in ADDR);
    return v mysid;

    input void v[ADDR j].tx(ADDR k, Seq msg) {
    output doTx(ADDR j, ADDR k, Seq msg) {
        ic oc {j ≠ k and not ongoing(v[j].tx(.))}
        txh[[j,k]].append(msg);
        v[j].tx(k, msg);
        oc ic {true}
        return;
    }

    input Seq v[ADDR j].rx() {
    output doRx(ADDR j) {
        ic oc {not ongoing(v[j].rx())}
        output (Seq msg, ADDR k) {
        Seq msg; ADDR k;
        [msg,k] ← v[j].rx();        // Note: v[j].rx returns [msg,k]
        oc ic {((rxh[[k,j]] ∘ [msg]) prefixOf txh[[k,j]]}
        rxh[[k,j]].append(msg);
        return msg;
        }
    }

    atomicity assumption {...}

    progress assumption condition {...}
} // FifoChannelInverse
```

Fig. 4.3 Connection-less fifo channel inverse program

4.3 Connection-less Lossy Channels

A connection-less lossy channel is like a connection-less fifo channel except that messages in transit can be lost. The service program differs from the fifo channel program in two ways. The first difference concerns the safety properties of the channel. Specifically, in the output condition of function rx, we replace "prefixOf" with "subsequenceOf". Unlike in the fifo case, the sequence of messages in transit from j to k is *not* uniquely determined by txh[[j,k]] and rxh[[j,k]]. For example, if the former is [a,b,c,b] and the latter is [a,b], then the sequence of messages in transit can be [c,b], [c], [b] or [].

The second difference concerns the progress assumption. The previous progress assumption is no longer tenable because a message can be lost. A reasonable alternative would be to assume that any message m repeatedly sent to an address is repeatedly delivered provided a user remains receiving at the destination. This can be expressed as follows, where "#sends of m to j" denotes the number of times m is sent to address j, and "#rcvs of m at j" denotes the number of times m is received at j:

$$(\text{forall}(\text{int } i: (\#\text{sends of m to j}) = i \; \textit{leads-to} \; (\#\text{sends of m to j}) > i)$$
$$\text{and } (\text{not ongoing}(v[j].rx) \; \textit{leads-to} \; \text{not ongoing}(v[j].rx)))$$
$$\Rightarrow \text{forall}(\text{int } i: (\#\text{rcvs of m at j}) = i \; \textit{leads-to} \; (\#\text{rcvs of m at j}) > i)$$

However this is a bit weaker than one often needs. Suppose the message is modified each time it is sent, e.g., by increasing a sequence number field. Then we expect at least one of the messages in this set to be eventually received. But this is *not* implied by the above assertion (because a different message is sent each time). It's easy to get the above assertion to state this stronger assumption: simply let m stand for the set of messages (rather than a single message) and let "m is sent (or received)" mean that any message in m is sent (or received).

The lossy channel program is obtained by modifying the fifo channel program to account for the above two differences. It is shown in Fig. 4.4. To improve readability of the progress assumption for receives, we introduce a helper assertion increasing(h,m), where h is a sequence and m is a set. It states that the number of elements of m in h grows without bound (which also implies that h is infinite).

4.4 Connection-less LRD Channels

A connection-less LRD channel program can be obtained from the lossy channel program simply by changing "subsequenceOf" to "in" in the output condition of v[j].rx(). This allows a transmitted message to be received at any time, regardless of its position in the transmitted sequence (reordering) or whether it has already been received (duplication). No other change would be needed.

```
service LossyChannel(Set ADDR) {  // Lossy channel. ADDR: addresses
   ic {ADDR.size ≥ 1}
   Map txh ← map([[j,k], []]: j,k in ADDR);
   Map rxh ← map([[j,k], []]: j,k in ADDR);
   Map v ← map([j, sid()]: j in ADDR);
   return v;

   input void v[ADDR j].tx(ADDR k, Seq msg) { // at j send msg to k
      ic {j ≠ k and not ongoing(v[j].tx(.))}
      txh[[j,k]].append(msg);
      oc {true}
      return;
   }

   input Seq v[ADDR j].rx() { // at j receive msg
      ic {not ongoing(v[j].rx())}
      output (Seq msg, ADDR k) {  // receive msg from k
         oc {(rxh[[k,j]] ∘ [msg]) subsequenceOf txh[[k,j]]}
         rxh[[k,j]].append(msg);
         return msg;
      }
   }

   atomicity assumption {input parts and output parts}

   // helper assertion: true iff number of m-elements in h is unbounded
   assertion increasing(Seq h, Set m) {
       forall(int i: set(j: j in h.keys, h[j] in m).size = i
                 leads-to  set(j: j in h.keys, h[j] in m).size > i)
   }

   progress assumption {
       forall(j in ADDR: ongoing(v[j].tx) leads-to  not ongoing(v[j].tx));

       // if rx always ready and msg set m is sent repeatedly
       //    then m received repeatedly
       forall(j,k in ADDR, m in Set<Seq>:
              (increasing(txh[[j,k]], m)
              and (not ongoing(v[j].rx) leads-to  ongoing(v[j].rx))
              ⇒ increasing(rxh[[j,k]], m)
       )
   }
}     // LossyChannel
```

Fig. 4.4 Connection-less lossy program

```
service LrdChannel(Set ADDR) {  // LRD channel. ADDR: addresses
   ic {ADDR.size ≥ 1}
   // txh[j]: sequence of messages sent to j from any address
   Map txh ← map([j, []]: j in ADDR);
   // rxh[j]: sequence of messages received at j from any address
   Map rxh ← map([j, []]: j in ADDR);
   Map v ← map([j, sid()]: j in ADDR);
   return v;

   input void v[ADDR j].tx(ADDR k, Seq msg) {  // at j send msg to k
      ic {j ≠ k and not ongoing(v[j].tx(.))}
      txh[k].append(msg);
      oc {true}
      return;
   }

   input Seq v[ADDR j].rx() {                    // at j receive msg
      ic {not ongoing(v[j].rx())}
      output (Seq msg) {
         oc {msg in txh[j]}
         rxh[j].append(msg);
         return msg;
      }
   }

   atomicity assumption {input parts and output parts}

   // helper assertion: same as in program LossyChannel
   assertion increasing(Seq h, Set m) {...}

   progress assumption {
      forall(j in ADDR: ongoing(v[j].tx) leads-to not ongoing(v[j].tx));

      // if msg set m is sent repeatedly and rx is always ready
      //   then m is received repeatedly
      forall(j in ADDR, m in Set<Seq>:
            (increasing(txh[j], m)
             and (not ongoing(v[j].rx) leads-to ongoing(v[j].rx)))
             ⇒ increasing(rxh[j], m))
   }
}     // LrdChannel
```

Fig. 4.5 Connection-less LRD channel program

However, we can get a simpler program by exploiting the fact that v[j].rx() can return any message that was sent to j from any address at any time in the past. So it suffices to record the messages sent to j from any address; transmit and receive histories for individual [j,k] pairs are not needed. Furthermore, the sequence of messages received at j is needed only for stating progress. An unexpected consequence of this is that the rx function *does not need the internal parameter* k, i.e., no internal nondeterminism. The resulting program is shown in Fig. 4.5.

4.5   Connection-oriented Fifo Channel

We now define a connection-oriented channel. Unlike connection-less channels, which provide only message transmit and receive functions, connection-oriented channels also provide functions for connection establishment and termination, collectively referred to as connection management. Practically all connection-oriented channels share the following. A user accesses a connection-oriented channel either as a **client** or as a **server**. A server user starts by becoming "accepting" at an address, i.e., becoming ready to accept any incoming connect request. A client user starts by requesting a connection to a remote address. If there is an accepting server user at that address, the client and the server would form a connection, each becoming *open* to the other. Each user is said to be a "peer" of the other. The users can then send and receive messages to each other, and then terminate the connection.

Within this basic framework, the specifics of connection management can vary greatly; e.g., the connection management that can be provided over a connection-less LRD channel is very different from what can be provided over a connection-less fifo channel. Here, we define a simple connection-oriented channel, one that is easily implemented over a fifo channel (see Exercise 4.10).

The service program for the connection-oriented channel variable is given in Figs. 4.6–4.8. It has the same parameter as a connection-less channel, namely ADDR, the set of addresses. To distinguish different connections between the same two addresses, each connect request is tagged with a unique "connect number". If the connect request results in a connection, the connect number serves to distinguish the connection instance and its transmit and receive histories. The program maintains the following variables.

- nc: integer, initially zero. Number of connect requests issued thus far. Used for generating connect numbers.
- txh, rxh: maps indexed by address-number pairs, initially empty. Entry txh[[j,n]] is the sequence of messages sent at address j in connection n. Entry rxh[[j,n]] is the sequence of messages received at address j in connection n.
- cs: connection status of address j. It takes the following values:

  – [CLOSED]: no user is at j.
  – [ACPTNG]: a server user is accepting at j for connect requests.

```
service ConnFifoChannel(Set ADDR) {  // connection-oriented fifo channel
   ic {ADDR.size ≥ 1}

   CLOSED ← 1; ACPTNG ← 2;
   OPENING ← 3; OPEN ← 4;
   int nc ← 0;                             // connect number counter
   Map cs ← map([j, [CLOSED]]: j in ADDR); // cs[j]: connection status of j
   Map txh ← map();                        // transmit histories
   Map rxh ← map();                        // receive histories
   Map v ← map([j, sid()]: j in ADDR);     // sid of access system at j
   return v;

   input ADDR v[ADDR j].accept() {         // at j become accepting
      ic {cs[j] = [CLOSED]}
      cs[j] ← [ACPTNG];
      output (ADDR k) {
         oc {cs[k][0,1] = [OPENING, j]}
         cs[j] ← [OPEN, k, cs[k][2]];      // open with k's connect number
         return k;
      }
   }

   input Seq v[ADDR j].connect(ADDR k) {   // at j request connection to k
      ic {cs[j] = [CLOSED] and k ≠ j}
      int n ← nc; nc ← nc+1;               // n: connect number
      cs[j] ← [OPENING,k,n];
      output (r) {
         oc {(r = 0 and cs[k] = [OPEN,j,n])     // connected
             OR (r = -1 and cs[k] ≠ [OPEN,j,n]) // rejected
         }
         if (r = 0) {
            cs[j][0] ← OPEN;
            txh[[j,n]] ← rxh[[j,n]] ← [];
         } else
            cs[j] ← [CLOSED];
         return r;
      }
   }

// continued
```

Fig. 4.6 Part 1: a connection-oriented fifo channel program

```
// ConnFifoChannel continued

    input void v[ADDR j].close() {           // at j request close connection
        ic {cs[j][0] = OPEN}
        [k,n] ← cs[j][1,2];                  // [remote address, connect number]
        oc {((ongoing(v[k].close) or cs[k] ≠ [OPEN,j,n])
            and rxh[[j,n]] = txh[[k,n]]
            and not (ongoing(v[j].tx(.)) or ongoing(v[j].rx))
        }
        cs[j] ← [CLOSED];
        return;
    }

    input void v[ADDR j].tx(Seq msg) {       // at j send msg to k
        ic {cs[j][0] = OPEN and not ongoing(v[j].tx(.))
            and not ongoing(v[j].close)}
        txh[j].append(msg);
        oc {true}
        return;
    }

    input Seq v[ADDR j].rx() {               // at j receive msg from k
        ic {cs[j][0] = OPEN and not ongoing(v[j].rx)}
        [k,n] ← cs[j][1,2];                  // [remote address, connect number]
        output (Seq rval, Seq msg) {
            oc {(rval = [-1] and rxh[[j,n]] = txh[[k,n]]
                and (ongoing(v[k].close) or cs[k] ≠ [OPEN,j,n]))
              OR (rval = [0,msg]
                    and (rxh[[j,n]] ∘ [msg]) prefixOf txh[[k,n]])}
            if (rval[0] = 0)
                rxh[[j,n]].append(msg);
            return rval;
        }
    }

// continued
```

Fig. 4.7 Part 2: a connection-oriented fifo channel program

- [OPENING,k,n]: a client user at j has issued a connect request to a remote
  address k with connect number n.
- [OPEN,k,n]: a (client or server) user at j is open to the user at k with connect
  number n.
- v: map indexed by address; v[j] is the sid of the access system at address j.

```
// ConnFifoChannel continued

    atomicity assumption [input parts and output parts]

    progress assumption [  // j, k range over addresses
        // progress assertion for v[j].accept left as an exercise
        (ongoing(v[j].accept) and ...) leads-to not ongoing(v[j].accept);

        // every connect and tx call eventually returns
        ongoing(v[j].connect) leads-to not ongoing(v[j].connect);
        ongoing(v[j].tx(.)) leads-to not ongoing(v[j].tx(.));

        // v[j].close returns if remote is closing or closed and j is receiving
        (ongoing(v[j].close) and cs[j][1,2] = [k,n]
        and (ongoing(v[k].close) or cs[k] ≠ [OPEN,j,n]))
            leads-to (not ongoing(v[j].close) or not ongoing(v[j].rx));

        // v[j].rx returns if there is an incoming message or if all
        // incoming messages have been received and remote is closing or closed
        (ongoing(v[j].rx) and cs[j][1,2] = [k,n]
        and (rxh[[j,n]].size < txh[[k,n]].size
            or (rxh[[j,n]] = txh[[k,n]]
                and (ongoing(v[k].close) or cs[k] ≠ [OPEN,j,n]))))
            leads-to not ongoing(v[j].rx)
    ]
}    // ConnFifoChannel
```

Fig. 4.8 Part 3: a connection-oriented fifo channel program

At each address j, the program has five input functions:

- Function v[j].accept() is called by a user to start accepting at address j for any incoming connect request. It is called only when j is closed. It is blocking. It returns a remote address k and sets j open to k with connect number n only if k is opening to j with connect number n.
- Function v[j].connect(k) is called by a user to request a connection to remote address k. It is called only when j is closed. It obtains a connect number n from nc and sets j opening to k. It returns 0 and becomes open to k only if k is open to j with connect number n. It returns –1 and sets j closed only if k is not open to j with connect number n. (The latter condition is too weak; see Exercise 4.9.)
- Function v[j].close() is called only when j is open (as client or server) to k. The call makes j "closing". It is blocking. It returns only when j has no ongoing tx or rx call, k is closing or has closed the connection, and all messages sent by k in this connection have been received.

- Function v[j].tx(msg) is called only if j is open to k and v[j].close is not ongoing. It transmits message msg to k.
- Function v[j].rx() is called only if j is open to k. It is blocking. It returns [0,msg] only if msg is the next message to be received in order from k. It returns [-1] only if k is closing or has closed the connection, and all messages sent by k in this connection have been received.

The progress assumption has an assertion for each function. Developing the assertion for v[j].accept is left as an exercise. For each of v[j].connect(k) and v[j].tx(.), the assertion says that the call eventually returns. For v[j].close, the assertion says that the call eventually returns provided k is closing or has closed the connection and j remains ready to receive incoming messages. For v[j].rx, the assertion says that the call eventually returns provided there is an incoming message or all messages have been received and k is closing or closed.

4.6 Multiplexing Ports onto Channels

This section presents a distributed program that uses a connection-less channel and multiplexes a set of ports at each address of the channel (similar to what UDP does over IP). The distributed program, called MultiplexorDist, is shown in Fig. 4.9. It has two parameters: ADDR, the set of addresses of the underlying channel; and PORT, the set of ports at each address.

The program first starts a connection-less channel with parameter ADDR and saves the returned sids in map c; entry c[j] has the sid of the channel access system at address j. The channel in the program is fifo, but it could just as well be lossy or LRD. The program then starts at each address j a multiplexor access system and saves the returned sid in v[j].

Each system v[j] is an instantiation of the await-structured program Multiplexor, shown in Fig. 4.10. The program sends and receives messages of the form [q,msg],

---

```
program MultiplexorDist(Set ADDR, Set PORT) {
    // ADDR: addresses of channel. PORT: ports at each address
    ia {ADDR.size ≥ 1 and PORT.size ≥ 1}
    Map c ← startSystem(FifoChannel(ADDR)); // c[j]: channel access system at j
    Map v ← map();                          // v[j]: multiplexor access sys-
tem at j
    for (j in ADDR)
        v[j] ← startSystem(Multiplexor(ADDR, PORT, j, c[j]));
    return v;
} // end MultiplexorDist
```

Fig. 4.9 Program of multiplexor access systems and channel

```
program Multiplexor(Set ADDR, Set PORT, ADDR aL, Sid cL) {
    // aL: local address. cL: sid of local channel access system
    ia {true}
    // rbuff[p]: sequence of received messages incoming to local port p
    Map rbuff ← map([p,[]]: PORT p);
    Tid tRx ← startThread(doRx());
    return mysid;

    // send msg to port pR at address aR
    input void mysid.tx(PORT pR, ADDR aR, Seq msg) {
        ia {aR ≠ aL}
        await (true)
            cL.tx(aR, [pR,msg]);
        return;
    }

    input Seq mysid.rx(PORT pR) {  // receive msg at port pR
        ia {aR ≠ aL}
•       await (rbuff[pR].size > 0) {
            Seq msg ← rbuff[pr][0];
            rbuff[pR].remove();
            return msg;
        }
    }

    function doRx() {     // executed by thread tRx
        while (true) {
•           Seq msg ← cL.rx();
            ia {msg in Tuple<PORT,Seq>}
            await (true)
                rbuff[msg[0]].append(msg[1]);
        }
    }
    atomicity assumption {awaits}
    progress assumption {weak fairness of threads}
}
```

Fig. 4.10 Program of multiplexor access system

where q is the destination port and msg is the user message. The program maintains a variable rbuff[p] for each port p in which it stores the sequence of user messages received for local port p. The program has the following functions:

• Input function tx(p,k,msg), to send user message msg to port p at destination address k. It calls c[j].tx(k, [p,msg]).

- Input function v[j].rx(p), to receive a user message at local port p. It removes a message from rbuff[p] and returns it to the user.
- Function doRx, executed by local thread tRx. It repeatedly receives a [q,msg] message from the channel and appends msg to rbuff[q].

Replacing the awaits with standard synchronization constructs is left as exercises. Defining a service program for MultiplexorDist is also left as an exercise.

4.7 Concluding Remarks

This chapter has defined three kinds of connection-less channels and one connection-oriented channel. The channels described in this chapter have "unicast" sends, where a transmitted message is to be delivered to a single address. One can also have "broadcast" and "multicast" sends [1, 2, 8]. A broadcast message is to be delivered to all addresses. A multicast message is to be delivered to a specified subset of addresses, with addresses typically being allowed to join and leave the subset. Broadcast channels are considered in Exercises 4.22 and 4.21.

4.7.1 Conventions

For a connection-less channel with an address j and a message msg, the predicate "msg receivable at j" is true iff the channel in its current state can deliver the message at j. Formally (below k ranges over addresses of the channel),

(msg receivable at j)
$$= \begin{cases} \text{forsome(k: rxh[[k,j]] } \circ \text{ [msg]) prefixOf txh[[k,j]]} & \text{if fifo channel} \\ \text{forsome(k: rxh[[k,j]] } \circ \text{ [msg]) subsequenceOf txh[[k,j]]} & \text{if lossy channel} \\ \text{(msg in txh[j])} & \text{if LRD channel} \end{cases}$$

If address j is fixed by the context, "msg receivable at j" is shortened to "msg receivable".

Let chan be an instantiation of service FifoChannel, let j and k be addresses of chan, and let msg be a message. Then we define the following

- chan.transit(j,k): sequence of messages in transit in chan from j to k.
- chan.numTransit(msg,j,k): number of msg instances in transit in chan from j to k.
- chan.numTransit(msg): number of msg instances in transit in chan (between any two addresses).

The above can defined formally. For example,

- chan.transit(j,k):
  [chan.txh[[j,k]][i]: i in chan.txh[[j,k]].keys, i ≥ chan.rxh[[j,k]].size]

End of conventions

Exercises

4.1. Write down the inverse of the lossy channel service.

4.2. Write down the inverse of the LRD channel service.

4.3. Modify program FifoChannel as follows. To each channel access system v[j], add an input function, say v[j].endLocal(), that shuts down address j without affecting any other address. That is, v[j].endLocal() can be called at any time, and after that neither v[j].tx(.) nor v[j].rx() can be called.

4.4. Modify your answer to Exercise 4.3 so that v[j].endLocal() also cancels any ongoing v[j].rx call. Let the latter return [0,msg] for success or [-1] for cancellation.

4.5. Modify program FifoChannel as follows. Let the program have a "special" address parameter, say j0. Let system v[j0] have an additional input function, say v[j0].endGlobal(), that shuts down all addresses; That is, v[j0].endGlobal() can be called at any time, and after that neither v[j].tx(.) nor v[j].rx() can be called at any address j.

4.6. Modify your answer to Exercise 4.5 so that v[j].endGlobal() also cancels any ongoing v[j].rx call. Let the latter return [0,msg] for success or [-1] for cancellation.

4.7. In program ConnFifoChannel (Fig. 4.7), is the connect number needed? Suppose we eliminate variable nc and its entry in cs[j] (when opening, open, or closing) and in the transmit and receive history indices. Does the resulting service program have undesirable evolutions?

4.8. Write down the inverse of program ConnFifoChannel.

4.9. Program ConnFifoChannel (Fig. 4.7) allows function v[j].connect(k) to return −1 in situations where it should not; in particular, it allows the implementation to return −1 even if k has been accepting throughout. Modify the program so that v[j].connect(k) returns −1 only if k was not accepting at some point during the v[j].connect(k) call.

4.10. Develop a distributed program that implements the connection-oriented channel ConnFifoChannel using a connection-less fifo channel FifoChannel over the same addresses. There would be two programs, say ConnChanDist and ConnChan (as with the multiplexor). ConnChanDist starts the connection-less fifo channel and an instantiation of ConnChan at each address.

(Hint: The ConnChan systems exchange messages over the connection-less fifo channel. Let v[j].connect(k) send a "connect" message from j to k. Let k respond to this with an "accept" or "reject" message. Treat closing in a similar way.)

4.11. Develop an appropriate progress assertion for function v[j].accept() in program ConnFifoChannel (Fig. 4.7).

(Hint: Determine a condition under which v[j].accept will surely become connected. You may need to maintain more state.)

4.12. Write a service program defining the service provided by program MultiplexorDist.

4.13. Refine the await-structured program Multiplexor (Fig. 4.10) so that it uses locks and condition variables instead of awaits.

4.14. Repeat Exercise 4.13 using semaphores instead of locks and condition variables.

4.15. Write a service program for the intended service of program MultiplexorDist.

4.16. Show that program MultiplexorDist implements the service defined in Exercise 4.15.

4.17. Develop an alternative fifo channel program in which txh[[j,k]] and rxh[[j,k]] are replaced by a single variable transit[[j,k]] that indicates the sequence of messages in transit from j to k (so receive removes a message from transit). Do you find this program more natural than the one in Fig. 4.2. Don't forget to capture the progress assumption.

4.18. Repeat Exercise 4.17 for the lossy channel program. Do you find it convenient to resort to internal nondeterminism? Do you find this program more natural?

4.19. Develop a fifo channel program that avoids internal nondeterminism. As mentioned at the end of Sect. 4.2, one way is to have the received message sequence at an address remain a prefix of a merge of the message sequences sent by the different users to that address. Here is an outline of the changes for address j:

- Introduce a variable, say aggRxh[j], that records the sequence of messages received at j from any sender (instead of recording it by sender, in rxh[[k,j]] for sender k).
- The output part of the input function v[j].rx() now has only one parameter, msg. The output condition requires aggRxh[j] ∘ [msg] to be a prefix of some merge of the sequences in bag(txh[k,j]: k in ADDR).
- Reformulate the progress assumptions in terms of aggRxh[j] and bag(txh[k,j]: k in ADDR). (Recall that there are two versions of the progress assumption: one which imposes fairness between senders, and one which does not.)

Which channel program do you find easier to understand, the one above (without internal nondeterminism) or the one in Fig. 4.4 (with internal nondeterminism).

4.20. Repeat Exercise 4.19 for lossy and LRD channels.

4.21. Define a **reliable broadcast channel** to be a channel such that: (1) every message sent is eventually delivered to all addresses (including the sender's address); and (2) all addresses receive messages in the same order. Develop a service program for such a channel. A skeleton is provided below.

```
service RelBroadcastChannel(Set ADDR) {  // reliable broadcast channel
    ic {ADDR.size ≥ 1}
    ....
    return v;  // v[j]: access system at j
    input void v[ADDR j].tx(Seq msg) {...}
    input Seq v[ADDR j].rx() {...}
    atomicity assumption {...}
    progress assumption {...}
} // RelBroadcastChannel
```

Your program must allow users at different addresses to call tx simultaneously. It must not require messages to be delivered in the global order in which they were sent; for example, given a sequence of sends, v1.tx(m1), v2.tx(m2), v3.tx(m3), it should allow the messages m1, m2, m3 to be received in any order. (Requiring receptions in the global send order would be horribly inefficient.)

4.22. Define an **atomic broadcast channel** to be a channel such that: (1) a message sent is either delivered to all addresses (including the sender's address), or not delivered to any address; (2) different addresses can receive messages in different order; and (3) a message repeatedly sent is eventually delivered. Develop a service program for such a channel. Use the skeleton given in Exercise 4.21 and be consistent with its constraints (e.g., allow simultaneous sends at different addresses, do not require an implementation to track the global order of sends).

4.23. Define a fifo channel whose set of addresses can be dynamically modified. Specifically, let ADDR be the set of all possible addresses of the channel and let addr be the subset of currently active addresses. At each address j, introduce two input functions: activate(), to make j active; and deactivate(), to make j inactive.

References

1. S. Banerjee, B. Bhattacharjee, C. Kommareddy, Scalable application layer multicast, in *Proceedings of the 2002 Conference on Applications, Technologies, Architectures, and Protocols for Computer Communications, SIGCOMM '02* (ACM, New York, 2002), pp. 205–217. doi:10.1145/633025.633045. http://doi.acm.org/10.1145/633025.633045
2. K.P. Birman, T.A. Joseph, Reliable communication in the presence of failures. ACM Trans. Comput. Syst. **5**(1), 47–76 (1987). doi:10.1145/7351.7478. http://doi.acm.org/10.1145/7351.7478
3. K.M. Chandy, L. Lamport, Distributed snapshots: determining global states of distributed systems. ACM Trans. Comput. Syst. **3**(1), 63–75 (1985). doi:10.1145/214451.214456. http://doi.acm.org/10.1145/214451.214456
4. K.M. Chandy, J. Misra, The drinking philosophers problem. ACM Trans. Program. Lang. Syst. **6**(4), 632–646 (1984). doi:10.1145/1780.1804. http://doi.acm.org/10.1145/1780.1804

5. D. Comer, *Internetworking with TCP/IP*, 4th edn. Vol 1: Principles, Protocols, and Architectures (Prentice-Hall, Upper Saddle River, 2000)
6. D.E. Knuth, Verification of link-level protocols. BIT **21**(1), 31–36 (1981)
7. L. Lamport, Time, clocks, and the ordering of events in a distributed system. Commun. ACM **21**(7), 558–565 (1978). doi:10.1145/359545.359563. http://doi.acm.org/10.1145/359545.359563
8. J.C. Lin, S. Paul, RMTP: a reliable multicast transport protocol, in *Proceedings of the Fifteenth Annual Joint Conference of the IEEE Computer and Communications Societies Conference on the Conference on Computer Communications – Volume 3, INFOCOM'96* (IEEE Computer Society, Washington DC, 1996), pp. 1414–1424. http://dl.acm.org/citation.cfm?id=1895726.1895798
9. L.L. Peterson, B.S. Davie, *Computer Networks: A Systems Approach*, 3rd edn. (Morgan Kaufmann, San Francisco, 2003)
10. A.U. Shankar, Verified data transfer protocols with variable flow control. ACM Trans. Comput. Syst. **7**(3), 281–316 (1989). doi:10.1145/65000.65003. http://doi.acm.org/10.1145/65000.65003
11. A.U. Shankar, S.S. Lam, An HDLC protocol specification and its verification using image protocols. ACM Trans. Comput. Syst. **1**(4), 331–368 (1983). doi:10.1145/357377.357384. http://doi.acm.org/10.1145/357377.357384

Chapter 5
Fifo Channels from Unreliable Channels

5.1 Introduction

Fifo, lossy, and LRD connection-less channels were presented in the previous
chapter. This chapter presents a distributed program that implements a connection-
less fifo channel between two addresses a1 and a2, given an *unreliable*, i.e., lossy
or LRD, connection-less channel connecting the two addresses. Henceforth we
omit the "connection-less" qualifier when referring to these channels. The program
has a component system at each address, which accepts messages from its local
user, transfers them over the unreliable channel to the remote component system,
which then delivers them in order to the remote user. Figure 5.1 illustrates the
configuration. In computer networking, such a program is referred to as a **data
transfer protocol** [4, 9, 10]. Following this terminology, we refer to the distributed
program as DtpDist and the program of each component system as Dtp, where "dtp"
is short for data transfer protocol. We refer to the messages exchanged between

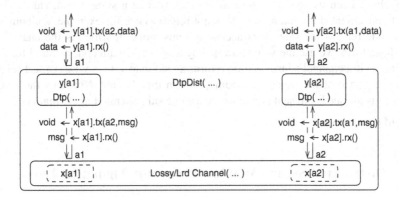

Fig. 5.1 The data transfer protocol between addresses a1 and a2, consisting of dtp systems y[a1]
and y[a2] interacting with channel access systems x[a1] and x[a2] below and users above

A.U. Shankar, *Distributed Programming: Theory and Practice*,
DOI 10.1007/978-1-4614-4881-5__5,
© Springer Science+Business Media New York 2013

the dtp users as "data blocks", and reserve the term "messages" for the messages exchanged between the dtp systems; the former would be sent inside the latter.

We develop the program in stages. Section 5.2 develops a distributed program, called SwpDist, that achieves *one-way* fifo data transfer, from a1 to a2, over the unreliable channel. A **source** system at a1 and a **sink** system at a2 employ the **sliding window protocol** with cyclic sequence numbers [4, 5, 7–10]. For readability, the source and sink are described at a so-called **algorithm level**, using informally-stated (but precise) rules rather than a program.

Section 5.3 analyzes the algorithm-level program SwpDist. The minimum size of the cyclic sequence number space for correct operation is obtained for each type of unreliable channel (lossy and LRD).

Section 5.4 translates the algorithm-level descriptions of the source and sink into await-structured programs and then into programs using locks and condition variables. The translation is straightforward. It preserves the atomicity of the algorithm-level description, and hence the results of the algorithm-level analysis. Ways to increase parallelism in the source and sink programs are described.

Section 5.5 takes two SwpDist programs, one in each direction, and merges them into the desired DtpDist program. Program Dtp is obtained by merging the source and sink at an address. The merge preserves the atomicity, and hence the properties, of SwpDist in each direction. It follows trivially that DtpDist implements FifoChannel(set(a1,a2)).

Section 5.7 shows how to add (TCP-style) connection termination to DtpDist. It turns out that achieving termination of the two dtp systems is not entirely trivial because the underlying channel is unreliable [2].

5.1.1 Conventions

Given types or sets $A_1, \cdots, A_n$, the construct union($A_1, \cdots, A_n$) denotes their union.

We have been using s.x to refer to a quantity x in a system with sid s. This is not convenient if s's main code does not return mysid; for example, a channel's main code returns the sids of its access systems, none of which is the channel's sid. Henceforth, we use the value returned by a system's main code as an id for the system; so if a channel's instantiation returns an sid map v, then v.txh[[j,k]] refers to the sequence of messages sent from j to k in the channel. Note that the value returned is unique because it contains at least one sid generated in the main code.

End of conventions

5.2 Distributed Sliding Window Program: Algorithm Level

This section develops a distributed program that employs the sliding window protocol over the unreliable channel to achieve fifo data transfer from a1 to a2. The distributed program, called SwpDist, is shown in Fig. 5.2. Parameters N, SW and RW are

```
program SwpDist(a1, a2, N, SW, RW) {
    ia {Val(a1,a2) and (a1 ≠ a2) and
        int(N,SW,RW) and (0 < SW,RW < N) and Φ}
    Map x ← startSystem(Lossy/LrdChannel(set(a1,a2)));
    y1 ← startSystem(Source(a1,a2,x[a1],N,SW));
    y2 ← startSystem(Sink(a2,a1,x[a2],N,RW));
    return map([a1,y1], [a2,y2]);
}
```

Fig. 5.2 Sliding window protocol program

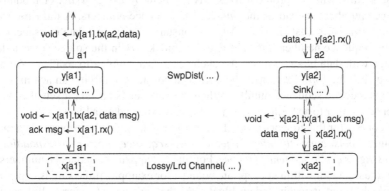

Fig. 5.3 Sliding window protocol: source and sink exchange data messages and ack messages over the unreliable channel to achieve fifo data transfer from a1 to a2

integers, and predicate Φ is a constraint on them which will be determined in due course. The program starts an unreliable channel with addresses a1 and a2, a source y[a1] at a1, and a sink y[a2] at a2. Its instantiation results in the configuration in Fig. 5.3. The rest of this section develops algorithm-level descriptions of the source and sink programs.

The source has an input function tx(a2,data) that the local user calls to pass data block data to the source. The source transfers the data block over the unreliable channel to the sink, retransmitting it until an acknowledgment is received. The user at the sink calls rx() to get a data block. The sink passes a data block data in the return after determining that data is the next in sequence to be delivered. An obvious way to achieve the latter is for the source to tag successive data blocks supplied by its user with increasing sequence numbers, and to include the sequence number in any message containing the data block.

The sequence numbers can also be used by the sink to acknowledge the reception of data blocks to the source. The accepted convention is for the ack to indicate the data block *next expected in sequence* rather than the received data block. (In networking jargon, the ack is "cumulative" and not "selective".) That is, suppose the sink receives data block j when it already has $0, \cdots, k-1$ but not k; if $j \neq k$ the sink responds with ack k, and if $j = k$ the sink responds with ack k+1. Finally, for good throughput, the source should be able to have several data blocks *outstanding*, i.e., sent but not yet acked, and the sink should be able to buffer data blocks received out of sequence. Note that if the sink has data blocks $0, \cdots, k-1, k+1, \cdots, j$ and receives data block k, then it responds with ack j+1.

The only drawback of the solution outlined in the previous two paragraphs is that the sequence numbers in the messages would grow without bound as more and more data blocks are transferred. This would greatly complicate fast (hardware) implementation of the component systems; it would also waste some channel bandwidth.

The sliding window protocol fixes this problem by using *cyclic*, or modulo-N, sequence numbers instead of the *unbounded* sequence numbers. A **data message** has the form [DAT,cn,data], where DAT is a constant signifying a data message, cn is a cyclic sequence number, and data is a data block. When the source sends a data message with data block j, it sets the cyclic sequence number to $\mod(j, N)$. An **ack message** has the form [ACK,cn], where ACK is a constant signifying an ack message and cn is a cyclic sequence number. When the sink sends an ack, it sets the cyclic sequence number to $\mod(j, N)$ where j is the next expected data block.

Of course, for this to work properly, when the sink (source) receives a data (ack) message, *it must correctly infer the unbounded sequence number corresponding to the message's cyclic sequence number*. For that to happen, the sequence numbers in transit must remain within appropriate bounds; for example, if the sink is expecting data block j and it receives data block j+N, the sink would incorrectly treat the received data block as data block j.

The sliding window protocol achieves this in an elegant way. The source maintains a **send window** corresponding to the sequence numbers of the data blocks that can be outstanding. The sink maintains a **receive window** corresponding to the sequence numbers of the data blocks that the sink is prepared to receive out of sequence. The parameters SW and RW indicate the sizes of the send and receive windows, respectively; obviously, each has to be less than N. Over time as data blocks are transferred, these two windows move towards increasing sequence numbers, always maintaining an overlap of at least one sequence number, and the sequence numbers in transit remain within a constant bound of the windows.

5.2.1 Source

Figure 5.5 gives the source program at the algorithm level. Variables ng, ns, na and sbuff are illustrated in Fig. 5.4. A total of ng data blocks, i.e., data blocks 0 through ng−1, have been generated by the local user thus far. Of these, data blocks 0 through na−1 have been sent and acked. Data blocks na through ns−1 are outstanding, i.e., sent at least once and not yet acked. Data blocks ns through ng−1 have not been sent. At all times, $na \le ns \le \min(ng, na+SW)$ holds; ng can be higher, equal, or lower than na+SW. The sequence numbers na through na+SW−1 constitute the send window.

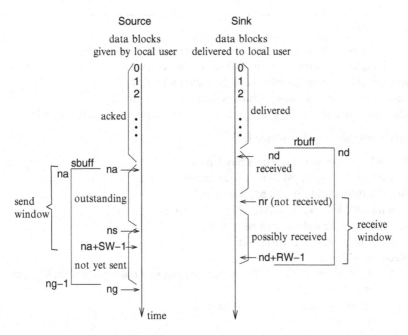

Fig. 5.4 Variables of the sliding window protocol

Map sbuff stores the data blocks na through ng-1, with sbuff[i] storing data block i. When the source gets a data block from its local user, it adds the block to sbuff with key ng and increments ng. The source sends a data message with data block ns only when ns < min(na+SW, ng) holds, after which it increments ns. The source can resend an outstanding data block at any time.

When the source receives an ack message [ACK,cn], it looks for a j in the send window that matches cn. Specifically, it sets j to na + mod(cn-na,N), which is the first number on or after na that matches cn, and checks if na < j ≤ ns holds. If it does, the source removes sbuff[na..j-1] and sets na to j.

Variable dbh records the sequence of all data blocks generated by the user. It is an auxiliary variable, needed only for stating desired properties. At all times, sbuff[i] equals dbh[i] for i in sbuff.keys.

5.2.2 Sink

Figure 5.6 gives the sink program at the algorithm level. Variables nd, nr and rbuff are illustrated in Fig. 5.4. The first nr data blocks have been received from the remote user. The first nd of these have been delivered to the local user. At all times, nd ≤ nr holds. The sequence numbers nr to nd+RW-1 constitute the receive window.

Source variables

- ng: initially 0. Number of data blocks generated by local user.
- ns: initially 0. Number of data blocks sent at least once.
- na: initially 0. Number of data blocks acknowledged.
- sbuff: map initially empty. Buffers data blocks na..ng−1.
- dbh: sequence of data blocks 0..ng−1; initially empty. Auxiliary variable.

Source rules (atomically executed)

- When local user generates data block data
      sbuff[ng] ← data; ng ← ng+1; dbh.append(data);
- Send sbuff[ns] only if ns < min(na+SW, ng)
      send [DAT, mod(ns,N), sbuff[ns]]; ns ← ns+1;
- Resend sbuff[k] only if k in na..ns−1
      send [DAT, mod(k,N), sbuff[k]];
- Receive [ACK, cn]:
      j ← na+mod(cn−na,N);   // j is first number on or after na that matches cn
      if (na < j ≤ ns) {
          for (k in na..j−1) sbuff.remove(k);
          na ← j;
      }

Fig. 5.5 Variables and rules of source

Sink variables

- nd: initially 0. Number of data blocks delivered to local user.
- nr: initially 0. Number of contiguous data blocks received.
- rbuff: map initially empty. Buffers received data blocks in nd..nd+RW−1.

Sink rules (atomically executed)

- Deliver data block rbuff[nd] to local user only if nd < nr
      rbuff.remove(nd); nd ← nd+1;
- Receive [DAT, cn, data]:
      j ← na+mod(cn−nr,N);   // j is first number on or after nr matching cn
      if ((nr ≤ j < nd+RW) and not (j in rbuff.keys)) {
          rbuff[j] ← data;
          while (nr in rbuff.keys)
                nr ← nr+1;
      }
      send [ACK, mod(nr,N)];

Fig. 5.6 Variables and rules of sink

Map rbuff buffers received data blocks nd through nd+RW-1. Its keys are a subset of nd..nd+RW-1, and rbuff[i], if present, should contain data block i. Data block nr has not been received (so nr is not in rbuff.keys). The sink delivers rbuff[nd] to the local user only if nd is less than nr, after which it removes the entry from rbuff and increments nd.

When the sink receives a data message [DAT,cn,data], it looks for a j in the receive window that matches cn. Specifically, it sets j to nr + mod(cn-nr,N), which is the first number on or after nr that matches cn, and checks if j < nd+RW holds. If it does, the sink saves the message's data in rbuff with key j (if not already present); if j equals nr, it increases nr to the next empty rbuff location. In any case, the sink sends an ack message.

5.2.3 Effective Atomicity of SwpDist

The body of SwpDist (Fig. 5.2) is effectively atomic. Even if the source, sink and channel undergo a sequence of interactions *x before* SwpDist executes return mysid, the state and input-output history of the aggregate SwpDist when SwpDist returns is the same as it would be if the source, sink and channel stay idle until after SwpDist returns and undergo *x subsequently*. (Keep in mind that interactions between the source, sink and channel are internal to SwpDist.) For example, suppose the source gets a data block from its local user and sends a message before the sink is created; the effect is the same as if the source gets the data block and sends the message after the sink is created but before the sink does anything.

5.3 Analysis of the Sliding Window Algorithm

This section proves that the sliding window program, SwpDist, achieves fifo data transfer from a1 to a2. Specifically, we will prove X_1 and X_2 below. For readability, we omit the sid prefixes y[a1] and y[a2] when referring to variables at the source and sink. There is no ambiguity because the source and sink have no variable name in common.

X_1 : *Inv* (nd < nr $\Rightarrow$ rbuff[nd] = dbh[nd])
X_2 : (U_1 and U_2 and U_3 and U_4)
    $\Rightarrow$ forall(k: nd = k < ng *leads-to* nd > k)
where

U_1 : forall(k: nd = k < nr *leads-to* nd > k)
U_2 : weak fairness for source sending sbuff[ns] and resending sbuff[na]
U_3 : (no ongoing source rx call) *leads-to* (ongoing source rx call)
U_4 : (no ongoing sink rx call) *leads-to* (ongoing sink rx call)

X_1 says that if the sink delivers a data block to the local user, then that data bock is the correct one to maintain fifo delivery. X_2 says that every data block generated by the source user is eventually delivered to the sink user (X_2 rhs) provided the sink user gets a data block when it is available (U_1), the source executes the rules for sending data blocks ns and na with weak fairness (U_2), and the source and sink remain ready to receive messages (U_3, U_4).

5.3.1 Correct Interpretation Conditions

We start the analysis by identifying additional properties that we expect of SwpDist. We expect every entry in rbuff, not just the entry for nd, to contain the correct data block. Formally, we expect $Inv A_1$, which implies X_1, to hold, where

A_1 : (k in rbuff.keys) $\Rightarrow$ rbuff[k] = dbh[k]

We expect the send and receive windows to move forward while always maintaining some overlap. More precisely, we expect a data block j to be acked at the source only after it has been received at the sink. The latter should happen only after data block j has been sent from the source at least once. The latter should happen only after data block j-SW has been acked, due to the send window size constraint. Putting all this together, we expect the following to be invariant.

A_2 : na $\leq$ nr $\leq$ ns $\leq$ na+SW

When the sink receives a data message, we want it to correctly interpret the received cyclic sequence number. To analyze this, we augment (for analysis only) each data message with an additional entry containing the unbounded sequence number of its data block. We say "data message j" to mean a data message with unbounded sequence number j (and cyclic sequence number mod(j,N)). When data message j is received, it is correctly interpreted if whenever j is in nr..nd+RW-1 (i.e., the data block is not discarded), j equals nr+mod(j-nr,N) (i.e., it is correctly matched).

What values of j ensure the above? If j lies in the receive window, it is correctly matched. If j is very much lower than nr or very much higher than nr+RW, then mod(j,N) wraps around and incorrectly matches a number in the receive window. Specifically, for decreasing j starting from nr (i.e., j = nr-1, nr-2, ...), the first number that is incorrectly matched is nr+RW-1-N (it gets mapped to nr+RW-1). So we want j $\geq$ nr+RW-N. Similarly, for increasing j starting from nr+RW-1, the first value that is incorrectly matched is nr+N (it gets mapped to nr). So we also want j $\leq$ nr+N-1. Combining the two bounds, we want A_3 below to be invariant. (Below, "data message j receivable" is short for "x.rxh[[a1,a2]]∘[data message j] subsequenceOf x.txh[[a1,a2]]", where x is the sid map returned by the unreliable channel's main code; recall the conventions in Sects. 4.7 and 5.1.)

A_3 : (data message j receivable) $\Rightarrow$ nr-N+RW $\leq$ j $\leq$ nr+N-1

When the source receives an ack message, we want it to correctly interpret the received cyclic sequence number. To analyze this, we augment each ack message with its unbounded sequence number, i.e., the value of nr when it was sent. We say "ack message j" to mean an ack message with unbounded sequence number j. When ack message j is received, it is correctly interpreted if whenever j is in na+1..ns (i.e., the ack is not discarded), j equals na+mod(j-na,N) (i.e., it is correctly matched). If j is in the range na+1..ns, it is correctly matched. As j gets away from this range, the first value that is incorrectly matched is ns-N on the lower side and na+N+1 on the upper side. So we want the following to be invariant:

A_4 : (ack message j receivable) $\Rightarrow$ ns-N+1 $\leq$ j $\leq$ na+N

Summarizing the development thus far, we want predicates A_1, A_2, A_3 and A_4 to be invariant. They hold initially (because na, ns, and nr are zero and dbh, rbuff, and the unreliable channel are empty). We next show that these predicates are preserved by each atomic step provided N is chosen appropriately. It suffices to show that each step preserves A_3 and A_4 assuming $A_2, A_3,$ and A_4 hold before the step. This is because A_3 and A_4 holding before a step ensures that A_2 and A_1 hold after the step; indeed, this is exactly how A_3 and A_4 were obtained.

5.3.2 Achieving Correct Interpretation over Lossy Channel

For a lossy channel, we show that each step preserves A_3 and A_4 provided SW+RW is at most N. That is,

Φ : N $\geq$ SW + RW

Consider A_3. It can be falsified in only two ways. One way is the transmission of a data message k which falsifies A_3's rhs (right-hand-side). Because k lies in na..ns-1, this preserves A_3's rhs if na $\geq$ nr-N+RW and ns-1 $\leq$ nr+N-1 hold. The first bound, na $\geq$ nr-N+RW, holds if na $\geq$ ns-N+RW (because ns $\geq$ nr), which holds if na $\geq$ na-N+RW+SW (because na $\geq$ ns-SW), which holds if N $\geq$ SW+RW. The second bound, ns-1 $\leq$ nr+N-1, holds if ns $\leq$ na+N (because nr $\leq$ ns), which holds because ns $\leq$ na+SW and SW < N.

The only other way to falsify A_3 is to increase nr to an extent that violates the lower bound in A_3's rhs for some data message j in transit. Let k_1 and k_2 be the values of nr before and after the data message reception, at say time t_1; so the received data block was k_1 and prior to t_1 data blocks $k_1+1, \ldots, k_2-1$ were buffered. For A_3 to be preserved, j $\geq k_2$-N+RW should hold prior to the reception, which is expressed by the following predicate:

A_5 : ((k in rbuff.keys) and (data message j receivable)) $\Rightarrow$ j $\geq$ k+1-N+RW

We now show that A_5 is invariant. Assume rbuff[k] is not empty at time t_1. So data block k was sent at some earlier time, say t_2 ($< t_1$). At that time, the value of ns, denoted by ns(t_2), satisfied ns(t_2) $\geq$ k+1. So na(t_2) $\geq$ k+1-SW, which implies na(t_2) $\geq$ k+1-N+RW (because N $\geq$ SW+RW). This means that any data message j sent after time

t_2, including those in transit at time t_1, satisfies $j \geq k+1-N+RW$. So A_5 is invariant, and hence A_3 is invariant.

A_4's invariance is simpler to argue. Because nr never decreases, successive ack transmissions have non-decreasing unbounded sequence numbers. Because acks in transit are never reordered, the sequence of j's in transit is non-decreasing and upper bounded by nr. Because na is the highest j received thus far, every ack message k in transit is lower bounded by na. Thus we have the following invariant, which implies A_4:

A_6 : (ack message j receivable) $\Rightarrow$ na $\leq$ j $\leq$ nr

Thus $N \geq SW+RW$ ensures that A_3, A_4, A_5, and A_6 are invariant, completing the safety proof. (To obtain an assertional proof of A_5 and A_6, some additional assertions are needed; see Exercises 5.2 and 5.3.)

5.3.3 Achieving Correct Interpretation over LRD Channel

What happens if the lossy channel is replaced by an LRD channel? Clearly, the sliding window protocol (or any protocol with bounded messages) cannot ensure fifo data transfer, because, for any given N, an LRD channel can always present the receiver with a message that will be incorrectly interpreted (e.g., the data message 0 when nr equals N).

But it can be made to work if the LRD channel has a maximum message lifetime, say L, and the source imposes a delay, say δ, between introducing new data blocks into the channel (i.e., between increments to ns). We show below that each step preserves A_3 and A_4 provided the following holds.

$$\Phi: \quad N \geq SW + RW + \frac{L}{\delta}$$

In practice, the L and δ time bounds come for free because every channel has a maximum bitrate (hence a minimum time between data block sends) and practically every channel has a maximum message lifetime, even if it is several orders higher than the average end-to-end delay.

Consider A_3. A_3's upper bound holds exactly as in the lossy channel case. Now consider A_3's lower bound. At time t_0, let data message j be receivable. So data message j was sent at some prior time t_1, where $t_1 > t_0 - L$. We want $j > nr(t_0) - N + RW$ to hold. It suffices if $j > ns(t_0) - N + RW$ holds (because $nr(t_0) \leq ns(t_0)$ holds). At time t_1, when data j was sent, j was at least $na(t_1)$ (otherwise j would not have been sent), which was at least $ns(t_1) - SW$. During the interval $[t_1, t_0]$, ns has increased by at most L/δ. So $j \geq ns(t_0) - L/\delta - SW$ holds. So the desired bound of $j > ns(t_0) - N + RW$ holds if $SW + L/\delta \leq N - RW$ holds, or equivalently, $N \geq SW + RW + L/\delta$.

Consider A_4. A_4's upper bound holds exactly as in the lossy channel case. Now consider A_4's lower bound. At time t_0, let ack message j be receivable. So ack j was sent at some time t_1 where $t_1 > t_0 - L$. We need to show that $j \geq ns(t_0) - N + 1$ holds.

At time t_1, when the ack j was sent, j equaled $nr(t_1)$, which was at least $na(t_1)$, which was at least $ns(t_1) - SW$. During the interval $[t_1, t_0]$, ns has increased by at most L/δ. So $j \geq ns(t_0) - L/\delta - SW$, which implies the desired bound given $N > SW + L/\delta$.

Thus A_3 and A_4 are invariant, and we are done. Note that the analysis for the LRD channel does not have any intermediate assertions (analogous to A_5 and A_6 for the lossy channel). To state such assertions, let alone give an assertional proof, we need a program model and assertion language in which real-time constraints can be expressed. This is straightforward, but we postpone it to later (Chap. 8).

5.3.4   Achieving Progress

We now prove X_2. i.e., assume $U_1 - U_4$ and prove X_2's rhs. The argument here applies to both lossy and LRD channels. We first prove that na and nr keep increasing as long as they lag ns.

P_1 : na $= k <$ nr $\leq$ ns *leads-to* na $> k$
P_2 : (na $= k =$ nr $<$ ns and nr $<$ nd+RW) *leads-to* nr $> k$
P_3 : (na $= k =$ nr $<$ ns and nr $=$ nd+RW) *leads-to* nr $> k$
P_4 : na $= k =$ nr $<$ ns *leads-to* nr $> k$
P_5 : na $= k <$ ns *leads-to* na $> k$
P_6 : nr $= k <$ ns *leads-to* nr $> k$

Proof of $P_1 - P_9$

P_1 holds as follows. Any action that falsifies the lhs (left-hand-side) establishes the rhs (right-hand-side), because all variables are non-decreasing and na $\leq$ nr $\leq$ ns is invariant. While the lhs holds, the source repeatedly sends data block k (via weak fairness (U_2)), hence the sink repeatedly receives them (via channel progress and sink ready to receive (U_4)), hence the sink repeatedly sends acks, hence the source eventually receives an ack (via channel progress and source ready to receive (U_3)), at which point the rhs is established.

P_2 holds as follows. Any action that falsifies the lhs establishes the rhs because all variables are non-decreasing and na $\leq$ nr is invariant. While the lhs holds, the source repeatedly sends data block k (via weak fairness (U_2)), hence the sink eventually receives one of them (via channel progress and sink ready to receive (U_4)) and stores it in rbuff (because nr is less than nd+RW), at which point the rhs is established.

P_3 holds because the sink user increases nd if it lags nr (U_1), which increases nd. This establishes P_2's lhs, which leads to P_2's rhs, which is the same as P_3's rhs.

P_2 and P_3 imply P_4.

P_4 and P_1 imply P_5.

P_5 and *Inv*(nr $\geq$ na) imply P_6. Suppose ns equals j where j is greater than k. Then na is less than or equal to k. So na will keep increasing (by P_5) until it equals or exceeds j, at which point nr will equal or exceed j.   □

Now all that remains is to bridge the gap between the "user-level" variables, nd and ng, and the sliding window variables, na, nr and ns. P_{11} below is the same as X_2's rhs.

P_7 : (ns = k < ng and ns < na+SW) *leads-to* ns > k
P_8 : (ns = k < ng and ns = na+SW) *leads-to* ns = k < ng and ns < na+SW
P_9 : ns = k < ng *leads-to* ns > k
P_{10} : nr = k < ng *leads-to* nr > k
P_{11} : nd = k < ng *leads-to* nd > k

Proof of P_7–P_8 P_7 holds because the source sends sbuff[ns] with weak fairness (U_2). P_8 holds because its lhs implies na < ns, which leads to na increasing (because of P_5). P_9 follows from the closure of P_7 and P_8. P_{10} follows from the closure of P_9 and P_6. P_{11} follows from the closure of P_{10} and U_1.   □

5.4 Distributed Sliding Window Program

We now translate the algorithm-level description of the source and sink (in Figs. 5.5 and 5.6) into await-structured programs and then into programs using locks and condition variables. These programs preserve the atomicity of the rules, hence the previous analysis remains valid.

5.4.1 Source and Sink Programs with Awaits

The await-structured source program, called Source, is shown in Figs. 5.7 and 5.8. (Ignore the comments "// 1", $\cdots$, "// 5"for now.) It has six parameters: aL, the local address; aR, the remote address; xL, the sid of the local unreliable channel access system; N, the cyclic sequence number size; SW, the send window size; and RW, the receive window size. Its main code defines variables ng, ns, na, sbuff and (auxiliary) dbh, exactly as in Fig. 5.5. It then starts three local threads executing functions doTxDat, doReTxDat and doRxAck. Function doTxDat sends a new data block. Function doReTxDat resends all outstanding data blocks. Function doRxAck receives an ack message and processes it. The program has one input function, mysid.tx(.), called by the local user to send a data block to the remote user. Note that each of these functions corresponds to a rule in Fig. 5.5, and is executed with the same (effective) atomicity. (The "•"s indicate atomicity breakpoints.)

The await-structured sink program, called Sink, is shown in Fig. 5.9. It has the same six parameters as the source program: aL, aR, xL, N, SW and RW. Its main code defines variables nd, nr and rbuff, exactly as in Fig. 5.6. It then starts a local thread executing function doRxDatTxAck. This function receives a data message, processes it, and then sends an ack response. It has one input function, mysid.rx(), called by the local user to receive a data block. Each of these functions corresponds to a rule in Fig. 5.6, and is executed with the same (effective) atomicity.

```
program Source(aL, aR, xL, N, SW, RW) {
   ia {Val(aL,aR) and aL ≠ aR and Sid(xL)
       and int(N,SW,RW) and (0 < SW,RW < N)}
   DAT ← 1; ACK ← 2;                                        // 1
   int ng ← 0;                                              // 1
   int ns ← 0;                                              // 1
   int na ← 0;                                              // 1
   Map sbuff ← map();                                       // 1
   Seq dbh ← [];   // auxiliary variable                    // 1
   Tid tSrcRx ← startThread(doRxAck());
   Tid tSrcTx ← startThread(doTxDat());
   Tid tSrcReTx ← startThread(doReTxDat());
   return mysid;

   input void mysid.tx(aR, Seq data) {
      ia {true}
      await (true) {
        sbuff[ng] ← data;                                   // 2
        ng ← ng+1;                                          // 2
        return;
      }
   }

   function void doTxDat() { // send new data
     while (true) {
     • await (ns < min(ng, na+SW)) {
         xL.tx(aR, [DAT, mod(ns,N), sbuff[ns]]);            // 3
         ns ← ns+1;                                         // 3
       }
     }
   }

   function void doReTxDat() { // resend data
     while (true) {
     • await (na ≤ ns-1)
         for (j in na..ns-1)                                // 4
           xL.tx(aR, [DAT, mod(j,N), sbuff[j]]);            // 4
     }
   }

// continued
```

Fig. 5.7 Part 1: source program (await-structured)

// Source continued

```
function void doRxAck() { // receive ack msg
  while (true) {
  • Seq msg ← xL.rx();
    ia {msg in Tuple<ACK, 0..N-1>}
    await (true) {
      int j ← na + mod(msg[1]-na, N);                   // 5
      if (na < j ≤ ns) {                                // 5
        for (k in na..j-1) sbuff.remove(k);             // 5
        na ← j;                                         // 5
      }
    }
  }
}
```

```
atomicity assumption {awaits}
progress assumption {weak fairness of threads}
} // Source
```

Fig. 5.8 Part 2: Source program (await-structured)

Because programs Source and Sink have the same effect and atomicity as the source and sink rules, the assertions established in Sect. 5.3 continue to hold for this program SwpDist.

5.4.2 Source and Sink Programs with Locks and Condition Variables

Programs SourceLCv and SinkLCv, shown in Figs. 5.10–5.12, implement the await-structured programs Source and Sink with locks and condition variables. Each boxed text stands for a code chunk from Source or Sink; for example, $\boxed{\text{Source.1}}$ refers to the lines from Source that are tagged with the comment "// 1". Program SinkLCv is obtained from Sink by applying the transformation in Theorem 3.1. Program SourceLCv is obtained from Source similarly, except that some scheduling constraints are imposed first, as explained next.

Program Source has three functions executed by local threads: doRxAck, doTxDat and doReTxDat. We want the first two functions to be executed without delay. But we do not want doReTxDat to be executed without delay, because that would result in needless retransmissions. Instead, data blocks should be retransmitted after rto time units since their previous transmission, where rto equals the expected roundtrip time from source to sink and back. For now, rto is a constant (but see Exercise 5.5).

```
program Sink(aL, aR, N, RW, xL) {

    ia {Val(aL,aR) and aL ≠ aR and Sid(xL)
        and int(N,SW,RW) and (0 < SW,RW < N)}

    DAT ← 1; ACK ← 2;                              // 1
    int nd ← 0;                                    // 1
    int nr ← 0;                                    // 1
    Map rbuff ← map();                             // 1
    Tid tSnkRx ← startThread(doRxDatTxAck());
    return mysid;

    input Seq mysid.rx() {
        ia {true}
    ● await (nd < nr) {
        Seq data ← rbuff[nd];                      // 2
        rbuff.remove(nd);                          // 2
        nd ← nd+1;                                 // 2
        return data;
        }
    }

    // receive data msg and send ack msg
    function void doRxDatTxAck() {
      while (true) {
      ● Seq msg ← xL.rx();
        ia {msg in Tuple<DAT,0..N-1,Seq>}
        await (true) {
          int j ← nr + mod(msg[1]-nr, N);          // 3
          if ((nr ≤ j < nd+RW)                     // 3
              and (not j in rbuff.keys)) {         // 3
            rbuff[j] ← msg[2];                     // 3
            while (nr in rbuff.keys)               // 3
              nr ← nr+1;                           // 3
            xL.tx(aR, [ACK,mod(nr,N)]);
          }
        }
      }
    }

    atomicity assumption {awaits}
    progress assumption {weak fairness of threads}

} // Sink
```

Fig. 5.9 Sink program (await-structured)

```
program SourceLCv(aL, aR, N, SW, xL) {
    ia {| Source.ia |}
    | Source.1 |
    Lock lckSrc;
    Condition(lckSrc) cvDat;
    int rto ← ...;  // retry timeout
    Tid tSrcRx ← startThread(doRxAck());
    Tid tSrcTx ← startThread(doTxDat());
    return mysid;

    input void mysid.tx(aR, Seq data) {
        ia {true}
        lckSrc.acq();
        | Source.2 |
        if (ns < na+SW)
            cvDat.signal();
        lckSrc.rel();
        return;
    }

    function void doTxDat() {
        while (true) {
            lckSrc.acq();
            if (na < min(ng,na+SW)) {
                while (na < min(ng,na+SW)-1) {
                    | Source.3 |
                }
              • cvDat.timedWait(rto);
            } else if (na < ns) {
                | Source.4 |
              • cvDat.timedWait(rto);
            } else
                cvDat.wait();
        }
    }
```

// continued

Fig. 5.10 Part 1: source program (locks, condition variables)

```
// SourceLCv continued

   function doRxAck() {
     while (true) {
     • Seq msg ← xL.rx();
       lckSrc.acq();                                    // 3
       ┌─────────┐
       │ Source.5│                                      // 3
       └─────────┘
           if (ns < ng) cvDat.signal();                 // 3
         lckSrc.rel();                                   // 3
       }
   }

   atomicity assumption {lckSrc, cvDat}
   progress assumption {weak fairness of threads}

} // SourceLCv
```

Fig. 5.11 Part 2: source program (locks, condition variables)

Program SourceLCv achieves this as follows. It has only two local threads. Thread
tSrcRx executes function doRxAck (as in Source). Thread tSrcTx executes a new
function doTxDat, which does the work of the old functions doTxDat and doReTxDat.
We use a lock, lckSrc, for atomicity and a condition variable, cvDat, for tSrcTx to
wait on. When tSrcTx wakes up, it does the following: if there are new data blocks
to send, it sends them all and does a *timed* wait; else if there are outstanding data
blocks, it sends them all and does a *timed* wait; else there is nothing to send and
it does a *regular* wait. The condition variable is signaled in mysid.tx if ns < na+SW
holds and in doRxAck if na increases and ns < na+SW holds.

5.4.3   Increasing Parallelism

There is very little concurrent activity in each of the programs SourceLCv and SinkLCv,
because almost all the code is run under the protection of a single lock. As described
in Sect. 3.6, performance can be improved by identifying conflicts in the code more
precisely and using locks to protect only those parts of the code. To illustrate,
suppose map sbuff is implemented such that *simultaneous accesses to entries with
different keys do not conflict* (e.g., if sbuff was implemented as a circular array).
This would greatly reduce conflicts:

• Functions mysid.tx and doRxAck would have no conflict. In particular, their
  accesses of sbuff have no overlapping keys (because every element in na..ns-1
  is less than ng).

```
program SinkLCv(aL, aR, N, RW, x) {
    ia {| Sink.ia |}
    | Sink.1 |
    Lock lckSnk;
    Condition(lckSnk) cvRxUser;
    Tid tSnkRx ← startThread(doRxDatTxAck());
    return mysid;

    input Seq mysid.rx() {
        ia {true}
        lckSnk.acq();
        if (nd = nr)
        • cvRxUser.wait();
        | Sink.2 |
        lckSnk.rel();
        return data;
    }

    function doRxDatTxAck() {
        while (true) {
        • Seq msg ← xL.rx();
            lckSnk.acq();                                   // 3
            | Sink.3 |                                      // 3
            if (nd < nr)                                    // 3
                cvRxUser.signal();                          // 3
            xL.tx(aR, [ACK, mod(nr,N)]);                    // 3
            lckSnk.rel();
        }
    }

    atomicity assumption {lckSnk, cvRxUser}
    progress assumption {weak fairness of threads}

} // SinkLCv
```

Fig. 5.12 Sink program (locks, condition variables)

• Functions mysid.tx and doTxDat would conflict only over ng. In particular, their accesses of sbuff have no overlapping keys (because ns never exceeds ng and mysid.tx updates sbuff[ng] before incrementing ng). Furthermore, if the underlying hardware provides atomic reads and writes of integer ng, then even a lock would not be needed here.

- Functions doRxAck and doTxDat would still conflict over variables na, ns, and sbuff[na..ns-1]. Without protection, doTxDat may retransmit sbuff[na..ns-1] while doRxAck is removing them because it received ack message ns. Still we would like to reduce doRxAck's wait for the lock so as to reduce the chance of the unreliable channel dropping an incoming ack message. One approach is to have doRxAck just update a copy of na, say naZ, and have doTxDat check naZ (i.e., drop sbuff[na..naZ-1] and update na to naZ) before sending data blocks. A lock can be avoided if the underlying hardware provides atomic reads and writes of integer naZ.

5.5 Data Transfer Protocol

Our original goal was to obtain a distributed program DtpDist, that implements a fifo channel between addresses a1 and a2 given an unreliable channel between a1 and a2. The sliding window program, SwpDist, achieves fifo data transfer from a1 to a2. So all that remains is to merge two sliding window systems, one in each direction. Program Dtp, executed by each component, consists of the source and sink programs, combined in some way.

Below, we will form program Dtp by merging the variables, threads, and functions of the source and sink, and accounting for the fact that the source and the sink share the same unreliable channel access system. (Another way is to let Dtp be the composite system of a source, a sink, and a "router" system; see Exercise 5.8.)

The parameters, input assumptions, and constants DAT and ACK in the source and sink programs do not conflict (they are the same). The variables, threads, and functions in the two programs do not conflict (they have different names). Thus merging is easy. Dtp's parameters are the source (or sink) parameters. Dtp's input assumption is the source (or sink) input assumption. Dtp.main becomes SourceLCv.main and SinkLCv.main in any order (with some adjustments noted below). The functions of Dtp are the functions of SourceLCv and SinkLCv. Note that Dtp gets two locks, lckSrc and lckSnk, allowing a SourceLCv thread and a SinkLCv thread to execute simultaneously. This is fine because the two parts have no shared resource except for the channel.

Now to account for the sharing of the unreliable channel access system, denoted by parameter xL of the source and sink programs. The channel requires that its users have at most one xL.tx call and at most one xL.rx call pending at any time. SourceLCv alone satisfies this because it has only thread, tSrcRx, that calls xL.rx. Similarly, SinkLCv alone satisfies this. But the merge of SourceLCv and SinkLCv would not satisfy this without some further synchronization.

The constraint on xL.tx can be met by letting lckSrc and lckSnk be the same lock. But this would be overkill, eliminating all parallelism between the source and sink. A better solution would be to introduce a lock, say lckTx, used only to protect x.tx calls. So Dtp.doTxDat, for example, would acquire lckSrc at the start, and acquire lckTx just before calling xL.tx and release it immediately after. And Dtp.doRxDat would do the same just before calling xL.tx.

```
program Dtp(aL, aR, xL, N, SW, RW) {
    ia { SourceLCv.ia }
    // source: DAT,ACK,ng,ns,na,sbuff,dbh,rto,lckSrc,cvDat,tSrcTx
    ┌─────────────────────────────────────────┐
    │ SourceLCv.main                          │
    │     without tSrcRx or return            │
    └─────────────────────────────────────────┘
    // sink: DAT,ACK,nd,nr,rbuff,lckSnk,cvRxUser
    ┌─────────────────────────────────────────┐
    │ SinkLCv.main                            │
    │     without tSnkRx or return            │
    └─────────────────────────────────────────┘
    Lock lckTx;                        // source, sink: protects xL.tx calls
    Tid tRx ← startThread(doRxDatAck());     // source, sink
    return mysid;
    // end main

    input void mysid.tx(aR, Seq data) {      // source
        ┌─────────────────────────────────────┐
        │ SourceLCv.mysid.tx.body            │
        └─────────────────────────────────────┘
    }

    function void doTxDat() {                // source
        ┌─────────────────────────────────────┐
        │ SourceLCv.doTxDat.body             │
        │     with xL.tx(.) replaced by      │
        │     lckTx.acq(); xL.tx(.); lckTx.rel() │
        └─────────────────────────────────────┘
    }

    input Seq mysid.rx() {                   // sink
        ┌─────────────────────────────────────┐
        │ SinkLCv.mysid.rx.body              │
        └─────────────────────────────────────┘
    }

// continued
```

Fig. 5.13 Part 1: program Dtp: component program of data transfer protocol

The constraint on xL.rx can be solved by having one thread receive messages from the channel (acks and data) and process them appropriately. This thread would do the work of tSrcRx and tSnkRx.

Program Dtp is shown in Figs. 5.13 and 5.14. Program DtpDist is shown in Fig. 5.15. The atomicity breakpoints of Dtp consist of the one explicitly shown in the figure and the ones in the code chunks inserted from SourceLCv and SinkLCv. Each (effectively) atomic step in program Dtp is identical to an atomic step of one of the two instances of SwpDist. Hence the assertions satisfied by program SwpDist continues to hold for each instance of SwpDist in program DtpDist.

// Dtp continued

```
function void doRxDatAck() {                     // source, sink
  while (true)
    Seq msg ← xL.rx();
    ia {msg in union(Tuple<DAT, 0..N-1, Seq>, Tuple<ACK, 0..N-1>)}
    if (msg[0] = ACK)
```

> SourceLCv.3
>   with xL.tx(.) replaced by
>   lckTx.acq(); xL.tx(.); lckTx.rel()

```
    else if (msg[0] = DAT)
```

> SinkLCv.3
>   with xL.tx(.) replaced by
>   lckTx.acq(); xL.tx(.); lckTx.rel()

```
  }
}
```

```
atomicity assumption {lckSrc, cvDat, lckTx, cvRxUser}

progress assumption {weak fairness of threads}
```

} // Dtp

Fig. 5.14 Part 2: program Dtp: component program of data transfer protocol

```
program DtpDist(a1, a2, N, SW, RW) {
  ia {Val(a1,a2) and (a1 ≠ a2) and
      int(N,SW,RW) and (0 < SW,RW < N) and Φ}
  Map x ← startSystem(Lossy/LrdChannel(set(a1,a2)));
  y1 ← startSystem(Dtp(a1,a2,x[a1],N,SW,RW));
  y2 ← startSystem(Dtp(a2,a1,x[a2],N,SW,RW));
  return map([a1,y1], [a2,y2]);
}
```

Fig. 5.15 Data transfer protocol program

5.6 Proving That DtpDist Implements FifoChannel

We now establish that DtpDist(a1,a2,N,SW,RW) implements FifoChannel(set(a1,a2)). Figure 5.16 shows the closed program X of DtpDist and the fifo channel inverse. The latter is available in Fig. 4.3. We have to show that program X satisfies assertions Y_0–Y_2 and Y_0'–Y_2', where Y_i' is Y_i with a1 and a2 interchanged.

```
program X(a1, a2, N, SW, RW) {
    ia [DtpDist.ia]
    inputs(); outputs();                        // closed system
    y ← startSystem(DtpDist(a1,a2,N,SW,RW));
    fci ← startSystem(FifoChannelInverse(set(a1,a2), y));
}
```

Fig. 5.16 Closed program of data transfer protocol and fifo channel inverse

Y_0 : *Inv* (thread at fci.doRx(a2).ic)
        $\Rightarrow$ (data = fci.txh[[a1,a2]][fci.rxh[[a1,a2]].size])
Y_1 : ongoing(y[a1].tx) *leads-to* not ongoing(y[a1].tx)
Y_2 : fci.txh[[a1,a2]].size $\geq$ i
        leads-to (fci.rxh[[a1,a2]].size $\geq$ i or not ongoing(y[a2].rx))

Y_0–Y_2 concern the fifo transfer from a1 to a2. Y_0'–Y_2' concern the fifo transfer from a2 to a1. Y_0 is the safety condition for the data block returned by y[a2].rx. Y_1 and Y_2 are the assertions in fci's progress condition. It suffices to prove Y_0–Y_2; then Y_0'–Y_2' would follow from symmetry.

Given the atomicity breakpoints, Y_0's lhs can be changed to y[a2].nd < y[a2].nr and data set to y[a2].rbuff[y[a2].nd]. Also note that the following hold always: (1) fci.txh[[a1,a2]] equals y[a1].dbh; (2) fci.txh[[a1,a2]].size equals y[a1].ng; and (3) fci.rxh[[a1,a2]].size equals y[a2].nd. Thus Y_0–Y_2 can be rewritten as follows.

Y_0 : *Inv* y[a2].nd < y[a2].nr
        $\Rightarrow$ y[a2].rbuff[y[a2].nd] = y[a1].dbh[y[a2].nd]
Y_1 : ongoing(y[a1].tx) *leads-to* not ongoing(y[a1].tx)
Y_2 : y[a1].ng $\geq$ i *leads-to* (y[a2].nd $\geq$ i or not ongoing(y[a2].rx))

We have already established that DtpDist satisfies X_1–X_2 for the a1 to a2 direction. Y_0 is identical to X_1. Thus DtpDist satisfies Y_0. Hence it satisfies Y_0' by symmetry.

Y_1 holds because y[a1].tx is non-blocking, loop-free, and executed with weak fairness. Y_1' holds by symmetry.

Y_2 is implied by X_2's rhs. Program X satisfies the assumptions U_1–U_4. Hence X satisfies Y_2. Y_2' holds by symmetry.

We are done.

5.7   Graceful-Closing Data Transfer Protocol

The data transfer protocol, as currently defined, does not have any way for the users to terminate the protocol operation. We now add graceful closing connection termination (as in TCP). We add an input function close() to program Dtp. The user calls close to become closing; after this it can not call tx but it can call rx (and should until condition 3 below holds). Function close returns only when (1) all the data sent by the local user has been acked, (2) the remote user has also called close, and (3) all the data sent by the remote user has been delivered to the local user.

We refer to this modified dtp program as the **graceful-closing dtp** program. It can be implemented as follows.

- Introduce two new messages: [IN], to indicate closing; and [FINACK], to ack a [FIN].
- Introduce three boolean flags: finRcvd, true iff [FIN] received; finAckRcvd, true iff [FINACK] received; and closed, true iff function close has returned. All are initially false.
- Defne function close as follows.

      wait for all outgoing data to be acked (i.e., na = ng);
      repeatedly send [FIN] until finAckRcvd is true;
      wait for finRcvd to be true;
      wait for all received data to be removed by the user (i.e., nd = nr);
      set closed to true;
      return;

- Modify function doRxDatAck to handle FIN and FINACK messages. Also, once closed is true, it only has to respond to FIN messages (because the remote dtp, if it is not closed, is closing and needs only to receive a FINACK). Thus change doRxDatAck's message handler (the part after "msg ← xL.rx") to the following.

      if not closed
        if msg is a DAT or ACK message then process as before;
        if msg is [FIN] then set finRcvd to true and send [FINACK];
        if msg is [FINACK] then set finAckRcvd to true;
      else if closed and msg is [FIN]
        then send [FINACK]

- Modify rx so that it returns a distinct value if a FIN has been received (hence the remote dtp is closing) and the local user has received all incoming data. The changes are as follows.

    - return [0,data] if there is a data block to receive, i.e., nr > nd.
    - return [-1] if finRcvd is true and all data blocks have been received, i.e., nr = nd.

Consider a distributed system of two graceful-closing dtp systems communicating over an unreliable channel (i.e., program DtpDist with program Dtp replaced by the graceful-closing dtp program). It satisfies the following (informally stated) assertions, where j and k identify the dtp systems, j.drxh is the sequence of data blocks received at j, k.dtxh is the sequence of data blocks sent at k, and so on. The first three are safety assertions and the rest are progress assertions.

- If j.rx returns [0,data] then j.drxh ∘ [data] is a prefix of k.dtxh.
- If j.rx returns [-1] then j.drxh equals k.dtxh and k is closing or closed.
- If j is closed then neither j.tx and j.rx are ongoing, j.drxh equals k.dtxh, and k is closing or closed.

- If j.tx is ongoing then eventually j.tx returns.
- If j.rx is ongoing and j.drxh $\neq$ k.dtxh then eventually j.rx returns.
- If j.rx is ongoing and j.drxh $=$ k.dtxh and k is closing or closed
  then eventually j.rx returns.
- If j is closing and k is closing or closed
  then eventually j becomes closed or j.rx is not ongoing.

5.8   Abortable Data Transfer Protocol

Note that the graceful-closing protocol terminates the connection but it does not terminate the dtp systems or the unreliable channel. Even after a dtp system has returned the close call, it must still be around to receive FIN messages and respond with FINACK messages. Otherwise the remote dtp system may never receive a FINACK and so never terminate itself. (However the dtp system can terminate all its threads and variables except for a single thread to handle FIN receptions.)

Is there a way to terminate both dtp systems after terminating the connection? Suppose we allow a closing dtp system, say y[a1], to terminate itself if it receives a FIN and does not receive a FINACK after a specified number of FIN retransmissions. Then the remote dtp system, y[a2], may never receive y[a1]'s FIN and hence would never terminate. If we allow y[a2] to terminate without receiving a FIN or a FINACK, then y[a1] may never receive a FIN so we should also allow y[a1] to terminate without receiving a FIN or a FINACK. But then the last data block exchanged between the users may never be acked; for example, if the user at y[a1] sends the last data block in the interaction between the users, then y[a1] may never receive the ack for that data block because y[a2] closes after receiving the data block and the ack is lost.

The only way to ensure that both y[a1] and y[a2] terminate is to allow a dtp system to terminate if it does not receive a FINACK within some K resends of FIN. It is customary to also do this if an ack to a data message is not received within K resends. Refer to the dtp program with this modification as the **abortable** dtp program. The service provided by this protocol is *not* the same as that of a fifo channel. For example, the safety property of fifo delivery of data blocks still holds but the progress property changes to: data sent is delivered *unless the underlying unreliable channel fails to deliver a message after K retransmissions*. Defining an appropriate service program is left as an exercise.

5.9   Concluding Remarks

This chapter developed a data transfer protocol that implements a two-address fifo channel making use of an unreliable (lossy or LRD) channel. We developed a sliding-window protocol that achieves one-way fifo data transfer, and then combined two of them, one in each direction, to form the data transfer protocol. The component systems were defined first at an algorithm level, then by await-structured programs, then by programs using locks and condition variables. We also showed how to increase parallelism in these programs.

The analysis of the sliding window protocol (in Sect. 5.3) comes from [10, 11]. A key step in the analysis is obtaining the "correct interpretation" conditions, i.e., conditions on the *unbounded* sequence numbers in transit so that the receiver can correctly deduce their values when only their *cyclic* version is available. Correct interpretation conditions have been obtained by Knuth [5] for the sliding window protocol over LRD channels with limited reordering, and by Oláh [7, 8] for other kinds of sliding window protocols (TCP PAWS, SNR) over LRD channels with maximum message lifetime. A mechanical verification of a sliding window protocol appears in [3].

The sliding window protocol here can be extended in various ways. The protocol given above uses cumulative acknowledgments. One can incorporate "selective" acknowledgments to indicate out-of-sequence data received [6–8, 10]. Selective acks allow the source to retransmit sooner only what is needed. They are optionally available in most protocols, including TCP, although they are usually not used.

The data blocks in the protocol can be of fixed or variable size; in the latter case, the data structure would contain a size entry. An alternative is to allow a message to have a variable number of fixed-size data blocks; if the data blocks are consecutive, the message needs only identify the sequence number of the first data block and the number of data blocks. TCP does this with an octet as the data block size.

In the sliding window protocol as currently specified, the time between successive retransmissions, i.e., parameter rto in program SourceLCv, is a constant. An rto that is too small causes needless retransmissions and can lead to congestion in the channel. An rto that is too large causes needless delay before retransmitting a message. For good performance, rto should be continuously updated to match the current roundtrip time. TCP does this [1, 4, 9]. (See Exercise 5.5.)

Flow control can be introduced between the source and the sink, so that the source does not send data faster than the sink can handle. This is easily done by dynamically varying the send window size: the sink regularly informs the source of its current receive-window size (using another entry in acknowledgment messages), and the source sets its send-window size accordingly [6, 10]. (See Exercise 5.7.) TCP does this.

Exercises

5.1. Modify program Source so that sbuff's size never exceeds a constant S. (Hint: When a call of mysid.tx makes sbuff's size reach S, block the return until sbuff's size becomes less than S. The latter would happen because of the progress property.)

5.2. In the analysis of the sliding window protocol with lossy channel (in Sect. 5.3), we gave an operational argument that A_5 is an invariant of program SwpDist. Provide an assertional proof of this. Specifically, obtain predicate(s) such that their conjunction B satisfies the following:

1. B holds immediately after the initialization of SwpDist.
2. for every non-initial atomic step e of SwpDist: e unconditionally establishes B and A_5 from B and A_2–A_6.

(Hint: Identify the atomic steps of X that affect A_5, and, for each step, determine any additional condition that needs to hold (immediately) before the step in order for A_5 to hold (immediately) after the step. These additional conditions will make up your B.

Pursuing this further, here are the atomic steps of SwpDist that affect A_5:

E1. Transmission of a data message.
E2. Reception of a data message.

Consider E1. Suppose data message (with unbounded sequence number) j1 is sent. In order for this to not falsify A_5, we want j1 $\geq$ k+1-N+RW to hold. We know that j1 is at least na. So we want the following to be invariant:

B_1 : (k in rbuff.keys) $\Rightarrow$ na $\geq$ k+1-N+RW

Now do the same thing with B_1: find out which atomic steps affect it and what is needed to preserve it.

Consider E2. Suppose the received data message is not added to rbuff. Then nothing else changes in SwpDist and A_5 is preserved (any data message that is receivable after the step was receivable before the step and hence satisfies A_5's rhs).

Suppose data message k1 is received and gets added to rbuff. If k1 is less than some k that was in rbuff before the step, then A_5 before the step implies A_5 after the step. So let k1 be the highest key in rbuff after the step. What must hold just before in order for A_5 to hold just after?

Keep doing this until you have a list of predicates, say B_1, B_2, $\cdots$, whose conjunction is the desired B.
End of hint)

5.3. Repeat Exercise 5.2 with A_5 replaced by A_6.

5.4. In the sliding window protocol as currently described, retransmissions are initiated by the source; that is, the source resends outstanding data messages and the sink sends ack messages only in response. Modify programs Source and Sink so that retransmissions are initiated by the sink; that is, the sink resends ack messages if it does not receive the data blocks it expects, and the source sends data messages only in response.

5.5. Modify program SourceLCv (in Figs. 5.10 and 5.11) so that rto adapts to a dynamically-measured roundtrip time of the channel. Introduce an input function tick(), which you can assume is called by the environment (e.g., operating system) once every time unit (e.g., 10 ms). For each outstanding data block (or some subset of them), introduce a "timer" variable to indicate the elapsed time since the data block was last sent. The value of this timer when the outstanding data block is acked gives a roundtrip time measurement. Use the roundtrip time measurements to obtain an estimate for the current roundtrip time.

5.6. Consider the sliding window protocol over an LRD channel. Do not assume any time constraints, i.e., no maximum message lifetime and no minimum delay between sending new data blocks. Instead assume that (1) a message in transit can overtake at most M messages, and (2) the sink sends an ack message for every data message it receives. Show that fifo data transfer is achieved if $N \geq SW + RW + M$. (Hint: See reference [5].)

5.7. Add flow control to the sliding window protocol by having the send window size at the source track the receive window size at the sink, rather than having it be constant at SW. This can done as follows.

- Augment ack messages with an additional entry indicating the receive window size; i.e., an ack message now has three entries, the first set to ACK (as before), the second set to mod(nr,N) (as before) and the third set to nd+RW-nr. Note that this entry ranges over 0..RW-1.
- At the source, introduce a variable sw that records the most recently received receive window size. Let the send window be na..na+sw, i.e., ns never exceeds na+sw.
- Have the source periodically send a data message even if sw=0 holds, so that it can learn when the receive window size at the sink becomes positive.

Obtain service programs for the source and the sink. Your protocol should ensure the following: (1) the source does not send data blocks which the sink cannot buffer; (2) data blocks are transferred as long as the receive window is not empty and the source has outstanding data blocks. Express these properties assertionally and establish that your protocol satisfies them. (Hint: See reference [10].)

5.8. The Dtp program in the text was obtained by merging the variables and functions of SourceLCv and SinkLCv. Another way to solve the problem is to let Dtp be a composite system of a source, a sink, and a router. The router gets inputs from the user, forwards them to the source or sink, and returns the response back to the user. It also receives messages from the channel and forwards them to the source or sink. A possible solution is outlined below.

```
program DtpX(aL, aR, xL, y, N, SW, RW) {
    ia {...}
    Sid ySrc ← Sid();
    Sid ySnk ← Sid();
    startSystem(y, Router(...));
    startSystem(ySrc, Source(...));
    startSystem(ySnk, Sink(...));
    return mysid;
}
```

Here, y, ySnk and ySrc are the sids of the Router, Source and Sink systems, respectively. The source and sink sids are dynamically chosen but they are chosen before Router is instantiated (so they can be passed as parameters to Router). Modify the source and sink programs so that separate channel access system sids can be used for sending and receiving, as follows: (1) replace the channel access system sid parameter x by two sid parameters, xTx and xRx; (2) change "x.tx(.)" to "xTx.tx(.)" and "x.rx()" to "xRx.tx()". Flesh out the Router program, either as a service program or an implementation program.

Can you solve the problem if the source and sink sids are not chosen before Router is instantiated?

5.9. Write a service program for the service provided by the graceful-closing data-transfer protocol (Sect. 5.7).

5.10. Write the dtp program for the graceful-closing data transfer protocol (Sect. 5.7).

5.11. Write a service program for the service provided by the abortable data-transfer protocol (Sect. 5.8). (Hint: Your service may have to be more conservative than what is implemented by the abortable protocol because the unreliable channel used by the protocol is not visible at the service.)

5.12. Write the dtp program for the abortable data transfer protocol (Sect. 5.8).

References

1. M. Allman, V. Paxson, E. Blanton, TCP congestion control. Technical report, RFC 5681, Internet Engineering Task Force, 2009. http://tools.ietf.org/html/rfc5681
2. D. Belsnes, Single-message communication. IEEE Trans. Commun. **24**(2), 190–194 (1976). doi:10.1109/TCOM.1976.1093283
3. D. Chkliaev, J. Hooman, E.P. de Vink, Verification and improvement of the sliding window protocol, in *TACAS 2003*, ed. by H. Garavel, J. Hatcliff. Lecture Notes in Computer Science (Springer, Berlin/New York, 2003), pp. 113–127
4. D. Comer, *Principles, Protocols, and Architectures*. Internetworking with TCP/IP, vol. 1, 4th edn. (Prentice-Hall, Englewood Cliffs, 2000)
5. D.E. Knuth, Verification of link-level protocols. BIT **21**(1), 31–36 (1981)
6. M. Mathis, J. Mahdavi, S. Floyd, A. Romanow, TCP selective acknowledgement options. Technical report, RFC 2018, Internet Engineering Task Force, 1996. http://tools.ietf.org/html/rfc2018
7. A.L. Oláh, Design and analysis of transport protocols for reliable high-speed communications. Ph.D. thesis, University of Twente, Enschede, the Netherlands, 1997. http://doc.utwente.nl/13676/
8. A.L. Oláh, S.M. Heemstra de Groot, Alternative specification and verification of a periodic state exchange protocol. IEEE/ACM Trans. Netw. **5**(4), 525–529 (1997). doi:10.1109/90.649467. http://dx.doi.org/10.1109/90.649467
9. L.L. Peterson, B.S. Davie, *Computer Networks: A Systems Approach*, 3rd edn. (Morgan Kaufmann Publishers Inc., San Francisco, 2003)

10. A.U. Shankar, Verified data transfer protocols with variable flow control. ACM Trans. Comput. Syst. **7**(3), 281–316 (1989). doi:10.1145/65000.65003. http://doi.acm.org/10.1145/65000.65003

11. A.U. Shankar, S.S. Lam, A stepwise refinement heuristic for protocol construction. ACM Trans. Program. Lang. Syst. **14**(3), 417–461 (1992). doi:10.1145/129393.129394. http://doi.acm.org/10.1145/129393.129394. Earlier version appeared in Stepwise Refinement of Distributed Systems, LNCS 430, Springer-Verlag, 1990

Chapter 6
Programs, Semantics and Effective Atomicity

6.1 Introduction

The previous chapters introduced SESF by way of examples. We now present the theory underlying SESF, starting with a semantics of programs and assertions in this chapter, compositionality in the next chapter, and the extension to real-time programs in the chapter after that.

Sections 6.2 and 6.3 summarize programs and service programs. Section 6.4 defines a semantics, i.e., a mathematical model, of program execution. A program is modeled by a state transition system, where each state is a value assignment of the program's variables, each transition is an execution of an atomic step of the program, and each path in the state transition system is an evolution of the program.

The remaining sections use the semantics to formalize various notions. Sections 6.5 and 6.6 define the evaluation of predicates and assertions. Section 6.7 defines the notions of "splitting" and "stitching" evolutions, which are needed in the next chapter for reasoning about compositionality.

Section 6.8 defines auxiliary variables. Section 6.9 defines effective atomicity, including the fundamental notion of commuting atomic steps. Section 6.10 gives a condensed treatment of proof rules. The last three sections are important for analysis of programs but orthogonal to the issue of compositionality.

In these three chapters dealing with theory, we will encounter sets, sequences, and other constructs as part of the semantics of programs rather than as part of programs. In these situations, we will be using a more mathematical notation and font, for example, $\langle i,j,k \rangle$ instead of [i,j,k], and $\{e(x) : x \text{ in } P\}$ instead of set(e(x): x in P). Also, we will use "wrt" as an abbreviation for "with respect to" in more situations than "safe wrt" and "complete wrt".

A.U. Shankar, *Distributed Programming: Theory and Practice*,
DOI 10.1007/978-1-4614-4881-5_6,
© Springer Science+Business Media New York 2013

6.2   Programs

A **program** has the following structure:

```
program <program name>(<program parameters>) { // header
    ia [<program input assumption predicate>]  // for analysis only
    <main>                                     // returns mysid
    <functions>
    <input functions>
    atomicity assumption [...]                 // for analysis only
    progress assumption [...]                  // for analysis only
}
```

An input function of a program has the form

```
input <return type> mysid.<function name>(<function parameters>) {
    ia [<input assumption predicate>]          // for analysis only
    <body>                                     // ends with return
}
```

The main code and functions are written in a generic programming syntax. The instructions can do the usual: access variables, call functions, start threads and systems, use synchronization constructs, and so on. **Input functions** are callable from, and only from, the environment. (There is no loss of generality, since one can define a regular function with the body of an input function.) The program and functions can have parameters. All parameters are read-only, i.e., not modified in the program. Assumptions about inputs from the environment are stated explicitly by **input assumptions**. The **atomicity assumption** indicates the operations that are assumed to be executed atomically by the underlying platform. The **progress assumption** indicates the progress expected of the underlying platform in scheduling the threads of the program. For implementation programs, it consists of fairness assertions only. The assumptions are for analysis only and not implemented. (The program may implement input assumptions, partly or entirely, for error reporting or efficient implementation.)

The program header indicates the program's name and any parameters. The program is instantiated when a thread in the environment executes a startSystem(.) call with the argument being the program name with any program parameters instantiated. At this point, a **basic system** is created and the instantiating thread enters the system and executes its main code, returning when it encounters a return instruction. (If the created system and the instantiating thread are in different address spaces, a "proxy" thread is created in the system to execute the main code on behalf of the instantiating thread. But the two threads can be treated as the same for purposes of analysis because the instantiating thread waits for the proxy thread to complete.)

Every basic system gets a unique **system id**, or **sid** for short, either assigned arbitrarily at creation time or chosen earlier and passed in the startSystem(.) call as an additional argument. The main code ends by returning the startSystem(.)

call, passing back a value that includes the system's sid and/or the sids of systems instantiated by the main code. (This ensures that the return value can be used to identify the created system in analysis.)

A call of an input function of a system has the form x.f(p), where x is the sid of the called system, f is the name of the function, and p is the instantiated parameters (if any) of the function. When an input function of the system is called by a thread in the environment, the thread enters the system and executes the function body, returning when it encounters a return instruction. (As in the case of instantiation, this may involve a "proxy" thread in the called system, but the two threads can be treated as the same for purposes of analysis.)

A thread in a basic system can create another thread in the system and start it executing a (non-input) function of the system, by executing a startThread(.) call with the argument being the function name with any function parameters instantiated. The thread gets a unique **thread id**, or **tid** for short, either chosen arbitrarily at creation time or chosen earlier and passed in the startThread(.) call as an additional argument. The startThread(.) call returns with the created thread's tid, while the created thread continues execution of its function. The latter terminates when it completes execution of its function.

The above are the only two ways to have threads in the system. Threads that have entered the system by calling its main code or input functions are referred to as **guest threads**. All other threads are **local threads**.

A system is terminated when endSystem() has been executed in it and the system is in an **endable** state, which means that (1) there are no guest threads in the system and (2) no local thread of the system is in a call to another system's function. At termination, all the system's (local) threads are terminated and the system's state is cleaned up.

There are two special variables, mysid and mytid, available in any program. In any instantiation of the program, mysid equals the sid of the system. At any point in the code of the system, mytid equals the tid of the thread executing the code. These variables cannot be modified by the program.

A basic system is said to become **faulty** if it executes an undefined operation, for example, division by zero, out-of-bound array reference, dereferencing a null pointer, calling a non-existing function, etc. We do not care what a system does after it becomes faulty; it may crash, execute abnormally, whatever. We say a system can **accept** an input at a point in an evolution if the system can receive the input at that point without becoming faulty. Equivalently, we say that the input is **acceptable** at that point.

Given a basic system x, the **aggregate system** x is the basic system x together with all the basic systems it has created, directly or indirectly. Thus when a basic system x creates a basic system y, the created system y is *outside* the basic system x and *inside* the aggregate system x. Given a program X, the **aggregate system** X refers to the aggregate system started when X is instantiated without renaming or constraining its parameters. When we talk about the evolutions and properties of a program X, we are referring to the evolutions and properties of its aggregate system.

A **composite system** is an *arbitrary* collection of one or more basic systems. Hence basic and aggregate systems are special cases of composite systems. A composite system M starts with the creation of a single basic system. During M's lifetime, it can acquire and lose basic systems. A basic system P can be added to M when P is created. P's creator may or may not be in M (whereas in an aggregate system, P's creator is in M). A basic system P leaves M when P is terminated.

The notion of a composite system is useful because definitions and properties of composite systems also apply to basic and aggregate systems. When we say "system" without qualifying it as basic or aggregate or composite (either explicitly or from context), then it usually doesn't matter.

6.2.1   Inputs and Outputs

The *environment* of a composite system consists of the systems that are not in the composite system. The **outputs** of a composite system are (1) the calls it does to input functions of systems in the environment, and (2) the returns it does to calls of its input functions by systems in the environment. We refer to the former as **output calls** and the latter as **output returns**. The **inputs** to a composite system are (1) the calls of its input functions by systems in the environment, and (2) the returns to its output calls by systems in the environment. We refer to the former as **input calls** and the latter as **input returns**. Note that interactions between basic systems of the composite system do not count towards its inputs or outputs.

Function startSystem is treated as an implicit input function of every basic system. Hence a startSystem call is an input of the created system and an output of the calling system; its parameters are the parameters of the instantiated program. A startSystem return is an output of the created system and an input of the calling system; its parameters are the returned value, which includes the created system's sid and/or the sids of systems instantiated by the main code.

6.2.2   Input Assumptions

An input assumption is associated with every input point of a program: start of the main code, start of every input function, and after every input return. An input assumption is expressed by the construct ia{.}, where the argument is a predicate in the input parameters and any program parameters and program variables defined at that point. If the ia{.} construct is missing at an input point, then it is implicit with an argument of true. In either case, type constraints on any input parameters are treated as part of the ia construct's argument, even though the type constraints may be stated elsewhere. (Typically, type constraints on input function parameters are stated in the input function headers. Type constraints on return value can be stated in the definition of the variable that collects the return value.)

We say a system **allows** an input, or equivalently that the input is **allowed**, at a point in an evolution if the corresponding input assumption holds at that point. Note that an input being "allowed" is not the same as the input being "acceptable".

The purpose of input assumptions is to establish properties of the program that would not hold otherwise, that is, properties that hold for the program assuming that it receives only allowed inputs. When the program is instantiated in another program, these properties would hold for the instantiation provided every input it gets (from its environment) is allowed. When writing a program, we typically formulate its input assumptions so that the program is fault-free and that certain code chunks are effectively atomic.

6.3 Service Programs

A service program is a program with special structure. Its purpose is twofold: it is the standard against which any implementation of the service is validated; and it serves as a canonical implementation when designing a larger system that make use of the service. A **service program** has the following structure:

```
service <program name>(<program parameters>) {
    ic {<program input condition predicate>}
    <main>
    <functions>
    <input functions>
    <output functions>
    atomicity assumption {...}
    <helper assertions>
    progress assumption {...}
}
```

A service program does not start systems or terminate systems, so startSystem or endSystem does not appear in the program. It starts a thread only at the beginning of an output function and terminates it at the end of the output function. Its only synchronization constructs are **input conditions**, expressed by the construct ic{.}, and **output conditions**, expressed by the construct oc{.}. The main code can generate sids (by calling sid) to use as the sid prefixes of input functions. The main code ends by passing back a value that includes the sid of this system and/or sids generated by the main code.

6.3.1 Input Functions

An input function of a service program consists of an "input part" followed by an "output part" as follows.

```
input <return type> <sid>.<function name>(<function parameters>) { // input part
    ic [<input condition predicate>]                              //    "    "
    <body>                                                        //    "    "
    output (<external parameters, internal parameters>) {         // output part
        oc [<output condition predicate>]                         //    "    "
        <body>                                                    //    "    "
        return <external parameters>;                             //    "    "
    } // end output part
} // end input function
```

The **input part** consists of three parts: (1) header, consisting of return type, sid, function name, and zero or more function parameters; (2) input condition ic[.]; and (3) **body**, consisting of code. The system id prefix, <sid>, in the header can be mysid but it may also be some other sid, specifically, the sid of an access system if the service has multiple access systems (as in the channel programs in Chap. 4). The input part is executed atomically when the input function is called if the input condition holds. If the input condition does not hold when the function is called, the program becomes faulty.

The **output part** consists of three parts: (1) header, consisting of the construct output(.) with zero or more **external parameters** and zero or more **internal parameters**; (2) output condition oc[.]; and (3) body, consisting of code ending in a return. The body is executed only if the output condition holds. At execution, the external and internal parameters can have any values that satisfy the output condition; thus the output condition effectively "assigns" values to these parameters. (There is no other constraint on their values because the output part's body, as with any code, does not update parameters.)

The external parameters form the return value; there are external parameters iff the function returns a non-void value. Note that the returned value depends on the output condition alone and not on the body (which, however, would influence future behavior). The internal parameters allow internal non-determinism. In principle, one can do without this feature. In practice, it can improve the readability of the service program (as illustrated in function rx of the fifo channel program in Sect. 4.2). If there are no parameters, the output(.) construct is usually omitted.

6.3.2   Output Functions

An **output function** is like an input function in reverse. It consists of an output part followed by an input part.

```
output <function name>(<external parameters>,    // output part
                      <internal parameters>) {  // output part
   oc {<output condition predicate>}             //   "    "
   <body>                                        //   "    "
   rval ← <sid>.<fname>(<fname parameters>);     // output part ends with call
                                                 // input part starts with rval
   ic {<input condition predicate>}              // input part
   <body>                                        //   "    "
   return;                                       //   "    " (optional)
} // end output function
```

The output part of an output function is conceptually the same as that of an input function, although it differs slightly in syntax. It consists of three parts: (1) header, consisting of function name, zero or more external parameters, and zero or more internal parameters; (2) output condition; and (3) body, consisting of code ending with an output call. The output part is executed atomically by a local thread only if the output condition holds. The local thread is created at the beginning of the output part (the startThread is implicit). At execution, the external and internal parameters are set to any values that satisfy the output condition. The parameters of the output call, i.e., <sid> and <fname parameters>, are the same as the external parameters.

This output part differs from the output part of an input function in two ways. First, it has a function name, <function name>, which is not present in the latter. The difference is cosmetic because the function name is used only for analysis. Second, this output part ends with a call whereas the other ended with a return. Again, there is no conceptual difference; both are outputs and only the external parameters are used in them.

The input part of an output function consists of three parts: (1) header that starts at the returned value rval; (2) input condition; and (3) body, consisting of code. The body is executed by the local thread when it returns from the call issued at the end of the output part. The local thread is terminated at the end of the input part. The return at the end of the input part can be omitted since an output function never returns a value and the thread is terminated.

All the output calls that the program makes to a particular function are grouped together in one output function; i.e., two output functions of the program will not have output calls with the same value of <sid>.<fname>. This makes the program easier to understand and simplifies inversion.

6.3.3 Atomicity and Progress Assumptions

The **atomicity assumption** of a service program is that the main code is atomic and each of the input and output parts is atomic. Thus the assumed atomicity is "maximal", in the sense that each atomic step involves an input or an output. Any function of the program can access any of the variables of the program (even if the service being defined has multiple access systems). Computational cost is not a concern. It is precisely this freedom from "physical-world" constraints that makes a service program easier to understand than a program that implements the service.

The **progress assumption** of a service program consists of progress assertions subject to the following restrictions (to simplify inversion). First, each progress assertion has the form of a predicate whose terms are restricted to be leads-to assertions (i.e., no fairness assertions). Second, in each leads-to assertion, the terms of the (lhs and rhs) predicates are restricted to expressions in the variables and parameters of the service program and expressions of the form "thread t in s.f(.)" or "not (thread t in s.f(.))", where s.f(.) is an input function of the service program or an output call (in an output function) of the service program. Note that if s.f(.) is an input function of the service program, thread t in s.f(.) says t is in the body of the input function. Whereas if s.f(.) is an output call of the service program, thread t in s.f(.) says t is in the call, which means it is in the body of input function s.f(.) somewhere in the environment of the service program.

"Helper" assertions are assertions used in defining the progress assertions (as illustrated in program LossyChannel in Fig. 4.4). They are defined using the assertion(.) construct (analogous to the function(.) construct).

The progress assumption must be **locally realizable**, i.e., realizable by the service without requiring inputs from the environment. For example, suppose variable x is incremented only in input functions and variable y is incremented in an output function. Then "$x=2$ *leads-to* $x=3$" would not be a valid progress assumption but "$(x=2$ *leads-to* $x=3) \Rightarrow (y=2$ *leads-to* $y=3)$" can be. (This issue does not arise with fairness assertions, which are intrinsically locally realizable.)

6.3.4 Usability and Fault-Freedom

A service program that has (output parts with) internal parameters must satisfy the following **usability condition**: for any input e and for any two finite evolutions x and y of the program such that x and y have the same input-output history, the program can accept e at the end of x iff it can accept e at the end of y. Otherwise the service program would be useless as a standard, because the environment, which does not see the internal state of the service, would not be able to avoid sending an unacceptable input to the service. The usability condition holds automatically for service programs without internal parameters, because such a service has no internal nondeterminism, i.e., two different evolutions x and y would have different input-output histories.

For proving properties of a service program, input conditions play the same role as input assumptions. That is, a service program satisfies a property if it satisfies the property assuming that every input to it satisfies the corresponding input condition. A service program must also be fault-free, i.e., fault-free assuming inputs satisfy the input conditions. Otherwise, it would be useless as a standard; nobody would be interested in a system that implements it.

6.4   State Transition Semantics of Systems

To reason about a program, i.e., its aggregate system, we need a mathematical model of its evolutions. We use a state transition model. Each evolution of the aggregate system is represented by a sequence of transitions, each transition corresponding to an atomic step, i.e., the atomic execution of a chunk of code. We now define the states, transitions and evolutions of a composite system M.

6.4.1   States

If M is a single basic system, each possible value assignment of the parameters, variables, and thread control points of M corresponds to a **state** of M. (Keep in mind that the set of parameters, variables and threads of a basic system can vary over time.) If M consists of several basic systems, each state of M is a collection of states of the basic systems in M; if s is a state of M and P is a basic system of M, then $s.P$ refers to the component of s pertaining to P.

An **initial state** of M is defined by a value assignment of the program parameters (if any) of a first basic system of M. The symbol fault represents the state of a system that has experienced a fault. Unless otherwise mentioned, the term "state" refers to a fault-free state. A composite system is treated as faulty if *even one of its basic systems is faulty*. This pessimistic view is consistent with our assumption that a faulty system can do anything (including sending invalid inputs to other systems).

6.4.2   Transitions

Each transition of M corresponds to an execution of an atomic step of M. It is denoted by a sequence of **start state** (i.e., state when the transition starts), input or output (if present in the step), and **end state** (i.e., state when the transition ends). Every transition starts in a fault-free state and ends either in a fault-free state or in fault if a fault is encountered during execution. Transitions are classified into basic internal, input, output, and composite internal, as described next.

A **basic internal transition** corresponds to an execution of an atomic step in which no input or output is involved, i.e., the transition is internal to a basic system. (Thread creation, thread termination and system termination are in this class.) If the transition is fault-free, it has the form $\langle s, t \rangle$ where s is the start state and t is the end state. If M is a composite system and the step belongs to a basic system P, then $t.Q$ equals $s.Q$ for every other basic system Q of M. If the transition is faulty, then t is fault.

An **input transition** corresponds to an execution of an atomic step in which M gets an input from the environment. If the transition is fault-free, it has the form

$\langle s,e,t \rangle$ where s is the start state, e is the input and M is ready for it in s, and t is the end state. If M is a composite system and the transition concerns a basic system P in M, then $t.Q$ equals $s.Q$ for every other system Q of M. If the transition is faulty, then t is fault. Depending on whether the input is a call or a return, the transition can be further qualified as an **input-call** transition or an **input-return** transition. In the latter case, if no value is returned then e is void.

An **output transition** corresponds to an execution of an atomic step in which M sends an output to its environment. If the transition is fault-free, it has the form $\langle s,e,t \rangle$ where s is the start state, e is the output, and t is the end state. If M is a composite system and the transition concerns a basic system P in M, then $t.Q$ equals $s.Q$ for every other system Q of M. If the transition is faulty, then t is fault. Depending on whether the input is a call or a return, the transition can be further qualified as an **output-call** transition or an **output-return** transition. In the latter case, if no value is returned then e is void.

A **composite internal transition** corresponds to an interaction between two basic systems of M, say a basic system P doing an output to a basic system Q. If the transition is fault-free, it has the form $\langle s,e,t \rangle$ where s is the start state, e is an output of P and an input of Q, and t is the end state. Here, $\langle s.P,e,t.P \rangle$ is an output transition of P, $\langle s.Q,e,t.Q \rangle$ is an input transition of Q, and $t.R = s.R$ for every basic system R in M other than P and Q. The transition is faulty if Q or P becomes faulty, in which case t is fault.

6.4.3 Evolutions

An evolution of M is a path in the state transition model starting from an initial state and consisting of at least one transition (which creates the first basic system in M). More precisely, a **finite evolution** is a finite sequence of transitions, $\langle t_0, t_1, \cdots, t_n \rangle$ where $n \geq 0$, transition t_0 is the input transition that creates the first basic system of M in this evolution, transition t_0's start state is an initial state, transitions $t_0, t_1, \cdots, t_{n-1}$ are fault-free, and, for every i, the end state of t_i equals the start state of t_{i+1}. If the final transition t_n is faulty, the evolution is faulty, otherwise it is fault-free. An **infinite evolution** is like a finite evolution except that it never ends and hence is fault-free.

An evolution that satisfies M's progress assumption is said to be **complete**. Depending on the progress assumption, a complete evolution can be finite or infinite. In any case, a complete evolution is fault-free (because a faulty evolution does not satisfy any assertion).

We say an evolution of M is **allowed** if every input in it is allowed; i.e., for every input transition $\langle s,e,t \rangle$ in the evolution, e's input assumption (or input condition, in case of a service) holds in state s. The set of allowed evolutions represents all the possible evolutions of M *assuming* that (1) the environment calls an input of M only when the input is allowed, and (2) whenever M does an output the target system exists and can accept it. Of course, if M is a closed system then nothing is being assumed (because M would have no inputs or outputs).

The set of allowed evolutions decides the correctness properties of *M*. Specifically, if *M* has a faulty allowed evolution then it does not satisfy any assertion. *M* satisfies a safety assertion iff every allowed evolution satisfies the assertion. In particular, *M* is fault-free iff every allowed evolution is fault-free. *M* satisfies a progress assertion iff it is fault-free and every complete allowed evolution satisfies the assertion.

We are also interested in the set of fault-free evolutions of *M*. This set, as we shall see, is relevant for compositionality. Note that an allowed evolution need not be fault-free, and a fault-free evolution need not be allowed. But for a service, an evolution is allowed iff it is fault-free. (Recall that a service program is fault-free and that an input condition triggers a fault iff it is executed when false.)

The faulty state, fault, does not satisfy any predicate (not even true). A faulty evolution does not satisfy any assertion (not even *Inv* true).

6.5 Predicates and their Evaluation

Predicates are used in programs and assertions to express properties of system states. A predicate is a boolean-valued construct of boolean-valued terms, propositional operators (not, and, or, ⇒ (implies), ⇔ (iff), *OR* (non-short-circuited or), and quantifiers (forall, forsome, forone). The propositional operators and, or and ⇒ are "short-circuit" evaluated from left to right. The terms in a predicate are boolean valued, but they typically involve non-boolean expressions in the system's quantities, for example, "(thread t on S)" or "(y[j]+f = 25)".

A forall predicate has the form forall(x in D: Q), where x is a parameter, D is the domain of values over which x can vary, and Q is a predicate (usually involving x). It says that every value of x in D satisfies Q. If Q has the form R ⇒ S, one can write the predicate as forall(x in D,R: S). By convention, the predicate evaluates to true if D evaluates to an empty domain.

A forsome predicate has the form forsome(x in D: Q), where x, D and Q are as above. It says that at least one value of x in D satisfies Q. A forone predicate has the form forone(x in D: Q), where x, D and Q are as above. It says that exactly one value of x in D satisfies Q. By convention, these predicates evaluate to false if D evaluates to an empty domain.

Quantified predicates can be nested, as in forall(x in D: forsome(y in E: Q)), which says "for every x in D, there is a y in E that satisfies Q)". Another example is forsome(y in E: forall(x in D: Q)), which says something stronger, namely, "there is a y in E that satisfies Q for every x in D". Nested quantifiers of the same type can be written more compactly by removing the nesting; for example, forall(x in D: forall(y in E: Q)) can be written as forall(x in D, y in E: Q). By convention, propositional operators bind more strongly than quantifiers.

In a predicate, a variable defined within the scope of a quantifier, e.g., x in forall(x in...), is said to be a **bound variable** of the predicate. A variable in the predicate that is not bound is said to be a **free variable**. The name of a bound variable can be changed without affecting the meaning of the predicate, as long as the new name does not conflict with an existing name in the predicate.

We use "." as a "don't-care" value to abbreviate the writing of predicates. Let predicate P contain a "." and let R denote the smallest predicate in P containing the ".". Then P is equivalent to P with with R replaced by forsome(x:R).

6.6 Assertions and their Evaluation

Assertions are used to express correctness properties of systems. A correctness property is an expression that evaluates to true or false for any evolution. There are two kinds of correctness properties: safety and progress. The informal distinction between them is that a safety property says that nothing bad happens, whereas a progress property says that something good eventually happens. Formally, a correctness property P is a safety property if, for any evolution x that does not satisfy P, there is no extension of x that will make it satisfy P. Whereas a correctness property P is a progress property if, for any evolution x that does not satisfy P, there is always an extension of x that will make it satisfy P.

We use a subset of temporal logic for expressing correctness properties, namely, invariant and unless assertions for safety properties, and fairness and leads-to assertions for progress properties. Below, we describe how these assertions are evaluated, first for any evolution of a system, and then for the system itself.

An **invariant assertion** has the form *Inv*P, where P is a predicate. *Inv*P (read "invariant P") means that P always holds for the system after it starts. Formally, an evolution satisfies *Inv*P if it is fault-free and every non-initial state in the evolution satisfies P.

An **unless assertion** has the form P *unless* Q, where P and Q are predicates. It means that if P holds at some instant after the system starts, then it continues to hold until Q holds. Formally, an evolution satisfies P *unless* Q if it is fault-free and for every non-initial state in the evolution that satisfies P and not Q, either that state is the last state in the evolution or the next state satisfies P or Q.

A **safety assertion**, in general, is a predicate with its terms replaced by invariant and/or unless assertions, for example, forall(int n: (*Inv*P) $\Rightarrow$ (Q *unless* R)). A safety assertion R holds for an evolution if the evolution is fault-free and R evaluates to true after each invariant and unless assertion S in R is replaced by true or false depending on whether or not the evolution satisfies S.

A safety assertion holds for a system if it holds for *every* allowed evolution of the system.

Weak fairness for a thread means that the thread is never starved of processor cycles. Formally, an evolution satisfies weak fairness for a thread if the evolution is fault-free and either (1) the evolution is finite and the thread is blocked in the last state of the evolution, or (2) the evolution is infinite and the thread executes infinitely often or is blocked infinitely often (i.e., at an infinite number of states).

Strong fairness for a thread means that, in addition to weak fairness, the thread eventually gets past any blocking statement provided the statement keeps getting unblocked. Formally, an evolution satisfies strong fairness for a thread if the evolution is fault-free and either (1) the evolution is finite and the thread is blocked in the last state of the evolution (same as weak fairness), or (2) the evolution is infinite and the thread executes infinitely often if it is unblocked infinitely often.

One can also associate (weak or strong) fairness with a chunk of code. This means that any thread has the appropriate fairness when on that chunk of code. Typically, if a platform provides strong fairness, it provides it only for some blocking constructs (e.g., lock acquires); it may even restrict this offering to certain threads.

A **leads-to assertion** has the form P *leads-to* Q, where P and Q are predicates. It means that if P holds at some instant, then Q holds at that instant or at some later instant. Formally, an evolution satisfies P *leads-to* Q if the evolution is fault-free and for every non-initial state in the evolution that satisfies P and not Q, some later state in the evolution satisfies Q.

A **progress assertion**, in general, is a predicate with its terms replaced by fairness assertions and/or leads-to assertions, for example, forall(int n: (X *leads-to* Y) $\Rightarrow$ (P *leads-to* Q)). A progress assertion R holds for an evolution if the evolution is fault-free and R evaluates to true after each fairness or leads-to assertion S in R is replaced by true or false depending on whether or not the evolution satisfies S.

A progress assertion holds for a system if the system is fault-free and the assertion holds for every *complete* allowed evolution of the system, i.e., holds for every allowed evolution that satisfies the progress assumption.

As in the case of predicates, a variable in an assertion is free or bound. An assertion concerning a system usually has its free variables be a subset of the variables and parameters of the system. However it is often convenient to allow free variables that are not variables or parameters of the system. When evaluating such an assertion, such free variables are assumed to be universally quantified. For example, consider the following assertion about a system:

P_1 : nd = k < ng *leads-to* nd > k

Here nd, k and ng are free variables. Suppose nd and ng are variables of the system, and k is neither a variable or parameter of the system. Then when P_1 is evaluated, it is treated as forall(int k: P_1).

All the types of assertions above satisfy the following: if an assertion holds for an evolution then it also holds when any finite sequence of identical states in the evolution is replaced by another finite sequence of the same state. We shall see later that this is important for compositionality. (An example of an assertion that does not have this property would be: if P holds in a state then either P is the last state in the evolution or the next state satisfies Q.)

6.7   Splitting and Stitching of Evolutions

Let composite system C be the union of disjoint composite systems $P_1, \cdots, P_N$, where by disjoint we mean that no two P_i and P_j share a basic system. We now formalize the notion that an evolution of C is made up of evolutions of $P_1, \cdots, P_N$ stitched together at matching interactions.

Definition (images of transitions and evolutions). Let C be a composite system. Let P be the composite system of a subset of the basic systems of C. For any transition t of C, the **image of t on P**, denoted $t.P$, is defined as follows: if t involves a transition of P, then $t.P$ is t with every state s in t replaced by $s.P$; if t does not involve a transition of P, then $t.P$ is the empty sequence. For any evolution x of C, the **image of x on P**, denoted $x.P$, is defined to be the sequence obtained by replacing every transition t by $t.P$.   □

Theorem 6.1 (evolution splitting).   *Let C be a composite system. Let P be the composite system of a subset of the basic systems of C. Let x be a fault-free evolution of C such that $x.P$ is not null. Then the following hold:*

(a) $x.P$ is a fault-free evolution of P.
(b) For any assertion B that does not involve systems of C other than those in P: x satisfies B iff $x.P$ satisfies B.
(c) If x is a complete evolution of C then $x.P$ is a complete evolution of P.   □

Proof. **Part (a):** Because x is fault-free, $x.P$ has no fault states. So it suffices to show that $x.P$ is an evolution of P. The proof is by induction on the number of transitions in x. The base case is when x consists of only one transition, namely the transition that creates the first basic system in C. The transition involves P iff this basic system is in P, in this case $x.P$ is an evolution of P consisting of the transition that starts P. Otherwise $x.P$ is the empty sequence.

Now for the induction step. Suppose the theorem holds for a finite evolution x. So $x.P$ is an evolution of P or an empty sequence. Let x be extended to z by a transition b of C. It suffices to show that $z.P$ is an evolution of P or the empty sequence.

Let s be the last state of x. Thus b starts with the state s.

Let b be a basic internal transition of C. If b involves P, then $b.P$ is a basic internal transition of P; hence $z.P$, which equals $x.P \circ b.P$, is an evolution of P (since $b.P$ starts from $s.P$). If b does not involve P, then $b.P$ is null and $z.P$ equals $x.P$ (which already satisfies the required condition).

Let b be an input transition of C. The argument is the same as for internal transition.

Let b be an output transition of C. The argument is the same as for internal transition.

Let b be a composite internal transition of C in which a basic system R does an output to a basic system S. If P contains R but not S, then $b.P$ is an output transition of P; hence $z.P$, which equals $x.P \circ b.P$, is an evolution of P. If P contains S but not R, then $b.P$ is an input transition of P; hence $z.P$, which equals $x.P \circ b.P$, is an evolution of P. If P contains both R and S, then $b.P$ is an composite internal transition of P; hence $z.P$, which equals $x.P \circ b.P$, is an evolution of P. If P contains neither R nor S, then $b.P$ is null and $z.P$ equals $x.P$.

Part (b): Assertion B depends only on the sequence of states and inputs and outputs of P. Because x is fault-free, $x.P$ is fault-free (from part a). The sequence of states of P in x is the same as in $x.P$ except that finite sequences of identical states may be replaced by a single instance of that state. So if B is an invariant, unless, or leads-to assertion, B holds for x iff it holds for $x.P$. For this to apply if B is a fairness assertion on a thread e, we also need that e is blocked at a state s of x iff e is blocked at $s.P$. This latter property holds because system composition does not affect the blocking condition of a thread of P.

Part (c): Let x be a complete evolution of C. So x satisfies the progress assumption of C, and hence the progress assumption of P. So $x.P$ satisfies the progress assumption of P (from part b). □

The converse also holds: any collection of system evolutions that make "compatible" sequence of calls to each other can be stitched together to form an evolution of their composite system. Let $P_1, \cdots, P_N$ be a collection of disjoint composite systems, i.e., no two P_i and P_j have a basic system in common. Let $x_1, \cdots, x_N$ be fault-free evolutions of systems $P_1, \cdots, P_N$, respectively. Let $ext(x_i)$ be the sequence of inputs and outputs of x_i. We say the evolutions $x_1, \cdots, x_N$ are **signature-compatible** if the sequences $ext(x_1), \cdots, ext(x_N)$ can be merged such that if an entry in the merged sequence comes from $ext(x_i)$ and is an output e to P_j, then the next entry in the merged sequence comes from $ext(x_j)$ and is an input e to P_j.

Theorem 6.2 (stitching evolutions). *Let $P_1, \cdots, P_N$ be a collection of disjoint composite systems. Let C be the composite system of the union of $P_1, \cdots, P_N$. Let x_i be a fault-free evolution of P_i, for $i = 1, \cdots, N$.*

(a) *There exists a fault-free evolution z of C such that $z.P_i = x_i$ for $i = 1, \cdots, N$ if and only if the evolutions $x_1, \cdots, x_N$ are signature-compatible.*

(b) *For any P_i and any assertion B that does not involve basic systems of C other than those in P_i: z satisfies B iff x_i satisfies B.*

(c) *Evolution z is a complete evolution of C iff x_i is complete evolution of P_i for $i = 1, \cdots, N$.* □

Proof. **Part (a)**

Case 1: Consider the "if" direction for $N = 2$, i.e., C consists of P_1 and P_2. Assume x_1 and x_2 are signature-compatible. We will show that they can be stitched together to form an evolution z of C. Because x_1 and x_2 are compatible, there is a compatible merge of $ext(x_1)$ and $ext(x_2)$. The proof is by induction on the number of P_1-P_2 interactions in this merge, where, as usual, a P_1-P_2 interaction is an output by one of them to the other.

The base case is when there are no P_1-P_2 interactions in the merge. Then any interleaving of the transitions in x_1 and x_2, e.g., $x_1 \circ x_2$, yields an evolution z of C such that $z.P_1 = x_1$ and $z.P_2 = x_2$.

Now assume that the result holds for upto some number of P_1-P_2 interactions, and consider evolutions x_1 and x_2 whose compatible merge has one more P_1-P_2 interaction. Let x_1' be the prefix of x_1 ending just before the last P_1-P_2 interaction, and let x_1'' be the suffix of x_1 following x_1'. Let x_2' be the prefix of x_2 ending just before the last P_1-P_2 interaction, and let x_2'' be the suffix of x_2 following x_2'. By the induction hypothesis, there is a finite evolution z' of C such that $z'.P_1 = x_1'$ and $z'.P_2 = x_2'$ hold. The last P_1-P_2 interaction is executable at the end of z'. Executing that (composite internal) interaction takes C to a state from where P_1 can execute the remaining transitions in x_1'' and P_2 can execute the remaining transitions in x_2''. These remaining transitions can be executed in any merged order because they do not interact with each other. Executing the P_1-P_2 interaction followed by the remaining transitions of x_1'' and x_2'' (in any merged order) extends z' to an evolution z that satisfies $z.P_1 = x_1$ and $z.P_2 = x_2$.

Case 2: The "only if" direction for $N = 2$ is easy. Given z such that $z.P_1 = x_1$ and $z.P_2 = x_2$, it is obvious that x_1 and x_2 are signature-compatible.

Case 3: The extension to a composite system C with components $P_1, P_2, \cdots, P_N$, where $N \geq 3$, is straightforward and is left as an exercise. One way to do it is apply the result for $N = 2$ to the intermediate composite systems $Q_2(P_1, P_2)$, $Q_3(Q_2, P_3)$, $\cdots$, $Q_N(Q_{N-1}, P_N)$, where $Q_i(Q_{i-1}, P_i)$ denotes a composite system Q_i of the union of Q_{i-1} and P_i.

Parts (b,c): Similar to parts (b,c) of Theorem 6.1. $\qquad\qquad\qquad\qquad\qquad\square$

6.8 Auxiliary Variables

When analyzing a program, it is often convenient to introduce hypothetical variables that record information about the program's behavior without influencing its evolutions (for example, thread ids). These variables, called **auxiliary variables**, are only for analysis, and are not implemented. To ensure that auxiliary variables do not affect the program's evolutions, they must satisfy the following **auxiliary variable condition**:

- Auxiliary variables do not appear in output conditions and their value is not used in updating a non-auxiliary variable. (A simple way to ensure this is to have auxiliary variables appear only in assignment statements, and if one appears in the right side of an assignment statement then the left side must be an auxiliary variable.)
- Statements involving auxiliary variables are fault-free. Each such statement is executed atomically with an existing statement (so no new control points are added).

Let Q be the program resulting by extending a program P with auxiliary variables. Then the evolutions of Q differ from those of P only in that each state of Q consists of a state of P and a state of the auxiliary variables. Thus the definition of image states and image evolutions is applicable here.

Theorem 6.3. *Let Q be a program P extended with auxiliary variables.*

(a) For any (faulty or fault-free) evolution x of Q, x.P is an evolution of P.
(b) For any evolution y of P, there exists an evolution x of Q such that x.P equals y.
(c) For any assertion Y whose free variables have no auxiliary variables, P satisfies
 Y iff Q satisfies Y.   □

Proof. **Part a.** For any evolution x of Q, $x.P$ is obtained by removing the auxiliary variable values from the states of x. Because the auxiliary variables do not give rise to a fault and do not affect output conditions or non-auxiliary variables, for every transition t in x, $t.P$ is a transition of P. Hence $x.P$ is an evolution of P.

Part b. Because the auxiliary variables do not give rise to a fault and do not affect blocking conditions or non-auxiliary variables, for each transition t in y, there is a transition u of Q such that $u.P = t$. Thus there is an evolution x of Q such that $x.P = y$.

Part c. If Q does not satisfy Y then there exists an evolution x of Q such that x does not satisfy Y. From part a, $x.P$ is an evolution of P. Because Y does not involve auxiliary variables, $x.P$ also does not satisfy Y. Hence P does not satisfy Y.

 If P does not satisfy Y then there exists an evolution y of P such that y does not satisfy Y. From part b, there exists an evolution x of Q such that $x.P = y$. Because Y does not involve auxiliary variables, x does not satisfy Y. Hence Q does not satisfy Y.   □

6.9 Effective Atomicity

Recall that under certain conditions a chunk of code S in an aggregate system is effectively atomic, i.e., can be treated as atomic for purposes of analysis, even though it may not be executed atomically by the underlying platform. Informally, for every evolution w of the system in which S is executed, there is an evolution w' in which S is executed atomically (i.e., without intervening executions of non-S statements) such that w and w' have the same input-output sequence. We now cover this rigorously. We present a sufficient condition in terms of "commuting" statements, which is implied by the sufficient conditions we have been using for effective atomicity. The notion of commuting statements turns out to be fundamental in the analysis of concurrent computations.

6.9.1 Defining Effective Atomicity

We say a code chunk S of an aggregate system is **sequentially executed** to mean that it is a finite sequence of statements and it is executed only by a thread going through its statements in sequence. We will develop conditions under which S is effectively atomic. Typically S is executed by at most one thread at any time. But it may also be executed by several threads simultaneously (such that the executions of different threads do not conflict).

We refer to an execution of S by a thread as an S-run. More precisely, an S-**run** is a finite sequence of transitions, $\langle t_1, t_2, \cdots \rangle$, in an evolution, where t_i is the transition due to the thread executing the ith atomic statement of S. An S-run need not be a contiguous fragment of the evolution, i.e., the end state of t_i need not equal the start state of t_{i+1}, because its transitions can be interleaved with transitions of other threads (perhaps even transitions of other S-runs). An S-run is said to be **whole** if it goes through all the statements in S; otherwise it is said to be **partial**.

S is defined to be **atomically executed** in an evolution w if each S-run in w is whole and its transitions are contiguous in w.

S is defined to be **effectively atomic** if, for every evolution w of the aggregate system, there is an evolution w' of the aggregate system such that:

- S is atomically executed in w'.
- w and w' have the same input-output sequence, i.e., $ext(w) = ext(w')$.
- If w is complete (satisfies progress assumption) then w' is complete.

The following theorem captures the benefits of effective atomicity.

Theorem 6.4. *Let a code chunk S of an aggregate system X be sequentially-executed and effectively atomic. Let X' be X but with S assumed to be atomic (i.e., atomically executed by the platform). Let P be a correctness property concerning only the external behavior of X, i.e., its input-output sequence. Then X satisfies P iff X' satisfies P.*   □

Proof. The *only if* direction (i.e., if X satisfies P then X' satisfies P) holds trivially because every evolution of X' is also an evolution of X.

The *if* direction (i.e., if X' satisfies P then X satisfies P) is easily proved by contradiction. Suppose P does not hold for X. Then X has an evolution w that does not satisfy P. Because S is effectively atomic, there is an evolution w' of X be such that S is atomically executed in w', $ext(w)$ equals $ext(w')$, and w' is complete if w is complete. Then w' does not satisfy P. But w' is also an evolution of X'. Hence P does not hold for X'. (If P is a progress property then w and w' would be complete evolutions.)   □

6.9.2 Commuting Statements

Given an atomic statement G, we say G-transition to mean a transition due to an execution of G.

Given atomic statements G and F in an aggregate system, we say $\langle G, F \rangle$ **commutes** if for every evolution w of the system, for every G-transition followed immediately by an F-transition of another thread in w, one can reverse the order of the two transitions and modify the states (and nothing else) in w so that the resulting sequence w' is also an evolution of the system. (Typically, when a G-transition, say $\langle r,g,s \rangle$, is commuted with a F-transition, say $\langle s,f,t \rangle$, only the state between them is modified. That is, if $w = \langle x, \langle r,g,s \rangle, \langle s,f,t \rangle, y \rangle$ then $w' = \langle x, \langle r,f,s' \rangle, \langle s',g,t \rangle, y \rangle$.)

Given a function $\mathcal{Z}(\cdot)$ on evolutions, we say $\langle G,F \rangle$ **commutes wrt** $\mathcal{Z}(\cdot)$ if $\mathcal{Z}(w)$ equals $\mathcal{Z}(w')$ in the above definition. For our purposes here, $\mathcal{Z}(\cdot)$ will be $ext(\cdot)$. But later we will encounter situations where commutation with other functions for $\mathcal{Z}(\cdot)$ will be useful.

Commutativity lets us coalesce the transitions of an S-run as follows. Let α denote an S-run in an evolution w. Let I and J be two successive atomic statements in S. Let α's I-transition be followed by one or more non-α transitions, followed by α's J-transition. If $\langle I,F \rangle$ commutes wrt $ext(\cdot)$ for every non-α statement F in the system, then by repeatedly swapping the I-transition and the following non-α transition, we can obtain an evolution w' in which I is immediately followed by J and $ext(w')$ equals $ext(w)$. Similarly, if $\langle F,J \rangle$ commutes wrt $ext(\cdot)$ for any non-α statement F in the system, then by repeatedly swapping the J-transition and the preceding non-α transition, we can obtain an evolution w' in which J is immediately preceded by I and $ext(w')$ equals $ext(w)$.

What remains is to handle evolutions with incomplete S-runs. Let I be a non-final atomic statement in S. We say I is **tail-droppable wrt** $\mathcal{Z}(\cdot)$ if for any evolution w that has a partial S-run ending with its I-transition, one can delete the I-transition and modify the states in w so that the resulting sequence w' is an evolution of the program and $ext(w')$ equals $ext(w)$. Similarly, let J be a non-first atomic statement in S and let K be its predecessor in S. We say J is **tail-appendable wrt** $\mathcal{Z}(\cdot)$ if for any evolution w of the program that has a partial S-run ending with its K-transition, one can insert the S-run's J-transition run after the K-transition and modify the states in w so that the resulting sequence w' is an evolution of the program and $ext(w')$ equals $ext(w)$.

Theorem 6.5. *Let S be a sequentially-executed code chunk in an aggregate system. Let K be an atomic statement in S. Let the following hold for every atomic statement I in S and every atomic statement F in the aggregate system that can be executed simultaneously with I:*

(a) If I comes before K in S then:

  (a1) $\langle I,F \rangle$ commutes wrt $ext(\cdot)$.
  (a2) I is tail-droppable wrt $ext(\cdot)$.

(b) If I comes after K in S then:

  (b1) $\langle F,I \rangle$ commutes wrt $ext(\cdot)$.
  (b2) I is tail-appendable wrt $ext(\cdot)$.

*Then S is effectively atomic and K is said to be an **anchor** of S.* □

Proof. Let w be an evolution of the system. Because S is sequentially executed, w contains zero or more whole S-runs and zero or more partial S-runs. (Each partial S-run would be executed by a different thread.)

Assume w has a partial S-run α. If α does not include the anchor transition, condition a2 tells us that we can drop α's transitions from w' without disturbing $ext(w')$. If α includes the anchor transition, condition b2 tells us that we can insert the transitions that would make α whole (i.e., let α's thread completely execute S) without disturbing $ext(w')$. Applying this to every partial S-run transforms w to an evolution w' without a partial S-run.

Assume w' has a whole S-run α. The transitions of α need not be contiguous in w'. But condition a1 allows the transitions of the pre-anchor statements of α to be moved to a later position (to the right) in w' until they are contiguous with α's anchor transition; i.e., for every atomic statement I in S preceding K, repeatedly swap the I-transition in α with the following non-α transition until the I-transition arrives immediately before the transition in α of its successor atomic statement in S (which may be the anchor). Similarly, condition b1 allows the transitions of the post-anchor statements in α to be moved earlier in w' until they are contiguous with α's anchor transition. Applying this to every S-run in w' results in an evolution w'' in which S is atomically executed (because every S-run is whole and its transitions are contiguous) and $ext(w'')$ equals $ext(w)$.   □

6.9.3 Some Simple Sufficient Conditions

We have previously made use of some simple conditions for effective atomicity. We now show that each of these conditions imply the requirements of Theorem 6.5. A code chunk S is said to **interfere** with code chunk R if (1) S and R conflict (i.e., one of them can write a variable that is simultaneously accessed by the other) or (2) S and R can do input or output simultaneously.

The following says that a code chunk S is effectively atomic if no other thread of the system program can execute a statement that interferes with S.

Theorem 6.6. *Let a code chunk S of an aggregate system X be sequentially-executed and and blockable only at the start. For every statement J that can be executed by another thread while S is being executed, let J not interfere with S. Then S is effectively atomic.*   □

Proof. Let S satisfies the requirements of Theorem 6.6. It suffices to show that S satisfies requirements a-b of Theorem 6.5. Define the anchor of S to be the first atomic statement of S. Then S satisfies conditions a-b because every non-anchor atomic statement I of S is mutually exclusive with any statement with which it interferes. (Details left as an exercise.)   □

The following says that S is effectively atomic even if it interferes with another code chunk provided all interference occurs only in one atomic statement of S.

Theorem 6.7. *Let a code chunk S of an aggregate system X be sequentially-executed and and blockable only at the start. Let K be an atomic statement in S*

such that for any statement J that can be executed simultaneously with S, J does not conflict with any statement of S other than K. Then S is effectively atomic and K is its anchor.   □

Proof. Let *S* satisfies the requirements of Theorem 6.7. Then *S* satisfies requirements a-b of Theorem 6.5 because every non-anchor atomic statement *G* of *S* is mutually exclusive with any statement with which it interferes. (Details left as an exercise.)   □

6.10   Proof Rules

Recall that assertions about programs can be proved either by operational arguments or by applications of proof rules. Proofs of the latter kind can be mechanically checked without any understanding of the program or the assertion being proved, although such understanding is needed to come up with the proof. This section describes proof rules briefly, starting with some necessary background concerning Hoare-triples.

6.10.1   Hoare-Triples

Hoare-triples express properties of program statements whose executions are not interfered with by the environment. A Hoare-triple has the form $\{P\}S\{Q\}$, where P and Q are predicates and S is a program statement. Predicates P and Q are referred to as the **precondition** and the **postcondition**, respectively, of the Hoare-triple.

- For a *non-blocking* statement S, the Hoare-triple $\{P\}S\{Q\}$ says that the execution of S starting from any state satisfying P always terminates (i.e., does not encounter a fault or infinite loop) in a state that satisfies Q, assuming that S's environment does not affect intermediate states of S's execution.
- For a *blocking statement* S consisting of *blocking condition* B and non-blocking code C (i.e., "await (B) C" or "oc {B} C"), the Hoare-triple $\{P\}S\{Q\}$ is defined to be $\{P \text{ and } B\}C\{Q\}$.

Here are some examples of Hoare-triples. Next to each we indicate whether or not it is valid.

- $\{true\}$ if $x \neq y$ then $x \leftarrow y+1$ $\{(x = y+1)$ or $(x = y)\}$ (valid)
- $\{x = n\}$ for i in $0..10$ do $x \leftarrow x+i$ $\{x = n+55\}$ (valid)
- $\{x = 3\}$ $x \leftarrow y+1$ $\{x=4\}$ (invalid; e.g., if $y = 1$ holds at start)
- $\{(x = 1)$ and $(y = 1)\}$ while $(x > 0)$ $x \leftarrow 2*x$ $\{y = 1\}$ (invalid; does not terminate)
- $\{true\}$ await $(x \neq y)$ $x \leftarrow y+1$ $\{x=y+1\}$ (valid)
- $\{true\}$ oc$\{x \geq 1\}$ $y \leftarrow 1/(2-x)$ $\{y=1/(2-x)\}$ (invalid; may divide by zero)

assignment	{P} x ← t {Q} holds if the following holds: • P ⇒ Q[x|t] where Q[x|t] is Q with every free occurrence of x replaced by t. (Rename bound variables to avoid any name conflicts.)
sequential composition	{P} S;T {Q} holds if the following hold for some predicate R: • {P} S {R} • {R} T {Q}
if-then-else	{P} if (B) S else T {Q} holds if the following hold: • {P and B} S {Q} • {P and not B} T {Q}
while	{P} while (B) S {Q} holds if the following hold, for some non-negative function T: • {P and B and T = n > 0} S {P and T < n } • (P and not B) ⇒ Q
await	{P} await B do S {Q} holds if the following holds: • {P and B} S {Q}
output-part	{P} oc {B} S {Q} holds if the following holds: • {P} await B do S {Q}

Fig. 6.1 Proof rules for Hoare-triples of some program constructs

Figure 6.1 shows proof rules for Hoare-triples for some program constructs. Proof rules for standard synchronization operations (on locks, condition variables, semaphores) can be obtained by replacing the operations by their equivalent await constructs (see Exercises 3.8–3.10) and then applying the given rules. A complete proof system would have a proof rule for every program construct and data type [4]. That is beyond the scope of this book.

Invariance induction

Inv P holds for program M if the following hold:

- for the initial atomic step e of M: {true} e {P}
- for every non-initial atomic step e of M: {P} e {P}

- -

Invariance induction

Inv P holds for program M if the following hold for some predicate R:

- *Inv* R
- for the initial atomic step e of M: {true} e {R $\Rightarrow$ P}
- for every non-initial atomic step e of M: {R and P} e {R $\Rightarrow$ P}

- -

Unless

P *unless* Q holds for program M if the following holds:

- for every non-initial atomic step e of M: {P and not Q} e {P or Q}

Fig. 6.2 Proof rules for safety assertions involving Hoare-triples

6.10.2 *Proof Rules for Safety Assertions*

We now give proof rules for inferring invariant and unless assertions for a program. There are two kinds of proof rules. One kind, referred to as **closure rules**, are for inferring assertions from other assertions. These do not involve Hoare-triples. The other kind are for inferring assertions from the program code (and perhaps other assertions). These involve establishing a Hoare-triple for *every* atomic (or effectively atomic) step of the program. The following convention is used:

$$\{P\}\ e\ \{Q\} = \begin{cases} \{P \text{ and } e.\text{ia}\}\ e\ \{Q\} & \text{if e is an input step of a program} \\ \{P \text{ and } e.\text{ic}\}\ e\ \{Q\} & \text{if e is an input step of a service program} \\ \{P\}\ e\ \{Q\} & \text{otherwise} \end{cases}$$

Figure 6.2 gives proof rules for inferring safety assertions from the program code. The first rule, called invariance induction, allows one to infer an invariant assertion from the program's code. Its soundness is easily proved. Let w be an allowed evolution of the program. The rule's first requirement ensures that the initial transition of w ends in a state satisfying P. The rule's second requirement ensures

Closure

Inv P holds if P holds.

Inv P holds if the following hold:

- *Inv* Q
- *Inv* (Q ⇒ P)

P *unless* Q holds if *Inv* (P ⇒ Q) holds.

P *unless* Q holds if the following hold:

- R *unless* S
- *Inv* (P ⇒ R)
- *Inv* (S ⇒ Q)

Fig. 6.3 Closure proof rules for safety assertions

that for every other transition, its ends state satisfies P if its start state satisfies P. Hence, by induction, every non-initial state in *w* satisfies *P*. Hence *Inv* P holds.

This rule does not allow one to take advantage of properties that have already been established. For example, suppose the program is known to satisfy *Inv* R for some predicate R. Then when checking the requirement for an atomic step e, one can assume that R holds in e's precondition and postcondition. The second rule in Fig. 6.2, also called invariance induction, captures this formally. Proving the soundness of this rule (and all upcoming rules) is left as an exercise.

The third rule in Fig. 6.2 allows one to infer an unless assertion from the program's code. As with the invariance induction rule, if an assertion *Inv* R has already been established, one can take advantage of it by changing the precondition to "R and P and not Q" and the postcondition to "R ⇒ (P or Q)".

Figure 6.3 gives some closure proof rules for inferring safety assertions from other safety assertions.

6.10.3 Proof Rules for Progress Assertions

We now give proof rules for establishing leads-to assertions for a program, starting with the rules for inferring from the program's code. For an atomic step e, let the

Weak-fair

P *leads-to* Q holds for program M if the following hold, where e is an atomic step of M subject to weak fairness:

- (P and not Q) $\Rightarrow$ e.enabled
- {P and not Q} e {Q}
- for every non-initial atomic step f of M: {P and not Q} f {P or Q}

Strong-fair

P *leads-to* Q holds for program M if the following hold, where e is an atomic step of M subject to strong fairness:

- (P and not Q and not e.enabled) *leads-to* (Q or e.enabled)
- {P and not Q} e {Q}
- for every non-initial atomic step f of M: {P and not Q} f {P or Q}

Fig. 6.4 Proof rules for leads-to assertions involving Hoare-triples

predicate e.enabled mean that a thread is at e and e is unblocked (if it has a blocking condition). Formally,

$$
\text{e.enabled} = \begin{cases} \text{thread at e} & \text{if e is nonblocking} \\ \text{(thread at e) and B} & \text{if e has blocking condition B (e.g., oc\{B\}S)} \end{cases}
$$

Figure 6.4 allows one to infer leads-to assertions from the program code and fairness assumptions. When applying these rules, we often use the shorthand "P **leads-to** Q **via** e" to mean that P, Q, and e satisfy the requirements of the weak-fair rule or the strong-fair rule (depending on the fairness of e). As usual, if an assertion *Inv* R has already been established, one can change each precondition X to "R and X" and each postcondition X to "R $\Rightarrow$ X".

Figure 6.5 gives some closure proof rules for inferring leads-to assertions from other assertions.

6.11 Concluding Remarks

This chapter presented the structure and semantics of programs, service programs, and assertions. It established some basic properties relating the evolutions of a composite system to the evolutions of its component systems. It formalized the notion of effective atomicity and introduced sufficient conditions based on

Closure

P *leads-to* (Q1 or Q2) holds if the following hold:

- P *leads-to* P1 or Q2
- P1 *leads-to* Q1

P *leads-to* Q holds if the following hold for some predicate R:

- (P and R) *leads-to* (R $\Rightarrow$ Q)
- *Inv* R

(P1 and P2) *leads-to* Q2 holds if the following hold for some predicate Q1:

- P1 *leads-to* Q1
- P2 *unless* Q2
- *Inv* (Q1 $\Rightarrow$ (not P2))

P *leads-to* Q holds if the following hold:

- P *unless* Q
- *Inv* (P $\Rightarrow$ R)
- R *leads-to* S
- *Inv* (S $\Rightarrow$ not P)

Well-founded closure

P *leads-to* Q holds if, for some function F on a lower-bounded partial order $(Z, \prec)$, the following hold:

- P *leads-to* (Q or forsome(x in Z: F(x)))
- forall(x in Z:
        F(x) *leads-to* (Q or forsome(w in Z: w $\prec$ x and F(w))))

Fig. 6.5 Closure proof rules for leads-to assertions

commuting statements. Finally, it gave a quick and very brief treatment of proof rules, touching on soundness and ignoring completeness.

The theoretical treatment here has been rather condensed because the thrust of this book is on application rather than theory. Each topic covered here has been examined in depth in the literature. Using state transition systems to define the semantics of concurrent systems is described in, e.g., [7, 9, 45, 48, 56, 57, 59–61, 79, 82]. A detailed coverage of predicate logic and its applications in computing is covered in, e.g., [12, 58]. Details of Hoare-logic and weakest preconditions can be found in, e.g., [4, 21, 26, 37, 40]. Their extension to concurrent programs can be seen in, e.g., [5, 69, 71]. Temporal logic and proof rules for safety and progress assertions are covered in, e.g., [3, 17, 51, 53, 56, 57, 59–63, 71–73, 76]. Applications of these proof rules, i.e., assertional reasoning, are found in, e.g., [1–3, 6–11, 13–18, 22–36, 38, 39, 41–44, 46, 47, 49, 55, 64–69, 74–78, 80–85]. Effective atomicity is examined in, e.g., [19, 20, 28, 50, 52, 54, 70].

References

1. C. Alaettinoglu, A.U. Shankar, Stepwise assertional design of distance-vector routing algorithms, in *Protocol Specification, Testing and Verification XII*, ed. by R.J. Linn Jr., M.M. Uyar. Proceedings of the IFIP TC6/WG6.1 Twelth International Symposium on Protocol Specification, Testing and Verification, Lake Buena Vista, 22–25 June 1992. IFIP Transactions, vol. C-8 (North-Holland, New York, 1992), pp. 399–413
2. G.R. Andrews, A method for solving synchronization problems. Sci. Comput. Program. 13(4), 1–21 (1989)
3. G.R. Andrews, F.B. Schneider, Concepts and notations for concurrent programming. ACM Comput. Surv. 15(1), 3–43 (1983). doi:10.1145/356901.356903. http://doi.acm.org/10.1145/356901.356903
4. K.R. Apt, Ten years of hoare's logic: a survey-part i. ACM TOPLAS 3, 431–483 (1981)
5. E.A. Ashcroft, Proving assertions about parallel programs. J. Comput. Syst. Sci. 10(1), 110–135 (1975). doi:10.1016/S0022-0000(75)80018-3. http://dx.doi.org/10.1016/S0022-0000(75)80018-3
6. R.J. Back, Invariant based programming: basic approach and teaching experiences. Form. Aspects Comput. 21, 227–244 (2009). doi:10.1007/s00165-008-0070-y
7. R.J.R. Back, F. Kurki-Suonio, Distributed cooperation with action systems. ACM Trans. Program. Lang. Syst. 10(4), 513–554 (1988). doi:10.1145/48022.48023. http://doi.acm.org/10.1145/48022.48023
8. R.J.R. Back, R. Kurki-Suonio, Decentralization of process nets with centralized control, in *Proceedings of the Second Annual ACM Symposium on Principles of Distributed Computing, PODC '83* (ACM, New York, 1983), pp. 131–142. doi:10.1145/800221.806716. http://doi.acm.org/10.1145/800221.806716
9. R.J.R. Back, K. Sere, Stepwise refinement of parallel algorithms. Sci. Comput. Program. 13(2–3), 133–180 (1990). doi:10.1016/0167-6423(90)90069-P. http://dx.doi.org/10.1016/0167-6423(90)90069-P
10. R.J. Back, K. Sere, Stepwise refinement of action systems. Software 12, 17–30 (1991)
11. R.J. Back, J.V. Wright, Contracts, games, and refinement. Inf. Comput. 156, 25–45 (2000). doi:10.1006/inco.1999.2820
12. M. Ben-Ari, *Mathematical Logic for Computer Science*, 2nd edn. (Springer, London, 2001)
13. M. Ben-Ari, *The Art of Multiprocessor Programming*, 2nd edn. (Addison-Wesley, San Francisco, 2006)
14. J.A. Carruth, J. Misra, Proof of a real-time mutual-exclusion algorithm. Parallel Process. Lett. 6(2), 251–257 (1996)
15. K.M. Chandy, J. Misra, The drinking philosophers problem. ACM Trans. Program. Lang. Syst. 6(4), 632–646 (1984). doi:10.1145/1780.1804. http://doi.acm.org/10.1145/1780.1804

16. K.M. Chandy, J. Misra, An example of stepwise refinement of distributed programs: quiescence detection. ACM Trans. Program. Lang. Syst. **8**(3), 326–343 (1986). doi:10.1145/5956.5958. http://doi.acm.org/10.1145/5956.5958

17. K.M. Chandy, J. Misra, *Parallel Program Design: A Foundation* (Addison-Wesley, Reading, 1989)

18. K.M. Chandy, J. Misra, Proof of distributed algorithms: an exercise, in *Developments in Concurrency and Communication*, ed. by C.A.R. Hoare (Addison-Wesley Longman Publishing Co., Inc, Boston, 1990), pp. 305–332. http://dl.acm.org/citation.cfm?id=107155.107171

19. E. Cohen, Modular progress proofs of asynchronous programs. Ph.D. thesis, University of Texas, Austin, 1993. UMI Order No. GAX93-23370

20. E. Cohen, L. Lamport, Reduction in tla, in *Proceedings of the 9th International Conference on Concurrency Theory, CONCUR '98* (Springer, London, 1998), pp. 317–331. http://dl.acm.org/citation.cfm?id=646733.701301

21. E.W. Dijkstra, Guarded commands, nondeterminacy and formal derivation of programs. Commun. ACM **18**(8), 453–457 (1975). doi:10.1145/360933.360975. http://doi.acm.org/10.1145/360933.360975

22. E.W. Dijkstra, A correctness proof for communicating processes—a small exercise. Technical report, Burroughs, Nuenen, 1977. EWD-607

23. E.W. Dijkstra, Two starvation-free solutions of a general exclusion problem. Technical report, Plataanstraat 5, 5671, AL Nuenen, 1978. EWD-625

24. E.W. Dijkstra, Finding the correctness proof of a concurrent program, in *Program Construction, International Summer School* (Springer, London, 1979), pp. 24–34. http://dl.acm.org/citation.cfm?id=647639.733356

25. E.W. Dijkstra, The distributed snapshot of k.m. chandy and l. lamport, in *Proceedings of the NATO Advanced Study Institute on Control Flow and Data Flow: Concepts of Distributed Programming* (Springer, New York, 1986), pp. 513–517. http://dl.acm.org/citation.cfm?id=22086.22099. Also EWD-864a

26. E.W. Dijkstra, *A Discipline of Programming*, 1st edn. (Prentice Hall PTR, Upper Saddle River, 1997)

27. E.W. Dijkstra, C.S. Scholten, Termination detection for diffusing computations. Inf. Process. Lett. **11**(1), 1–4 (1980)

28. E.W. Dijkstra, L. Lamport, A.J. Martin, C.S. Scholten, E.F.M. Steffens, On-the-fly garbage collection: an exercise in cooperation. Commun. ACM **21**(11), 966–975 (1978). doi:10.1145/359642.359655. http://doi.acm.org/10.1145/359642.359655

29. E.W. Dijkstra, W.H.J. Feijen, A.J.M. van Gasteren, Derivation of a termination detection algorithm for distributed computations. Inf. Process. Lett. **16**(5), 217–219 (1983). Also EWD 840

30. N.J. Drost, J.V. Leeuwen, *Assertional Verification of a Majority Consensus Algorithm for Concurrency Control in Multiple Copy Databases* (Springer, New York, 1988). doi:10.1007/3-540-50403-6_48

31. M.R. Drost, A.A. Schoone, Assertional verification of a reset algorithm. Technical report, DSpace at Utrecht University [http://dspace.library.uu.nl:8080/dspace-oai/request] (Netherlands), 1988, http://igitur-archive.library.uu.nl/math/2006-1214-201542/UUindex.html

32. W.H.J. Feijen, A.J.M. van Gasteren, *On a Method of Multiprogramming* (Springer, New York, 1999)

33. D. Ginat, Adaptive ordering of contending processes in distributed systems. Ph.D. thesis, University of Maryland, Computer Science Department, College Park, 1989. CSTR-2335

34. D. Ginat, A.U. Shankar: An assertional proof of correctness and serializability of a distributed mutual exclusion algorithm based on path reversal. Technical report, University of Maryland, Computer Science Department, 1988. CSTR-2104

35. D. Ginat, A.U. Shankar, A.K. Agrawala, An efficient solution to the drinking philosophers problem and its extensions, in *Distributed Algorithms*, ed. by J.C. Bermond, M. Raynal. Lecture Notes in Computer Science, vol. 392 (Springer, Berlin/Heidelberg, 1989), pp. 83–93. http://dx.doi.org/10.1007/3-540-51687-5_34.10.1007/3-540-51687-5_34

36. D. Gries, An exercise in proving parallel programs correct. Commun. ACM **20**(12), 921–930 (1977). doi:10.1145/359897.359903. http://doi.acm.org/10.1145/359897.359903
37. D. Gries, *The Science of Programming*, 1st edn. (Springer, Secaucus, 1987)
38. B. Hailpern, S. Owicki, Modular verification of computer communication protocols. IEEE Trans. Commun. **31**(1), 56–68 (1983). doi:10.1109/TCOM.1983.1095720
39. M. Herlihy, N. Shavit, *The Art of Multiprocessor Programming* (Morgan Kaufmann Publishers, San Francisco, 2008)
40. C.A.R. Hoare, An axiomatic basis for computer programming. Commun. ACM **12**(10), 576–580 (1969). doi:10.1145/363235.363259. http://doi.acm.org/10.1145/363235.363259
41. E. Knapp, An exercise in the formal derivation of parallel programs: maximum flows in graphs. ACM Trans. Program. Lang. Syst. **12**(2), 203–223 (1990). doi:10.1145/78942.78945. http://doi.acm.org/10.1145/78942.78945
42. D.E. Knuth, Verification of link-level protocols. BIT **21**(1), 31–36 (1981)
43. R.A. Krzysztof, E.R. Olderog, *Verification of Sequential and Concurrent Programs* (Springer, New York, 1991)
44. P. Ladkin, L. Lamport, B. Olivier, D. Roegel, Lazy caching in tla. Distrib. Comput. **12**(2–3), 151–174 (1999). doi:10.1007/s004460050063. http://dx.doi.org/10.1007/s004460050063
45. S.S. Lam, A.U. Shankar, Specifying modules to satisfy interfaces: a state transition system approach. Distrib. Comput. **6**(1), 39–63 (1992). doi:10.1007/BF02276640. http://dx.doi.org/10.1007/BF02276640
46. L. Lamport, Proving the correctness of multiprocess programs. IEEE Trans. Softw. Eng. **3**(2), 125–143 (1977)
47. L. Lamport, An assertional correctness proof of a distributed algorithm. Sci. Comput. Program. **2**(3), 175–206 (1982)
48. L. Lamport, Specifying concurrent program modules. ACM Trans. Program. Lang. Syst. **5**(2), 190–222 (1983). doi:10.1145/69624.357207. http://doi.acm.org/10.1145/69624.357207
49. L. Lamport, A fast mutual exclusion algorithm. ACM Trans. Comput. Syst. **5**(1), 1–11 (1987). doi:10.1145/7351.7352. http://doi.acm.org/10.1145/7351.7352
50. L. Lamport, A theorem on atomicity in distributed algorithms. Distrib. Comput. **4**, 59–68 (1990). http://dx.doi.org/10.1007/BF01786631. 10.1007/BF01786631
51. L. Lamport, The temporal logic of actions. ACM Trans. Program. Lang. Syst. **16**(3), 872–923 (1994). doi:10.1145/177492.177726. http://doi.acm.org/10.1145/177492.177726
52. L. Lamport, How to make a correct multiprocess program execute correctly on a multiprocessor. IEEE Trans. Comput. **46**(7), 779–782 (1997). doi:10.1109/12.599898. http://dx.doi.org/10.1109/12.599898
53. L. Lamport, *Specifying Systems: The TLA+ Language and Tools for Hardware and Software Engineers* (Addison-Wesley Longman, Boston, 2002)
54. L. Lamport, F.B. Schneider, Pretending atomicity. Technical report, Cornell University, Ithaca, 1989
55. N.A. Lynch, *Distributed Algorithms* (Morgan Kaufmann Publishers, San Francisco, 1996)
56. N.A. Lynch, M.R. Tuttle, Hierarchical correctness proofs for distributed algorithms, in *Proceedings of the Sixth Annual ACM Symposium on Principles of Distributed Computing, PODC '87* (ACM, New York, 1987), pp. 137–151. doi:10.1145/41840.41852. http://doi.acm.org/10.1145/41840.41852
57. N.A. Lynch, M.R. Tuttle, An introduction to input/output automata. Technical report, MIT/LCS/TM-373 (1988). Also CWI-Quarterly, 2(3):219–246, September 1989
58. Z. Manna, *Introduction to Mathematical Theory of Computation* (McGraw-Hill, New York, 1974)
59. Z. Manna, A. Pnueli, Adequate proof principles for invariance and liveness properties of concurrent programs. Sci. Comput. Program. **4**(3), 257–289 (1984). doi:10.1016/0167-6423(84)90003-0. http://dx.doi.org/10.1016/0167-6423(84)90003-0
60. Z. Manna, A. Pnueli, *The Temporal Logic of Reactive and Concurrent Systems* (Springer, New York, 1992)

61. Z. Manna, A. Pnueli, *Temporal Verification of Reactive Systems: Safety* (Springer, New York, 1995)
62. J. Misra, A Discipline of Multiprogramming. ACM Comput. Surv. **28**(4es) (1996). doi:10. 1145/242224.242286. http://doi.acm.org/10.1145/242224.242286
63. J. Misra, *A Discipline of Multiprogramming: Programming Theory for Distributed Applications* (Springer, Secaucus, 2001)
64. S.L. Murphy, A.U. Shankar, A note on the drinking philosophers. ACM TOPLAS **10**(1), 178–188 (1988)
65. S.L. Murphy, A.U. Shankar, Connection management for the transport layer: service specification and protocol verification. IEEE Trans. Commun. **39**(12), 1762–1775 (1991). doi:10.1109/ 26.120163. Earlier version in Proceedings ACM SIGCOMM '87 Workshop, Stowe, Vermont, August, 1987
66. A.L. Oláh, Design and analysis of transport protocols for reliable high-speed communications. Ph.D. thesis, University of Twente, Enschede, 1997. http://doc.utwente.nl/13676/
67. A.L. Oláh, S.M.H. de Groot, Assertional verification of a connection management protocol, in *Proceedings of the IFIP TC6 Eighth International Conference on Formal Description Techniques VIII* (Chapman and Hall, London, 1996), pp. 401–416. http://dl.acm.org/citation. cfm?id=646214.681518
68. A.L. Oláh, S.M.H. de Groot, Alternative specification and verification of a periodic state exchange protocol. IEEE/ACM Trans. Netw. **5**(4), 525–529 (1997). doi:10.1109/90.649467. http://dx.doi.org/10.1109/90.649467
69. S. Owicki, D. Gries, An axiomatic proof technique for parallel programs – i. Acta Inform. **6**, 319–340 (1976)
70. S. Owicki, D. Gries, Verifying properties of parallel programs: an axiomatic approach. Commun. ACM **19**(5), 279–285 (1976). doi:10.1145/360051.360224 http://doi.acm.org/10. 1145/360051.360224
71. S. Owicki, L. Lamport, Proving liveness properties of concurrent programs. ACM Trans. Program. Lang. Syst. **4**(3), 455–495 (1982). doi:10.1145/357172.357178. http://doi.acm.org/ 10.1145/357172.357178
72. A. Pnueli, The temporal logic of programs, in *Proceedings of the 18th Annual Symposium on Foundations of Computer Science, SFCS '77* (IEEE Computer Society, Washington, DC, 1977), pp. 46–57. doi:10.1109/SFCS.1977.32. http://dx.doi.org/10.1109/SFCS.1977.32
73. A. Pnueli, The temporal semantics of concurrent programs, in *Proceedings of the International Sympoisum on Semantics of Concurrent Computation* (Springer, London, 1979), pp. 1–20. http://dl.acm.org/citation.cfm?id=647172.716123
74. A.A. Schoone, Verification of connection-management protocols. Technical report, DSpace at Utrecht University [http://dspace.library.uu.nl:8080/dspace-oai/request] (Netherlands), 1987. http://igitur-archive.library.uu.nl/math/2006-1214-201341/UUindex.html
75. A.U. Shankar, Verified data transfer protocols with variable flow control. ACM Trans. Comput. Syst. **7**(3), 281–316 (1989). doi:10.1145/65000.65003. http://doi.acm.org/10.1145/ 65000.65003
76. A.U. Shankar, An introduction to assertional reasoning for concurrent systems. ACM Comput. Surv. **25**(3), 225–262 (1993). doi:10.1145/158439.158441. http://doi.acm.org/10.1145/ 158439.158441
77. A.U. Shankar, S.S. Lam, An HDLC protocol specification and its verification using image protocols. ACM Trans. Comput. Syst. **1**(4), 331–368 (1983). doi:10.1145/357377.357384. http://doi.acm.org/10.1145/357377.357384
78. A.U. Shankar, S.S. Lam, Time-dependent distributed systems: proving safety, liveness and real-time properties. Distrib. Comput. **2**, 61–79 (1987). http://dx.doi.org/10.1007/BF01667079. 10.1007/BF01667079
79. A.U. Shankar, S.S. Lam, A stepwise refinement heuristic for protocol construction. ACM Trans. Program. Lang. Syst. **14**(3), 417–461 (1992). doi:10.1145/129393.129394. http:// doi.acm.org/10.1145/129393.129394. Earlier version appeared in Stepwise Refinement of Distributed Systems, LNCS 430, Springer, 1990

80. A.U. Shankar, D. Lee, Minimum-latency transport protocols with modulo-n incarnation numbers. IEEE/ACM Trans. Netw. **3**(3), 255–268 (1995). doi:10.1109/90.392385. http://dx. doi.org/10.1109/90.392385

81. M.G. Staskauskas, The formal specification and design of a distributed electronic funds-transfer system. IEEE Trans. Comput. **37**(12), 1515–1528 (1988). doi:10.1109/12.9730. http:// dx.doi.org/10.1109/12.9730

82. K. Suonio, *A Practical Theory of Reactive Systems: Incremental Modeling of Dynamic Behaviors* (Springer, Secaucus, 2005). (Texts in Theoretical Computer Science. An EATCS Series)

83. G. Tel, Assertional verification of a timer-based protocol. Technical report, DSpace at Utrecht University [http://dspace.library.uu.nl:8080/dspace-oai/request] (Netherlands), 1987. http:// igitur-archive.library.uu.nl/math/2006-1214-201352/UUindex.html

84. G. Tel, F. Mattern, The derivation of distributed termination detection algorithms from garbage collection schemes. ACM Trans. Program. Lang. Syst. **15**(1), 1–35 (1993). doi: 10.1145/151646.151647. http://doi.acm.org/10.1145/151646.151647

85. G. Tel, R.B. Tan, J. van Leeuwen, The derivation of graph marking algorithms from distributed termination detection protocols. Sci. Comput. Program. **10**(2), 107–137 (1988). doi:10.1016/ 0167-6423(88)90024-X. http://dx.doi.org/10.1016/0167-6423(88)90024-X

Chapter 7
Implements and Compositionality

7.1 Introduction

This chapter presents the core of SESF theory in four parts. Section 7.2 defines what it means for program A to implement program B in terms of the evolutions of A and B. Section 7.3 establishes compositionality: if program A implements program B, then replacing an instantiation of B in any program C by an instantiation of A preserves all the properties of program C (excluding, of course, internal properties of the replaced instantiation of B). Section 7.4 presents the program version of "A implements B" for the case where B is a service program without internal parameters. Briefly, A implements B iff the composite system of A and B-inverse satisfies B-inverse's input conditions and progress condition. Section 7.5 extends the program version of "A implements B" to the case where B is a service program with internal parameters, essentially by converting the internal parameters into external parameters.

7.1.1 Conventions

In this chapter, the term "system" refers to an aggregate system, unless otherwise stated. We now recall some definitions.

A system **allows** an input e in a state s, or e is **allowed** in s, if e is an input of the system and e's input assumption (or input condition, if a service) holds in s. A system **can accept** an input e in a state s, or e is **acceptable** in s, if e is an input of the system and the system does not become faulty when it receives e in s. A transition is said to be **enabled** at the end of an evolution if the final state of the evolution is the start state of the transition.

For any evolution x of an aggregate system, $ext(x)$ denotes the sequence of inputs and outputs of x. (Entries of composite internal transitions in x, if any, do not appear in $ext(x)$).

A.U. Shankar, *Distributed Programming: Theory and Practice*, 173
DOI 10.1007/978-1-4614-4881-5__7,
© Springer Science+Business Media New York 2013

Given a program B and an evolution x of a program A, we say x is **safe wrt** B to mean that x is fault-free and either $ext(x)$ is empty or there is an evolution y of B such that $ext(x)$ equals $ext(y)$. Given a non-empty sequence p of inputs and outputs, we say $x \circ p$ is **safe wrt** B to mean that x is fault-free and there is an evolution y of B such that $ext(x) \circ p$ equals $ext(y)$.

Given a program B and an evolution x of a program A, we say x is **complete wrt** B to mean that x is fault-free and either $ext(x)$ is empty or there is a complete evolution y of B (i.e., satisfying B's progress assumption) such that $ext(x)$ equals $ext(y)$.

Let C be a composite system and P be the composite system of a subset of the basic systems of C. For any transition t of C, the **image of t on P**, denoted $t.P$, is t with every state s in t replaced by $s.P$ if t involves a transition of P, and the empty sequence otherwise. For any evolution x of C, the **image of x on P**, denoted $x.P$, is the sequence obtained by replacing every transition t by $t.P$.

End of conventions

7.2   Implements

Definition (implements). Program A **implements** program B, also stated as "A satisfies the **implements conditions wrt** B", if the following hold:

Safety condition:

- (Instantiation) For every value of B's program parameters (if any): if B's instantiation is fault-free then A's instantiation is fault-free.
- (Input) For every finite evolution x of A such that x is safe wrt B, and for every input e of B such that $x \circ \langle e \rangle$ is safe wrt B: A can accept e in the last state of x.
- (Internal) For every finite evolution x of A such that x is safe wrt B, for every (composite or basic) internal transition t of A that is enabled in the last state of x: t is fault-free.
- (Output) For every finite evolution x of A such that x is safe wrt B, for every output transition t of A that is enabled in the last state of x: t is fault-free and $x \circ \langle e \rangle$, where e is the output in t, is safe wrt B.

Progress condition:

- For every evolution x of A such that x is safe wrt B: if x satisfies A's progress assumption then x is complete wrt B.   □

The safety instantiation condition ensures that A can be instantiated successfully wherever B is instantiated successfully. The safety input condition ensures that A is ready to accept any input that would keep the behavior safe wrt B. The safety internal and safety output conditions ensure that any activity initiated by A keeps the behavior safe wrt B. The safety conditions together ensure that as long as the environment does not give an input to A that would be unsafe wrt B, every possible evolution of A is fault-free and safe wrt B. The progress condition says that every possible evolution of A is complete wrt B provided the underlying platform satisfies A's progress assumption.

Note that the definition of "A implements B" does not say anything about the input assumptions of A. It does not require that every input that is safe wrt B also be allowed by A. It requires A to be fault-free if its inputs are safe wrt B, but it does not require that A be fault-free. One may prefer A to satisfy the stronger requirements, which results in the following stronger version of the implements safety condition.

Definition (implements strong-safety condition). Program A satisfies the **implements strong-safety condition wrt** program B if the following hold:

- (fault-freedom) A is fault-free (i.e., each of its allowed evolutions is fault-free).
- (instantiation) For every value of B's program parameters (if any): if B's instantiation is fault-free then A's input assumption holds.
- (input) For every finite evolution x of A such that x is safe wrt B, and for every input e of B such that $x \circ \langle e \rangle$ is safe wrt B: A allows e at the end of x.
- (output) For every finite evolution x of A such that x is safe wrt B, for every output e that A can do in the last state of x: $x \circ \langle e \rangle$ is safe wrt B.   □

7.3 Compositionality

We now establish that if a program implements another program, then in any context an instantiation of the latter program can be replaced by an instantiation of the former without disturbing any property not involving the internals of the replaced system. More precisely, let program $\mathcal{A}'$ implement program $\mathcal{A}$, and let $\mathcal{C}$ be any program that starts (perhaps only in some evolutions) an instantiation, say A, of $\mathcal{A}$. Let $\mathcal{C}'$ be $\mathcal{C}$ except that the instantiation A of $\mathcal{A}$ is replaced by an instantiation of $\mathcal{A}'$; i.e., $\mathcal{A}$ is changed to $\mathcal{A}'$ in the appropriate startSystem statement. We want $\mathcal{C}'$ to satisfy the following conditions. First, if $\mathcal{C}$ implements a program $\mathcal{D}$ then $\mathcal{C}'$ also should implement $\mathcal{D}$. Second, for any assertion P not involving the state of A (but perhaps involving the inputs and outputs of A), if $\mathcal{C}$ satisfies P assuming its inputs are safe wrt $\mathcal{D}$ then $\mathcal{C}'$ should satisfy P assuming its inputs are safe wrt $\mathcal{D}$. All this is formalized in the following theorem, which is proved in Sect. 7.6.

Theorem 7.1 (compositionality). *Let programs $\mathcal{A}'$, $\mathcal{A}$, $\mathcal{C}$, $\mathcal{C}'$, and $\mathcal{D}$ satisfy the following:*

- *$\mathcal{A}'$ implements $\mathcal{A}$.*
- *$\mathcal{C}$ implements $\mathcal{D}$.*
- *$\mathcal{C}$ starts (perhaps only in some evolutions) an instantiation A of $\mathcal{A}$.*
- *$\mathcal{C}'$ is $\mathcal{C}$ with A replaced by an instantiation A' of $\mathcal{A}'$.*

Let $\widehat{\mathcal{C}}$ denote the composite system consisting of the aggregate system $\mathcal{C}$ minus the aggregate system A. Then the following hold:

(a) C' implements D.

(b) If an evolution x' of C' is safe wrt D, then there is an evolution x of C such that $x.\widehat{C}$ equals $x'.\widehat{C}$.

(c) If an evolution x' of C' is safe wrt D and satisfies C''s progress assumption, then there is an evolution x of C such that $x.\widehat{C}$ equals $x'.\widehat{C}$ and x satisfies C's progress assumption.   □

Parts b and c are just a way of stating that for any assertion P not involving the state of A, if C satisfies P assuming C's inputs are safe wrt D, then C' satisfies P assuming C''s inputs are safe wrt D.

7.4   Program Version of Implements for Services without Internal Parameters

Given a service *without internal parameters* and a candidate implementation, we now express the conditions for the candidate implementation to implement the service in terms of their programs. Throughout this section, let B(x) denote the service program with parameters x, and let A(x,y) denote the candidate implementation program with parameters x and y. Program A may not use all the parameters in x, in which case those parameters can be removed from A's header.

The first step is to transform service program B(x) to its inverse program; the latter has the same evolutions as B(x) but with inputs and outputs interchanged. The structure of service programs allows this to be done mechanically, by changing input functions into output functions and vice versa. Figure 7.1 shows the transformation.

The first row in Fig. 7.1 shows the changes to the header and main code. The program name is changed to any conflict-free name. Any program parameters, denoted by *sparams* in the figure, are retained. An additional program parameter, say *xrval*, is added, which will be set to the value *rval* returned by the main code of the candidate implementation being tested, except that any mysid in *rval* is changed to a new parameter, say impsid, in *xrval*. The service inverse needs *xrval* to call input functions of the candidate implementation.

The second row in Fig. 7.1 shows how an input function of the service is changed to an output function of the service inverse.

- The input part of the service function becomes the output part of the service-inverse function. In the function header, input becomes output, the function name is changed to any conflict-free name, the parameters (if any) are retained, and the return type is removed. The input condition becomes an output condition. The body remains the same but it now ends with an output call to the candidate implementation's input function. The call's sid prefix, *xsid*, is impsid if *sid* is mysid, otherwise *xsid* is *sid*. (So it has the same *value* as the sid prefix, *sid*, in the original input function header.)

Service program	$\Longrightarrow$	Service inverse program

- -

```
service SrvName(sparams) {          service SrvNameInverse(sparams, xrval) {
  ic {predicate}         ⟹          ic {predicate}
  code                               code
  generate sids;                     generate sids;
  return rval;                       return rval mysid;
```

                                    // xrval is rval [mysid | impsid]

- -

```
input Rtype sid.fname(fparams) {    output doFname(xsid, params) {
  ic {predicate1}        ⟹            oc {predicate1}
  code1                               code1
  output (rval) {                     Rtype rval ← xsid.fname(fparams);
    oc {predicate2}                   ic {predicate2}
    code2                             code2
    return rval;                      return;
  }                                 }
}
```

                                    // xsid is impsid if sid is mysid
                                    // else xsid is sid

- -

```
output doFname(sid, params) {       input Rtype sid.fname(fparams) {
  oc {predicate1}                     ic {predicate1}
  code1                  ⟹            code1
  Rtype rval ← sid.fname(fparams);    output (rval) {
  ic {predicate2}                       oc {predicate2}
  code2                                 code2
  return;                               return rval;
}                                     }
                                    }
```

- -

```
atomicity assumption {...}     ⟹     atomicity assumption {...}
```

- -

```
progress assumption {assertions}   ⟹   progress condition {
                                          assertions [mysid | impsid]
                                        }
```

Fig. 7.1 Transforming a service program to its inverse program

```
program AB̄(x,y) {
    ia {f(x,y)}              // B(x).ic ⇒ forsome(y: f(x,y))
    inputs(); outputs();     // closed system
    atomic {
        a ← startSystem(A(x,y));
        b̄ ← startSystem(B̄(x,a));
    }
}
```

Fig. 7.2 Closed program of candidate implementation and service inverse

- The output part of the service function becomes the input part of the service-inverse function. The first step is to store the returned value (if any) of the output call in a variable of the same name as the input function's output parameter, *rval*. The output condition becomes an input condition. The body remains the same except that any return value is removed. (Note that the body can involve *rval*.)

The third row in Fig. 7.1 shows how an output function of the service is changed to an input function of the service inverse. The transformation is exactly the reverse of what happens to a service's input function, i.e., same as the second row but with the arrow going from right to left. (The issue of *xsid* does not arise here.)

The fourth row in Fig. 7.1 shows that there is no change to the atomicity assumption. Each input part and each output part is still atomic.

The fifth row in Fig. 7.1 shows the changes to the progress assumption. The assertions are the same except that any mysid is changed to impsid, and "progress assumption" is changed to "progress condition".

Let B̄(a,x) denote the inverse program of service B(x), as defined by the transformations in Fig. 7.1. The next step is to define the *closed* program of instantiations of the candidate implementation A(x,y) and the service inverse B̄(a,x). This program, denoted AB̄(x,y), is shown in Fig. 7.2. Program AB̄(x,y)'s input assumption, denoted by f(x,y) in the figure, must not constrain B(x).ic. More precisely, for every value of x that satisfies B(x).ic, there must be a value of y that satisfies f(x,y); i.e., predicate B(x).ic ⇒ forsome(y: f(x,y)) must hold.

The following theorem expresses the conditions for "A(x,y) implements B(x)" in terms of correctness properties of program AB̄(x,y).

Theorem 7.2 (program-based implements). *Let programs* B(x), B̄(a,x), A(x,y) *and* AB̄(x,y), *or* AB̄ *for short, be as defined above. Then the following hold:*

(a) A(x,y) satisfies the implements safety condition wrt B(x)
   iff AB̄ *is fault-free*
   iff AB̄ *satisfies* Inv((thread at b̄.ic{P}) ⇒ b̄.P)
      for every input condition ic{P} *in* b̄.
(b) A satisfies the implements progress condition wrt B
   iff AB̄ *satisfies* b̄'s *progress condition.*
(c) A satisfies the implements strong-safety condition wrt B *iff*

- *(fault-freedom)* A *is fault-free.*
- *(output) For every input condition* ic[P] *in* $\overline{b}$:
    $A\overline{B}$ *satisfies* $Inv((\text{thread at } \overline{b}.\text{ic[P]}) \Rightarrow \overline{b}.P)$.
- *(input) For every input assumption* ia[P] *in* a:
    $A\overline{B}$ *satisfies* $Inv((\text{thread at a.ia[P]}) \Rightarrow \text{a.P})$.   □

Theorem 7.2 is proved in Sect. 7.7, except for the last "iff" in part a, which we prove now. If an assertion $Inv((\text{thread at } \overline{b}.\text{ic[P]}) \Rightarrow \overline{b}.P)$ is not satisfied by $A\overline{B}$, then there is an evolution in which $\overline{b}$ gets a disallowed input, which means that $\overline{b}$, and hence $A\overline{B}$, becomes faulty. Conversely, if $A\overline{B}$ becomes faulty then it does not satisfy any assertion.

7.5   Program Version of Implements for Services with Internal Parameters

We now develop a program version of "A implements B" for the case where B is a service with internal parameters. The basic idea is (1) to modify B to a service without internal nondeterminism by augmenting its outputs with internal parameters, and (2) to modify A to implement this modified B by augmenting its outputs with the corresponding internal parameters in B. The previous program version of the implements relation (for services without internal nondeterminism) can then be applied to the modified A and the modified B. The rest of this section restates this rigorously.

The modification to B is straightforward. For every output function that has internal parameters, add the internal parameters to its output call; i.e., if f(x,u,v) is an output function with output x.e(u) and internal parameter v, then replace output x.e(u) by x.e(u,v). Similarly, for every input function whose output part has internal parameters, add the internal parameters to its output return; i.e., if the output part does return rval and has internal parameter v, then replace output return rval by return [rval,v]. We refer to the modified B as B **externalized**, and denote it by $\widehat{B}$. Note that $\widehat{B}$ has no internal nondeterminism and its outputs differ from those of B.

The modification to A is similar but not as simple, because in addition to augmenting its outputs with internal parameters, one has to introduce code that assigns values to these new parameters. We refer to the modified A as A **externalized**, and denote it by $\widehat{A}$. Consider an output call x.e(a) in A. Suppose that the corresponding output call x.e(u) in B has become x.e(u,v) in $\widehat{B}$, where v is an internal parameter in B. Then call x.e(a) in A has to become call x.e(a,b) in $\widehat{A}$, where b is a value of parameter v. Furthermore, $\widehat{A}$ should choose the value b such that extending the current evolution of $\widehat{A}$ with x.e(a,b) is safe wrt $\widehat{B}$. Auxiliary variables may be introduced in $\widehat{A}$ for use in computing these values. This motivates the following definition.

Definition (externalizer). An A-to-B **externalizer** is a function in the variables of A such that, given any finite evolution x of A that is safe wrt B and any output e that A can do at the end of x, the externalizer returns a value of the internal parameters of the corresponding output in B. Auxiliary variables can be added to A to be used in the externalizer function.   □

An externalizer is just like any regular function of A, except that it does not affect the evolution of A but only returns some information about its current evolution, i.e., makes external some internal state of A. Given an A-to-B externalizer ψ, define A **externalized with** ψ, denoted by $\widehat{A}_\psi$, to be A augmented by ψ and with every output augmented with the value of ψ; i.e., every output call x.e(u) is replaced by x.e(u,ψ), and every output return return u is replaced by return [u,ψ]. Thus, if A has the same outputs as B, then $\widehat{A}_\psi$ has the same outputs as $\widehat{B}$.

The following two theorems are proved in Sect. 7.8. The first theorem states that A implements B if there is an A-to-B externalizer ψ such that $\widehat{A}_\psi$ implements $\widehat{B}$. The second theorem states that if A implements B then there exists such an externalizer. Finding an externalizer is not a mechanical procedure, but given it one can use Theorem 7.2 to obtain a program-based version of "$\widehat{A}_\psi$ implements $\widehat{B}$".

Theorem 7.3 (externalizer implies implements). *Given a program* A, *a service program* B *with internal parameters, and an* A-to-B *externalizer* ψ, *the following hold:*

(a) *If the safety condition of "$\widehat{A}_\psi$ implements $\widehat{B}$" holds then the safety condition of "A implements B" holds.*

(b) *If the progress condition of "$\widehat{A}_\psi$ implements $\widehat{B}$ holds" then the progress condition of "A implements B" holds.*   □

Theorem 7.4 (implements implies externalizer). *Given a program* A *and a service program* B *with internal parameters, if* A *implements* B *then there exists an* A-to-B *externalizer* ψ *such that* A_ψ *implements* $\widehat{B}$.   □

7.6   Proof of Theorem 7.1

The assumptions of Theorem 7.1 are restated below for ease of reference. Throughout this section, A', A, C', C, A', A, $\widehat{C}$ and D are as stated below.

- Program A' implements program A.
- Program C starts (perhaps in only some evolutions) an instantiation A of A.
- Program C' is C with A replaced by an instantiation A' of A'.
- $\widehat{C}$ is the composite system of the aggregate system of C minus the aggregate system A.
- Program C implements a program D.

We first establish the following lemma.

Lemma 7.1. *If an evolution x' of C' is safe wrt D then the image $x'.A'$ is safe wrt A.*   □

Proof. The proof is by induction on the number of transitions in x'. For the base case, we show that C''s instantiation is fault-free. If C''s instantiation does not start A' then it is the same as C's instantiation; this is fault-free because C implements $\mathcal{D}$. If C''s instantiation starts A' then it is the same as C's instantiation with A's creation replaced by A''s creation; this is fault-free because $\mathcal{A}'$ implements $\mathcal{A}$.

For the induction step, assume that the lemma holds for evolutions of n transitions and consider an evolution y' of C' that is safe wrt $\mathcal{D}$ and has $n+1$ transitions. Let t' be the last transition in y' and let x' be the prefix of y' excluding the last transition, i.e., $y' = x' \circ \langle t' \rangle$. Then x' is an evolution of C' that has n transitions and is safe wrt $\mathcal{D}$ (because it is a prefix of y'). So by the induction hypothesis, $x'.A'$ is safe wrt A. Hence there is a fault-free evolution x_A of A such that $ext(x_A) = ext(x'.A')$. Evolutions x_A and $x'.\widehat{C}$ are signature-compatible (because $x'.A'$ and $x'.\widehat{C}$ are signature-compatible). Hence x_A and $x'.\widehat{C}$ can be stitched together to form a fault-free evolution, say x, of C such that $x.A = x_A$ and $x.\widehat{C} = x'.\widehat{C}$.

Now consider the different cases of t'.

Let t' not involve A', i.e., $t'.A'$ is null. Then $t'.\widehat{C}$ is a transition of $\widehat{C}$ that is enabled at the end of $x'.\widehat{C}$ and hence at the end of $x.\widehat{C}$. If $t'.\widehat{C}$ is an output or internal transition of $\widehat{C}$, it is fault-free (because C implements $\mathcal{D}$ and x' is safe wrt $\mathcal{D}$). If $t'.\widehat{C}$ is an input transition of $\widehat{C}$, it is fault-free (because C implements $\mathcal{D}$ and y' is safe wrt $\mathcal{D}$). So y' is fault-free. So $y'.A'$ is fault-free. It is safe wrt A because $x'.A'$ is safe wrt A and t' does not involve A' and hence does not involve A.

Let t' be an output transition of C' involving A', i.e., $t'.A'$ is an output transition of A'. Then $y'.A'$ is fault-free and safe wrt A (because $\mathcal{A}'$ implements $\mathcal{A}$ and $x'.A'$ is safe wrt A).

Let t' be an internal transition of C' involving only A'. The previous argument for the case where t' is an output transition also works here.

Let t' be an input transition involving A', i.e., $t'.A'$ is an input transition of A' and its input, say e, is also an input of $\mathcal{D}$. (This case includes the creation of A' by a system outside C'.) Because y' is safe wrt $\mathcal{D}$ (from assumption), $x' \circ \langle e \rangle$, and hence $x \circ \langle e \rangle$, is safe wrt $\mathcal{D}$, and so A can accept e at the end of x (because A is part of C and C implements $\mathcal{D}$). So $x.A \circ \langle e \rangle$ is safe wrt A. So A' can accept e at the end of $x'.A'$ (because $\mathcal{A}'$ implements $\mathcal{A}$). So $t'.A'$ is fault-free. So $y'.A'$ is safe wrt A.

Let t' be a composite internal transition in which A' does an output e to $\widehat{C}$, i.e., $t'.A'$ is an output transition of A', $t'.\widehat{C}$ is an input transition of $\widehat{C}$, and e is an input of $\widehat{C}$. Then $x' \circ \langle e \rangle$ is safe wrt A (because $\mathcal{A}'$ implements $\mathcal{A}$). Also $t'.\widehat{C}$ is fault-free (because A can output e at the end of x and C can accept this because it implements $\mathcal{D}$). So t' is fault-free. So y' is safe wrt A.

Let t' be a composite internal transition in which $\widehat{C}$ calls an input e of A', i.e., $t'.A'$ is an input transition of A' and $t'.\widehat{C}$ is an output transition of $\widehat{C}$. (This case includes the creation of A' by a basic system in $\widehat{C}$.) Because C implements $\mathcal{D}$ and x is safe wrt $\mathcal{D}$, $t'.\widehat{C}$ is fault-free. Hence A can accept e at the end of $x.A$. Hence A' can accept e at the end of $x'.A'$ (because $ext(x'.A')$ equals $ext(x.A)$ and $\mathcal{A}'$ implements $\mathcal{A}$). $\square$

7.6.1 Proof of Safety Parts of Theorem 7.1

We now establish the safety condition of "C' implements D" and part b of the theorem.

Instantiation: We have already established that C''s instantiation is fault-free (base case of proof of Lemma 7.1).

Part b of theorem: Let x' be a finite evolution of C' that is safe wrt D. So $x'.A'$ is safe wrt A (by Lemma 7.1). So there is a finite fault-free evolution x_A of A such that $ext(x'.A')$ equals $ext(x_A)$. So there is a finite fault-free evolution x of C such that $x.\widehat{C}$ equals $x'.\widehat{C}$ and $ext(x.A)$ equals $ext(x_A)$. This establishes part b of the theorem.

In the remainder of this proof, x', x_A and x are as defined above. To repeat:

- x' is a finite evolution of C' that is safe wrt D.
- x_A is a finite fault-free evolution of A such that $ext(x'.A')$ equals $ext(x_A)$.
- x is a finite fault-free evolution of C such that $x.\widehat{C}$ equals $x'.\widehat{C}$ and $ext(x.A)$ equals $ext(x_A)$.

Input: Let e be an input of D such that $x' \circ \langle e \rangle$ is safe wrt D. Then $x \circ \langle e \rangle$ is safe wrt D. Thus C can accept e at the end of x (because C implements D). In particular, if e is an input of $\widehat{C}$, then $\widehat{C}$ can accept e at the end of x, hence at the end of $x'.\widehat{C}$, hence at the end of x'. If e is an input of A, then A can accept e at the end of x hence at the end of $x'.A$. Hence A' can accept e at the end of $x'.A'$ (because A' implements A) and hence at the end of x'. So in either case, C' can accept e. This establishes input condition of C' implements D.

Internal: Let t' involve an internal transition of $\widehat{C}$ that is enabled at the end of x'. Then $t'.\widehat{C}$ is enabled at the end of x and hence is fault-free (because C implements D). Hence t' is fault-free. Hence $x' \circ \langle t' \rangle$ is fault-free and safe wrt D (because x' is safe wrt D and t' is internal).

Let t' be an internal transition of A' that is enabled at the end of x'. Then $t'.A'$ is fault-free (because $x'.A'$ is safe wrt A and A' implements A). Hence t' is fault-free. Hence $x' \circ \langle t' \rangle$ is fault-free and safe wrt D (because x' is safe wrt D and t' is internal).

Let t' be a composite internal transition of C' in which $\widehat{C}$ calls input e of A'. Then $t'.\widehat{C}$ is enabled at the end of $x.\widehat{C}$. Hence A can accept e at the end of x (because x' is safe wrt D and C implements D). So A' can accept e at the end of x' (because $x'.A'$ is safe wrt A and A' implements A). Hence t' is fault-free. Hence $x' \circ \langle t' \rangle$ is fault-free and safe wrt D (because x' is safe wrt D and t' is internal).

Let t' be a composite internal transition of C' in which A' calls input e of $\widehat{C}$. Then $t'.A'$ is fault-free (because $x'.A'$ is safe wrt A and A' implements A). Also $t'.\widehat{C}$ is fault-free (because A has an evolution, say z_A, such that $ext(z_A) = ext(x_A) \circ \langle e \rangle$, and $\widehat{C}$ can accept this at the end of x (otherwise C would not implement D)). Hence t' is fault-free. Hence $x' \circ \langle t' \rangle$ is fault-free and safe wrt D (because x' is safe wrt D and t' is internal). This establishes internal safety condition of C' implements D.

Output: Let t' be an output transition of C' involving $\widehat{C}$ doing an output e. Then $t'.\widehat{C}$ is an output transition of $\widehat{C}$ which is enabled at the end of $x.\widehat{C}$. Hence $x \circ \langle t'.\widehat{C} \rangle$ is safe wrt $\mathcal{D}$ (because $\mathcal{C}$ implements $\mathcal{D}$). Hence $x' \circ \langle t'.\widehat{\mathcal{C}} \rangle$ is safe wrt $\mathcal{D}$. Hence $x' \circ \langle t' \rangle$ is safe wrt $\mathcal{D}$.

Let t' be an output transition of C' involving A' doing an output e. Then $t'.A'$ is an output transition of A'. Hence $t'.A'$ is fault-free and A can output e at the end of x (because $\mathcal{A}'$ implements $\mathcal{A}$ and $x'.A'$ is safe wrt A). Hence $x \circ \langle e \rangle$ is safe wrt $\mathcal{D}$ (because $\mathcal{C}$ implements $\mathcal{D}$). Hence $x' \circ \langle t' \rangle$ is safe wrt $\mathcal{D}$. This establishes internal safety condition of C' implements $\mathcal{D}$.   □

7.6.2 *Proof of Progress Parts of Theorem 7.1*

We establish the progress condition of C' implements $\mathcal{D}$ and part c of the theorem. Let x' be an evolution of C' such that x' is safe wrt $\mathcal{D}$ and x' satisfies C''s progress assumption. Then $x'.A'$ is safe wrt A (by Lemma 7.1) and satisfies A''s progress assumption (by Theorem 6.1). Hence $x'.A'$ is complete wrt A (because $\mathcal{A}'$ implements $\mathcal{A}$). So there is an evolution x_A of A such that $ext(x_A)$ equals $ext(x'.A')$ and x_A satisfies A's progress assumption. So x_A and $x'.\widehat{\mathcal{C}}$ can be stitched together (by Theorem 6.2) to yield an evolution x of C such that x is safe wrt $\mathcal{D}$, $ext(x)$ equals $ext(x')$, and x satisfies the progress assumption of A and $\widehat{\mathcal{C}}$. Hence x is complete wrt $\mathcal{D}$ (because $\mathcal{C}$ implements $\mathcal{D}$).   □

7.7 Proof of Theorem 7.2

The assumptions of Theorem 7.2 are restated below for ease of reference, along with some notation:

- A is a program.
- B is a service program without internal parameters.
- $\bar{B}$ is B-inverse.
- $A\bar{B}$ is the closed program with instantiation a of A and instantiation $\bar{b}$ of $\bar{B}$.
- For any evolution x, let $inverse(x)$ denote x with input transitions changed to output transitions and vice versa.

The following lemma holds immediately from the definitions of $\bar{B}$ and $A\bar{B}$, and evolution stitching (Theorem 6.2).

Lemma 7.2. *Given fault-free evolutions x_A of A and x_B of B such that $ext(x_A) = ext(x_B)$, the following hold:*

- *$inverse(x_B)$ is an evolution of $\bar{B}$.*
- *$inverse(x_B)$ is signature-compatible with x_A.*
- *There exists an evolution $x_{A\bar{B}}$ of $A\bar{B}$ such that $x_{A\bar{B}}.a = x_A$ and $x_{A\bar{B}}.\bar{b} = inverse(x_B)$.*
                                                □

The following lemma covers one direction of part a of Theorem 7.2.

Lemma 7.3. *If* $A\overline{B}$ *is fault-free then the safety condition of "*A *implements* B*" holds.*
                                                                                                    □

Proof. The proof is by contradiction. Assume that the safety condition of A implements B does not hold. We need to show that $A\overline{B}$ is faulty.

Suppose the instantiation condition does not hold. Then A's instantiation is faulty, which makes $A\overline{B}$'s instantiation faulty, and hence $A\overline{B}$ is faulty.

Suppose the input condition does not hold. Then there exists a finite evolution x_A of A and an input e of B such that $x_A \circ \langle e \rangle$ is safe wrt B but A cannot accept it. Because $x_A \circ \langle e \rangle$ is safe wrt B there exists a finite fault-free evolution y_B of B such that $ext(y_B)$ equals $ext(x_A) \circ \langle e \rangle$. Let t_B be the last transition in y_B and let x_B be the prefix of y_B excluding this last transition, that is, $y_B = x_B \circ \langle t_B \rangle$ and $ext(x_B) = ext(x_A)$. Then, by Lemma 7.2, there exists an evolution $x_{A\overline{B}}$ of $A\overline{B}$ such that $x_{A\overline{B}}.a = x_A$ and $x_{A\overline{B}}.\overline{b} = inverse(x_B)$. So $\overline{B}$ can call input e at the end of $x_{A\overline{B}}$, which A cannot accept (by the above supposition), causing $A\overline{B}$ to become faulty.

Suppose the internal or output condition does not hold. Then there exists a finite evolution x_A of A and a transition t_A such that x_A is safe wrt B but $x_A \circ \langle t_A \rangle$ is not safe wrt B. Because x_A is safe wrt B there exists a finite fault-free evolution x_B of B such that $ext(x_B) = ext(x_A)$. So by Lemma 7.2, there exists an evolution $x_{A\overline{B}}$ of $A\overline{B}$ such that $x_{A\overline{B}}.a = x_A$ and $x_{A\overline{B}}.\overline{b} = inverse(x_B)$. So A can execute transition t_A at the end of $x_{A\overline{B}}$.

Suppose $x_A \circ \langle t_A \rangle$ is not safe wrt B because t_A is faulty. Then this faulty transition is also possible in $A\overline{B}$. Suppose $x_A \circ \langle t_A \rangle$ is not safe wrt B because t_A does an output e and $x_A \circ \langle e \rangle$ is not safe wrt B. Then e is not accepted by B at the end of $x_{A\overline{B}}.B$ (otherwise B would have an evolution that extends $inverse(x_{A\overline{B}}.B)$ by e). So in either case, $A\overline{B}$ would have a faulty evolution.   □

The following lemma covers the other direction of part a of Theorem 7.2. It relies on B(x) having *no internal parameters* (and hence no internal non-determinism).

Lemma 7.4. *If the safety condition of* A *implements* B *holds then* $A\overline{B}$ *is fault-free.*   □

Proof. The proof is by contradiction. Assume that $A\overline{B}$ has a faulty evolution $y_{A\overline{B}}$. We need to show that the safety condition of A implements B does not hold.

Suppose $y_{A\overline{B}}$ consists only of the instantiation transition. Then A's instantiation is faulty (because $A\overline{B}$'s instantiation consists of the instantiations of A and $\overline{B}$, and the latter is the same as B's instantiation, which is fault-free).

Suppose $y_{A\overline{B}} = x_{A\overline{B}} \circ \langle t_{A\overline{B}} \rangle$, where $x_{A\overline{B}}$ is fault-free and $t_{A\overline{B}}$ is faulty. Then $x_{A\overline{B}}.a$ is a fault-free evolution of A and $x_{A\overline{B}}.\overline{b}$ is a fault-free evolution of $\overline{B}$. So $inverse(x_{A\overline{B}}.\overline{b})$ is a fault-free evolution of B and $ext(inverse(x_{A\overline{B}}.\overline{b}))$ equals $ext(x_{A\overline{B}}.a)$. So $x_{A\overline{B}}.a$ is safe wrt B.

Suppose $t_{A\overline{B}}$ involves an internal or output transition of A and is faulty. Then $t_{A\overline{B}}.a$ is faulty and can be executed at the end of $x_{A\overline{B}}.a$. So the safety condition of A implements B does not hold.

Suppose $t_{A\bar{B}}$ involves an input e of A which $\bar{B}$ outputs and A cannot accept. Then $x_{A\bar{B}}.a \circ \langle e \rangle$ is safe wrt B but A cannot accept the input e at the end of evolution $x_{A\bar{B}}.a$. So the safety condition of A implements B does not hold.

Suppose $t_{A\bar{B}}$ involves a output e done by A such that $t_{A\bar{B}}.B$ is faulty. Because B is a service, the only way for $t_{A\bar{B}}.B$ to be faulty is if $\bar{b}$ does not allow e at the end of $x_{A\bar{B}}.\bar{b}$. So B cannot call e at the end of $inverse(x_{A\bar{B}}.\bar{b})$. Furthermore, *because B has no internal non-determinism*, B has no other evolution with the same external input-output sequence as $inverse(x_{A\bar{B}}.\bar{b})$. So $x_{A\bar{B}} \circ \langle e \rangle$ is not safe wrt B. So the safety condition of A implements B does not hold.   □

Lemmas 7.3 and 7.4 imply Theorem 7.2a.

Now for the progress part of the theorem.

Lemma 7.5. *Given that $A\bar{B}$ is fault-free, $A\bar{B}$ satisfies $\bar{B}$'s progress condition iff the progress part of A implements B holds.*   □

Proof. Again, the proof for each direction is by contradiction.

Suppose the safety part of A implements B holds but not the progress part. Then there exists an evolution x_A of A that is safe wrt B, satisfies A's progress assumption, but is not complete wrt B. So there exists an evolution x_B of B such that $ext(x_A) = ext(x_B)$ and x_B does not satisfy B's progress assumption. Then $inverse(x_B)$ and x_A can be stitched together to form an evolution $x_{A\bar{B}}$ of $A\bar{B}$ such that $x_{A\bar{B}}.a = x_A$ and $x_{A\bar{B}}.\bar{b} = inverse(x_B)$. Evolution $x_{A\bar{B}}$ is fault-free, satisfies A's progress assumption but not $\bar{B}$'s progress condition (because x_B does not satisfy B's progress assumption). Hence $A\bar{B}$ does not satisfy $\bar{B}$'s progress condition.

Suppose $A\bar{B}$ does not satisfy B's progress assumption, i.e., there exists an evolution $x_{A\bar{B}}$ of $A\bar{B}$ such that $x_{A\bar{B}}$ is fault-free, satisfies A's progress assumption, but does not satisfy B's progress assumption. Then $x_{A\bar{B}}.a$ is an evolution of A that satisfies A's progress assumption, and $x_{A\bar{B}}.\bar{b}$ is an evolution of $\bar{B}$ that does not satisfy B's progress assumption. The latter implies that $inverse(x_{A\bar{B}}.\bar{b})$ is an evolution of B that does not satisfy B's progress assumption. Furthermore, because B has no internal non-determinism, B has no other evolution with the same external input-output sequence as $inverse(x_{A\bar{B}}.\bar{b})$. So $x_{A\bar{B}}$ is not complete wrt B, but it is safe wrt B and satisfies A's progress assumption. So the progress condition of A implements B does not hold.   □

This completes the proof of parts a and b of Theorem 7.2. The proof of part c is practically identical, and is left as an exercise.

7.8 Proof of Theorems 7.3 and 7.4

The assumptions of Theorems 7.3 and 7.4 are restated below for ease of reference, along with some notation:

- A is a program.
- B is a service program with internal parameters.
- $\widehat{B}$ denotes B externalized.
- ψ is an A-to-B externalizer.
- $\widehat{A}_\psi$ denotes A externalized with ψ.
- For every quantity x (state, transition, etc.) in A, let $\widehat{x}$ denote the corresponding quantity in $\widehat{A}_\psi$, and vice versa.
- For every quantity x in B, let $\widehat{x}$ denote the corresponding quantity in $\widehat{B}$, and vice versa.

Lemma 7.6. *Let $\widehat{A}_\psi$ implement $\widehat{B}$. Let x be an evolution of A. If x is safe wrt B then $\widehat{x}$ is safe wrt $\widehat{B}$.*   □

Proof. By induction on the number of transitions in x. For the base case, suppose x consists only of an initial transition t, i.e., the input transition creating A. Then $\widehat{x}$ is x with every state in it "hatted" (any difference would be due to auxiliary variables). Thus $\widehat{x}$ is safe wrt $\widehat{B}$.

Assume the lemma holds for an evolution of n transitions. Let y be an evolution of A of $n+1$ transitions such that y is safe wrt B. Let its last transition be p and let x be y excluding the last transition, i.e., $y = x \circ \langle p \rangle$. Evolution x is safe wrt B (because y is safe wrt B). Hence $\widehat{x}$ is safe wrt $\widehat{B}$ (induction hypothesis).

Suppose u is an input transition $\langle s, e, t \rangle$. Then $\widehat{u}$ equals $\langle \widehat{s}, e, \widehat{t} \rangle$, and it is a fault-free input transition of $\widehat{A}_\psi$ enabled at the end of $\widehat{x}$ (because ψ does not inhibit any extension of x). Thus $\widehat{y}$, which equals $\widehat{x} \circ \langle \widehat{u} \rangle$, is fault-free. Also $\widehat{x} \circ \langle e \rangle$ is safe wrt $\widehat{B}$ (because $x \circ \langle e \rangle$ is safe wrt B). Hence $\widehat{y}$ is safe wrt B.

Suppose u is an internal transition $\langle s, t \rangle$. The argument is the same as the previous one for an output transition (except that e is absent).

Suppose u is an output transition $\langle s, e, t \rangle$. Then u is fault-free (because y, being safe wrt B, is fault-free). Hence $\widehat{u}$, which equals $\langle \widehat{s}, \widehat{e}, \widehat{t} \rangle$, is a fault-free output transition of $\widehat{A}_\psi$ (because ψ does not inhibit any extension of x). Hence $\widehat{y}$, which equals $\widehat{x} \circ \langle \widehat{u} \rangle$, is fault-free and safe wrt $\widehat{B}$ (because $\widehat{A}_\psi$ implements $\widehat{B}$).   □

Proof of part a of Theorem 7.3. Let $\widehat{A}_\psi$ satisfy the implements safety condition wrt $\widehat{B}$. We need to show that A satisfies the implements safety condition wrt B. Let x be a finite evolution of A that is safe wrt B.

Let e be an input of B. Let $x \circ \langle e \rangle$ be safe wrt B. We need to show that A can accept e at the end of x. From Lemma 7.6, evolution $\widehat{x}$ of $\widehat{A}_\psi$ is safe wrt $\widehat{B}$. Because e is an input, $\widehat{e}$ is the same as e and the step that receives e in $\widehat{B}$ is the same as in B. Hence $\widehat{x} \circ \langle e \rangle$ is safe wrt $\widehat{B}$. Hence $\widehat{A}_\psi$ can accept e at the end of $\widehat{x}$ (because $\widehat{A}_\psi$ satisfies the implements safety condition wrt $\widehat{B}$). Hence A can accept e at the end of x (because ψ does not inhibit or enable a step in $\widehat{A}_\psi$).

Let $\langle s, e, t \rangle$ be an output transition of A that is enabled at the end of x. We need to show that this transition is fault-free and $x \circ \langle e \rangle$ is safe wrt B. From the construction of $\widehat{A}_\psi$, $\langle \widehat{s}, \widehat{e}, \widehat{t} \rangle$ is an output transition of $\widehat{A}_\psi$ that is enabled at the end of $\widehat{x}$. Hence $\langle \widehat{s}, \widehat{e}, \widehat{t} \rangle$ is fault-free and $\widehat{x} \circ \langle \widehat{e} \rangle$ is safe wrt $\widehat{B}$ (because $\widehat{A}_\psi$ implements $\widehat{B}$). Hence $\langle s, e, t \rangle$ is fault-free (because ψ does not inhibit or enable $\widehat{A}_\psi$) and $x \circ \langle e \rangle$ is safe wrt B (because $\widehat{x} \circ \langle \widehat{e} \rangle$ is safe wrt $\widehat{B}$).

The argument for an internal transition $\langle s,t \rangle$ of A enabled at the end of x is similar to that for an output transition. □

Proof of part b of Theorem 7.3. Let x be an evolution of A that is safe wrt B and satisfies the progress assumption of A. We need to show that x is complete wrt B. Because A and $\widehat{A}_\psi$ have the same progress assumption, $\widehat{x}$ satisfies the progress assumption of $\widehat{A}_\psi$. Hence $\widehat{x}$ is complete wrt $\widehat{B}$ (because $\widehat{A}_\psi$ implements $\widehat{B}$). Because B and $\widehat{B}$ have the same progress assumption (the progress assumption of $\widehat{B}$ does not distinguish between different values of internal parameters), an evolution of B is complete wrt B iff its "hatted"-version is complete wrt $\widehat{B}$. Thus x is complete wrt B. □

Proof of Theorem 7.4. Assume A implements B holds. We now come up with an A-to-B externalizer ψ such that $\widehat{A}_\psi$ satisfies the implements condition wrt $\widehat{B}$. The idea is as follows. Function ψ maintains an instantiation $\widehat{b}$ of $\widehat{B}$, which it keeps synchronized to the history of inputs and outputs that $\widehat{A}_\psi$ has done so far. Whenever $\widehat{A}_\psi$ is about to do an output whose "unhatted" part is, say e, function ψ chooses an output $\widehat{e}$ that $\widehat{b}$ can do.

We now state this formally. Function ψ does the following:

- Initially, when $\widehat{A}_\psi$ is instantiated, function ψ creates an instantiation $\widehat{b}$ of $\widehat{B}$.
- When $\widehat{A}_\psi$ receives an input $\widehat{e}$, function ψ executes the corresponding input part of $\widehat{b}$.
- When $\widehat{A}_\psi$ is about to do an output whose "unhatted" part is e (i.e., the part of $\widehat{A}_\psi$ excluding ψ is about to output e), function ψ sets the output to any output $\widehat{e}$ that the output part of $\widehat{b}$ corresponding to e can output. (At least one such $\widehat{e}$ exists because A implements B and because the sequence of unhatted inputs and outputs of $\widehat{A}_\psi$ thus far is safe wrt B.)

Thus an appropriate externalizer exists. Of course, in practice, one would usually invent a simpler externalizer, one that does not need to maintain $\widehat{b}$. □

7.9 Concluding Remarks

This chapter defined the core of SESF theory. We defined the meaning of "program A implements program B" in terms of the evolutions of A and B. We showed that this definition provides compositionality. There are many such formalizations in the literature, for example, [1–16]. We then expressed the definition of A implements B in terms of the programs of A and B. Such "program-based" formulations are found in most of the works cited previously.

Our program-based formulation of "*A* implements *B*" restricts *B* to be a service program. This restriction simplifies the program-based implementation conditions specifically because threads are explicit in our programs. Whereas most other formalizations use a "programming language" in which threads are implicit: a program is written as a bag of atomic steps with blocking conditions, any of which can be executed when it is unblocked. In such an approach, implementation programs have the same structure as service programs, and nothing is gained by having the program-based formulation of "*A* implements *B*" restrict *B* to be a service program.

The internal non-determinism in our service programs is somewhat restricted in that a service can make a non-deterministic choice only when it does an output. Because of this, an externalizer for a candidate implementation can be defined using auxiliary variables that record the history of the implementation. If services were allowed to have more general internal non-determinism, for example, non-deterministic code in input parts, then one would also need so-called "prophecy" variables [1] to define an externalizer.

Exercises

7.1. Show that Theorem 7.2 does not hold if B has internal nondeterminism, by coming up with examples of A and B for which the theorem does not hold.

7.2. Does compositionality (Theorem 7.1) hold if the implements safety condition is changed to the implements strong-safety condition. In particular, if system *A* satisfies the implements strong-safety condition wrt system *B* and system *B* satisfies the implements strong-safety condition wrt system *C*, then does *A* satisfy the implements strong-safety condition wrt system *C*.

References

1. M. Abadi, L. Lamport, The existence of refinement mappings. Theor. Comput. Sci. **82**(2), 253–284 (1991). doi:10.1016/0304-3975(91)90224-P. http://dx.doi.org/10.1016/0304-3975(91)90224-P
2. M. Abadi, L. Lamport, Composing specifications. ACM Trans. Program. Lang. Syst. **15**(1), 73–132 (1993). doi:10.1145/151646.151649. http://doi.acm.org/10.1145/151646.151649. Also in Stepwise Refinement of Distributed Systems, LNCS 430, Springer-Velag, 1990
3. R. johan Back, J.V. Wright, Contracts, games, and refinement. Inf. Comput. Control **156**, 25–45 (2000). doi:10.1006/inco.1999.2820
4. R.J.R. Back, F. Kurki-Suonio, Distributed cooperation with action systems. ACM Trans. Program. Lang. Syst. **10**(4), 513–554 (1988). doi:10.1145/48022.48023. http://doi.acm.org/10.1145/48022.48023
5. R.J.R. Back, R. Kurki-Suonio, Decentralization of process nets with centralized control, In: *Proceedings of the Second Annual ACM Symposium on Principles of Distributed Computing*,

PODC '83. (ACM, New York, 1983), pp. 131–142. doi:10.1145/800221.806716. http://doi.acm.org/10.1145/800221.806716

6. R.J.R. Back, K. Sere, Stepwise refinement of parallel algorithms. Sci. Comput. Program. **13**(2–3), 133–180 (1990). doi:10.1016/0167-6423(90)90069-P. http://dx.doi.org/10.1016/0167-6423(90)90069-P

7. K.M. Chandy, J. Misra, An example of stepwise refinement of distributed programs: quiescence detection. ACM Trans. Program. Lang. Syst. **8**(3), 326–343 (1986). doi:10.1145/5956.5958. http://doi.acm.org/10.1145/5956.5958

8. K.M. Chandy, J. Misra, *Parallel Program Design: A Foundation* (Addison-Wesley, Reading, 1989)

9. S.S. Lam, A.U. Shankar, Specifying modules to satisfy interfaces: a state transition system approach. Distrib. Comput. **6**(1), 39–63 (1992). doi:10.1007/BF02276640. http://dx.doi.org/10.1007/BF02276640

10. L. Lamport, Specifying concurrent program modules. ACM Trans. Program. Lang. Syst. **5**(2), 190–222 (1983). doi:10.1145/69624.357207. http://doi.acm.org/10.1145/69624.357207

11. L. Lamport, A simple approach to specifying concurrent systems. Commun. ACM **32**(1), 32–45 (1989). doi:10.1145/63238.63240. http://doi.acm.org/10.1145/63238.63240

12. L. Lamport, The temporal logic of actions. ACM Trans. Program. Lang. Syst. **16**(3), 872–923 (1994). doi:10.1145/177492.177726. http://doi.acm.org/10.1145/177492.177726

13. N.A. Lynch, M.R. Tuttle, Hierarchical correctness proofs for distributed algorithms, in *Proceedings of the Sixth Annual ACM Symposium on Principles of Distributed Computing, PODC '87* (ACM, New York, 1987), pp. 137–151. doi:10.1145/41840.41852. http://doi.acm.org/10.1145/41840.41852

14. Z. Manna, A. Pnueli, Adequate proof principles for invariance and liveness properties of concurrent programs. Sci. Comput. Program. **4**(3), 257–289 (1984). doi:10.1016/0167-6423(84)90003-0. http://dx.doi.org/10.1016/0167-6423(84)90003-0

15. A.U. Shankar, S.S. Lam, A stepwise refinement heuristic for protocol construction. ACM Trans. Program. Lang. Syst. **14**(3), 417–461 (1992). doi:10.1145/129393.129394. http://doi.acm.org/10.1145/129393.129394. Earlier version appeared in Stepwise Refinement of Distributed Systems, LNCS 430, Springer-Verlag, 1990

16. K. Suonio, *A Practical Theory of Reactive Systems: Incremental Modeling of Dynamic Behaviors* (Springer, Secaucus, 2005). (Texts in Theoretical Computer Science. An EATCS Series)

Chapter 8
SESF for Time-Constrained Programs

8.1 Introduction

This chapter extends SESF to time-constrained programs, that is, programs whose statements are subject to time constraints. A **time constraint** for a statement of a program specifies bounds on the time at which the statement is executed, relative to times at which statements of the program have been executed in the past. There are two kinds of time constraints: "only-within" constraints and "deadline" constraints. An **only-within constraint** for a statement A states that A executes only within some time interval, for example, only after some time T or only before some time T. A **deadline constraint** for a statement A states that A ends execution within some time T. Practically any time constraint of interest can be expressed as a combination of only-within and deadline constraints.

Clearly, in order for a program to satisfy desired time constraints, the underlying platform must enforce time constraints of its own. Time constraints that are assumed to be enforced by the underlying platform are referred to as **timing assumptions**. Time constraints that are to be satisfied by the program are referred to as **timing properties**. The effect of a program's timing assumptions is to eliminate some of the evolutions that the program would otherwise have, thereby allowing it to satisfy additional correctness properties, including timing properties. Timing assumptions satisfied by threads, perhaps in different systems, give rise to global correctness and timing properties. We have already seen an example of this with the sliding window protocol, where fifo data transfer over LRD channels is achieved assuming an upper bound on message lifetime and a lower bound on data message transmission time (Sect. 5.3).

Handling time-constrained programs requires a few extensions to the theory. Each evolution of a program should indicate not only the sequence of steps taken but also the times at which they occurred, so that one can reason about the timing behavior of the program. This is done by augmenting the program model with a variable called τnow that indicates the **current time**, and a function called τage that can increase τnow at any point. Given these, timing properties can be expressed by

A.U. Shankar, *Distributed Programming: Theory and Practice*,
DOI 10.1007/978-1-4614-4881-5_8,
© Springer Science+Business Media New York 2013

regular assertions, and timing assumptions can be expressed by blocking conditions. Consequently, time-constrained programs become regular programs and the results of the previous two chapters—semantics, implements definition, compositionality property, and program version of implements—carry over to time-constrained programs.

The following sections describe how a program is augmented with τnow and τage, how its timing properties and timing assumptions are expressed, how the resulting program is equivalent to a regular program, and how the results of the previous two chapters carry over. Examples of time-constrained service programs and time-constrained implementation programs are given. Timing assumptions of service programs can describe arbitrary constraints. Whereas timing assumptions of implementation programs are limited to bounds on the time taken to execute chunks of code, because this is what operating systems and compilers typically support.

Conventions For notational convenience in expressing time constraints, we use ∞ to denote a value higher than any number, and $-\infty$ to denote a value lower than any number. In particular, the following hold for any number x: $-\infty < x < \infty$, $x + \infty = \infty$, and $x - \infty = -\infty$. **End of conventions**

8.2   Time-Constrained Programs

A time-constrained program is a regular program, say S, with constraints on the elapsed time between specified statement executions. To express these time constraints, we introduce in the environment of S a real-valued variable τnow that indicates the current time and an "ageing" function τage(δ) that increments τnow by an arbitrary amount δ. Variable τnow is readable by every basic system in the aggregate system of S. In particular, a basic system can record the time when it executes a statement by simultaneously reading τnow.

Recall that τnow and τage are defined outside program S. The program of τnow, τage and S is referred to as the **explicit-time version of** S and is denoted S_τ. A preliminary outline of S_τ follows:

```
program S(.)τ {  // outline of explicit-time S
   real τnow ← 0;
   sys ← startSystem(S(.));
   return mysid;

   output τage(δ) {
      oc {δ > 0 and ...}  // '...' to be filled in
      τnow ← τnow+δ;
      ic {true}
   }
}
```

Program S_τ is a hypothetical program whose sole purpose is to define the evolutions of the time-constrained program S. Function τage is classified as an output function because any change to τnow is immediately visible to all basic systems in S, and because there is always an implicit thread attempting to execute it. The program semantics defined earlier (in Sect. 6.4) is applicable to S_τ. Briefly, each state of S_τ consists of a value assignment to τnow and a state of S. The transitions of S_τ consist of regular transitions of S and **ageing** transitions, due to executions of τage. Ageing transitions change τnow and nothing else. Regular transitions, also referred to as **non-ageing** transitions, do not change τnow. Each evolution of S_τ is a sequence of transitions, which now include ageing transitions.

We mentioned that any basic system in S_τ can record the time when it executes a statement by simultaneously reading τnow. Variables that store such values are referred to as **epoch variables**. Given epoch variables and τnow, time constraints can be expressed by assertions or by blocking conditions on statements of S. Our choice is to use assertions for timing properties and blocking conditions for timing assumptions, as explained next.

8.2.1 Modeling Time Constraints

We show by example how time constraints can be expressed by assertions. Let A and B be two statements of program S such that each is executed at most once in any evolution and B is executed only after A is executed. Here are three constraints on the elapsed time between A's execution and B's execution:

C1: B *is not* executed *before* T seconds have elapsed since A's execution (only-within constraint).

C2: B *is not* executed *after* T seconds have elapsed since A's execution (only-within constraint).

C3: B *is* executed *before* T seconds have elapsed since A's execution (deadline constraint).

To express these constraints formally, introduce epoch variables, say tA and tB, in S to record the times when A and B are executed, respectively. Let tA be initialized to ∞ and assigned τnow as a side effect of A's execution. Let tB be defined similarly with respect to B. Then the above constraints can be expressed by the following assertions:

C1: *Inv* (tA $\neq \infty$ and tB $\neq \infty$) $\Rightarrow$ (tB $>$ tA+T)
C2: *Inv* (tA $\neq \infty$ and tB $\neq \infty$) $\Rightarrow$ (tB $<$ tA+T)
C3: *Inv* (tA $\neq \infty$ and τnow $\geq$ tA+T) $\Rightarrow$ (tB $\neq \infty$ and tB $<$ tA+T)

Establishing that the program satisfies a timing property is then equivalent to establishing that the program satisfies the corresponding assertion. There are several points worth noting. First, C1 and C2 do not involve τnow. This makes sense because an only-within time constraint can always be satisfied by allowing time to pass by.

Second, C3 does involve τnow, and increasing τnow sufficiently will falsify it. This makes sense because a deadline time constraint can be satisfied only by meeting the deadline. Because of our conventions regarding "∞", C3's predicate can be shortened to (τnow $\geq$ tA+T) $\Rightarrow$ (tB < tA+T). Third, the above assertions are all safety assertions. Progress assertions are not needed to express real-time properties.

8.2.2   Modeling Timing Assumptions

Recall that a timing assumption is a time constraint that is assumed to be enforced by the underlying platform (whereas a timing property is a time constraint that is to be satisfied by the program). We could express timing assumptions in the same way as timing properties, i.e., by assertions. The difference would be that, in analysis, one would assume that these assertions hold (rather than trying to establish them). But having invariant assumptions in the program would make the program a bit different syntactically from a regular (non-time-constrained) program. In particular, the rules for inverting service programs would need some changes.

To directly reuse the previous results for non-time-constrained programs, we should express the invariant assumptions by blocking conditions on statements. Essentially, a statement should be blocked if its execution would violate an invariant assumption. To illustrate, the above constraints C1, C2 and C3 are expressed by introducing the following blocking conditions on statements. (A statement is executed only if its blocking condition holds.)

C1: Blocking condition for statement B: τnow > tA+T
C2: Blocking condition for statement B: τnow < tA+T
C3: Blocking condition for τage(δ): (tA $\neq$ ∞ and tB = ∞) $\Rightarrow$ (τnow+δ < tA+T)

Only-within timing assumptions are expressed by blocking statements of S, whereas deadline timing assumptions are expressed by blocking τage, i.e., adding an additional conjunct to τage's output condition. The latter may seem odd, but keep in mind that it is just a way to eliminate evolutions that don't meet the deadline assumptions.

We now have all the pieces to complete the picture of a time-constrained program S. As shown in Fig. 8.1, a time-constrained (implementation or service) program S is a regular program augmented as follows. First, the statements of S, as part of their execution, can record the value of τnow (and store it in epoch variables). Second, the statements can have blocking conditions involving τnow (and epoch variables); these represent only-within timing assumptions. Third, program S can have a **deadline assumption** consisting of a predicate involving τnow and epoch variables; this represents a deadline not to be violated by ageing. Program S_τ, the explicit-time version of S, is as before except that τage(δ) is now blocked from falsifying the deadline assumption of any basic system in the aggregate system of S.

Time-constrained program is a regular program in which:

- statements can simultaneously record the value of τnow
- statements can have "only-within" blocking conditions involving τnow
- the program can have a deadline assumption consisting of a predicate involving τnow

Explicit-time version of time-constrained program S:

```
program S(.)τ {  // explicit-time version of S(.)
    real τnow ← 0;
    sys ← startSystem(S(.));
    return mysid;

    output τage(δ) {
        oc {(δ > 0) and deadline[τnow | τnow+δ]}
        τnow ← τnow+δ;
        ic {true}
    }
}
```

Fig. 8.1 A time-constrained program and its explicit-time version; deadline is the conjunction of the deadline assumptions of all basic systems in sys, and deadline[τnow | τnow+δ] is deadline with τnow replaced by τnow+δ

The deadline assumption of a program must be **locally realizable**, by which we mean the following: there is a positive real E such that for any finite evolution x ending in a state where the deadline prevents τnow from being increased, x can be extended by non-input transitions to a state where τnow can be increased by at least E. Otherwise the deadline assumption would be impossible to satisfy regardless of the underlying platform's computing power.

8.3 Time-Constrained Service Programs

This section illustrates the material in the previous section with examples of time-constrained message-passing services. The first example defines a **LRD channel with maximum message lifetime** L, which means that a message (including any duplicate) cannot be received L seconds after it was sent. This is an only-within constraint. The program is obtained by modifying the original LRD channel program (in Fig. 4.5) as follows. First, every message in the send history, txh, is augmented with the time at which the message was sent. Second, a message can be received only if its send time lags the current time by less than L. The resulting program is given in Fig. 8.2, with the modified parts underlined.

```
service LrdChannelMaxLife(Set ADDR, real L) {
    // ADDR: addresses. L: max msg lifetime
    ic {ADDR.size ≥ 1}
    Map txh ← map([j, []]: j in ADDR);  // [msg,t] pairs sent to j from any address
    Map rxh ← map([j, []]: j in ADDR);  // messages received at j from any address
    v ← map([j,sid()]: j in ADDR);    // v[j]: channel access system at address j
    return v;

    input void v[ADDR j].tx(ADDR k, Seq msg) {      // at j send msg to k
        ic {j ≠ k and not ongoing(v[j].tx(.))}
        txh[j].append([msg,τnow]);
        oc {true}
        return;
    }

    input Seq v[ADDR j].rx() {                       // at j receive msg
        ic {not ongoing(v[j].rx())}
        output (Seq msg) {
            oc {forsome(real t, t > τnow−L: [msg,t] in txh[j])}
            rxh[j].append(msg);
            return msg;
        }
    }

    atomicity assumption {input parts and output parts}

    assertion increasing(Seq h, Set m) {...}        // as in LrdChannel
    progress assumption {...}                        // as in LrdChannel
}       // LrdChannelMaxLife
```

Fig. 8.2 LRD channel with maximum message lifetime (showing changes to LrdChannel)

The second example is a **point-to-point fifo channel with maximum message delay** D. A point-to-point fifo channel is a one-way fifo channel between two addresses, say from address a1 to another address a2. It has only two input functions: tx(a2, msg) at a1 and rx() at a2. A point-to-point fifo channel with maximum delay D means that a message is received within D seconds since it was sent provided a user thread is ready to receive it. This is a deadline constraint.

The program is obtained from the fifo channel program for two addresses. First, we retain only the functions and variables needed for a one-way channel (e.g., txh and rxh need not be maps). Second, every message in the send history, txh, is augmented with the time at which the message was sent (as in the LRD case). Third, a deadline is imposed that every message in transit is younger than D seconds. Because the channel is fifo, a message is in transit iff rxh.size < txh.size, and the

```
service PpFifoChannelMaxDelay(Val a1, Val a2, D, RGAP, TGAP) {
    // D: max delay. RGAP: max non-receiving duration.
    // TGAP: min inter-tx duration
    ic {(a1 ≠ a2) and (D,RGAP,TGAP positive real) and RGAP < min(D,TGAP)}

    Seq txh ← seq();            // [msg,t] pairs sent from a1
    Seq rxh ← seq();            // msgs received at a2
    real rxRetEpoch ← 0;        // when rx was last returned
    real maxRxGap ← 0;          // max continuous interval without ongoing rx call
    real txCallEpoch ← 0;       // when tx was last called
    y1 ← sid(); y2 ← sid();     // y1, y2: access systems at a1, a2
    return [[a1,y1], [a2,y2]];

    input void y1.tx(Val a2, Seq msg) {     // at a1 send msg to a2
        ic {not ongoing(y1.tx(.))
            and (τnow > txCallEpoch+TGAP)}
        txCallEpoch ← τnow;
        txh.append([msg,τnow]);
        oc {true}
        return;
    }

    input Seq y2.rx() {                      // receive msg at a2
        ic {not ongoing(y1.tx(.))}
        maxRxGap ← max(maxRxGap, τnow - rxRetEpoch);
        output (Seq msg) {
            oc {(rxh ∘ [msg]) prefixOf [m[0]: m in txh]}
            rxh.append(msg);
            rxRetEpoch ← τnow;
            return msg;
        }
    }

    deadline assumption {
        (maxRxGap < RGAP
        and (not ongoing(y2.rx) ⇒ τnow - rxRetEpoch < RGAP))
            ⇒ ((txh.size > rxh.size) ⇒ (τnow - txh[rxh.size][1] < D))
    }

    atomicity assumption {input parts and output parts}

    progress assumption {forall(int i: txh.size ≥ i leads-to rxh.size ≥ i)}

} // PpFifoChannelMaxDelay
```

Fig. 8.3 Fifo channel with maximum delay (time-related parts are underlined)

send time of the oldest such message is txh[rxh.size][1]. So it suffices if this send time is higher than τnow − D. Fourth, the deadline must be locally realizable. One option is to always have a thread ready to receive, but this requires at least two rx calls to be ongoing simultaneously. A more sensible option is to have an upper bound, say RGAP, on the duration when no thread is receiving, and a lower bound, say TGAP, on the time between successive message sends. Clearly, RGAP < D and RGAP < TGAP must hold. (If the latter does not hold, an unbounded number of messages can queue up at the receiver.)

The resulting program is given in Fig. 8.3, with the underlined parts indicating the time-constrained parts. Three variables maintain timing information. Variable rxRetEpoch indicates the time when rx last returned; it's initialized to 0. Variable maxRxGap indicates the largest interval in the past between an rx call and the previous rx return; it's initialized to 0. Variable txCallEpoch indicates the time when tx was last called; it's initialized to 0.

The deadline assumption is an implication. The antecedent, to be satisfied by the environment, has two conjuncts. The first conjunct, (maxRxGap < RGAP), says that every past non-receiving duration is less than RGAP. The second conjunct, (not ongoing(y2.rx) ⇒ (τnow − rxRetEpoch < RGAP)), says that if no rx call is ongoing then the last rx return occurred later than RGAP ago. The consequent of the deadline assumption says that if there are messages in transit, then the oldest such message is no older than D seconds.

Note that the deadline assumption does not replace the progress assumption. The former is a safety constraint on how an evolution of the program can grow. The latter says that it will eventually grow under certain circumstances.

8.4   Implements and Compositionality

The semantics of a time-constrained program S is the semantics of its explicit-time program S_τ. A state of S_τ consists of a state of S and a value of τnow. A transition of S_τ is either a transition of S or an ageing transition. A transition of S has the form $\langle s,t \rangle$ or $\langle s,e,t \rangle$, where s is the start state, e is an input or output, t is the end state, τnow has the same value in s and t, and s satisfies the only-within blocking condition (if any) on the atomic step that gives rise to the transition. An ageing transition has the form $\langle s, \tau\mathrm{age}(\delta), t \rangle$, where the end state t is the same as the start state s except that τnow is increased by δ, and t satisfies S's deadline assumption (if any).

The implements relation and compositionality results for regular programs apply to S_τ, provided we treat $\tau\mathrm{age}(\delta)$ as an output function, whose execution delivers an input (the new value of τnow) to all basic systems in its environment, including those in S. The definitions of $ext(\cdot)$, "safe wrt", "complete wrt", and "A_τ implements B_τ" are *exactly* as before. For example, $ext(x)$ for an evolution x of S_τ is still the sequence of inputs and outputs in x, where each ageing transition $\langle s, \tau\mathrm{age}(\delta), t \rangle$ in x contributes a $\tau\mathrm{age}(\delta)$ entry in $ext(x)$.

Let A and B be two time-constrained programs. Then A **implements** B is defined to mean A_τ implements B_τ, where the latter is defined exactly as before (in Sect. 7.2). In particular, the ageing step of A_τ must satisfy the safety output condition:

- For every finite evolution x of A_τ that is safe wrt B_τ, for every ageing transition $\langle s, \tau age(\delta), t \rangle$ of A_τ enabled at the last state of x:

  - The transition is fault-free (i.e., A.deadline is well defined).
  - $x \circ \langle \tau age(\delta) \rangle$ is safe wrt B_τ (i.e., the new value of τnow does not invalidate B.deadline).

Compositionality (Theorem 7.1) remains valid exactly as before. For example, given time-constrained programs A, B and C, if A_τ implements B_τ and B_τ implements C_τ, then A_τ implements C_τ.

8.4.1 Program Version of Implements

Let B(x) denote a time-constrained service program with parameters x, and let A(x,y) denote a (time-constrained) candidate implementation program with parameters x and y. The program version of "$A(x,y)_\tau$ implements $B(x)_\tau$" can be obtained exactly as in the non-time-constrained situation (Chap. 7). First, one obtains $B(x)_\tau$ inverse; here, $B(x)_\tau$'s ageing function would become an input function and B's deadline assumption would become a deadline *condition*. Then one would show that the closed program of instantiations of $A(x,y)_\tau$ and $B(x)_\tau$ inverse is fault-free and satisfies the latter's deadline condition and progress condition.

But there is a simpler way to get the desired closed program. Simply instantiate B(x) inverse, denoted $\bar{B}(x)$, inside A_τ (along with an instantiation of A), and trigger a fault if function τage falsifies $\bar{B}(x)$'s deadline. This simpler program, denoted $A\bar{B}(x,y)_\tau$ and referred to as the **explicit-time closed program** of A and B inverse, is shown in Fig. 8.4.

Theorem 8.1 (program-based implements for time-constrained programs). *Let programs* B(x), $\bar{B}(a,x)$, A(x,y) *and* $A\bar{B}(x,y)_\tau$ *be as defined above. Then the following hold:*

(a) Safety condition of "A implements B" holds iff $A\bar{B}(x,y)_\tau$ *is fault-free.*
(b) Progress condition of "A implements B" holds iff $A\bar{B}(x,y)_\tau$ *satisfies* $\bar{B}$'s *progress condition.* □

The extensions to implements-with-strong-safety and to service programs with internal parameters can be handled exactly as before.

```
program AB̄(x,y)_τ {
    ia {f(x,y)}                    // B.ic(x) ⇒ forsome(y: f(x,y))
    inputs(); outputs();
    atomic {
        a ← startSystem(A(x,y));
        b̄ ← startSystem(B̄(a,x));
    }
    return mysid;

    output τage(δ) {
        oc {(δ > 0) and a.deadline[τnow | τnow + δ]}
        τnow ← τnow + δ;
        ic {not b̄.deadline}
    }
}
```

Fig. 8.4 Explicit-time closed program of A and B inverse

8.5   Timing Assumptions for Implementation Programs

Timing assumptions of service programs are not subject to any restrictions other than having to be locally realizable. That is appropriate for service programs but not for programs that implement services. Timing assumptions for implementation programs should be limited to bounds on the time taken by a thread to execute code chunks of a bounded number of instructions. Furthermore, a thread should not be subject to a deadline timing assumption when it is *blocked*, i.e., at a lock's acq when the lock is unavailable, or at a condition variable's wait when a signal is not pending, or at a semaphore's P when the semaphore's value is zero. (Note how this is similar to restricting the progress assumptions of a system program to fairness assumptions.) Finally, a thread should no longer be subject to a program's timing assumptions when it exits the program (via an output call or output return). (Of course, the program that it enters may subject it to a timing assumption).

Below are the constructs we use to define timing assumption for system programs. These constructs would be inserted in code at appropriate points and would give rise to only-within and/or deadline constraints when threads encounter them. The constructs have a parameter L and/or a parameter U, where L is a non-negative number, U is a positive number or ∞, and U is higher than L if both appear in a construct.

- delay(L,U): When a thread arrives at this construct, the underlying platform must ensure that the thread gets past this construct after L seconds and before U seconds have elapsed since the thread arrived at the construct.
- ddl[U]: When a thread arrives at this construct, the underlying platform must ensure that the thread (gets past this construct and) reaches a timing assumption

construct or exits the program within U seconds, unless U is ∞, in which case the construct frees the thread from any prior deadline constraint. The sequence of instructions from this construct to the next timing assumption construct or program exit must be bounded if U is not ∞.

- <block>(U), where <block> is any blocking construct, for example, lck.acq(U), cond.wait(U), and sem.P(U). When a thread arrives at this construct, the underlying platform ensures that the thread gets past the construct within U seconds since the thread arrived at the construct or the construct last became unblocked, whichever was later. In other words, at most U seconds can elapse while the thread is at the construct and the construct is *continuously* unblocked.

Parameter L imposes an only-within constraint unless it is zero, in which case it imposes no constraint. Parameter U imposes a deadline constraint unless it is ∞ or it is in a blocking construct that is blocked, in which case it imposes no constraint.

8.5.1 Transforming Timing Constructs into Blocking Conditions

To analyze a system program S with timing assumption constructs, the constructs are first transformed into blocking conditions involving τnow. For this, we introduce two variables for every thread t:

- t.taReset: Equals ∞ whenever t is not subject to a timing assumption. Otherwise equals the value of τnow when t last became subject to a timing assumption. When t is started, t.taReset is set according to the first statement it is to execute.
- t.taSlack: Equals ∞ whenever t is not subject to a deadline assumption. Otherwise equals the parameter U of the timing assumption construct that t is subject to. When t is started, t.taSlack is set according to the first statement it is to execute.

These variables are updated when thread t comes to a timing assumption construct or executes a timing assumption construct or becomes unblocked at a <block>(U) construct (due to another thread executing the unblocking action). Figure 8.5 shows the updates for delay(L,U) (first row), for ddl(U) (second row), for an output call or output return (third row), and for lock lck (remaining rows). Note that updates are needed for lck.rel and lck.acq(), even though these are not timing assumption constraint, because they affect the deadline of threads waiting at lck.acq(U). The updates for condition variable and semaphores are left as exercises.

After program S is transformed as described above, its explicit-time version S_τ can be generated exactly as before (in Fig. 8.1). Each thread t gives rise to a deadline assumption $\tau now < t.taReset + t.taSlack$. The constraint is vacuous if t.taReset or t.taSlack equals ∞. The deadline assumption defined by an instance s of a system program, i.e., s.deadline, is thus given by the following:

forall(t in s.threads: $\tau now < t.taReset + t.taSlack$)

```
delay(L,U);        ⟹    atomic {
                            mytid.taReset ← if (L = 0 and U = ∞) ∞ else τnow;
                            mytid.taSlack ← U;
                        }
                        await((mytid.taReset = ∞) or (τnow > mytid.taReset+L));
```

- -

```
ddl(U);            ⟹    atomic {
                            mytid.taReset ← if (U = ∞) ∞ else τnow;
                            mytid.taSlack ← U;
                        }
```

- -

```
<output>           ⟹    atomic {<output> ddl{∞}}
(call or return)
```

- -

```
Lock lck;          ⟹    Sid lck.acqd ← null;    // tid that has lck
                        Set lck.waiting ← set(); // tids waiting on lck
```

- -

```
lck.acq(U);        ⟹    atomic {
                            if (lck.acqd = mytid) fault;
                            lck.waiting.add(mytid);
                            mytid.taReset ←
                                if (lck.acqd = null and U ≠ ∞) τnow else ∞;
                            mytid.taSlack ← U;
                        }
                        await (lck.acqd = null) {
                            lck.acqd ← mytid;
                            for (t in lck.waiting) t.taReset ← ∞;
                            lck.waiting.remove(mytid);
                        }
```

- -

```
lck.acq();         ⟹    lck.acq(∞);
```

- -

```
lck.rel();         ⟹    atomic {
                            if (lck.acqd ≠ mytid) fault;
                            lck.acqd ← null;
                            for (t in lck.waiting) t.taReset ← τnow;
                        }
```

Fig. 8.5 Expressing timing constructs in terms of thread variables

8.6 Time-Constrained Implementation Program

Figure 8.6 shows a system program with timing assumptions. It is the simple lock program from Sect. 2.2 with ddl constructs separating all straight-line code chunks other than the main code. There are five explicit ddl constructs and two implicit ones, one with each return. Here are the (deadline) timing assumptions they impose.

- ddl[U1] at a0: When thread t arrives at a0, within U1 seconds it must get to a3 or get back to a0 (which one happens depends on the value of xreq[xp]).
- ddl[U2] at a3: when thread t arrives at a3, within U2 seconds it must get back to a3 or get to a0.
- ddl[U3] at a5: when a (guest) thread arrives at a5, within U3 seconds it must get to a6.
- ddl[U4] at a6: when a (guest) thread arrives at a6, within U4 seconds it must get to a6 or execute a7 (and exit this program).
- ddl[U5] at a8: when a (guest) thread arrives at a8, within U5 seconds it must execute a9 (and exit this program).

8.7 Concluding Remarks

This chapter extended SESF to time-constrained programs. The idea of modeling and verifying a time-constrained system by introducing a variable indicating the current time has been around for a while, e.g., [1–4, 7–10]. Early works used integer-valued current time [8–10], but later approaches all use real-valued current time. Reference [4] models timing constraints on blocking constructs by lower and upper bounds on the elapsed time since the construct was last unblocked. Examples of assertional analysis for time-constrained programs include, e.g., [3, 5, 6, 9, 10].

Exercises

8.1. An LRD channel with a minimum message delay D is an LRD channel in which a message (including any duplicate) cannot be received before D seconds since it was sent. Obtain the service program of such a channel. Obtain the service program of an LRD channel with maximum message life L and minimum message delay D.

8.2. Obtain a time-constrained version of the simple lock service SimpleLockService (in Fig. 2.2) that has the following timing assumption: if every user holds the lock for at most MaxEat seconds, then every request is satisfied within MaxWait seconds, where MaxEat and MaxWait are parameters of the service program. (Hint: Augment SimpleLockService with epoch variables and timing assumptions. Constrain MaxEat and MaxWait so that any deadline assumptions are locally realizable.)

```
system TimedSimpleLock(int N) { // time-constrained lock for users 0, ..., N-1
   ic {N ≥ 1}
   boolean[N] xreq← false;
   boolean xacq ← false;
   int xp ← 0;
   Tid t ← startThread(serve());
   return mysid;

   function serve() {
     forever do {
        ddl{U1}
a0:  if xreq[xp] then {
a1:      xacq ← true;
a2:      xreq[xp] ← false;
a3:      while (ddl{U2} xacq) do skip;
      }
a4:  if xp = N-1 then xp ← 0 else xp ← p+1;
     }
   }

   input mysid.acq() {
      ic {mytid in 0..N-1}
      ddl{U3}
a5: xreq[mytid] ← true;
a6: while (ddl{U4} xreq[mytid]) do skip;
a7: return;  // implicit ddl{∞}
   }

   input mysid.rel() {
      ic {mytid in 0..N-1}
      ddl{U5}
a8: xacq ← false;
a9: return;  // implicit ddl{∞}
   }

   atomicity assumption {reads and writes of xacq, xreq[0], ..., xreq[N-1]}

   progress assumption {weak fairness for every thread}
}
```

Fig. 8.6 Simple lock program with timing assumptions (shown underlined)

8.3. Show that program TimedSimpleLock (in Sect. 8.5) implements the service you have defined in Exercise 8.2 for appropriate bounds on their timing assumption parameters.

8.4. Obtain a service program for a clock. The program should have three parameters:

- x: sid of a system to which it issues a "tick".
- R: positive real number indicating the resolution of the clock (e.g., 0.1 s).
- D: positive real number indicating the maximum drift rate (e.g., 10^{-5}).

The program should have a single output function that calls x.tick() once every R seconds within a maximum drift of D; i.e., if t1 and t2 are the values of τnow at two successive x.tick() calls, then $R(1-D) < (t1-t2) < R(1+D)$ should hold.

8.5. In Sect. 5.3 we established that the sliding window protocol satisfies the implements safety condition wrt a lossy channel and wrt an LRD channel with maximum message lifetime. Part of the analysis for the LRD case was operational, i.e., the proof of invariance of A_3 and A_4 (in subsection "Achieving correct interpretation over LRD channel"). Give an assertional proof of this part. Specifically, do the following:

- Let program SwpDistTimed be the time-constrained version of SwpDist obtained as follows:

  - Use LrdChannelMaxLife (Fig. 8.2) for its unreliable channel.
  - In program Source, introduce an epoch variable, say tNs, to ensure that successive increments of ns are at least minNs seconds apart; i.e., include "τnow > tNs+minNs" in doTxDat.oc and "tNs ← τnow" in doTxDat's input part.

- Develop a set of predicates such that their conjunction, say C, satisfies the following with respect to the explicit-time version of program SwpDist.

  - C holds initially.
  - $\{C,A_2,A_3,A_4\}\,e\,\{C,A_3,A_4\}$ holds for every atomic step e of SwpDist with LRD channel.

(Hint: The predicates in C will be similar to those developed for the lossy channel case (i.e., A_5 and A_6 in Sect. 5.3 and the predicates in Exercises 5.2 and 5.3) and will involve the transmit times of data and ack messages. You may find it convenient to have an auxiliary variable that records the successive times of increments to ns.)

References

1. M. Abadi, L. Lamport, An old-fashioned recipe for real time. ACM Trans. Program. Lang. Syst. **16**(5), 1543–1571 (1994). doi:10.1145/186025.186058. http://doi.acm.org/10.1145/186025.186058

2. A. Bernstein, P.K. Harter Jr., Proving real-time properties of programs with temporal logic. SIGOPS Oper. Syst. Rev. **15**(5), 1–11 (1981). doi:10.1145/1067627.806585. http://doi.acm. org/10.1145/1067627.806585

3. J.A. Carruth, J. Misra, Proof of a real-time mutual-exclusion algorithm. Parallel Process. Lett. **6**(2), 251–257 (1996)

4. M. Merritt, F. Modugno, M.R. Tuttle, Time-constrained automata (extended abstract), in *Proceedings of the 2nd International Conference on Concurrency Theory, CONCUR '91* (Springer, London, 1991), pp. 408–423. http://dl.acm.org/citation.cfm?id=646726.703043

5. A.L. Oláh, Design and analysis of transport protocols for reliable high-speed communications. Ph.D. thesis, University of Twente, Enschedem, 1997. http://doc.utwente.nl/13676/

6. A.L. Oláh, S.M. Heemstra de Groot, Alternative specification and verification of a periodic state exchange protocol. IEEE/ACM Trans. Netw. **5**(4), 525–529 (1997). doi:10.1109/90. 649467. http://dx.doi.org/10.1109/90.649467

7. A.U. Shankar, Verified data transfer protocols with variable flow control. ACM Trans. Comput. Syst. **7**(3), 281–316 (1989). doi:10.1145/65000.65003. http://doi.acm.org/10.1145/65000. 65003

8. A.U. Shankar, S.S. Lam, Time-dependent distributed systems: proving safety, liveness and real-time properties. Distrib. Comput. **2**, 61–79 (1987). http://dx.doi.org/10.1007/ BF01667079. 10.1007/BF01667079

9. A.U. Shankar, S.S. Lam, A stepwise refinement heuristic for protocol construction. ACM Trans. Progr. Lang. Syst. **14**(3), 417–461 (1992). doi:10.1145/129393.129394. http://doi.acm. org/10.1145/129393.129394. Earlier version appeared in Stepwise Refinement of Distributed Systems, LNCS 430, Springer-Verlag, 1990

10. G. Tel, Assertional verification of a timer-based protocol. Technical report, DSpace at Utrecht University [http://dspace.library.uu.nl:8080/dspace-oai/request] (Netherlands), 1987. http:// igitur-archive.library.uu.nl/math/2006-1214-201352/UUindex.html

Chapter 9
Lock Using Peterson's Algorithm

9.1 Introduction

In Chap. 2, we defined a lock service program, SimpleLockService(N), for users (with tids) 0, ..., N − 1, and a program, SimpleLock(N), that implemented the service. That implementation assumed only read-write atomicity and weak fairness, but it had an "arbiter" thread that continuously scanned for user requests. One would prefer an implementation where the only threads are those of the users, so that its code is executed only when a user has a pending request or is returning the lock. Such implementations can be readily obtained from any solution to the classical mutual exclusion, or "mutex", problem.

The **mutex** problem is as follows. Given a program that has "critical sections" and is executed concurrently by N threads, to obtain "entry" and "exit" procedures to surround each critical section such that: (1) at most one thread is inside a critical section at any time; (2) any thread that starts executing the entry procedure eventually enters its critical section provided no thread stays indefinitely inside a critical section; (3) only read-write atomicity of memory words is assumed; and (4) there is no overhead when no thread is interested in accessing a critical section (this rules out arbiter-based solutions). The classical mutual exclusion problem was formulated in 1962 by Dijkstra. Dekker presented a solution for two threads in the early 1960s, and Dijkstra presented a solution for N threads in 1965 [1, 2]. Many solutions have been developed since then, e.g., [3, 4, 6].

The simplest two-thread solution is Peterson's algorithm [5], developed about 20 years after the first two-user solution. This chapter presents a program that uses Peterson's algorithm to implement the lock service for two users. The N-user case is covered in the next chapter.

A.U. Shankar, *Distributed Programming: Theory and Practice*,
DOI 10.1007/978-1-4614-4881-5__9,
© Springer Science+Business Media New York 2013

Conventions

We follow the common terminology of saying a user is "thinking" if it is not interested in the lock, "hungry" if it has a lock request pending, and "eating" if it has acquired the lock.

For thread i and step s, the construct i.s refers to the execution of step s by thread i.

In this chapter, parameter i ranges over $0..1$, and parameter j equals $1 - i$.

End of conventions

9.2   Lock Program and Implements Conditions

Peterson's algorithm solves the mutex problem for two threads, referred to as thread 0 and thread 1. The two threads interact via three binary-valued variables: th[0], which is true iff thread 0 is thinking; th[1], which is true iff thread 1 is thinking; and turn, which indicates the thread that has priority whenever both threads are hungry at the same time. When thread i becomes hungry, it sets th[i] to false, sets turn to the other thread, say j, and busy waits as long as the other thread is not thinking and is favored by turn, i.e., as long as not th[j] and turn $=$ j is valid. When one of these conditions stops holding, thread i becomes eating. When thread i stops eating, it sets th[i] to true.

The lock program based on Peterson's algorithm is shown in Fig. 9.1. Its structure is similar to that of program SimpleLock(N) (in Fig. 2.1), but without the "arbiter" thread t that continuously scans for user requests. Our goal is to establish that LockPeterson() implements the lock service SimpleLockService(N) (Fig. 2.2) for $N = 2$. The lock service inverse program for $N = 2$ is shown in Fig. 9.2. (It's taken from Figs. 2.3–2.4.) Figure 9.3 shows the closed program Z of instantiation lck of the lock program and instantiation lsi of the service inverse. We have to establish that Z satisfies the following assertions.

Y_1 : *Inv* (thread at lsi.doAcq.ic) $\Rightarrow$ (not acqd[0] and not acqd[1])
Y_2 : forall(i in 0..1: (thread i in lck.rel) *leads-to* (not i in lck.rel))
Y_3 : forall(i in 0..1: ,(thread i in lck.end) *leads-to* (not i in lck.end))
Y_4 : forall(i in 0..1: acqd[i] *leads-to* not acqd[i])
      $\Rightarrow$ forall(i in 0..1: (thread i on lck.acq) *leads-to* acqd[i])

Y_1 is due to lsi.doAcq's input condition. The input conditions of lsi.doRel and lsi.doEnd are vacuous, hence do not give rise to assertions. Y_2, Y_3 and Y_4 are lsi's progress condition.

```
program LockPeterson() { // users 0,1
   ia {true}
   // th[i] true iff user i is thinking
   boolean[2] th ← true;
   // turn: 0..1. winner during contention
   int turn ← 0;  // 1 is ok also
   return mysid;

   input mysid.acq() {
i1:    ia {mytid in 0..1}
s1:    th[mytid] ← false;
       // j is other user's tid
s2:    int j ← 1-mytid;
s3: •  turn ← j;
       // wait if j is hungry or eating
       // and has priority
       while
s4:      ( • not th[j]
s5:        and • turn = j);
       return;
   }

   input mysid.rel() {
i2:    ia {mytid in 0..1}
s6:    th[mytid] ← true;
       return;
   }

   input void mysid.end() {
      ia {true}
      endSystem();
   }

   atomicity assumption {reads and writes
                  of turn, th[0], th[1]}

   progress assumption {weak fairness for
                           every thread}
}
```

Fig. 9.1 Lock program from Peterson algorithm; '•'s are atomicity breakpoints

```
program SimpleLockServiceInverse
                   (2, Sid lck) {
   ic {true}
   boolean[2] acqd ← false;
   ending ← false;
   return mysid;

   output doAcq() {
      oc {not ending
            and (mytid in 0..1)
            and not acqd[mytid]}
      lck.acq();
      ic {not acqd[0]
            and not acqd[1]}
      acqd[mytid] ← true;
      return;
   }

   output doRel() {
      oc {not ending
            and (mytid in 0..1)
            and acqd[mytid]}
      acqd[mytid] ← false;
      lck.rel();
      ic {true}
      return;
   }

   output doEnd() {
      oc {not ending}
      ending ← true;
      lck.end();
      ic {true}
      return;
   }

   atomicity assumption {
      input parts and
      output parts}

   progress condition {...}
}
```

Fig. 9.2 Lock service inverse for N = 2

```
program Z() {
  inputs(); outputs();    // closed system
  lck ← startSystem(LockPeterson());
  lsi ← startSystem(SimpleLockServiceInverse(2,lck));
}
```

Fig. 9.3 Closed program of lock and inverse lock service

9.3 Proving the Implements Conditions

We now establish that Z satisfies Y_1–Y_4. We first identify effectively-atomic steps in Z. Threads 0 and 1 are the only threads executing in Z. Variable acqd[i] is accessed only by thread i, so it is not conflicted. The only variables that can be accessed by both threads are th[0], th[1] and turn, all in lck. Here is a partitioning of the code in which each step contains at most one access to any of these variables. The resulting atomicity breakpoints are indicated, as usual, by the '•'s in Fig. 9.1. The atomicity breakpoints for the lock service inverse are, as always, at the output conditions.

- Step Z.main: consisting of lck's main and lsi's main.
- Step s3.
- Step s4 with th[j] = false: from s4 to start of s5.
- Step s5 with turn = j: from s5 to start of s4.
- Step doAcq call: from doAcq start to start of s3 (in input function acq).
- Step s4 with th[j] = true: from s4 to end of doAcq's input part.
- Step s5 with turn ≠ j: from s5 to end of doAcq's input part.
- Step doRel: from start of doRel to end of doRel (including the execution of lck.rel).
- Step doEnd: from start of doEnd to end of doEnd (including the execution of lck.end).

9.3.1 Proving the Safety Condition: Y_1

Given Z's atomicity breakpoints, a thread i comes to lsi.doAcq.ic iff it is at s4 and th[j] is false or it is at s5 and turn is not i. Thus Y_1 is equivalent to $Inv A_1(i)$, where:

$A_1(i)$: (thread i on s4..s5) and (th[j] or turn ≠ j)
            ⟹ (not acqd[0] and not acqd[1])

Our goal is to establish $Inv A_1(i)$. An operational proof is relatively straightforward, and is left as an exercise. Below we give an assertional proof. The following are invariant; each predicate individually satisfies the invariance induction rule.

$A_2(i)$: th[i] ⟹ not acqd[i]
$A_3(i)$: (i on s3..s5) ⟹ not acqd[i]
    A_4 : turn in 0..1

$A_1(i)$'s lhs consists of the conjuncts (i on s4..s5) and (th[j] or turn $\neq$ j). The first conjunct and $A_3(i)$ imply not acqd[i]. The first disjunct of the second conjunct, th[j], and $A_2(j)$ imply not acqd[j]. Thus $Inv A_1(i)$ holds if $Inv A_5(i)$ holds, where:

$A_5(i)$: ((i on s4..s5) and (turn $\neq$ j)) $\Rightarrow$ not acqd[j]

The only possible steps that can falsify $A_5(i)$ are i.s3 and j.s3 (these may establish $A_5(i)$'s lhs), and j.s4 with th[j] = true and j.s5 with turn $\neq$ j (these falsify $A_5(i)$'s rhs). Step i.s3 establishes (i on s4..s5), but it also sets turn to j, thus falsifying $A_5(i)$'s lhs. Step j.s3 establishes turn = i, but it also establishes j on s4, which, because of $A_3(j)$, implies not acqd[j], hence establishing $A_5(i)$'s rhs. Step j.s4 with th[i] = true happens only if th[i] is true, which implies that i is not on s4..s5 (due to $A_3(i)$'s invariance), thus falsifying $A_5(i)$'s lhs. Step j.s5 with turn $\neq$ i happens only if turn = j holds (from A_4), but this falsifies $A_5(i)$'s lhs. Thus A_5 satisfies the invariance induction rule given the invariance of A_2, A_3, and A_4. We are done.

9.3.2 Proving the Progress Condition: Y_2–Y_3

Y_2 holds trivially because the body of lck.rel has no loops and is executed with weak fairness. Y_3 holds in the same way. Y_4 has the form "$P_0(0)$ and $P_0(1)$ $\Rightarrow$ $P_1(0)$ and $P_1(1)$", where

$P_0(i)$: acqd[i] *leads-to* not acqd[i]
$P_1(i)$: (i on lck.acq) *leads-to* acqd[i]

We have to establish that Z satisfies $P_1(i)$ assuming $P_0(0)$ and $P_0(1)$. Because step doAcq call is atomic, thread i is on lck.acq iff it is on s3..s5. Also, if thread i is on s3 then it eventually gets to s4. Thus it suffices to establish the following:

$P_2(i)$: (i on s4..s5) *leads-to* acqd[i]

Suppose thread i is on s4..s5 and turn = i holds. Then thread i eventually exits the loop because only thread i can falsify turn = i. So we have the following:

$P_3(i)$: ((i on s4..s5) and (turn = i)) *leads-to* acqd[i]

Suppose thread i is on s4..s5, and turn = j and th[j] hold, i.e., thread j is thinking. Then eventually one of two things happen: (1) thread i executes acq.s4 return (exiting the loop); or (2) thread j executes doAcq call, setting th[j] false and turn to i. So we have

$P_4(i)$: ((i on s4..s5) and (turn = j) and th[j])
            leads-to (acqd[i] or (turn = i))

If turn = i holds, then $P_3(i)$'s lhs holds (because thread i stays in the while loop until it gets the lock). So $P_4(i)$ and $P_3(i)$ together yield the following:

$P_5(i)$: ((i on s4..s5) and (turn = j) and th[j]) *leads-to* acqd[i]

Suppose thread i is on s4..s5, and turn $= j$ holds and th[j] is false, i.e., thread j is hungry (on s4..s5) or eating. If thread j is hungry, then $P_3(j)$ ensures that it starts eating. Assumption $P_0(j)$ ensures that it eventually becomes thinking, at which point th[j] becomes true and the lhs of $P_5(i)$ holds. Summarizing, the following hold:

$P_6(i)$: ((i on s4..s5) and (turn $= j$) and (not th[j]))
      leads-to ((i on s4..s5) and turn $= j$ and ((j on s3..s5) or acqd[j]))
      leads-to (" " " " " "   and acqd[j])   [from $P_3(j)$]
      leads-to (" " " " " "   and th[j])   [from $P_0(j)$]
      leads-to acqd[i]   [from $P_5(i)$]

$P_1(i)$ follows from $P_6(i)$, $P_5(i)$, and $P_3(i)$. We are done.

9.4 Concluding Remarks

Perhaps the most surprising aspect of Peterson's algorithm is that it took about 20 years after the first two-thread mutex solution to come up with such a simple solution. Prior two-thread solutions were significantly more complicated. It is not clear how to generalize Peterson's algorithm to solve the N-thread mutex problem.

Exercises

9.1. Develop a timed version of program LockPeterson and show that it satisfies the time-constrained simple lock service in Exercise 8.2 for two users.

References

1. E.W. Dijkstra, Cooperating sequential processes. Technical report, Burroughs, Nuenen, The Netherlands, 1965. EWD-123
2. E.W. Dijkstra, Solution of a problem in concurrent programming control. Commun. ACM **8**(9), 569 (1965). doi: 10.1145/365559.365617. http://doi.acm.org/10.1145/365559.365617
3. M.A. Eisenberg, M.R. McGuire, Further comments on dijkstra's concurrent programming control problem. Commun. ACM **15**(11), 999 (1972). doi: 10.1145/355606.361895. http://doi.acm.org/10.1145/355606.361895
4. L. Lamport, A new solution of dijkstra's concurrent programming problem. Commun. ACM **17**(8), 453–455 (1974). doi: 10.1145/361082.361093. http://doi.acm.org/10.1145/361082.361093
5. G.L. Peterson, Myths about the mutual exclusion problem. Inf. Process. Lett. **12**(3), 115–116 (1981)
6. G. Taubenfeld, The black-white bakery algorithm and related bounded-space, adaptive, local-spinning and fifo algorithms, in *DISC* (Association for Computing Machinery, New York, 2004), pp. 56–70

Chapter 10
Lock Using the Bakery Algorithm

10.1 Introduction

As noted in the previous chapter, given a solution to the mutex problem, one can obtain a program that implements the simple lock service on a platform with read-write atomicity and weak fairness, without resorting to an "arbiter" thread. This was illustrated by using Peterson's algorithm to implement the simple lock service for two users. This chapter repeats the exercise using a mutex solution for N users, resulting in a program that implements SimpleLockService(N) for any N.

There are many mutex solutions for N threads, e.g., [1–5]. Here, we use Lamport's **bakery algorithm** solution [4] . Threads have ids 0, 1, $\cdots$, N – 1. They share integer variables num[0], $\cdots$, num[N – 1], where num[i] is writeable by thread i and readable by all other threads. Variable num[i] is zero when thread i is thinking, and positive otherwise. The num values of non-thinking threads determine the order in which the threads enter the critical section, with smaller num values having higher priority.

When a thread i becomes hungry, it scans the num values of the other threads and sets num[i] to a value higher than the scanned num values. After setting num[i], thread i scans the num values of the other threads once again, but this time when thread i encounters a positive num[j] less than num[i], it waits until num[j] becomes zero or higher than num[i] (signifying that j has left the critical section). When thread i completes this second scan, it enters the critical section. Upon leaving the critical section, it zeros num[i].

The above description is an over-simplification because it implicitly assumes that the first scan done by a hungry thread is atomic. In reality, only reads and writes of a num value are atomic. This complicates matters. Two hungry threads whose first scans overlap in time can end up with the same num value, for example, if both threads read num[0], $\cdots$, num[N – 1] in their first scans *before* either of them updates its num. In this case, the procedure described above would result in two threads waiting on each other forever in their second scans. Another complication is that when thread i reads num[j] in its second scan, thread j may be in the middle of its first scan. Thread i may read num[j] to be zero and hence not wait on num[j].

A.U. Shankar, *Distributed Programming: Theory and Practice*,
DOI 10.1007/978-1-4614-4881-5__10,
© Springer Science+Business Media New York 2013

However, the final value of num[j] may end up being less than num[i], and so thread j, in its second scan, would not wait on num[i], resulting in both threads being in the critical section at the same time.

The ingenuity of the bakery algorithm lies in how it handles these complications. For ease of understanding, we develop the lock program using the bakery algorithm in two stages. The first stage assumes that a hungry user's first scan is atomic, corresponding to the over-simplified description given above. The second stage relaxes this assumption, showing how the bakery algorithm handles the complications mentioned above.

It turns out, amazingly enough, that the bakery algorithm does not require reads to be atomic: when a read and a write overlap, the read can return any value. But it also has a drawback: its num values can increase without bound. Taubenfeld's **black-white bakery algorithm** [5] fixes this problem in an elegant way, but it requires reads to be atomic.

Conventions

We follow the common terminology of saying a user is "thinking" if it is not interested in the lock, "hungry" if it has a lock request pending, and "eating" if it has acquired the lock.

The bakery mechanism makes use of lexicographic ordering of two-tuples, so we extend the relational operator $<$ appropriately. Specifically, $[a_1, a_2] < [b_1, b_2]$ is defined to be "$a_1 < b_1$ or ($a_1 = b_1$ and $a_2 < b_2$)".

In the rest of this chapter, parameters i and j range over $0..N-1$.

End of conventions

10.2   Simplified Bakery Lock Program and Implements Conditions

The lock program based on the simplified bakery algorithm is shown in Fig. 10.1. Our goal is to establish that LockSimplifiedBakery(N) implements the lock service SimpleLockService(N) (Fig. 2.2). The lock service inverse, SimpleLockServiceInverse(N), is shown in Fig. 10.2 (repeated from Figs. 2.3 and 2.4). Figure 10.3 shows the closed program Z of instantiation lck of the lock program and instantiation lsi of the service inverse. We have to establish that Z satisfies the following assertions.

Y_1 :   *Inv* (thread at lsi.doAcq.ic) $\Rightarrow$ forall(i in $0..N-1$: not acqd[i])

Y_2 :   forall(i in $0..N-1$: (thread i in lck.rel) *leads-to* (not i in lck.rel))

Y_3 :   forall(i in $0..N-1$: (thread i in lck.end) *leads-to* (not i in lck.end))

Y_4 :   forall(i in $0..0..N-1$: acqd[i] *leads-to* not acqd[i])

          $\Rightarrow$ forall(i in $0..0..N-1$: (thread i on lck.acq) *leads-to* acqd[i])

```
program LockSimplifiedBakery(N) {
    ia {int N ≥ 1}
    // num[i] = 0 iff user i is thinking
    int[N] num ← 0;
    return mysid;

    input mysid.acq() {
        ia {mytid in 0..N-1}
s1:     num[mytid] ← max(num[0],
                         num[1],
                         ...,
                         num[N-1]) + 1;
        for (p in 0..N-1)
s2:         do { • int x ← num[p];
s3:         } while (x ≠ 0 and
                     x < num[mytid]);
        return;
    }

    input mysid.rel() {
        ia {mytid in 0..N-1}
s4:     num[mytid] ← 0;
        return;
    }

    input void mysid.end() {
        ia {true}
        endSystem();
    }

    atomicity assumption {
        s1, reads and writes of
        num[0], ..., num[N-1]
    }

    progress assumption {
        weak fairness for every thread
    }

} // end LockSimplifiedBakery
```

Fig. 10.1 Lock program from the simplified bakery algorithm

```
program SimpleLockServiceInverse
                (int N, Sid lck) {
    ic {N ≥ 1}
    boolean[N] acqd ← false;
    ending ← false;
    return mysid;

    output doAcq() {
        • oc {not ending
             and (mytid in 0..N-1)
             and not acqd[mytid]}
        lck.acq();
        ic {forall(j in 0..N-1:
                    not acqd[j])}
        acqd[mytid] ← true;
        return;
    }

    output doRel() {
        • oc {not ending
             and (mytid in 0..N-1)
             and acqd[mytid]}
        acqd[mytid] ← false;
        lck.rel();
        ic {true}
        return;
    }

    output doEnd() {
        • oc {not ending}
        lck.end();
        ic {true}
        return;
    }

    atomicity assumption {...}

    progress condition {...}
}
```

Fig. 10.2 Lock service inverse

```
program Z() {
  ia (int N ≥ 1}
  inputs(); outputs();    // closed system
  lck ← startSystem(LockSimplifiedBakery(N));
  lsi ← startSystem(SimpleLockServiceInverse(lck, N));
}
```

Fig. 10.3 Closed program of lock and service inverse

We now identify effectively-atomic steps in Z. Threads 0 through N-1 are the only threads in Z, and num[0], ..., num[N-1] are the only variables accessed by more than one thread. Here is a partitioning of the code in which each step contains at most one conflict. The resulting atomicity breakpoints are indicated by the '•'s in Fig. 10.1.

- Step Z.main: consisting of lck's main and lsi's main.
- Step doAcq call: from doAcq start to start of s2 (in input function acq). All conflicts are in s1, which is atomic.
- Step s2 iteration: from s2 back to s2, when s3's while-condition is true *or* p is less than N-1. The only conflict is num[p]'s access in s2. There is *no conflict* in num[mytid]'s access in s3 because num[mytid] can be modified only by thread mytid and that does not happen while thread mytid is on s2..s3.
- Step s2 return: from s2 to end of doAcq, when s3's while-condition is false *and* p equals N-1). The only conflict is num[p]'s access in s2.
- Step doRel: from start of doRel to end of doRel (including the execution of lck.rel). The only shared access is in s4.
- Step doEnd: from start of doEnd to end of doEnd (including the execution of lck.end).

10.3 Proving the Implements Conditions for Simplified Bakery

We now establish that Z satisfies Y_1–Y_4. Our analysis will be more concise than in previous chapters, in that some straightforward properties will be claimed without proof.

We expect hungry users to eat in the order of their num values, with smaller num values having higher priority. This motivates us to consider the *hypothetical* queue of (the tids of) non-thinking users ordered by their num values, with the user having the smallest num value at the head of the queue. This queue is empty iff every user is thinking. A user joins the queue *at the tail* upon becoming hungry and executing s1; because s1 is atomic, no two non-thinking users have the same num value. A user leaves the queue upon completing eating and executing doRel. These are the only two ways in which the queue changes.

We will show that the user at the head of the queue, i.e., with the smallest num value, is the only user that can eat. Furthermore, we will show that the user at the head is not blocked by any other user, and so it will eventually eat, after which all the users in the queue move one step closer to eating.

Define ahead(i) to be the set of users ahead of user i in the queue if i is non-thinking, and the empty set if i is thinking. Define passed(i,j) to be true iff user i is non-thinking and has completed execution of the do-while body with i.p = j since i last became hungry. A hungry user i *does not know* which, or how many, users are ahead of it in the queue, but it *does know* which users it has passed. Formally, define ahead(i) and passed(i,j) as the following functions:

- ahead(i): set(j:j in 0..N−1; 0 < num[j] < num[i])
- passed(i,j): (acqd[i] or ((thread i at s2) and i.p > j))

10.3.1 *Proving the Safety Condition:* Y_1

Given Z's atomicity breakpoints, a thread i comes to 1si.doAcq.ic iff it is at s2 and can execute step s2 return. Thus Y_1 is equivalent to $Inv\,A_0(i)$, where:

$A_0(i)$: (i on s2) and i.p = N−1
       and (num[i.p] = 0 or num[i.p] > num[i])
       $\Rightarrow$ forall(j in 0..N−1: not acqd[j])

For any non-thinking user i and any user j, we expect that i has passed j only if either j is thinking (num[j] = 0) or j is behind i in the queue (num[j] > num[i] > 0). Formally,

$A_1(i,j)$: (i $\neq$ j and passed(i,j)) $\Rightarrow$ (num[j] = 0 or (num[j] > num[i] > 0))

$Inv\,A_1(i,j)$ holds because $A_1(i,j)$ holds initially and is preserved by every atomic step. In particular, the following hold. Steps of users other than i or j do not affect $A_1(i,j)$. Step i.doAcq call falsifies passed(i,j). Steps i.s2 iteration and i.s2 return each establish the antecedent only if the consequent holds. Step i.doRel falsifies passed(i,j). Step j.doAcq call establishes the consequent. Steps j.s2 iteration and j.s2 return each has no affect on $A_1(i,j)$. Step j.doRel establishes the consequent.

$A_1(i,j)$ implies the desired A_0. Briefly, for any two i and j, $A_1(i,j)$ and $A_1(j,i)$ imply that acqd[i] and acqd[j] cannot hold as follows. If acqd[i] is true, then passed(i,j) holds and hence $A_1(i,j)$'s consequent holds. Similarly, if acqd[j] is true, then $A_1(j,i)$'s consequent holds. The two consequents, and the property that any user at doRel.oc has a non-zero num value, yield num[j] > num[i] and num[i] > num[j], which is a contradiction. We are done.

To flesh out the above proofs into assertional proofs, one needs to explicitly state and establish some straight-forward properties which are implicit in the above analysis, for example, Inv (thread t in lck.acq $\Rightarrow$ i in 0..N-1).

10.3.2 Proving the Progress Condition: Y_2–Y_3

Y_2 and Y_3 hold trivially because they have no loops and are executed with weak fairness. Y_3 holds if every thread on lck.acq eventually returns assuming every user that has the lock eventually releases it.

A user i at the head of the queue, i.e., with the smallest non-zero num, eventually eats because it does not wait indefinitely on s2 iteration. (The only way that num[j], j $\neq$ i, can change is if j executes s1, in which case num[j] becomes higher than num[i].) Hence the following holds:

$L_1(i)$: (num[i] $\neq$ 0 and ahead(i).size = 0) *leads-to* acqd[i]

Because eating is finite, if i has the lock it eventually executes doRel. This and L_1 imply the following:

$L_2(i)$: (num[i] $\neq$ 0 and ahead(i).size = 0) *leads-to* not acqd[i]

Now consider a non-thinking user i that is not at the head of the queue. Its position does not worsen, because users join the queue only at the tail. Its position eventually decreases because the user at the head eventually leaves the queue (from L_2). So we have

$L_3(i)$: (num[i] $\neq$ 0 and (ahead(i).size = k > 0))
        leads-to ((num[i] $\neq$ 0) and ahead(i).size < k)

The closure of L_3 and L_2 yields that every hungry user eventually eats.

10.4 Original Bakery Lock Program and Implements Conditions

We now consider the original bakery algorithm, that is, assuming atomicity of reads and writes of individual num[i]'s but not the atomicity of s1. As described earlier, this introduces two complications not present in the simplified bakery algorithm.

The first complication is that two non-thinking users can end up with equal num values. This is overcome by introducing a tie-breaking rule so that ties are resolved in a consistent manner. The priority of a non-thinking user i is now given by the two-tuple [num[i],i] under lexicographic ordering; that is, [k1,k2] < [j1,j2] if k1 < j1 or k1 = j1 and k2 < j2. So user i passes user j if it finds num[j] = 0 or [num[i],i] < [num[j],j] holding.

The second complication is that a thread i, when deciding whether to pass another thread j, may read num[j] while j is in the middle of updating it, and thereby obtain some "intermediate" value of num[j] that causes i to wrongly pass j; that is, i passes j now but [num[j],j] ends up being smaller than [num[i],i], and so j passes i while the latter has the lock. This complication is overcome by introducing a boolean flag choosing[i] for each user i, indicating whether i is in the middle of choosing its num value. When user i becomes hungry, it sets choosing[i] to true before reading the num values of the other users, and sets choosing[i] to false after setting its num[i].

When user i attempts to pass user j, it first waits until it finds choosing[j] to be false, and only then does it start checking num[j]. So it is still possible for thread i to read an unstable num[j], but this can happen only if j started choosing its value after i finished choosing its value. So num[j] will stabilize eventually to a value higher than num[i]. Hence there is no danger of i passing j now and j passing i later while i is still eating. As before, user i enters the critical section after going past every other user, and zeroes num[i] upon leaving the critical section.

The resulting lock program is shown in Fig. 10.4. It differs from the simplified bakery program (Fig. 10.1) as follows: array choosing in the main code; statements t1, t2, t3; the last conjunct of s3; and the atomicity breakpoints in s1 (which is no longer atomic). The lock service inverse program is repeated next to the lock program in Fig. 10.5. The closed program Z of the lock and service inverse is as in Fig. 10.3, except that LockSimplifiedBakery is replaced by LockBakery. As before, we have to establish that Z satisfies assertions Y_1–Y_4.

10.5 Proving the Implements Condition for Original Bakery

We follow the same procedure as with the simplified bakery program. Our analysis is in terms of the hypothetical queue of non-thinking users ordered by their [num,tid] pairs. As in the simplified case, a user leaves the queue only from the head. *Unlike* the simplified case, users can join this queue at *any* position. In particular, if users i and j have overlapping choosing durations, then it is possible that j completes choosing (i.e., reaches t2) after i completes choosing and yet num[j] is smaller than num[i]; this would happen, for example, if j.s1 read num[i] before i.s1 read num[j]. Thus hungry user i would be preempted by user j entering the queue ahead of i. However we shall see that hungry user i can be preempted by user j *at most once*.

Define ahead(i) and passed(i,j) as in the simplified case:

- ahead(i): set(j: j in $0..N-1$; num[j] $\neq 0$ and [num[j],j] < [num[i],i])
- passed(i,j): (acqd[i] or ((i at s2) and i.p > j))

For a hungry user i that has finished choosing its num value (i.e., on t3..s3), let peers[i] be the set of (tids of) users that (1) were choosing when i finished choosing, and (2) have not yet finished choosing. These are the only users that can overtake i in the queue. Formally, define peers[i] as an auxiliary variable as follows:

```
program LockBakery(N) {
  ia {int N ≥ 1}
  // num[i] = 0 iff user i is thinking
  int[N] num ← 0;
  // choosing[i] true if user i on s1
  boolean[N] choosing ← false;
  return mysid;

  input mysid.acq() {
    ia {mytid in 0..N-1}
t1: choosing[mytid] ← true;
s1: • num[mytid] ← max( • num[0],
                        • num[1],
                        • ...,
                        • num[N-1]) + 1;
t2: • choosing[mytid] ← false;
    for (p in 0..N-1)
t3:   while ( • choosing[p]) no-op;
s2:   do { • int x ← num[p];
s3:   } while (x ≠ 0 and
            (x < num[mytid] or
             (x = num[mytid] and p < mytid)));
    return;
  }

  input mysid.rel() {
    ia {mytid in 0..N-1}
    num[mytid] ← 0;
    return;
  }

  input void mysid.end() {
    ia {true}
    endSystem();
  }

  atomicity assumption {reads and writes of
    choosing[i], num[i], for i in 0..N-1}

  progress assumption {weak fairness
                       for every thread}
} // end LockBakery
```

Fig. 10.4 Lock program from the original bakery algorithm

```
program SimpleLockServiceInverse
              (int N, Sid lck) {
  ic {N ≥ 1}
  boolean[N] acqd ← false;
  ending ← false;
  return mysid;

  output doAcq() {
  • oc {not ending
       and (mytid in 0..N-1)
       and not acqd[mytid]}
    lck.acq();
    ic {forall(j in 0..N-1:
               not acqd[j])}
    acqd[mytid] ← true;
    return;
  }

  output doRel() {
  • oc {not ending
       and (mytid in 0..N-1)
       and acqd[mytid]}
    acqd[mytid] ← false;
    lck.rel();
    ic {true}
    return;
  }

  output doEnd() {
  • oc {not ending}
    lck.end();
    ic {true}
    return;
  }

  atomicity assumption {...}

  progress condition {...}
}
```

Fig. 10.5 Lock service inverse

- Insert the following in the main code:
    ```
    Set peers ← set();   // auxiliary variable
    ```
- Insert the following after t2, to be atomically executed with t2:
    ```
    peers[i] ← set(j: j in 0..N-1, choosing[j]);
    for (j in 0..N-1)
        peers[j].remove(i); // remove any i from peers[j]
    ```
- Insert the following in doAcq input part:
    ```
    peers[i] ← set();   // empty peers[i]
    ```

Note that peers[i] is empty when i is not on t3..s3, and i is in peers[j], $j \neq i$, only when i is on s1..t2.

10.5.1 Proving the Safety Condition: Y_1

Given Z's atomicity breakpoints, Y_1 is equivalent to $Inv\,C_0(i)$, where:

$C_0(i)$:   ((i on s2) and i.p = N-1
         and (num[p] = 0 or [num[i.p],i.p] > [num[i],i]))
         $\Rightarrow$ forall(j in 0..N-1: not acqd[j])

We expect that if i has passed j then either (1) j is thinking, or (2) j is choosing and it started choosing after i finished choosing, or (3) j has a stable non-zero num and is behind i in the queue. In any case, j would not be in peers[i]. We also expect that if i is at s2 with i.p = j and j is choosing, then j started choosing only after i completed choosing. Again, j would not be in peers[i]. Formally,

$C_1(i,j)$:   (i $\neq$ j and passed(i,j))
        $\Rightarrow$ ((not j in peers[i])
           and (not acqd[j] or (j on s1..t2)
              or (num[j] > 0 and [num[j],j] > [num[i],i])))
$C_2(i,j)$:   (i $\neq$ j and (i on s2) and i.p = j and choosing[j])
        $\Rightarrow$ (j not in peers[i])

$Inv\,C_2(i,j)$ holds because $C_2(i,j)$ holds initially and is preserved by every step. In particular, the following holds. Step i.t3 with i.p = j preserves $C_2(i,j)$ because i comes to s2 only if choosing[j] is false. Step i.s2 with i.p = j preserves it because nothing changes if the while test succeeds and the predicate holds vacuously if it fails (because i.p = j no longer holds). Step j.doAcq call preserves it because j, having just started choosing, is not in any user's peers set at this point. Every other step either does not affect the predicate or establishes it vacuously.

$Inv\,C_1(i,j)$ holds because $C_1(i,j)$ holds initially and is preserved by every step assuming $Inv\,C_2(i,j)$. In particular, the following hold. Step i.t2 zeros p and so falsifies the antecedent (passed(i,j)). Step i.s2 with i.p = j affects the predicate only if the while test succeeds, in which case it establishes the consequent. Step j.s2 with j.p = i does not affect the predicate because it cannot pass its while test because [num[j],j] > [num[i],i] holds (from $C_1(i,j)$'s consequent) prior to its execution. Every other step either does not affect the predicate or establishes it vacuously.

The desired safety assertion C_0 follows from $C_1(i,j)$ and $C_1(j,i)$, just as in the case of the simplified algorithm.

10.5.2   Proving the Progress Condition: Y_2–Y_3

Unlike in the simplified algorithm, ahead(i).size for a non-thinking user i is not monotonically decreasing, and so it is not an adequate metric for progress. But the two-tuple [peers[i].size, ahead(i).size] under lexicographic ordering is an adequate metric. The following hold while thread i is non-thinking:

D_1 : [peers[i].size,ahead(i).size] = [k1,k2] > [0,0]
         unless ([peers[i].size,ahead(i).size] < [k1,k2])

D_2 : peers[i].size = k1 > 0 *leads-to* peers[i].size < k1

D_3 : [peers[i].size,ahead(i).size] = [0,0] *leads-to* acqd[i]

D_4 : [peers[i].size,ahead(i).size] = [0,0] *leads-to* not acqd[i]

D_5 : [peers[i].size,ahead(i).size] = [k1,k2] > [0,0]
         leads-to [peers[i].size,ahead(i).size] < [k1,k2]

D_1 holds because (1) peers[i] can only decrease (no user joins peers[i]), and (2) any increase to ahead(i) is simultaneously accompanied by a decrease in peers[i] (because only a user in peers[i] can enter the queue ahead of i). D_2 holds because every user in peers[i] eventually leaves (since t1..t2 is non-blocking and threads have weak fairness). D_3 holds because i does not get blocked at s2 for any i.p. D_4 holds from D_3 and the assumption that eating is bounded. D_5 holds if k1 > 0 because of D_2 and D_1. D_5 holds if k1 = 0 and k2 > 0 because of D_4 for the user at the head of the queue. The desired progress assertion follows from D_5 and D_3.

10.6   Concluding Remarks

A distinctive feature of the bakery algorithm is that every variable is written by only one thread. Hence simultaneous writes to the same variable never occur. This is unlike almost all other mutex solutions (e.g., Peterson's algorithm allows simultaneous writes to turn). Thus the underlying platform does not have to ensure the atomicity of concurrent writes. The bakery algorithm has an even more beautiful property. It works *regardless of the value obtained by a read that overlaps a write*! In other words, a read need not be atomic. To see this, consider the possible read-write overlaps.

- Suppose choosing[j] is read by thread i (in t3) while being updated by thread j (in t1 or t2). Thread i reads either true or false. (Because choosing[j] is a boolean, thread i will interpret whatever it reads as a boolean.) In either case, the value read is consistent with the read being atomic. For example, if j is on t1 and i reads true, this is consistent with i.t1 happening atomically just after j.t1.

- Suppose thread i reads num[j] (in s2) and gets the value n while thread j is in the thread of updating num[j] (in s1) to a final value of m. Because the read overlaps with the write, n can be any non-negative integer. Suppose n is lower than m. Then thread i may needlessly busy wait on j in s2;s3, but this anomaly does not last because i repeatedly reads num[j] and it will get the correct value m once j completes its write. Suppose n is higher than m. Then thread i may pass thread j in s2, but this is ok because j started choosing after num[i] was stable. So i would have passed j even if it had read the correct final value m.
- Suppose thread i reads num[j] (in s2) and gets the value n while thread j is updating num[j] to 0 in rel. Again, the value n that i reads does not matter as long as it is treated as a non-negative integer. (The argument is similar to the above case.)

But the bakery algorithm also has an undesirable property. The num values *can increase without bound*; this happens when users keep acquiring and releasing the lock while there is always at least one non-thinking user. There is no simple way to bound the num values.

The **black-white bakery algorithm** [5] solves this problem in an elegant way. However, it has a binary-valued variable that can be simultaneously written. The algorithms maintains two queues of non-thinking users, a "black" queue and a "white" queue, and a binary-valued flag that is either black or white. The flag indicates the queue that is currently *open*; the other queue is *closed*. An arriving user reads the flag, joins the open queue, and sets its num based on users in its queue. Users within a queue are ordered by their num-id pairs. Users in the open queue defer to users in the closed queue. When a user eats, it sets the flag to the opposite color of the user; if this is the first user to eat out of the users currently in its queue, the queue goes from open to closed. Each evolution of the algorithm has the following structure.

1. Initially both queues are empty and the flag is, say, white.
2. Arriving users join the white queue. When the first of these users eats, the white queue becomes closed and the black queue becomes open (and is empty).
3. Arriving users join the black queue. They defer to users in the white queue. When the white queue becomes empty, the first of the users in the black queue eats. At this point the black queue becomes closed, and the white queue becomes open (and is empty).
4. Arriving users join the white queue. They defer to users in the black queue. When the black queue becomes empty, the first of the users in the white queue eats. At this point the white queue becomes closed, and the black queue becomes open (and is empty). Go to 3.

Because a queue is empty when it becomes open, the first arrival to it gets a num value of 1. This ensures that the num values do not exceed N.

Exercises

10.1. Give assertional proofs of safety and progress for the simplified bakery algorithm, by adding any additional assertions needed to instantiate the proof rules.

10.2. Repeat Exercise 10.1 for the (original) bakery algorithm.

10.3. In the original bakery algorithm, each of the "for" loops scans the threads in the order $0, \ldots, N-1$. Is any order acceptable? (Note that if the answer is yes, thread i can start $N-1$ threads and scan the num values of the other threads in parallel.)

10.4. Write down a lock program based on the black-white bakery algorithm, described in Sect. 10.6, and prove that it implements the lock service.

References

1. E.W. Dijkstra, Cooperating sequential processes. Technical report, Burroughs, Nuenen, 1965. EWD-123
2. E.W. Dijkstra, Solution of a problem in concurrent programming control. Commun. ACM **8**(9), 569 (1965). doi:10.1145/365559.365617. http://doi.acm.org/10.1145/365559.365617
3. M.A. Eisenberg, M.R. McGuire, Further comments on dijkstra's concurrent programming control problem. Commun. ACM **15**(11), 999 (1972). doi:10.1145/355606.361895. http://doi.acm.org/10.1145/355606.361895
4. L. Lamport, A new solution of dijkstra's concurrent programming problem. Commun. ACM **17**(8), 453–455 (1974). doi:10.1145/361082.361093. http://doi.acm.org/10.1145/361082.361093
5. G. Taubenfeld, The black-white bakery algorithm and related bounded-space, adaptive, local-spinning and fifo algorithms, in *DISC* (ACM, New York, 2004), pp. 56–70

Chapter 11
Distributed Lock Service

11.1 Introduction

This chapter presents a **distributed lock service**, that is, a lock whose users may be spread over different locations (e.g., users at different computers of a network). At each location there is an access system through which users access the lock. (In contrast, SimpleLockService (in Chap. 2) is centralized because all users access the service at one system.)

The service has one parameter, the set of addresses of the locations at which the lock can be accessed. At each address j, the program has an access system with two input functions: acq(), to request the lock; and rel(), to release the lock. Figure 11.1 illustrates the service. For brevity, we do not consider termination; it can be added in exactly the same way as was explained for connection-less channels (Sect. 4.2).

11.2 Service Program

The service program is given in Fig. 11.2. Parameter ADDR is the set of addresses of the locations at which the lock can be accessed. The main code defines the following. Variable eating is null if no one has the lock; otherwise it stores the tid of the user currently holding the lock. Variable users is a map indexed by addresses such that users[j], for address j, is the set of tids of users currently accessing the

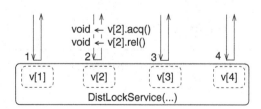

Fig. 11.1 Distributed lock service over addresses 1, 2, 3 and 4, with access system v[j] at address j

A.U. Shankar, *Distributed Programming: Theory and Practice*,
DOI 10.1007/978-1-4614-4881-5__11,
© Springer Science+Business Media New York 2013

```
service DistLockService(Set ADDR) { // distributed lock over addresses ADDR
   ic {ADDR.size ≥ 1}
   Tid eating ← null;                // user with lock if not null
   Map users ← map();               // users[j]: user at address j
   // v[j]: sid of access system at address j
   Map v ← map([j,sid()]: j in ADDR);
   return v;
   // end main

   input void v[ADDR j].acq() {
      ic {mytid ≠ eating}
      users[j].add(mytid);
      oc {eating = null}
      eating ← mytid;
      return;
   }

   input void v[ADDR j].rel() {
      ic {mytid = eating and (mytid in users[j])}
      users[j].remove(mytid);
      eating ← null;
      oc {true}
      return;
   }

   atomicity assumption {input parts and output parts}

   progress assumption {
      // v[j].rel call eventually returns
      forall(Tid u, ADDR j:
              (thread u in v[j].rel) leads-to (not u in v[j].rel));

      // if no one holds the lock forever then no one starves
      (eating ≠ null leads-to eating = null)
      ⇒ forall(Tid u, ADDR j:
                  (thread u in users[j]) leads-to u = eating);
   }

} // end DistLockService
```

Fig. 11.2 Distributed lock service program

service at j, i.e., the users at j that are waiting for the lock and the eating user (if any) that acquired the lock at j. Variable v is a map from addresses to sids such that v[j] stores the sid of the access system at address j.

Each access system v[j] has two input functions. v[j].acq, to acquire the lock; and v[j].rel, to release the lock. Function v[j].acq can be called only by a non-eating user. This is equivalent to saying that the caller is not in users[k] for any address k (because a user in users(k) is either eating or blocked at v[k].acq's output condition). Function v[j].rel can be called only by an eating user that acquired the lock at addresss j.

11.2.1 Service Inverse

The inverse of the service program is shown in Fig. 11.3. It is obtained from the lock service in the usual way. Map v returned by the service's main is added as a parameter. Input functions are changed to output functions. The progress "assumption" is renamed to be a progress "condition".

11.3 Concluding Remarks

The literature has numerous algorithms that implement a distributed lock given a fifo channel connecting the access systems, e.g., [1–9]. We will examine some in later chapters, but for now we outline two simple solutions and point out some optimizations.

The first solution we outline is essentially a centralized solution in which a particular access system, say v[0], controls the lock. Calls to acq and rel are converted to messages and sent to v[0]. System v[0] queues acq-call messages serves them in first-come-first-serve order. When the lock is available, it removes the acq-call message at the head of the queue and sends back an acq-return message. When a rel-call message is received, system v[0] responds with a rel-return message and treats the lock as available.

The second solution we outline is a distributed version of the simple lock solution in Chap. 2. A "token" message circulates among the access systems in some fixed order. When an access system v[j] receives the token, it does the following. If no local acq calls are ongoing then v[j] forwards the token to the next access system. Otherwise, v[j] returns an ongoing acq call, waits for a rel call, and then forwards the token to the next access system.

Both solutions have disadvantages. In the first solution, system v[0] can be a bottleneck. In the second solution, every system periodically does work on behalf of the lock, even if it has no interest in the lock. One would like a solution in which the resolution of a request involves only those systems that are currently non-thinking. We will see a solution that comes close to this ideal in Chap. 16.

~~service DistLockService(Set<Val> ADDR) {~~
program DistLockServiceInverse(Set<Val> ADDR, Map<ADDR,Sid> v) {

```
    ic {ADDR.size ≥ 1}
    Tid eating ← null;                    // user with lock if not null
    Map users ← map();                    // users[j]: user at address j
    Map v ← map({j,sid()}: j in ADDR);    // v[j]: access system at address j
    return v mysid;
    // end main

    input void v[ADDR j].acq() {
    output doAcq(ADDR j) {
        ie oc {mytid ≠ eating}
        users[j].add(mytid);
        v[j].acq();
        oe ic {eating = null}
        eating ← mytid;
        return;
    }

    input void v[ADDR j].rel() {
    output doRel(ADDR j) {
        ie oc {mytid = eating and (mytid in users[j])}
        users[j].remove(mytid);
        eating ← null;
        v[j].rel();
        oe ic {true}
    }

    atomicity assumption {input parts and output parts}

    progress assumption condition {
        forall(Tid u, ADDR j:
                (thread u in v[j].rel) leads-to  (not u in v[j].rel));

        (eating ≠ null leads-to eating = null)
           ⇒ forall(Tid u, ADDR j:
                   (thread u in users[j]) leads-to  u = eating);
    }

} // end LockServiceInverse
```

Fig. 11.3 Distributed lock service inverse program

Exercises

11.1. Obtain an await-structured program that implements the lock service by fleshing out the first solution outlined in the concluding remarks.

11.2. Implement your await-structured program in Exercise 11.1 with locks and condition variables.

11.3. Obtain an await-structured program that implements the lock service by fleshing out the second solution outlined in the concluding remarks.

11.4. Implement your await-structured program in Exercise 11.3 with locks and condition variables.

References

1. S. Banerjee, P. Chrysanthis, A new token passing distributed mutual exclusion algorithm. Int. Conf. Distrib. Comput. Syst. **0**, 717 (1996). doi:http://doi.ieeecomputersociety.org/10.1109/ICDCS.1996.508024
2. D. Ginat, A.U. Shankar, An assertional proof of correctness and serializability of a distributed mutual exclusion algorithm based on path reversal. Technical report, University of Maryland, Computer Science Department, 1988. CSTR-2104
3. L. Lamport, Time, clocks, and the ordering of events in a distributed system. Commun. ACM **21**(7), 558–565 (1978). doi:10.1145/359545.359563. http://doi.acm.org/10.1145/359545.359563
4. M. Maekawa, A $\sqrt{n}$ algorithm for mutual exclusion in decentralized systems. ACM Trans. Comput. Syst. **3**(2), 145–159 (1985). doi:10.1145/214438.214445. http://doi.acm.org/10.1145/214438.214445
5. M. Mizuno, M.L. Neilsen, R. Rao, A token based distributed mutual exclusion algorithm based on quorum agreements, in *Proceedings of International Conference on Distributed Computing Systems* (IEEE, LosAlamitos, 1991), pp. 361–368
6. M.L. Neilsen, M. Mizuno, A dag-based algorithm for distributed mutual exclusion, in *Proceedings of International Conference on Distributed Computing Systems* (IEEE, LosAlamitos, 1991), pp. 354–360
7. G. Ricart, A.K. Agrawala, An optimal algorithm for mutual exclusion in computer networks. Commun. ACM **24**(1), 9–17 (1981). doi:10.1145/358527.358537. http://doi.acm.org/10.1145/358527.358537
8. I. Suzuki, T. Kasami, A distributed mutual exclusion algorithm. ACM Trans. Comput. Syst. **3**(4), 344–349 (1985). doi:10.1145/6110.214406. http://doi.acm.org/10.1145/6110.214406
9. M. Trehel, M. Naimi, A distributed algorithm for mutual exclusion based on data structures and fault tolerance, in *6th Annual International Phoenix Conference on Computers and Communication*, Scottsdale, 1987, pp. 35–39

Chapter 12
Distributed Lock Using Timestamps

12.1 Introduction

This chapter uses Lamport's timestamp mechanism [3] to solve a "distributed request scheduling" problem. It then refines the solution to a distributed program that implements the distributed lock service (Chap. 11) over a fifo channel.

The timestamp mechanism allows systems attached to a fifo channel to achieve a total order on statement executions that is consistent with causality. The mechanism is simple. Each system has an integer **clock** variable (which need not be a real-time clock) and an id (which need not be an sid or tid). When a system executes a statement that is to be ordered, it increases its clock and sends to all other systems a message containing a description of the statement, its clock value, and its id. The clock value is referred to as the **timestamp** of the statement execution. When a system receives this message, it increases its clock to a value higher than the message's timestamp.

A statement execution x is ordered before a statement execution y iff (1) x's timestamp is less than y's timestamp, or (2) their timestamps are equal and x's system's id is lower than y's system's id. In other words, x is ordered before y if x's timestamp-id pair is *lexicographically* smaller than y's timestamp-id pair. We refer to a timestamp-id pair as an **extended timestamp**.

Given statement executions x and y, we say x **causally precedes** y if (1) x and y happened in that order within the same system, (2) x sent a message that y received, or (3) there is a sequence of such causal precedences leading from x to y, i.e., transitive closure of the first two relations. The extended-timestamp ordering is consistent with causality: x's timestamp is less than y's timestamp if x causally precedes y.

Causal precedence is a *partial* order on statement executions. If x and y are not causally related, i.e., neither causally precedes the other, there is no way for the systems to determine which actually happened first (without using real-time clocks or communicating outside the fifo channel). The best one can hope for is for all

A.U. Shankar, *Distributed Programming: Theory and Practice*,
DOI 10.1007/978-1-4614-4881-5__12,
© Springer Science+Business Media New York 2013

systems to agree on some arbitrary ordering of x and y. This is what the timestamp mechanism provides.

Section 12.2 describes the "distributed request scheduling" problem and solves it using the timestamp mechanism. Distributed locks are a special case of distributed request scheduling. Section 12.3 presents the distributed lock solution at the algorithm level, and proves that it satisfies desired correctness properties. Section 12.4 translates the algorithm-level description into a program that implements the distributed lock service. The proof of the implementation conditions follows trivially from the algorithm-level analysis. Section 12.5 refines the solution so that timestamps can be cyclic.

Conventions

We use i, j and k as parameters that range over addresses.

For readability, we say "system j" to mean the system at address j (instead of using its sid). Similarly, we refer to a quantity x in system j as j.x.

For brevity, we use the address of a system as its id for timestamping purposes.

Set minus is denoted by "\". So given sets A and B, the construct A\B is the set of entries in A that are not in B.

End of conventions

12.2 Request Scheduling Problem and Solution Using Timestamps

The **request scheduling problem** is as follows. Consider a collection of systems attached to a fifo channel. Users issue requests to the systems. Each request is to be "served" by the local system. Requests can conflict. Conflicting requests should not be served simultaneously (by the same system or by different systems). We want a mechanism that informs each system when to serve a request issued by its user. Note that the problem corresponds to that of a distributed lock if every two requests conflict; serving a request then corresponds to holding the lock. The problem corresponds to a distributed readers-writers lock if requests are classified into reads and writes and a write request conflicts with every other request.

The solution using the timestamp mechanism is as follows. Each system j maintains the following variables.

- clk: timestamping clock; initially 0.
- rts: map over addresses other than j. Entry rts[k] stores the highest timestamp received from k; initially 0.
  Let αRts denote min([rts[k],k]: k in rts.keys), i.e., the minimum extended timestamp induced by rts.

- req: set containing [x,t,k] for every request x with extended timestamp [t,k] that system j has received or generated and perceives as unserved; initially empty.

The systems exchange "request", "release" and "ack" messages. A request message has the form [REQ,x,t,k], where REQ is a constant, x is a request (issued by a user), t is its timestamp, and k is the sender's address. A release message has the form [REL,x,t,k], where REL is a constant and x, t and k are as in the request message. An ack message has the form [ACK,t,k], where ACK is a constant, and t and k are the sender's clock value and address.

System j obeys the following (atomically executed) rules.

- When user issues request x:
  clk ← clk+1;
  add [x,clk,j] to req;
  send [REQ,x,clk,j] to every other system.
- Start serving request [x,t,j] only if
  ([x,t,j] in req)
  and (for every [y,s,k] in req such that x conflicts with y: [t,j] ≤ [s,k])
  and [t,j] ≤αRts
- Finish serving request [x,t,j]:
  remove [x,t,j] from req;
  send [REL,x,t,j] to every other system.
- Receive [REQ,x,t,k]:
  clk ← max(clk, t+1); rts[k] ← t;
  add [x,t,k] to req;
  send [ACK,clk,j] to k.
- Receive [ACK,t,k]:
  clk ← max(clk, t); rts[k] ← t.
- Receive [REL,x,t,k]:
  remove [x,t,k] from req.

Because clocks are non-decreasing and the channel is fifo, system j will never receive a timestamp from system k that is less than j.rts[k]. Consequently, every request with extended timestamp less than αRts has entered j.req and leaves j.req only after it has been served. Thus when system j starts serving a request [x,t,j], there is no unserved conflicting request with smaller timestamp anywhere in the distributed system. Thus conflicting requests are not served simultaneously. Every request is eventually served if every request's service is bounded because all systems learn when a request's service ends (via the release messages), at which point the next conflicting request, if any, can be served.

(*Note*: When system j receives a request message [REQ,x,t,k], it need not send an ack if it has already sent, or will soon send, a request or release message to k with a higher extended timestamp than [t,k]. Also, because what matters is the extended-timestamp order rather than the timestamp order, system j can set its clk to max(clk,t), instead of max(clk,t+1), if j is greater than k.)

12.3   Distributed Lock Program: Algorithm Level

This section presents a distributed lock program obtained by specializing the request scheduling solution for the case where every two requests conflict. The distributed program, called LockTsDist, is shown in Fig. 12.1. It has one parameter, the set of addresses of the distributed lock. It starts a fifo channel with these addresses, then a lock component system at each address, then returns the sid map of the lock component systems. The resulting configuration is illustrated in Fig. 12.2.

Each lock component system is an instantiation of a program LockTs. In this section, the activity at each address is described at an algorithm level. Let "system j" denote the composite system of the users and the LockTs system at address j. System j will have at most one user request participating in the timestamp mechanism. (Until that request's service ends, system j will buffer any other user request.) We say system j is "thinking", "hungry" or "eating" to mean the usual: it becomes hungry when it introduces a request into the timestamp mechanism, eating when it starts to serve the request, and thinking when it finishes serving the request.

```
program LockTsDist(Set ADDR) {       // distributed lock program
    ia {ADDR.size ≥ 1}

    // c[j]: sid of channel access system at address j
    c ← startSystem(FifoChannel(ADDR));

    // v[j]: will hold sid of lock system at address j
    // LockTs: lock component program
    Map v ← map();
    for (j in ADDR)
        v[j] ← startSystem(LockTs(ADDR,j,c[j]));
    return v;
} // end LockTsDist
```

Fig. 12.1 Distributed program of lock component systems and fifo channel

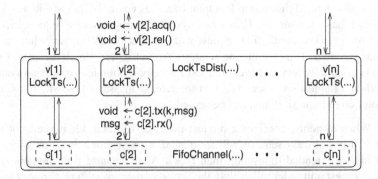

Fig. 12.2 Distributed lock using timestamps and fifo channel with addresses 1, ⋯, n

Variables of system j

- clk ← 0. Timestamp clock.
- rts ← map([k,0]: k ≠ j).
  // rts[k] is max timestamp received from k
- req ← map().
  // req[k] exists iff j knows of ongoing request [req[k], k]
- status: thinking, hungry or eating; initially thinking.

Helper functions of system j

- αRts: min([rts[k], k]: k ≠ j)
  // minimum extended timestamp induced by rts
- αReq: min([req[k], k]: k in req.keys)
  // minimum extended timestamp induced by req

Rules of system j (atomically executed)

- Become hungry only if thinking:
  clk ← clk+1;
  req[j] ← clk;
  send [REQ, clk, j] to every other system.
- Become eating only if hungry
  and [req[j], j] =αReq ≤αRts.
- Become thinking only if eating:
  remove entry for j from req;
  send [REL, j] to every other system.
- Receive [REQ,t,k]:
  clk ← max(clk, t+1); rts[k] ← t;
  req[k] ← t;
  send [ACK,clk,j] to k.
- Receive [ACK,t,k]:
  clk ← max(clk, t); rts[k] ← t.
- Receive [REL,k]:
  remove entry for k from req;

Fig. 12.3 Variables and rules of system j in timestamp-based distributed lock

The variables and rules of system j are given in Fig. 12.3. The request, release and ack messages are simpler than before (because all requests conflict and a system has at most one ongoing request). A request message has the form [REQ,t,k] where [t,k] is the extended timestamp of the request. A release message has the form [REL,k] where k is the sender's address. An ack message has the form [ACK,t,k] where t and k are the sender's clock value and address. System j maintains variables clk, rts and req as in the request scheduling problem, except that req is now a map over addresses. Entry req[k] exists and equals t iff a request with extended timestamp [t,k] was generated or received by j and is still unserved from system j's perspective. Denote by αReq the minimum [req[k], k] over all req[k] entries.

When system j becomes hungry, it increments its clock, sends the request message [REQ,clk,j] to every other system, and sets req[j] to clk. System j starts eating when the extended timestamp of its request, [req[j], j], equals αReq and is less than or equal to αRts (the minimum extended timestamp induced by rts). When system j stops eating, it sends a release message [REL,j] to every other system, where REL is a constant. When system j receives request message [REQ,t,k], it updates clk and rts[k], sets req[k] to t, and sends an ack message. When system j receives a release message [REL,k], it removes the entry for k from req.

12.3.1 Analysis

We first prove that at most one system is eating at any time. The following hold invariantly. (Because req is a map indexed by address, "[k,t] in req" corresponds to the informal "extended timestamp [t,k] 'in' req".)

A_1 : (([j,s] in k.req) and j $\neq$ k)
$\qquad \Rightarrow$ ([j,s] in j.req) or ([REL,j] in transit to k)

A_2 : (j eating)
$\qquad \Rightarrow$ [j.req[j], j] = j.αReq $\leq$ j.αRts

A_3 : ((j eating) and (k eating)) $\Rightarrow$ j = k

A_4 : ((j hungry) and [j.req[j], j] = j.αReq $\leq$ j.αRts)
$\qquad \Rightarrow$ (no one eating)

Proof of Inv.A_1–A_4 *Inv A_1* holds as follows. Entry [j,s] joins k.req when message [REQ,s,j] arrives at k, which happens after [j,s] joins j.req. It leaves k.req when message [REL,j] arrives at k, which happens after [j,s] has left j.req.

Inv A_2 holds as follows. A_1's rhs becomes true when A_1's lhs becomes true. It stays true as long as j is eating because [s,j] $\leq$ j.αRts, which holds when j becomes eating, ensures that j will not receive a request (or any message) with extended timestamp less than [s,j].

Inv A_3 holds as follows. Suppose j and k are different and are both eating. Let j.req[j] be s, let k.req[k] be t, and, without loss of generality, let [s,j] be less than [t,k]. Because j is eating, [s,j] $\leq$ j.αRts holds (from A_2). Hence j has received all requests with extended timestamps less than [s,j], including [t,k]. Because k is eating, [k,t] is still in j.req (from A_1). Hence [s,j] is not the smallest extended timestamp induced by j.req, contradicting A_2.

Inv A_4 is implied by (and is just a restatement of) *Inv A_3*. A_4's lhs says that system j can become eating. So A_4 says that if j can become eating then no one is eating. If this were not true, then j becoming eating would falsify A_3. $\square$

Next to show that every hungry system becomes eating if every eating system becomes thinking. We will prove the following.

P_1 : (U_1 and U_2 and U_3)
$\qquad \Rightarrow$ ((j hungry) *leads-to* (j eating))

where

U_1 : forall(k: (k eating) *leads-to* (k thinking))   // eating is finite
U_2 : weak fairness for the 'become-eating' rule
U_3 : (no ongoing rx call) *leads-to* (ongoing rx call)
$\qquad\qquad\qquad\qquad\qquad$ // system j always ready to receive messages

We start by defining the following auxiliary quantities.

- $\overline{hst}$:   global history of extended timestamps of requests in increasing order.
- $\overline{ne}$:   number of entries in $\overline{hst}$ that have finished eating.

Because $\overline{hst}$ is sorted by extended timestamp, a new entry can join it at a position other than the tail. But the prefix $\overline{hst}[0..\overline{ne}-1]$, consisting of the entries that have finished eating, grows only at the tail.

Assume U_1–U_3 for the rest of this section. When system j becomes hungry with extended timestamp [s,j], it adds [s,j] to $\overline{hst}$ and sends a [REQ,s,j] message to every other system k. System k receives this message (because of channel progress and U_3) and sends an ack response. System j receives the ack (because of channel progress and U_3), at which point [j.rts[k],k] is updated to exceed [s,j]. Other steps cannot prevent this from happening (but they can make this happen earlier). Thus the following holds:

P_2 : ([j,s] in j.req) *leads-to* (([j,s] in j.req) and [s,j] $\le$ j.αRts)

Once P_2's rhs holds, the [s,j] entry occupies a "stable" position in $\overline{hst}$, i.e., its distance to the head of $\overline{hst}$ does not increase. Suppose j is not eating.

1. If $\overline{ne}$ is zero and $\overline{hst}[\overline{ne}]$ equals [s,j], then no one has yet eaten yet and system j's become-eating rule is unblocked and remains so. System j eventually starts eating (by U_2).
2. If $\overline{ne}$ is greater than zero and $\overline{hst}[\overline{ne}]$ equals [s,j], then the request at $\overline{hst}[\overline{ne}-1]$ has finished eating and its release message is in transit to j; it will arrive (by channel progress and U_3), at which point argument 1 applies.
3. If $\overline{hst}[\overline{ne}+n]$ equals [s,j] for some n greater than zero, then there is another request at position $\overline{hst}[\overline{ne}]$. That request will eat (by arguments 1 and 2), then stop eating (by U_1), after which $\overline{hst}[\overline{ne}+n-1]$ equals [s,j], i.e., [s,j] is now one step closer to position $\overline{ne}$. So eventually [s,j] will be at position $\overline{ne}$, after which it will eat.

We have established the following.

P_3 : (([j,s] in j.req) and [s,j] $\le$ j.αRts) *leads-to* (j eating)

Combining P_2 and P_3 yields P_1's rhs.

12.4   Distributed Lock Program

We now cast the rules of system j (in Fig. 12.3) into an await-structured program LockTs. We prove that the resulting distributed program LockTsDist implements the distributed lock service (Chap. 11). Program LockTs is shown in Figs. 12.4 and 12.5. Implementing the awaits with standard synchronization constructs is left as an exercise.

The program has three parameters: ADDR, set of addresses of all the component systems; aL, local address (of this component system); and cL, sid of the local channel access system. It has two input functions, mysid.acq and mysid.rel. The boxes are comments containing fragments of the distributed lock service inverse matching the LockTs code at the left. The first box shows the service inverse's main. The second box, to the right of input function mysid.acq, shows the body of the matching output function mysid.doAcq from the service inverse. The third box plays the same role for input function mysid.rel.

The main code defines types for request, ack and release messages. It defines helper functions, αRts, which returns the minimum extended timestamp induced by rts, and αReq, which returns the minimum extended timestamp in req. It then defines the variables clk, rts and req, exactly as in the algorithm-level description, and starts a local thread, tRx, executing function doRx.

Function doRx is executed by local thread tRx. It repeatedly receives a message and processes it. If it receives a request message, it inserts the message's timestamp in req, updates rts and clk, and sends an ack message. If it receives an ack message, it updates rts and clk. If it receives a release message, it removes the corresponding entry from req.

Input function mysid.acq can be called by any thread that does not already have the lock. In particular, it can be called by several threads at the same time. The function consists of two awaits, at a1 and a2.

- A thread gets past await a1 only if aL is not in req.keys, i.e., only if this system has no ongoing request in the timestamp mechanism. In executing the await, the thread gets a new timestamp from clk, saves the timestamp in req[aL], sends out the corresponding request message to all other addresses (recall that "\" denotes set minus), and waits at a2. Thus at most one thread can be at await a2.
- A thread gets past await a2 only if (1) the extended timestamp of its request, [req[aL], aL], is the minimum of the extended timestamps induced by req and (2) either ADDR has only one entry (i.e., this is the only system) or [req[aL], aL] is less than the minimum extended timestamp induced by rts. When it gets past the await, it returns from this input function. It now has the lock, and req[aL] remains equal to the timestamp of its request.

Input function mysid.rel removes the entry for aL from req, sends a release message to every other system, and returns. At this point, if threads are waiting at mysid.acq's await a1, one of them gets past the await. Await a1 has strong fairness,

```
program LockTs(Set ADDR, ADDR aL, Sid cL) {      // lock component system
    // aL: address of this system. cL: sid of local channel access system
    ia {true}
    // types
    REQ ← 1; ACK ← 2; REL ← 3;
    type ReqMsg = Tuple<REQ,int,ADDR>;           // request messages
    type AckMsg = Tuple<ACK,int,ADDR>;           // ack messages
    type RelMsg = Tuple<REL,ADDR>;               // release messages
    // variables
    int clk ← 0;
    Map rts ← map([j,0]: j in ADDR, j ≠ aL);
    Seq req ← map();
    // thread to do receives and ACK sends
    Tid tRx ← startThread(doRx());
    return mysid;
    // end main

    // helper functions
    function Seq αRts() { // min xts "in" rts
        return min([rts[k], k]: k in ADDR, k ≠ aL);
    }

    function Seq αReq() { // min xts "in" req
        return min([req[k], k]: k in req.keys);
    }

    input void mysid.acq() {
        ia {true}
a1: •  await (not (aL in req.keys)) {
            clk ← clk + 1;
            req[aL] ← clk;
            for (j in ADDR\set(aL))
                cL.tx(j,[REQ,clk,aL]);
        }
a2: •  await ([req[aL], aL] =αReq()
                and (ADDR.size = 1
                    or [req[aL], aL] ≤αRts()));
        return;
    }

// continued
```

```
DistLockServiceInverse(ADDR,v)
    // main

    ic {Set(ADDR)
        and ADDR.size ≥ 1
        and Map<ADDR,Sid>(v)}
    Tid eating ← null;
    // users[j]: user threads at j
    Map users ← map();
    return mysid;
```

```
DistLockServiceInverse
    // doAcq(aL)

    oc {(aL in ADDR)
        and (mytid ≠ eating)}
    users[aL].add(mytid);
    v[aL].acq();
    ic {eating = null}
    eating ← mytid;
```

Fig. 12.4 Part 1: program LockTs. Boxes are comments containing fragments of the distributed lock service inverse

```
// continuing LockTs
```

```
    input void mysid.rel() {
        ia {true}
        await (true) {
            req.remove(aL);
            for (j in ADDR\set(aL))
                cL.tx(j,[REL, aL]);
            return;
        }
    }
```

```
DistLockServiceInverse
// doRel(aL)
oc {(aL in ADDR)
        and (mytid in users[aL])
        and (mytid = eating)}
users[aL].remove(mytid);
eating ← null;
v[aL].rel();
ic {true}
```

```
    function doRx() { // executed by thread tRx
        while (true) {
        ● Seq msg ← cL.rx();
            ia {msg in union(ReqMsg,AckMsg,RelMsg)}   // REQ/ACK/REL msg
            await (true) {
                if (msg[0] = REQ) {
                    req[msg[2]] ← rts[msg[2]] ← msg[1];
                    clk ← max(clk,msg[1]+1);
                    cL.tx(msg[2],[ACK,clk,aL]);
                } else if (msg[0] = ACK) {
                    rts[msg[2]] ← msg[1];
                    clk ← max(clk,msg[1]);
                } else if (msg[0] = REL)
                    req.remove(msg[1]);
            }
        }
    }
```

```
    atomicity assumption {awaits}

    progress assumption {weak fairness of threads,
                        strong fairness of await a1}
} // end LockTs
```

Fig. 12.5 Part 2: program LockTs of lock component system

so every thread at a1 eventually arrives at a2 as long as req keeps getting its entry for aL removed.

12.4.1   Proving the Implements Conditions

Our goal is to establish that LockTsDist(ADDR) implements DistLockService(ADDR) (in Fig. 11.2). Figure 12.6 shows the closed program Z of LockTsDist and

DistLockServiceInverse. (The latter is in Fig. 11.3; it is also available from the boxes in Figs. 12.4.) Note that Z.ia does not constrain DistLockService.ic. We have to establish that Z satisfies the following assertions.

B_1 : *Inv* (thread at lsi.doAcq(j).ic) $\Rightarrow$ lsi.eating = null
B_2 : (thread u in j.rel) *leads-to* (not u in j.rel)
B_3 : (lsi.eating $\neq$ null *leads-to* lsi.eating = null)
$\qquad \Rightarrow$ ((thread u in lsi.users[j]) *leads-to* lsi.eating = u)

In proving that program Z satisfies B_1–B_3, we also have to prove that the fifo channel c is used correctly, which we do now. Channel c's instantiation (in program LockTsDist, Fig. 12.1) is correct because ADDR is a set (from Z(ADDR).ia). Function c[j].rx() is used correctly: at most one call is ongoing at any time because it is called by only one thread (v[j].tRx). Function c[j].tx(.,.) is used correctly: at most one call is ongoing at any time because it is called within an await of v[j]; the destination address is always different from j.

Now back to proving that Z satisfies B_1–B_3. Note that if ADDR has exactly one entry (i.e., exactly one LockTs system), then it is obvious that Z satisfies B_1–B_3. Henceforth, for notational convenience, assume that ADDR has at least two entries.

Note that system v[j] in program Z is equivalent to system j (in Fig. 12.3) if we treat the arrival of a thread to j.a2 as corresponding to j becoming hungry, the departure of a thread from j.a2 as corresponding to j becoming eating, and the removal of j from j.req.keys as corresponding to j becoming thinking. Under this equivalence, program Z is equivalent to the distributed program in in Sect. 12.3. Thus program Z satisfies the assertions *Inv* (A_1–A_4) and P_1–P_3 established there, under the following "translations".

- "j hungry" becomes "thread at a2".
- "j eating" becomes "(j in j.req.keys) and not (thread at j.a2)".
- "no one eating" corresponds to "lsi.eating = null".
- "j thinking" becomes "not (j in j.req.keys)".

Here are the translated A_4 and P_1.

A_4' : ((thread at j.a2) and [req[j], j] = min([req[k], k]: k)
$\qquad$ and [req[j], j] $\leq$ j.αRts)
$\qquad \Rightarrow$ lsi.eating = null

```
program Z(Set ADDR) {
    ia [DistLockService(ADDR).ic]
    inputs(); outputs();
    v ← startSystem(LockTsDist(ADDR)); // v[j]: lock access system at j
    lsi ← startSystem(DistLockServiceInverse(ADDR,v));
} // end Z
```

Fig. 12.6 Closed program of timestamp-based distributed lock and distributed lock service inverse

P_1' : $(U_1$ and U_2 and $U_3)$
$\Rightarrow$ ((thread at j.a2) *leads-to* not (thread at j.a2))

Program Z satisfies B_1 because $Inv\,A_4'$ implies B_1.

Program Z satisfies B_3 because P_1' implies B_3. Details are as follows. U_1 is implied by B_3's lhs. U_2 holds because await a2 is executed with weak fairness. U_3 holds because thread tRx, in executing doRx, returns to cL.rx each time it leaves cL.rx. Thus program Z satisfies P_1''s rhs, i.e., every thread at j.a2 eventually returns. Because the await at j.a1 has strong fairness, every thread at j.a1 eventually reaches j.a2. Thus B_3 holds.

B_2 holds because j.rel does not loop or block and is executed with weak fairness.

12.5   Using Cyclic Timestamps

One drawback of the distributed lock solution in Sects. 12.3 and 12.4 is that it is not clear how to bound the timestamps in messages (see Exercises 12.4–12.6). This section presents a simple refinement of program LockTs that overcomes this drawback. In the original program, a hungry system j eats when (1) its request's extended timestamp, say [t,j], equals j.αReq, and (2) j has received from every other system an extended timestamp higher than [t,j]. Now there is an additional requirement: (3) j eats only after it receives an ack to its request from every system.

This simplifies matters. First, requirement 3 subsumes requirement 2, because an ack to request [t,j] would have a timestamp higher than t. Second, there is no need for an ack, from say k, to contain a timestamp, because the presence of the ack implies that its timestamp, if it had one, would exceed t, which is all that j needs to know about k. Thus j need not implement map rts. It only needs to keep track of which acks are yet to be received for request [t,j]. Third, there is no need for an ack to contain the sender's id, because j can simply wait to receive an ack from every other system, i.e., ADDR.size - 1 number of acks.

Figure 12.7 shows how the the resulting lock component program, called LockTs2, is obtained from program LockTs. Map variable rts is replaced by integer variable na, indicating the number of acks received since becoming hungry. Variable na is zeroed when the program becomes hungry (i.e., thread comes to a2), and incremented when an ack is received. The program becomes eating when [req[aL], aL] $=\alpha$Req and na = ADDR.size - 1 hold. Ack messages lose their last two entries.

12.5.1   Analysis

Consider a distributed system of LockTs2 systems communicating over a fifo channel. As the distributed system evolves, the timestamps exchanged grow without bound. In order to replace these unbounded timestamps by cyclic timestamps, we need

```
program LockTs2(Set ADDR, ADDR aL, Sid cL) {        // lock component system
    ...
    ~~Map rts ← map([j,0]: j in ADDR, j ≠ aL);~~
    int na ← 0;       // number of acks received becoming non-thinking
    ...

    input void mysid.acq() {
        ...
a1: • await (...) {
        ...
        na ← 0;
    }
a2: • await ([req[aL], aL] =αReq()
            ~~and (ADDR.size = 1 or [req[aL], aL] ≤αRts())~~
            and na = ADDR.size - 1);
        return;
    }

    input void mysid.rel() {...}

    function doRx() {
        ...
            if (msg[0] = REQ) {
                ...
                ~~cL.tx(msg[2],[ACK,clk,aL]);~~
                cL.tx(msg[2],[ACK]);
            } else if (msg[0] = ACK)
                ~~rts[msg[2]] ← msg[1];~~
                ~~clk ← max(clk,msg[1]);~~
                na ← na+1;
                ...

    atomicity assumption {...}
    progress assumption {...}
} // end LockTs2
```

Fig. 12.7 Program LockTs2, obtained from LockTs after deletions and additions (*underlined*)

constant lower and upper bounds on the unbounded timestamps in transit with respect to a number available at a system. This would allow the unbounded timestamps to be replaced by their modulo-M values for an appropriate M such that a system can correctly infer the unbounded timestamp from the cyclic timestamp in a received message.

We start by defining the following auxiliary variables. The first two are global to the distributed system and the third is local to component i.

- $\overline{\text{hst}}$: global history of extended timestamps of requests in increasing order; initially has the entry [0,0] (to simplify notation). (Apart from the initial entry, this is exactly the same as $\overline{\text{hst}}$ in Sect. 12.3.)
- $\overline{\text{ne}}$: Number of completed eating sessions; initially zero and incremented at every rel call. Thus $\overline{\text{hst}}[\overline{\text{ne}}]$ is the extended timestamp of the last request to finish eating; it's initially [0,0].
- i.ne: Number of completed eating sessions as perceived by system i; initially zero and incremented at every i.rel call and every release message reception.

Suppose a [REQ,t,j] message is in transit. The message was sent when j became hungry with timestamp t. Furthermore, j has not started eating since then, because that would happen only after j receives acks to all its [REQ,t,j] messages, which would mean that no [REQ,t,j] messages are in transit. Hence [t,j] is higher than $\overline{\text{hst}}[\overline{\text{ne}}]$, which means that t is not less than $\overline{\text{hst}}[\overline{\text{ne}}][0]$. Also, if [REQ,t,j] message is in transit then [t,j] is in $\overline{\text{hst}}$, so t does not exceed the timestamp of the last entry in $\overline{\text{hst}}$. Thus $Inv\,C_1$ holds, where:

C_1 : ([REQ,t,j] receivable) $\Rightarrow$ $\overline{\text{hst}}[\overline{\text{ne}}][0] \leq t \leq \overline{\text{hst}}.\text{last}[0]$

Next we bound the difference between successive timestamps in $\overline{\text{hst}}$. We prove that $Inv\,C_2$ and $Inv\,C_3$ hold, where

C_2 : forsome(x in $\overline{\text{hst}}$: x[0] $\leq$ i.clk $\leq$ x[0]+1)
C_3 : forall(p, p+1 in $\overline{\text{hst}}$.keys: $\overline{\text{hst}}[p][0] \leq \overline{\text{hst}}[p+1][0] \leq \overline{\text{hst}}[p][0]+2$)

Proof of Inv C_2 and Inv C_3 $Inv\,C_2$ holds as follows. Initially C_2 holds because i.clk is 0 and $\overline{\text{hst}}$ contains [0,0]. C_2 is preserved when i issues a request, because a timestamp with the new value of i.clk is added to $\overline{\text{hst}}$. C_2 is preserved when i receives a [REQ,t,j] message with t+1 > i.clk because $\overline{\text{hst}}$ contains a [t,j] entry and i.clk is set to t+1. C_2 is preserved by every other step.

$Inv\,C_3$ holds as follows. Initially C_3 holds. C_3 is affected only when a request is issued. Suppose j becomes hungry when j.clk equals t. [t+1,j] is added to $\overline{\text{hst}}$. Because C_2 holds prior to this, there is an entry x in $\overline{\text{hst}}$ such that x[0] $\leq$ t $\leq$ x[0]+1. Thus t+1 $\leq$ x[0]+2 holds. $\qquad\qquad\square$

There are ADDR.size number of systems in total. A system can have at most one unsatisfied request in $\overline{\text{hst}}$ at any time. Thus there are at most ADDR.size number of entries in $\overline{\text{hst}}$ after position $\overline{\text{ne}}$. This and C_3 implies that $\overline{\text{hst}}.\text{last}[0]$ differs from $\overline{\text{hst}}[\overline{\text{ne}}][0]$ by at most 2×ADDR.size. So $Inv\,C_4$ holds, where:

C_4 : ([REQ,t,j] receivable) $\Rightarrow$ $\overline{\text{hst}}[\overline{\text{ne}}][0] \leq t \leq \overline{\text{hst}}[\overline{\text{ne}}][0] + 2\times\text{ADDR.size}$

We have obtained fixed lower and upper bounds on timestamps in transit, but these bounds are with respect to $\overline{\text{hst}}[\overline{\text{ne}}][0]$ and the latter is not always available to a system. In particular, system j finds out that system k has finished eating only when j receives k's release message. Thus j.ne, the number of completed eating sessions as perceived by system j, can lag $\overline{ne}$. The difference between them equals the number of release messages incoming to system j. Thus $InvC_5$ holds, where

C_6 : $\overline{ne} - i.ne\ =\ $ (number of release messages incoming to i)

The maximum number of release messages incoming to i is upper bounded by ADDR.size. From this and C_3, we have $InvC_7$ holding, where

C_7 : $\overline{hst[ne][0]} - 2 \times ADDR.size \leq \overline{hst[i.ne]} \leq \overline{hst[ne][0]}$

Combining this and C_4 yields $InvC_8$, where

C_8 : ([REQ,t,j] receivable) $\Rightarrow$ $\overline{hst[i.ne][0]} \leq t \leq \overline{hst[i.ne][0]} + 4 \times ADDR.size$

C_8 tells us that every timestamp in transit lies in the range

$$[i.tse .. i.tse + 4 \times ADDR.size]$$

where i.tse denotes the timestamp of the last request that i removed from its req (or 0 if no such request exists). Thus the timestamps can be made modulo-M for any M at least $4 \times ADDR.size$. Program LockTs2 would be modified as follows.

- Define variable tse initialized to 0; it stores the *unbounded* timestamp of the last request removed from req.
- When an entry [k,ct] is removed from req, update tse to tse + mod(ct-tse, M).
- When a request message is sent, its timestamp is set to mod(clk, M).
- When a request message is received, the (cyclic) timestamp, say ct, in the message, is treated as the unbounded timestamp tse + mod(ct-tse, M).

12.6 Concluding Remarks

The timestamp mechanism provides a way for systems interacting over a fifo channel to impose a total ordering of statement executions that is consistent with causality. It is used in various distributed contexts, e.g., [1, 3, 4]. We used it to solve the request scheduling problem: requests are associated with extended timestamps, and conflicting requests are served in extended-timestamp order. We cast the solution for the case where all requests conflict into a distributed program that implements the distributed lock service. One drawback of the solution is that it is not clear how to bound the timestamps in messages [2] (J. Stuckman, 2010, Bounding timestamps, Private correspondence).

We then refined the solution so that cyclic timestamps can be used. The refinement was to impose an additional condition that a hungry system can eat only after receiving acks for its request messages from all other systems. The solution can be further refined as follows. When a request with extended timestamp [t,j] is received by a hungry system whose request has a lower extended timestamp than [t,j], the system delays sending the ack until its request is served (instead of sending an ack immediately and a release after its request is served). The result is the Ricart-Agrawala algorithm [5].

Solutions based on the timestamp mechanism have a significant drawback. All the component systems participate in the resolution of a request x, even component systems that have no requests outstanding during the entire lifetime of x. Compare this to the naive solution in which all requests are sent to a dedicated system which constructs a schedule for serving requests (see Exercise 12.2). In the naive solution, non-requesting systems are not disturbed. Thus it would appear that the naive solution is superior to the timestamp-based solution. Is that really so?

Exercises

12.1. Implement the awaits in program LockTs with locks and condition variables. (Hint: The straightforward implementation would use one lock and two associated condition variables, say condReqTs for the wait at a1 and condAcqRet for the wait at a2. Variable condReqTs can be signaled in mysid.rel. Variable condAcqRet can be signaled at the end of doRx.)

12.2. In Exercise 11.1, we developed a centralized solution to the distributed lock service. Compare that solution with the timestamp-based solution with respect to: number of messages sent per lock request; number of messages sent by (and received at) a component system; maximum number of successive message hops per lock request. Suppose one thread is very slow compared to the others (e.g., slow processor or low-bandwidth access to the channel). How does this affect the performance of the distributed system.

12.3. Use the timestamp mechanism to implement the reliable broadcast channel from Exercise 4.21. (Hint: Associate an extended timestamp with every user message sent, and deliver user messages in order of extended timestamps.)

12.4. Consider the distributed lock program (Sect. 12.3). Are the timestamps that i receives from j within some constant upper bound of $i.rts[j]$? That is, is there an integer constant U (which may depend on ADDR.size) such that the following is invariant:

D_1 : ([.,t,j] receivable at i) $\Rightarrow$ (t $\leq$ i.rts[j] + U)

If you answer yes, supply a suitable constant U and establish $Inv\,D_1$. If you answer no, give, for any constant U, an evolution that violates D_1.

12.5. Repeat Exercise 12.4 using i.tse instead of i.rts[j], where i.tse is the timestamp of the last request that i removed from its req or 0 if no such request exists (as defined in Sect. 12.5). That is, is there integer constant U (which may depend on ADDR.size) such that the following is invariant:

D_2 : ([.,t,j] receivable at i) $\Rightarrow$ (t $\leq$ i.tse + U)

12.6. Repeat Exercise 12.5 but with a lower bound instead of an upper bound. That is, is there integer constant L (which may depend on ADDR.size) such that the following is invariant:

D_3 : ([.,t,j] receivable at i) $\Rightarrow$ (t $\geq$ i.tse - L)

12.7. Formalize the request scheduling problem (in Sect. 12.2) as a service. (Hint: It would be similar to the distributed lock service, except that conflicts would be determined by the requests.)

12.8. Develop a distributed program that implements your request scheduling service in Exercise 12.7. (Hint: A reasonable starting point is the timestamp solution (in Sect. 12.2) to the request scheduling problem.)

12.9. In the distributed lock solution using component program LockTs, when system j receives a message [REL,k], it removes the entry for k, say [k,t], from j.req. Suppose we modify LockTs so that system j removes every entry [i,s] in j.req such that [s,i] is less than [t,k].

(a) Would the distributed program with the modified LockTs still implement the distributed lock service?
(b) If so, make any needed modifications to the analysis in Sect. 12.3.

12.10. Repeat Exercise 12.9 with component program LockTs2 (instead of LockTs). In your answer to part b, cover the analyses in Sects. 12.3 and 12.5.

References

1. P.A. Bernstein, N. Goodman, Concurrency control in distributed database systems. ACM Comput. Surv. **13**(2), 185–221 (1981). doi:10.1145/356842.356846. http://doi.acm.org/10.1145/356842.356846
2. C. Fidge, Logical time in distributed computing systems. Computer **24**(8), 28–33 (1991). doi:10.1109/2.84874. http://dx.doi.org/10.1109/2.84874
3. L. Lamport, Time, clocks, and the ordering of events in a distributed system. Commun. ACM **21**(7), 558–565 (1978). doi:10.1145/359545.359563. http://doi.acm.org/10.1145/359545.359563
4. M.M.K. Martin, D.J. Sorin, A. Ailamaki, A.R. Alameldeen, R.M. Dickson, C.J. Mauer, K.E. Moore, M. Plakal, M.D. Hill, D.A. Wood, Timestamp snooping: an approach for extending smps, in *Proceedings of the Ninth International Conference on Architectural Support for Programming Languages and Operating Systems, ASPLOS-IX* (ACM, New York, 2000), pp. 25–36. doi:10.1145/378993.378998. http://doi.acm.org/10.1145/378993.378998
5. G. Ricart, A.K. Agrawala, An optimal algorithm for mutual exclusion in computer networks. Commun. ACM **24**(1), 9–17 (1981). doi:10.1145/358527.358537. http://doi.acm.org/10.1145/358527.358537

Chapter 13
Channel with Termination Detection Service

13.1 Introduction

It is often the case in a distributed computation that we want a particular component system of the computation to determine when and if the computation has terminated, for example, whether a routing update has reached all the routers in a network. Stating this independently of the specific distributed computation leads to the "distributed termination detection" problem [1]: given a generic distributed computation, say X, to obtain another distributed computation, say Y, that executes alongside X on the same platform, does not disturb X, and informs a particular system, which we call the "sink" system, when and if X has terminated. More precisely, each system in X is either "active" or "inactive". An active system can do local computation, send and receive messages, and become inactive. An inactive system does nothing except become active upon receiving a message. The computation X is said to have terminated if all its systems are inactive and none of its messages are in transit. There are many elegant solutions to this problem, e.g., [1–4].

This chapter formalizes the termination detection problem as a service, specifically, as an enhanced fifo channel in which, in addition to message sends and receives, each user informs the service when it becomes inactive, and the service informs the sink user when all users are inactive and no messages are in transit. We refer to this service as a **termination-detection channel**. Implementations of this service are shown later in this chapter and in Chap. 14.

13.2 Service Program

Figure 13.1 illustrates the service. The service program, called TdChannel, is given in Figs. 13.2 and 13.3. It is an extension of the fifo channel program (in Fig. 4.2). The program has three parameters. The first parameter, ADDR, is the set of addresses,

A.U. Shankar, *Distributed Programming: Theory and Practice*,
DOI 10.1007/978-1-4614-4881-5_13,
© Springer Science+Business Media New York 2013

```
                      | ↑
     void ← v[1].isTerminated()                    | ↑                                    | ↑
          void ← v[1].tx(k,msg)    void ← v[2].tx(k,msg)                      void ← v[n].tx(k,msg)
          msg ← v[1].rx()          msg ← v[2].rx()        • • •              msg ← v[n].rx()
          void ← v[1].inactive()   void ← v[2].inactive()                   void ← v[n].inactive()
          1 ↓                      2 ↓                                       n ↓
        ┌─ ─ ─ ─┐                ┌─ ─ ─ ─┐        • • •                    ┌─ ─ ─ ─┐
        ¦ v[1]  ¦                ¦ v[2]  ¦                                 ¦ v[n]  ¦
        └─ ─ ─ ─┘                └─ ─ ─ ─┘                                 └─ ─ ─ ─┘
                                   TdChannel( ... )
```

Fig. 13.1   Termination-detection channel with addresses 1..n and sink at 1

exactly as in the fifo channel. The next two parameters are specific to termination
detection. Parameter a0 is the address of the sink user. Parameter initActive is a set
containing all the addresses whose users are initially active.

The main code defines four maps: txh, rxh, v and active. The first three maps are
as in the fifo channel. Maps txh and rxh are indexed by address pairs and store the
transmit and receive histories; they are used to achieve fifo delivery of messages.
Map v is indexed by address; entry v[j] stores the sid of the access system at
address j. The fourth map, active, is specific to termination detection. It is a map
from addresses to booleans. Entry active[j] is true iff the user at j is active. There
is a helper function, terminated(), which is true iff all users are inactive and there
are no messages in transit.

At each address j, the program has three input functions, tx, rx and inactive.
The first two are as in the fifo channel: v[j].tx(k,msg) sends message msg to address
k; and v[j].rx() returns a received message. The third function, v[j].inactive(), is
called to indicate that the local user has become inactive. There is an additional input
function at the sink's address: v[a0].isTerminated(), which returns iff terminated
holds, i.e., all users are inactive and there are no messages in transit. Functions rx
and isTerminated are blocking.

13.3   Concluding Remarks

The termination-detection channel consists of two parts, a message-passing part
and a termination-detection part, with the latter overlaid on the former. We could
have defined a termination-detection service separately from the message-passing
service. But such a termination-detection service would be cumbersome because it
would need to learn from its users whether messages are in transit (since that is part
of the termination condition).

We now outline a distributed program that uses a fifo channel and employs
polling to implement a termination-detection channel over the addresses of the fifo
channel. There is a "td" system at each address of the fifo channel. The td system

```
service TdChannel(Set ADDR, ADDR a0, Set<ADDR> initActive) {
    // ADDR: addresses. a0: address of sink user.
    // initActive: set of addresses whose users are active initially
    ic {ADDR.size ≥ 1}
    // txh[[j,k]]: sequence of messages sent at j to k
    Map txh ← map([[j,k],[]]: j,k in ADDR);
    // rxh[[j,k]]: sequence of messages received at k from j
    Map rxh ← map([[j,k],[]]: j,k in ADDR);
    // active[j]: true iff user at j is active
    Map active ← map([j,(j in initActive): j in ADDR);
    // v[j]: sid of access system at j
    Map v ← map([j,sid()]: j in ADDR);
    return v;
    // end main

    // helper function
    function boolean terminated() {
        return forall(j in ADDR: not active[j]) and
               forall(j,k in ADDR: txh[[j,k]] = rxh[[j,k]]);
    }

    input void v[ADDR j].tx(ADDR k, Seq msg) { // at j transmit msg to k
        ic {active[j] and j ≠ k and not ongoing(v[j].tx(.))}
        txh[[j,k]].append(msg);
        oc {true}
        return;
    }

    input Seq v[ADDR j].rx() { // at j receive msg
        ic {not ongoing(v[j].rx())}
        output (Seq msg, ADDR k) {
            oc {(rxh[[k,j]] ∘ [msg]) prefixOf txh[[k,j]]}
            rxh[[k,j]].append(msg);
            active[j] ← true;
            return msg;
        }
    }

// continued
```

Fig. 13.2 Part 1: termination-detection channel

```
// TdChannel continued
```

```
input void v[ADDR j].inactive() { // at j user says it is inactive
    ic {active[j] and not ongoing(v[j].inactive())}
    active[j] ← false;
    oc {true}
    return;
}
```

```
input void v[a0].isTerminated() { // returns upon termination
    ic {not ongoing(v[a0].isTerminated())}
    oc {terminated()}
    return;
}
```

```
atomicity assumption {input parts and output parts}
```

```
progress assumption {
    // every call to v[j].tx returns
    forall(j in ADDR:
            ongoing(v[j].tx) leads-to not ongoing(v[j].tx));
```

```
    // every call to v[j].inactive returns
    forall(j in ADDR:
            ongoing(v[j].inactive) leads-to not ongoing(v[j].inactive));
```

```
    // every message sent is delivered if the destination is receiving
    forall(j,k in ADDR, i in int:
            txh[[k,j]].size ≥ i
                leads-to (rxh[[k,j]].size ≥ i or not ongoing(v[j].rx)));
```

```
    // every call to v[a0].isTerminated returns
    // if the application has terminated
    (ongoing(v[a0].isTerminated) and terminated())
                leads-to not ongoing(v[a0].isTerminated);
}
```

```
} // TdChannel
```

Fig. 13.3 Part 2: termination-detection channel

relays messages between the local user and the local fifo channel access system, and maintains the following "td state": number of messages transmitted; number of messages received; and whether the local user is active. Periodically the td system at the sink polls the other td systems (over the fifo channel) and obtains their td states. If this collection of td states indicates that all users are inactive and that the total number of messages transmitted equals the total number of messages received, then the td system at the sink signals termination. Otherwise, it repeats the procedure after a while. The main disadvantage of this solution is the overhead of polling. The next chapter shows a solution without polling.

Exercises

13.1. Obtain the inverse program of TdChannel.

13.2. Flesh out the implementation outlined in Sect. 13.3, into a program.

13.3. The termination-detection channel presented above has fifo message-passing. Define a termination-detection channel with lossy message-passing.

13.4. Obtain a distributed program that implements the termination-detection channel in Exercise 13.3 using a lossy channel with the same set of addresses.

13.5. Does it make sense to define a termination-detection channel with LRD message-passing.

References

1. E.W. Dijkstra, C.S. Scholten, Termination detection for diffusing computations. Inf. Process. Lett. **11**(1), 1–4 (1980)
2. E.W. Dijkstra, W.H.J. Feijen, A.J.M. van Gasteren, Derivation of a termination detection algorithm for distributed computations. Inf. Process. Lett. **16**(5), 217–219 (1983). Also EWD 840
3. F. Mattern, Algorithms for distributed termination detection. Distrib. Comput. **2**(3), 161–175 (1987). http://dblp.uni-trier.de/db/journals/dc/dc2.html#Mattern87
4. G. Tel, F. Mattern, The derivation of distributed termination detection algorithms from garbage collection schemes. ACM Trans. Progr. Lang. Syst. **15**(1), 1–35 (1993). doi: 10.1145/151646. 151647. http://doi.acm.org/10.1145/151646.151647

Chapter 14
Termination Detection for Diffusing Computations

14.1 Introduction

This chapter presents a distributed program that implements the termination-detection channel (Chap. 13) over the addresses of a fifo channel for the case where only the sink user is active initially. (Recall that the sink user is the one that is informed when termination is detected.) Dijkstra and Scholten [2] refer to a distributed computation with only one initially active user as a **diffusing computation** (because it "diffuses" out from the initially active user). They have an elegant solution to the termination detection of diffusing computations [2], and we employ that solution.

The termination detection solution is itself a diffusing computation. It maintains a distributed dynamic tree that includes all active users and is rooted at the user that is initially active. The tree grows whenever a user not on the tree becomes active and shrinks whenever a user at a leaf of the tree becomes inactive. Termination is detected by the user that is initially active when the tree becomes empty. Because trees have many uses in distributed computing (just as in sequential computing), the distributed tree-growing algorithm underlying the solution is a useful building block of distributed programs.

Section 14.2 presents the distributed program at the algorithm level, i.e., with the component systems described by rules. The distributed program is shown to satisfy desired properties. Section 14.3 translates the algorithm-level description of the component systems into a program. This is straightforward. Section 14.4 establishes that the resulting distributed program implements the termination detection channel. This also is straightforward, given the analysis in Sect. 14.2.

A.U. Shankar, *Distributed Programming: Theory and Practice*,
DOI 10.1007/978-1-4614-4881-5__14,
© Springer Science+Business Media New York 2013

14.1.1   Conventions

We use i, j and k as parameters that range over addresses. We say "system j" to mean the system at address j. We refer to a quantity x in system j as "j.x".

Now for some graph-theoretic definitions. A **directed graph**, or **digraph** for short, is a 2-tuple, where the first entry is a set of **nodes** and the second entry is a bag of directed **edges** on the nodes, with each edge being a 2-tuple of nodes. Because the edges are specified by a bag (rather than a set), there can be one or more edges from a node to itself or to another node. (Such graphs are also referred to as multi-digraphs.)

A **directed path** in a digraph is a sequence of nodes with at least two entries such that for every two successive nodes u and v in the sequence, [u,v] is an edge. An **undirected path** is the same except that for successive nodes u and v in the sequence, [u,v] or [v,u] is an edge; i.e., an edge can be traversed along or against its direction. A directed (undirected) **cycle** is a directed (undirected) path whose starting and ending nodes are the same.

An **out-tree** is a digraph that has no undirected cycles and has a node u such that there is a directed path from u to every other node. Node u is referred to as the **root** node of the out-tree.

The above can be formally stated by predicates. For example, the first predicate below states that parameter G is a digraph. The second predicate states that p is a directed path in a digraph G. Fleshing out the remaining two constructs is left as an exercise.

```
diGraph(G):   Tuple<.,.>(G) and Set(G[0]) and Tuple<G[0],G[0]>(G[1])
dPath(p,G):   diGraph(G) and Seq<X>(p) and p.size ≥ 2
     and forall(i in [0..p.size-2]: [p[i],p[i+1]] in G[1])
outTree(G):   "digraph G is an out-tree"
root(G):   "the root of out-tree G"
```

End of conventions

14.2   Distributed Program: Algorithm Level

This section develops a distributed program, called TdDiffusingDist, that detects termination assuming only one initially active user. The program is shown in Fig. 14.1. It has two parameters: ADDR, the set of addresses of the termination detection channel being implemented; and a0, the address of the initially active user, which is also the address of the sink. The program starts a fifo channel with parameter ADDR, and stores the sids of the channel access systems in map c. It then starts a termination-detection component system at each address, storing their sids in map v. The resulting configuration is shown in Fig. 14.2.

```
program TdDiffusingDist(Set ADDR, ADDR a0) {
    // ADDR: addresses of fifo channel.  a0: address of sink
    ic {ADDR.size ≥ 1}
    // c[j]: sid of channel access system at j
    c ← startSystem(FifoChannel(ADDR));
    // v[j]: termination detection component system at j
    Map v ← map();
    for (j in ADDR)
        v[j] ← startSystem(TdDiffusing(ADDR,j,a0,c[j]));
    return v;
} // TdDiffusingDist
```

Fig. 14.1 Distributed program of termination-detection component systems and fifo channel

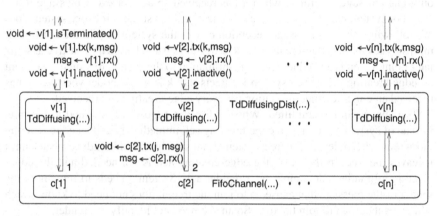

Fig. 14.2 Configuration of the termination-detection channel implementation with addresses 1..n and sink at 1

Each component system is an instantiation of a program TdDiffusing. In this section, the component systems are described at an algorithm level. Let "system j" denote the composite system of the user and the TdDiffusing system at address j. A system is active iff its user is active. The distributed program maintains a distributed dynamic out-tree that includes all active systems and is rooted at a0. So when system a0 finds the out-tree to be empty, it can be assured of termination detection. Initially only a0 is in the out-tree. The tree grows whenever a system not on the tree becomes active and shrinks whenever a system at a leaf of the tree becomes inactive.

When a system k that is not on the out-tree receives a message from a system j, system k becomes active and the directed edge [j,k] is added to the out-tree, making k a leaf node of the out-tree. This active session of system k has one of three possible futures:

- System k can remain active forever (perhaps also sending and receiving messages). Then k remains a node of the out-tree forever.
- System k can become inactive without sending any messages (although it may have received messages). Because system k has not sent a message, it has not caused another address to join the out-tree and hence k has remained a leaf node. Thus k can be removed from the out-tree when system k becomes inactive.
- System k becomes inactive after having sent messages (and perhaps also having received messages). Address k can be removed only after ensuring that k is a leaf node and that there are no outgoing messages from system k in transit (otherwise their reception may cause k to become a non-leaf node).

How can system k detect the conditions in the third case? To detect whether there are outgoing messages from system k in transit, it suffices if every system sends an ack in response to a message reception. Then system k detects that it has no outgoing messages in transit when it has received an ack for every message it has sent. For system k to detect whether k is a leaf node, it suffices if every system does the following: when a message reception causes the system to join the out-tree, it marks its ack as an "edge-creating" ack; when the system leaves the out-tree at some later point, it sends an "edge-deleting" intimation to the system to which it last sent an edge-creating ack. Then system k detects that k is a leaf node whenever it has received an edge-deleting intimation for every edge-creating ack received.

The above can be simplified. When a directed edge [k,j] is added to the tree, instead of system j sending an edge-creating ack immediately and an edge-deleting intimation when it leaves the tree, system j can simply withold sending the ack until it leaves the tree. In this case, the edge-creating ack is not needed and the edge-deleting intimation can simply be a regular ack. System j needs to remember the sender of the message that caused j to join the tree; it does not need to know which addresses it caused to join the tree. So an ack need not identify the sender.

The resulting program of a system j is given in Fig. 14.3, at the level of variables and atomically-executed rules. The systems exchange data messages and ack messages. A data message has the form [DAT,j,msg], where DAT is a constant, j is the sender address, and msg is a message of the original diffusing computation (i.e., a user message). An ack message has the form [ACK], where ACK is a constant.

System j maintains the following variables. A boolean active that is true iff system j is active. A sequence engager that is empty if j is not on the tree and otherwise contains the address of the system that last activated system j. An integer unAcked that indicates the number of unacked DAT messages that system j has sent. A system is on the tree iff its engager is not empty. A non-sink system on the tree leaves the tree when its active is false and its unAcked is zero, by sending an ack to its engager's entry and setting engager to empty. This can happen only after receiving an ack or becoming inactive.

Variables of system j

- active: boolean; initially true iff j is a0.
- engager: sequence; initially [a0] if j = a0 otherwise [].
- unAcked: integer; initially 0.

Rules of system j (atomically executed)

- Become inactive only if active:
      active ← false
- Send [DAT,j,msg] to k, k ≠ j, only if active:
      unAcked ← unAcked+1
- Receive [DAT,k,msg]:
      active ← true;
      if engager = [] then engager ← [k]
      else {send [ACK] to k}
- Receive [ACK]:
      unAcked ← unAcked−1
- Disengage only if (not active and unAcked = 0 and engager ≠ []):
      if j = a0 then signal termination
      else {send [ACK] to engager[0]; engager ← []}

Fig. 14.3 Variables and rules of system j

14.2.1   Analysis

For brevity in stating desired properties, we introduce the following notation. (They can be defined formally given the conventions in Sect. 4.7.)

- numDAT(j): number of DAT messages in transit outgoing from address j.
- numACK(j): number of ACK messages in transit incoming to address j.

We now prove that the distributed program TdDiffusingDist satisfies A_1 and A_2.

A_1 : *Inv* (a0.unAcked = 0 and not a0.active)
            ⇒ forall(j: not j.active and numDAT(j) = 0)

A_2 : (weak fairness for 'disengage' rule)
          ⇒ (forall(j: not j.active and numDAT(j) = 0)
              leads-to (a0.unAcked = 0 and not a0.active))

The analysis is straightforward given the previous discussion. For brevity in analysis, we introduce some more notation.

- eNodes: set(j: j.engager ≠ [])   // set of "engaged" nodes
- eEdges: bag([k.engager[0], k]: k ≠ a0, k.engager ≠ [])
                                                          // set of "engagement" edges
- eGraph: [eNodes, eEdges]   // "engagement" digraph

Thus eGraph denotes the digraph formed by the engaged nodes and the engagement edges. Initially eGraph consists of node a0 and no edges. We now prove that predicates B_1–B_3 below are invariant and imply A_1. B_1 says that eGraph remains an out-tree rooted at a0. B_2 says that a system's unAcked equals the total number of outgoing data messages, outgoing engagement edges, and incoming acks.

B_1 : outTree(eGraph) and root(eGraph) = a0
B_2 : j.unAcked = numDAT(j) + numACK(j) + sum([j,k]: [j,k] in eEdges)
B_3 : j.engager = [] $\Rightarrow$ (not j.active and j.unAcked = 0)

Proof of Inv B_1–B_3 and A_1 B_1–B_3 holds initially and is unconditionally preserved by every rule execution. Details follow. A [DAT,j,.] message reception at system k decreases numDAT(j) and either increases numACK(j) or adds [j,k] to eEdges. An ack reception at j decreases numACK(j) and j.unacked. The removal of an engagement edge [j,k] increases numACK(j). The sending of a data message by j increases numDAT(j) and j.unAcked.

A_1's predicate is implied by B_1–B_3 as follows. Assume A_1's predicate's lhs, i.e., not a0.active and a0.unAcked = 0. The latter and B_1 implies that eEdges is empty and eGraph consists only of node a0. Hence for every j other than a0, system j is inactive and j.unAcked is zero (from B_3), hence numDAT(j) is zero (from B_2). The same is also true for a0 (from A_1's predicate's lhs). Thus all nodes are inactive and no data messages are in transit, which is A_1's predicate's rhs.   □

Proof of A_2. Assume A_2's lhs, i.e., the disengage rule is executed with weak fairness. Assume A_2's rhs' lhs holds, i.e., all systems are inactive and no data messages are in transit. We need to show that a0.unAcked eventually becomes zero. Assume eEdges is not empty. Then eNodes has a leaf node. That node has no outgoing data messages and no outgoing engagement edges. So eventually it receives acks for its data messages (from Inv B_2 and channel progress), at which point its unAcked becomes zero and remains zero (because all systems are inactive). Hence it eventually leaves eNodes (by weak fairness for its disengage rule). Thus eEdges keeps shrinking until it becomes empty, at which point a0.unAcked is zero (from Inv B_2).   □

14.3   Distributed Program

We now cast variables and rules in Fig. 14.3 into a program TdDiffusing, and show that the resulting distributed program TdDiffusingDist implements the termination-detection channel. Program TdDiffusing is given in Figs. 14.4 and 14.5. The boxes are comments containing fragments of the termination detection service inverse matching the LockTs code at the left.

The program has four parameters: ADDR, the addresses of the component systems; aL, the local address, i.e., of this component system; a0, the address of the sink; and cL, the sid of the local channel access system. The main code defines variables

```
program TdDiffusing(Set ADDR, ADDR aL, ADDR a0, Sid cL) {
    // aL: local address. a0: sink address
    // cL: sid of local channel access system
    ic {true}
```

```
    //types and constants
    ACK ← 1; DAT ← 2;
    // ack messages
    type AckMsg = Tuple<ACK>;
    // data messages
    type DatMsg = Tuple<DAT,ADDR,Seq>;

    // variables
    boolean active ← (aL = a0);
    Seq engager ←
        if (aL = a0) [a0] else [];
    int unAcked ← 0;
    // user receive queue
    Seq rxq ← seq();
    Tid tRx ← startThread(doRx());
    return mysid;
```

```
TdChannelInverse main
ic {ADDR.size ≥ 1}
txh ← map([[j,k],[]]: j,k);
rxh ← map([[j,k],[]]: j,k);
active ←
    map([j,(j in initActive)]
        : j);
return mysid;


function boolean terminated() {
    return
        forall(j: not active[j]) and
        forall(j,k:
            txh[j,k] = rxh[j,k]);
}
```

```
    input void mysid.tx(ADDR aR, Seq msg) {
        ia {true}
    • await (true) {
            cL.tx(aR, [DAT,aL,msg]);
            unAcked ← unAcked+1;
            return;
        }
    }
```

```
TdChannelInverse doTx(aL,aR,msg)
oc {active[aL] and aL ≠ aR
    and not ongoing(v[aL].tx)}
txh[[aL,aR]].append(msg);
v[aL].tx(aR, msg);
ic {true}
```

```
    input Seq mysid.rx() {
        ia {true}
    • await (rxq.size > 0) {
            msg ← rxq[0];
            rxq.remove();
            return msg[2];
            // return msg[2,1];   // match doRx
        }
    }
```

```
TdChannelInverse doRx(aL)
oc {not ongoing(v[aL].rx)}
[msg, k] ← v[aL].rx();
ic {((rxh[[k,aL]] ∘ [msg])
        prefixOf txh[[k,aL]]}
rxh[[k,aL]].append(msg);
active[aL] ← true;
```

```
// continued
```

Fig. 14.4 Part 1: program TdDiffusing

```
// TdDiffusing continued

    input void mysid.inactive() {
        ia {active}
    • await (true) {
            if (rxq = []) {
                active ← false;
                if (aL ≠ a0 and unAcked = 0) {
                    cL.tx(engager[0], [ACK]);  // disengage
                    engager ← [];
                }
            }
        }
        return;
    }
}

    input void mysid.isTerminated() {
        ia {aL = a0}        // only at a0
    • await (not active and unAcked = 0);
        return;
    }
```

```
TdChannelInverse doInactive(aL)

oc {active[aL] and
      not ongoing(v[aL].inactive)}
active[j] ← false;
v[aL].inactive();
ic {true}
```

```
TdChannelInverse
 doIsTerminated(aL)

oc {aL = a0 and
   not ongoing(v[aL].terminated)}
v[aL].isTerminated();
ic {terminated()}
```

```
    function void doRx() {  // receive message from channel
        while (true) {
        • Seq msg ← cL.rx();
            ia {msg in union(AckMsg,DatMsg)}  // ACK or DAT msg
            await (true)
                if (msg[0] = DAT) {
                    rxq.append(msg);
                    active ← true;
                    if (engager = [])
                        engager ← [msg[1]];
                    else
                        cL.tx(msg[1], [ACK]);
                } else if (m[0] = ACK) {
                    unAcked ← unAcked - 1;
                    if (aL ≠ a0 and unAcked = 0 and not active) {
                        cL.tx(engager[0], [ACK]);  // disengage
                        engager ← [];
                    }
                }
            }
        }
    }

    atomicity assumption {awaits}
    progress assumption {weak fairness of threads}

} // TdDiffusing
```

Fig. 14.5 Part 2: program TdDiffusing

active, engager and unAcked, exactly as in Fig. 14.3. It then defines a sequence variable rxq, for storing received data messages that are waiting to be picked up by the local user. It then starts a local thread tRx executing a function doRx, which receives messages from the channel and processes them.

We want the (effectively) atomic steps of the program to correspond to the rules in Fig. 14.3, so that the properties proved in Sect. 14.2 can be assumed to hold here without further analysis. So the program must update active and engager together upon receiving a data message (because that is what happens in the rules). This update can be done when the data message enters rxq or when it leaves rxq. We take the first option here and leave the second option as an exercise. This implies that variable active should apply to the combination of the user and rxq. It makes sense to treat rxq as "active" iff it is not empty. Hence, the program will maintain the following:

Variable active is true iff the user is active *or* rxq is not empty.

We can now explain the functions of the program. There are four input functions: tx, rx, inactive, and terminated; the last is callable only if aL equals a0. Function tx(aR,msg) puts user message msg in a data message, sends the data message (via cL.tx), and increments unAcked. Function rx waits for rxq to be non-empty, then removes the data message at rxq's head and returns the user message in the data message. (The return statement is replaced by the one in the box when this program executed in the context of program Z below.) Function inactive sets active to false if rxq is empty, and then disengages this system if it is not the sink system and unAcked is zero. Function isTerminated executes only at address a0. It returns only when a0.unAcked is zero and a0.active is false.

Function doRx, executed by local thread tRx, receives a message from the fifo channel. If the message is [DAT,k,msg], it appends the message to rxq, sets engager to k if it was empty and otherwise sends an ack to k. If the message is [ACK], it decrements unAcked and then disengages this system if it is not the sink system and active is false.

Program TdDiffusing does not code the "disengage" rule as a separate function nor does it have a separate thread to execute it. Instead, whenever a step causes the "disengage" rule to become unblocked, the step then executes the rule. (Thus program TdDiffusing actually has coarser atomicity than the rules in Fig. 14.3.)

14.4   Proving the Implements Conditions

We now establish that TdDiffusingDist(ADDR,a0) implements TdChannel(ADDR,a0, initActive) (in Figs. 13.2 and 13.3) for initActive = set(a0). Figure 14.6 shows the closed program Z of instantiation v of TdDiffusingDist and instantiation si of TdChannelInverse. The latter is available from the boxes in Figs. 14.4 and 14.5 (and also from Exercise 13.1). Z.ia does not constrain TdChannel.ic except for requiring that the sink user be the only user initially active. We have to establish that Z satisfies assertions C_1–C_6 below. C_1–C_2 are concerned with the fifo message transfer aspect

---

```
program Z(Set ADDR, ADDR a0) {
  ia {TdChannel(ADDR, a0, set(a0)).ic}
  inputs(); outputs();
  v ← startSystem(TdDiffusingDist(ADDR,a0));
  si ← startSystem(TdChannelInverse(ADDR, a0, set(a0), v));
} // Z
```

Fig. 14.6 Closed program of TdDiffusing and TdChannelInverse

of the service. (Note that the internal nondeterminism in the service's rx function becomes "externalized" (Sect. 7.5) in the service inverse and in the implementation's "boxed" return.) C_3–C_6 are concerned with the termination detection aspect of the service.

C_1 : *Inv* (thread at si.doRx(j).ic)
$\Rightarrow$ si.rxh[[k,j]] ∘ [msg] prefixOf si.txh[[k,j]]
// [msg,k] provided by $\boxed{\text{v[j].rx.return}}$

C_2 : si.txh[[k,j]].size $\geq$ i
leads-to (si.rxh[[k,j]].size $\geq$ i or not ongoing(v[j].rx))

C_3 : *Inv* (thread at si.doIsTerminated().ic) $\Rightarrow$ si.terminated()

C_4 : (ongoing(v[a0].isTerminated) and si.terminated()
leads-to not ongoing(v[a0].isTerminated))

C_5 : ongoing(v[j].tx) *leads-to* not ongoing(v[j].tx)

C_6 : ongoing(v[j].inactive) *leads-to* not ongoing(v[j].inactive)

14.4.1 Proof of C_1–C_2

C_1 and C_2 follow trivially from the fact that the underlying channel is fifo and rxq simply buffers received data messages in order. More formally, the following captures the relationship between the user messages in transit in the service inverse si and the data messages in transit in the fifo channel c.

D_1 : si.transit(j,k)
= [msg[2]: msg in k.rxq, msg[1] = j]   // user messages from j in k.rxq
∘ [msg[2]: msg in c.transit(j,k), msg[0,1] = [DAT,j]]
//user messages in fifo channel from j to k

D_1 is unconditionally preserved by every atomic step. Hence *Inv* D_1 holds, and it implies C_1.

C_2 holds as follows. Thread tRx, which executes function doRx, is always ready to receive messages from the fifo channel. Hence every data message in the fifo channel incoming to j is appended to j.rxq eventually. From there, it is eventually received by a user thread in function j.rx, unless there is no such thread in which case C_2 holds vacuously.

14.4.2 Proof of C_3–C_6

C_5 holds trivially because v[j].tx is nonblocking and the executing thread has weak fairness. C_6 holds in the same way. What remains is to establish C_3–C_4. We show that they follow from the properties A_1 and A_2 established for the algorithm-level distributed program. C_3 and C_4 are restated as C'_3 and C'_4 below, after accounting for Z's effective atomicity and after expanding si.terminated (with its definition in Fig. 13.2).

C'_3 : *Inv* (a0.unAcked = 0 and not a0.active)
$\quad\quad\quad \Rightarrow$ forall(j: not si.active[j])
$\quad\quad\quad\quad\quad$ and forall(j,k: si.txh[[j,k]] = si.rxh[[j,k]])
C'_4 : (forall(j: not si.active[j])
$\quad\quad\quad$ and forall(j,k: si.txh[[j,k]] = si.rxh[[j,k]]))
$\quad\quad\quad$ *leads-to* (not a0.active and a0.unAcked = 0)

Program Z satisfies assertions A_1 and A_2, established in Sect. 14.2 (because Z's steps have the same effect and atomicity as the rules in Fig. 14.3). Those assertions are restated below in the context of Z as A'_1 and A'_2.

A'_1 : *Inv* (a0.unAcked = 0 and not a0.active)
$\quad\quad\quad \Rightarrow$ forall(j: not j.active and numDAT(j) = 0)
A'_2 : (weak fairness for 'disengage' rule)
$\quad\quad\quad \Rightarrow$ forall(j: not j.active and numDAT(j) = 0)
$\quad\quad\quad$ *leads-to* (a0.unAcked = 0 and not a0.active)

D_2 below captures the fact that variable active in program TdDiffusing covers both the local user and rxq. Program Z satisfies *Inv* D_2 because each of its atomic steps unconditionally preserves D_2.

D_2 : j.active $\Leftrightarrow$ (si.active[j] or j.rxq $\neq$ []]

Proof of C'_3. C'_3 is implied by A'_1 and *Inv* D_2 as follows. Assume C'_3's predicate's lhs. This is the same as A'_1's predicate's lhs. Thus A'_1's predicate's rhs holds, i.e., not j.active and numDAT(j) = 0 hold for every j. From not j.active and D_2, we have not si.active[j] and j.rxq = [] holding for every j. From numDAT(j) = 0 and k.rxq = [], we have si.transit(j,k) = [] holding for every [j,k] pair. Thus si.active[j] is false for every j and si.transit(j,k) is empty for every [j,k] pair. Hence C'_3's rhs holds. $\quad\quad\quad\quad\square$

Proof of C'_4. Recall that program TdDiffusing executes the "disengage" rule atomically with the become-inactive step or receive-ack step that establishes the condition for disengaging. Thus program TdDiffusing satisfies A'_2's lhs. Thus it satisfies A'_2's rhs.

C_4' is implied by A_2' rhs and $InvD_2$ as follows. Assume C_4''s rhs' lhs, i.e., not si.active[j] holds for every j and si.txh[[j,k]] equals si.rxh[[j,k]] for every [j,k] pair. The latter and $InvD_2$ imply that numDAT(j) is zero and k.rxq is empty. Hence A_2''s rhs' lhs holds. Hence A_2''s rhs' rhs eventually holds. This implies C_4''s rhs (because of $InvD_2$).   □

14.5 Concluding Remarks

There are many elegant solutions to the problem of distributed termination detection, e.g., [1–4]. The algorithm and analysis in this chapter are taken from [2]. The analysis there develops the algorithm and the desired invariants in incremental steps. Also, it assumes that message transfers are instantaneous, i.e., a message sent by one system is immediately transfered to the receiving system. That is actually more general than the case considered here, because each "point-to-point link" in the channel can be treated as a system (see Exercise 14.6).

Exercises

14.1. Implement program TdDiffusing using locks and condition variables.

14.2. Implement program TdDiffusing using semaphores.

14.3. Program TdDiffusing has local thread tRx execute doRx, in which it repeatedly calls cL.rx and processes the received message. Can we dispense with rxq and have this work be done instead by the user thread executing mysid.rx? In particular, suppose input function mysid.rx is modified to do the following:

- Call cL.rx and wait for returned data or ack message.
- If [DAT,i,msg] do the following (as before): if engager is empty then set it to [i] else respond with an ack; return msg (instead of appending it to rxq).
- If [ACK] do the following: decrement unAcked; disengage if unAcked is zero and active is false; go back to the cL.rx call (instead of returning).

Would this work? If not, come up with an evolution that falsifies C_1 or C_3. If yes, come up with any modifications to E_1–E_6 so that they continue to satisfy the invariance proof rule and imply C_1–C_3.

14.4. In the termination detection algorithm, the reception of a [DAT,i,msg] message requires updating active and either updating engager or sending an ack. Program TdDiffusing does this processing in function doRx, when the data message is removed from the fifo channel. Can this processing be done when the user message is received from rxq? Specifically, suppose program TdDiffusing is modified as follows.

- In function doRx, after cL.rx returns [DAT,i,msg]: append msg to rxq but do not update Tactive or engager or send an ack.
- In function mysid.rx, when rxq is not empty: remove the entry at rxq's head, update Tactive and either engager or send an ack.

Would this work? If not, come up with an evolution that falsifies C_3 or C_4. If yes, come up with a proof in which A_1 and A_2 are reused.

14.5. Flesh out the definitions of predicates outTree(G) and root(G).

14.6. Let P refer to the termination detection algorithm described in Sect. 14.2. Let Q refer to the special case of P in which message transfers are instantaneous; specifically, when system j sends a message to system k, the message is received atomically with the send.

Show that any instance p of P can be mapped to an instance q of Q such that x is an evolution of p iff it is an evolution of q. (Hint: Treat the fifo channel in P as a collection of systems, d(j,k), for every address pair [j,k], where d(j,k) holds the sequence of messages in transit from j to k and has two input functions, tx at j and rx at k. Update d(j,k)'s termination detection variables (engager, etc.) appropriately.)

References

1. E.W. Dijkstra, W.H.J. Feijen, A.J.M. van Gasteren, Derivation of a termination detection algorithm for distributed computations. Inf. Process. Lett. **16**(5), 217–219 (1983). Also EWD 840
2. E.W. Dijkstra, C.S. Scholten, Termination detection for diffusing computations. Inf. Process. Lett. **11**(1), 1–4 (1980)
3. F. Mattern, Algorithms for distributed termination detection. Distrib. Comput. **2**(3), 161–175 (1987). http://dblp.uni-trier.de/db/journals/dc/dc2.html#Mattern87
4. G. Tel, F. Mattern, The derivation of distributed termination detection algorithms from garbage collection schemes. ACM Trans. Progr. Lang. Syst. **15**(1), 1–35 (1993). doi: 10.1145/151646. 151647. http://doi.acm.org/10.1145/151646.151647

Chapter 15
Object-Transfer Service

15.1 Introduction

It is often the case in a distributed computation that the component systems of the computation share a set of objects, each characterized by an id and a mutable value, for example, a set of intermediate results. A system can acquire an object, make changes to its value, and release the object. Over time the object passes from system to system, changing its value. When a system acquires an object, its value should be what it was at its last release. Other than this last requirement, an object is just like a token.

This chapter formalizes the above as a distributed service, referred to as the **object-transfer service**. The service spans a set of addresses, with an access system at each address, as illustrated in Fig. 15.1. Each access system has three input functions: acq(oid), to acquire object oid and get its value; rel(oid,oval), to release object oid with value oval; and rxReq(), to receive a request for an object. With respect to acquires and releases, an object is like a lock with an associated value. But unlike a lock, a user releases an object only upon receiving a request for it (whereas a user releases a lock when it no longer needs the lock). We refer to the user holding an object as the current **owner** of the object.

Because an object is just like a token with a value, the service can be implemented over a fifo channel using any distributed token-passing algorithm, e.g., [1–7]. We will outline some straightforward implementations at the end of this chapter.

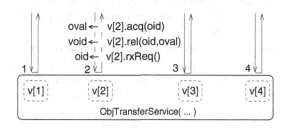

Fig. 15.1 Object transfer service spanning addresses 1, 2, 3, 4, with access system v[j] at address j

A.U. Shankar, *Distributed Programming: Theory and Practice*,
DOI 10.1007/978-1-4614-4881-5__15,
© Springer Science+Business Media New York 2013

The next chapter presents another, much more efficient, implementation. Later chapters use the object-transfer service to implement a distributed shared-memory service.

Convention: Construct disjoint(...) takes a list of sets (or bags) as its argument and is true iff the sets (or bags) are disjoint.

15.2   Service Program

The object-transfer service program is given in Figs. 15.2 and 15.3. The service has four parameters: ADDR, the set of addresses of the service; OID, the set of ids of the objects; OVAL, the set of possible values of an object; and initObjs, map over ADDR where initObjs[j] is the set of ids of objects whose initial owner is at j. The program input condition requires that initObjs partition the set OID, i.e., every entry in OID is owned initially by exactly one user.

The program maintains the following variables. Variable objs is a map over ADDR such that objs[j] is the set of objects held by j's user. Variable reqs is a map over ADDR such that reqs[j] is the set of objects for which j's user has received requests; it is a subset of the objects held or being acquired by j's user. Variable val is a map over OID such that oid is in val.keys iff object oid is in the service and val[oid] is its value when it was last released to the service.

At each address j, the access system v[j] has three input functions: v[j].acq(oid), v[j].rel(oid,oval), and v[j].rxReq().

Function v[j].acq(oid) is called to acquire object oid. It is called only if j's user does not have oid and does not have an ongoing call to v[j].acq(oid) (but it can have ongoing v[j].acq calls for other objects). It returns the object's value, at which point j's user becomes the owner of the object.

Function v[j].rel(oid,oval) is called to release object oid with value oval to the service. It is called only in response to a received request for oid and only if j has object oid.

Function v[j].rxReq() is called to receive a request for an object that is either owned or being requested by j's user. It is called only if there is no other ongoing call to v[j].rxReq(). We allow rxReq to return oid while v[j].acq(oid) is still ongoing because simultaneous calls to v[j].acq(oid) and rxReq are allowed. Even if the implementation waits for v[j].acq(oid) to return before allowing rxReq to return oid, the rxReq's return may complete before acq(oid)'s return.

The progress assumption consists of three assertions. The first assertion says that a rel call eventually returns. The second assertion says that if the owner of an object maintains an ongoing rxReq call, then the owner is informed whenever another user requests the object. The third assertion says if a user requests an object then the user eventually gets the object provided the current owner of the object (1) receives a request for the object and (2) subsequently releases the object. Typically, a user would satisfy condition 1 by satisfying the second assertion's lhs (i.e., maintain an ongoing rxReq call if it holds an object).

```
service ObjTransferService(ADDR, OID, OVAL, initObjs) {

    ic {Set(ADDR,OID,OVAL) and Map<ADDR,Set<OID>>(initObjs)
        and min(ADDR.size,OID.size,OVAL.size) ≥ 1
        and ADDR.size = initObjs.size
        and disjoint(initObjs[i]: i in ADDR)
        and union(initObjs[i]: i in ADDR) = OID}

    // objs[j]: set of ids of objects held by j's user
    Map objs ← initObjs;

    // reqs[j]: set of ids of objects at j requested by service for other users
    Map reqs ← map([j,set()]: j in ADDR);

    // oid in val.keys iff object oid is in the service with value val[oid]
    Map val ← map();

    // v[j]: sid of access system at address j
    Map v ← map([j,sid()]: j in ADDR);
    return v;
    // end main

    input OVAL v[ADDR j].acq(OID oid) {
        ic {not ongoing(v[j].acq(oid))
            and not (oid in objs[j])}
        output (rval) {
            oc {(oid in val.keys) and rval = val[oid]}
            val.remove(oid);
            objs[j].add(oid);
            return rval;
        }
    }

    input void v[ADDR j].rel(OID oid, OVAL oval) {
        ic {(oid in objs[j]) and (oid in reqs[j])}
        objs[j].remove(oid);
        reqs[j].remove(oid);
        val[oid] ← oval;
        oc {true}
        return;
    }

// continued
```

Fig. 15.2 Part 1: Object-transfer service program

```
// program ObjTransferService continued

    input OID v[ADDR j].rxReq() {
      ic {not ongoing(v[j].rxReq())}
      output (oid) {
        oc {((oid in objs[j]) or ongoing(v[j].acq(oid)))
            and not (oid in reqs[j])}
        reqs[j].add(oid);
        return oid;
      }
    }

    atomicity assumption {input parts and output parts}

    progress assumption {
        // every rel call returns
        ongoing(v[j].rel(oid,oval))  leads-to  not ongoing(v[j].rel(oid,oval))

        // if a user requests an object then the owner is informed eventually,
        // provided the object's owner maintains an ongoing rxReq call.
        (objs[j].size > 0  leads-to  ongoing(v[j].rxReq))
         ⇒ (((oid in objs[j]) and ongoing(v[k].acq(oid)))
                leads-to  (oid in reqs[j]))

        // an acquire of an object is satisfied provided its current owner
        // releases the object when it receives a request for the object
        forall(ADDR j:
                (((oid in objs[j]) and ongoing(v[k].acq(oid)))
                    leads-to  (oid in reqs[j]))
                and ((oid in reqs[j])  leads-to  not (oid in reqs[j])) )
         ⇒ forall(ADDR j:
                    ongoing(v[j].acq(oid))  leads-to  not ongoing(v[j].acq(oid)))
    }
} // end ObjTransferService
```

Fig. 15.3 Part 2: Object-transfer service program

15.3   Concluding Remarks

We now outline three distributed algorithms to implement the object-transfer service over addresses 1, $\cdots$, n. Each algorithm is executed by a set of systems, v[1], $\cdots$, v[n], attached to a fifo channel with addresses 1, $\cdots$, n. For brevity, each algorithm manages only one object; multiple objects can be managed with a separate instance of the algorithm for each object.

Algorithm 1 has a fixed system, say v[1], track the system that currently owns the object, by having every system inform v[1] whenever it receives the object. When system v[i] wants the object, it informs v[1], which relays the request to the current owner, which eventually sends the object to v[i]. Any further requests for the object are buffered at v[1] until v[i] informs v[1] that it has the object, at which point one request is relayed to v[i]. Thus v[1] allows at most one request to reach the current owner, and buffers any further requests in a local queue. One disadvantage of this algorithm is that all object transfers involve v[1], which can become a bottleneck.

Algorithm 2 improves upon Algorithm 1. It reduces (but does not eliminate) the traffic at v[1] by buffering requests in a "distributed" queue spread across the systems. The distributed queue is implemented as follows. System v[1] has a variable, say last, that records the last requester of the object; it would point to the current owner, say v[i], iff v[1] has not received a request since v[i]'s request. When system v[j] requests the object, v[j] informs v[1], which relays the request to the system pointed to by last and changes last to point to v[j]. With this approach, a requesting system may have to buffer a request when it does not (yet) have the object, but it need not inform v[1] when it gets the object.

Algorithm 3 avoids having a fixed system, namely v[1], track the object's location. Instead, when a system acquires the object, it informs all other systems of the new location. When a system wants the object, it sends its request directly to the current owner. There is no centralized coordinator. However, it's not clear whether this better than Algorithm 2 because now each object transfer requires sending messages to *every* system, even those that have no interest in the object. Also, a distributed queue of requests is still needed (why?).

Fleshing out the above three algorithms is left as an exercise. In the next chapter, we will see a variation of Algorithm 2 that is far superior to the above algorithms.

Exercises

15.1. Obtain the inverse of the object transfer service.

15.2. Flesh out the Algorithm 1 outline in Sect. 15.3 to an algorithm-level description of the distributed system. That is, obtain the variables and rules of each system (analogous to Fig. 14.3 for the termination detection algorithm).

15.3. Flesh out the algorithm-level description obtained in Exercise 15.2 into a distributed program that implements the object-transfer service.

15.4. Flesh out the Algorithm 2 outline in Sect. 15.3 to an algorithm-level description of the distributed system.

15.5. Flesh out the algorithm-level description obtained in Exercise 15.4 into a distributed program that implements the object-transfer service.

15.6. Flesh out the Algorithm 3 outline in Sect. 15.3 to an algorithm-level description of the distributed system.

15.7. Flesh out the algorithm-level description obtained in Exercise 15.6 into a distributed program that implements the object-transfer service.

15.8. The object-transfer service as currently defined has a fixed set of objects. Modify the service so that the service initially has no objects but users can add objects to the service. Specifically, at each access system v, introduce an input function v[j].register(oid) to add to the service an object oid residing initially with v's user.

15.9. Modify the service in Exercise 15.8 so that an object can be removed from the service. Specifically, at each access system v, introduce an input function v[j].unregister(oid) that a user calls to remove object oid from the service.

15.10. The object-transfer service allows the service to return a v[j].rxReq call with oid as long as the following conditions hold: (1) the local user is requesting or holds the object; and (2) the request has not yet been passed to the user. Add a third condition that some other user is requesting the object, i.e., a v[k].acq(oid) call is ongoing. (Hint: This may not be as simple as it sounds.)

References

1. S. Banerjee, P. Chrysanthis, A new token passing distributed mutual exclusion algorithm. Int. Conf. Distrib. Comput. Syst. **0**, 717 (1996). doi: http://doi.ieeecomputersociety.org/10.1109/ICDCS.1996.508024
2. M. Mizuno, M.L. Neilsen, R. Rao, A token based distributed mutual exclusion algorithm based on quorum agreements, in *Proceedings of the International Conference on Distributed Computing Systems*, Arlington, pp. 361–368 (1991)
3. M. Naimi, M. Trehel, A. Arnold, A log(n) distributed mutual exclusion algorithm based on path reversal. J. Parallel Distrib. Comput. **34**(1), 1–13 (1996)
4. M.L. Neilsen, M. Mizuno, A dag-based algorithm for distributed mutual exclusion, in *Proceedings of the International Conference on Distributed Computing Systems*, Arlington, pp. 354–360 (1991)
5. I. Suzuki, T. Kasami, A distributed mutual exclusion algorithm. ACM Trans. Comput. Syst. **3**(4), 344–349 (1985). doi:10.1145/6110.214406. http://doi.acm.org/10.1145/6110.214406

6. P. Thambu, J. Wong, An efficient token-based mutual exclusion algorithm in a distributed system. J. Syst. Softw. **28**(3), 267–276 (1995). doi:10.1016/0164-1212(94)00061-Q. http://www.sciencedirect.com/science/article/pii/016412129400061Q

7. M. Trehel, M. Naimi, A distributed algorithm for mutual exclusion based on data structures and fault tolerance, in *6th Annual International Phoenix Conference on Computers and Communication*, Scottsdale, pp. 35–39 (1987)

Chapter 16
Object Transfer Using Path Reversal

16.1 Introduction

This chapter presents a distributed program that implements the object-transfer service (in Chap. 15) over the addresses of a fifo channel. The component systems of the program employ a distributed "path-reversal" algorithm [1, 3–6] to track the current location of an object. Each system maintains for each object a **last pointer** that is either nil or points to another system. To a first approximation, the path of last pointers leading out of any system ends at the system holding the object, i.e., the last pointers form an in-tree. To acquire the object, a system j sends a request that gets forwarded along the last pointer path leading out of j until it reaches the system with the object, say system k. At each hop, the system receiving j's request sets its last pointer to j.

The evolutions of the distributed program are quite simple if at most one request is in transit at any time. Then the sequence of last pointer redirections results in a **path reversal** in the in-tree of last pointers. The amortized cost of a path reversal is $\log N$ message sends, where N is the number of systems [2, 5]. However when multiple requests are issued simultaneously, the last pointer redirections of their path reversals are interleaved, resulting in rather complex evolutions. It is not obvious whether the distributed program still works, let alone whether it still has an amortized cost of $\log N$ [1].

Section 16.2 presents the distributed program for one object with a fixed value. The component systems are described at the algorithm level, i.e., by rules instead of a program. Example evolutions are presented in terms of evolving digraphs. Sections 16.3 and 16.4 prove that the distributed program ensures that every request for the object is eventually satisfied provided no one holds on to the object indefinitely. Section 16.5 establishes the "serializability" property that every evolution (even if it has multiple requests in transit simultaneously) is equivalent to an evolution in which at most one request is in transit, and hence has an amortized message cost of $\log N$ per request. Section 16.6 presents the distributed program that implements the object transfer service. It consists of an instance of the program

A.U. Shankar, *Distributed Programming: Theory and Practice*,
DOI 10.1007/978-1-4614-4881-5_16,
© Springer Science+Business Media New York 2013

in Sect. 16.2 for each object. Section 16.7 establishes that this program implements the object transfer service. This essentially follows from the properties proved in Sects. 16.3 and 16.4.

16.1.1   Conventions

We use j and k as parameters that range over the addresses of the fifo channel. We say "system j" to mean the system at address j. We refer to a quantity x in system j as "j.x".

The analysis involves digraphs over the addresses. For readability, when stating predicates involving these digraphs, we will often use informal (but rigorous) terminology, for example, saying

"digraph X has exactly one undirected path between every two nodes"

instead of the more formal

"forall(j,k, j≠k: forone(Seq p: uPath(p,X) and p[0] = j and p.last = k))"

An **in-tree** is a digraph that has no undirected cycles and has a node u such that there is a directed path from every other node to u. Node u is referred to as the root node of the in-tree.

End of conventions

16.2   Distributed Path-Reversal Program

This section presents a distributed program, called PathReversalDist, that achieves object transfer for *one* object of a *fixed* value. The program is given in Fig. 16.1. It has two parameters: ADDR, the addresses of the service; and a0, the initial address of the object. It starts a fifo channel with addresses ADDR, and then starts a component

```
program PathReversalDist(Set ADDR, ADDR a0) {  // object initially at a0
   ia {ADDR.size ≥ 1}
   Sid c ← startSystem(FifoChannel(ADDR));
   Map v ← map();
   for (j in ADDR)
       v[j] ← startSystem(PathReversal(ADDR, j, c[j], a0));
   return v;
} // end PathReversalDist
```

Fig. 16.1 Distributed program of path-reversal component systems and fifo channel

---

Variables of system j

- 1st ← nil if j = a0 otherwise a0.
- nxt ← nil.
- status: thinking, hungry or eating; initially eating if j = a0 otherwise thinking.

Rules of system j (atomically executed)

- Become hungry only if thinking: // $H(j)$
  send [REQ,j] to 1st; set 1st to nil.
- Receive [OBJ]: // $E(j)$
  become eating
- Become thinking only if eating and nxt is non-nil: // $T(j)$
  send object to nxt; set nxt to nil.
- Receive [REQ,k]: // $R(j,k)$
  if 1st is not nil then {send [REQ,k] to 1st; set 1st to k}
  else set nxt and 1st to k.

Fig. 16.2 Variables and rules of system j. Labels $H(j)$, $E(j)$, $T(j)$ and $R(j,k)$ are used in the serializability analysis

system at each address. Each component system is an instantiation of a program PathReversal, which we describe only at the algorithm level. Let "system j" denote the component system at address j.

The systems exchange request messages and "object-carrying" messages. A request message is a tuple [REQ,j] where REQ is a constant and j is the address of the system that *issued* the request (not the system that *last* sent the request, if it was forwarded). An object-carrying message is a tuple [OBJ] where OBJ is a constant.

We say a system is *eating* if it has the object, *hungry* if it has an ongoing request for the object, and *thinking* otherwise. The system cycles through these states. Each system j has a variable 1st, which is its last pointer, and a variable nxt, referred to as its **next pointer**. Each ranges over addresses and a nil value different from any address. Variable 1st equals the address in the *last* request message received by system j after it last became hungry. It is nil if no such request message has been received. Variable nxt is nil either if system j is thinking or if it is non-thinking and has not received a request message since it last became non-thinking. Otherwise, nxt equals the address in the *first* request message received by system j after becoming non-thinking.

The request messages and last pointers are the key to the algorithm. When a system j becomes hungry, it sends [REQ,j] to its 1st and sets 1st to nil. When a system receives [REQ,j], it does the following: (1) if its 1st is non-nil, it forwards the request to 1st and sets 1st to j; (2) if its 1st is nil, it sets its nxt and 1st to j. If an eating system's nxt is non-nil, it (eventually) sends the object to nxt (becoming thinking) and sets nxt to nil.

Figure 16.2 gives the variables and the atomically-executed rules of system j. We will see that the initial condition on the last pointers can be relaxed. Specifically, a non-eating system's 1st need not equal a0; it suffices if the path of last pointers leading out of the system ends in a0.

Although the algorithm is simple to describe, its evolutions, in the general case when multiple requests are simultaneously ongoing, are not simple. To get some insight, we will first look at some restricted cases of evolutions before considering the general case. We will view the state of the distributed system as a digraph over addresses formed by the non-nil last pointers, non-nil next pointers and request messages in transit. For readability, we use the following terminology.

- "[j,k] is a **last edge**": j.1st is not nil and equals k (i.e., (j.1st = k ≠ nil)).
- "[j,k] is a **next edge**": j.nxt is not nil and equals k.
- "[j,k] is a **request edge**": message [REQ,j] is in transit to k.

Recall that a digraph is a 2-tuple, with the first entry being a set of nodes and the second being a set of edges, each a 2-tuple of nodes. Digraph LNR is defined as follows.

LNR : [ADDR, bag([j,k]: [j,k] is a last edge, next edge or request edge)]

Convention: When drawing an instance of LNR, last edges are solid, next edges are dashed, and request edges are dotted, and the circle is the object. Note that LNR can have multiple edges between nodes.

16.2.1   Serial Evolutions with at Most One Hungry System at Any Time

We refer to an evolution of the distributed path-reversal algorithm as **serial** if at most one request is in transit at any time. We start by looking at serial evolutions in which at most one system is hungry. Figure 16.3 illustrates the changes to LNR in a serial evolution involving systems at addresses 1, ···, 6, over the course of one request being satisfied. When a system j becomes hungry, a [REQ,j] message gets forwarded, hop by hop, along the directed path of last edges in LNR from j to the eating system, say k. At each hop, the receiving system sets its 1st to j. Finally the request arrives at system k, which sets its 1st and nxt to j. Later system k stops eating, sends the object to its nxt (i.e., j), and sets its nxt to nil.

Let L be the digraph over addresses consisting of last edges only. Initially, L is an in-tree rooted at the address, say k, of the eating system. When a system j becomes hungry, a [REQ,j] message gets forwarded along the directed path in L from j to k, with the receiving system at each hop setting its 1st to j. At the end L has changed as follows: each node on the path in the old L from j's parent to the root k has now become a child of j, which is the root of the new L. This transformation of L is referred to as a **path reversal**. Thus a serial evolution consists of a sequence of path reversals of L.

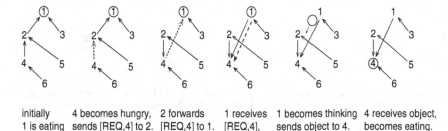

initially 1 is eating	4 becomes hungry, sends [REQ,4] to 2.	2 forwards [REQ,4] to 1.	1 receives [REQ,4],	1 becomes thinking sends object to 4.	4 receives object, becomes eating.

Fig. 16.3 LNR in a serial evolution with at most one hungry node at any time. Last edges are *solid*, next edges are *dashed*, request edges are *dotted*, and the *circle* is the object

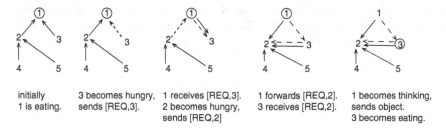

initially 1 is eating.	3 becomes hungry, sends [REQ,3].	1 receives [REQ,3]. 2 becomes hungry, sends [REQ,2]	1 forwards [REQ,2]. 3 receives [REQ,2].	1 becomes thinking, sends object. 3 becomes eating.

Fig. 16.4 LNR in a serial evolution with more than one hungry system at a time

Each path reversal consists of a sequence of last edge redirections, each involving one message send. An individual path reversal consists, in the worst case (when L is a single path), of $N-$ edge redirections, where N is the number of nodes. However, the amortized number of edge redirections per path reversal is $\log N$; that is, in any sequence of path reversals, the total number of edge redirections divided by the total number of path reversals, is at most $\log N$ [2,5] (see Exercise 16.4). Hence any serial evolution has an amortized cost of $\log N + 1$ message sends, where the "+1" is for the transfer of the object.

16.2.2 Serial Evolutions with Multiple Hungry Systems at a Time

Now let us consider a serial evolution in which more than one system can be hungry; i.e., a system becomes hungry only when no request message is in transit but other systems can be hungry or eating. Figure 16.4 illustrates such an evolution. L evolves in exactly the same way as previously, when at most one system is hungry at any time. What is different here is that the next edges can form a path of more than two nodes. The head node of the next path, i.e., the node that has no incoming next pointer, has the object in hand or in transit to it. All the other nodes of the next path

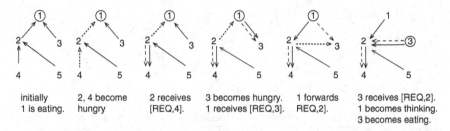

initially 1 is eating.	2, 4 become hungry	2 receives [REQ,4].	3 becomes hungry. 1 receives [REQ,3].	1 forwards REQ,2].	3 receives [REQ,2]. 1 becomes thinking. 3 becomes eating.

Fig. 16.5 LNR in a non-serial evolution

are hungry. (Previously, the next edges formed a path of at most two nodes and the head was always eating.) The last node of the next path, i.e., the node whose next pointer is nil, is also the root of L. The amortized message cost is the same as it would be if each request is issued only when no other system is non-thinking.

16.2.3   Non-serial Evolutions

Now consider the general case where there are no constraints on when requests are initiated. Different requests can be in transit simultaneously, and a hungry system whose request message is in transit may receive a request message from another system. Thus, the edge redirections of different path reversals in L can be interleaved in time. Figure 16.5 illustrates a concurrent evolution.

Things are not so clear now. Does L remain acyclic? Can a request message arrive at its issuer? The next edges can form several paths (e.g., path [1,3] and path [2,4] in the fourth LNR in Fig. 16.5), and only one of them has the object at its head. Does a hungry system eventually join this particular next path? Is the amortized message cost the same as in serial evolutions. We will establish that all these do indeed hold.

16.3   Algorithm Analysis: Safety Properties

We start by noting some obvious properties. There is always exactly one instance of the object. If a system's next pointer is not nil, it is non-thinking and its last pointer is not nil. If a system is thinking, its last pointer is non-nil (hence rule $H(j)$ is fault-free). Thus $Inv\,A_1$–A_3 holds. (Proof: A_1–A_3 holds initially and is preserved by every rule.)

A_1 : forone(j: either (j eating) or ([OBJ] in transit to j))
A_2 : j.nxt $\neq$ nil $\Rightarrow$ (j.lst $\neq$ nil and (j not thinking))
A_3 : (j thinking) $\Rightarrow$ j.lst $\neq$ nil

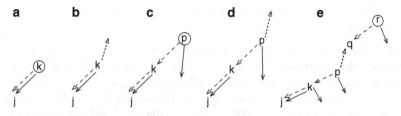

Fig. 16.6 Some snapshots just after [REQ,j] stops at system k

We next establish some safety properties that will be used in proving that every hungry system j eventually eats. Consider the chain of events triggered when system j becomes hungry. It issues a [REQ,j] message that keeps getting forwarded until it reaches a system, say k, whose last pointer is nil. System k sets its last and next pointers to j. At this point, j joins a next-edge path behind k. Figure 16.6 illustrates some of the possibilities. If system k is eating (Fig. 16.6a), it will send the object to j when it stops eating. If system k is hungry, then either system k's request message is in transit to some system and k is at the head of its next-edge path (Fig. 16.6b), or node k has already joined the next-edge path headed by some other system, say p. System p either has the object in hand or in transit to it (Fig. 16.6c), or it has a request message in transit "on behalf" of all systems in its next-edge path (which now includes j) (Fig. 16.6d). When that request message reaches a system, say q, whose last pointer is nil (Fig. 16.6e), the next-edge path containing j gets appended to the next-edge path containing q. This keeps happening until j joins the next-edge path whose head system has the object. Once this happens, j will eventually eat because the object will make its way down the next-edge path.

The above discussion gives insight into the algorithm but it is not a rigorous argument. For example, it implicitly assumes L remains acyclic, otherwise a system's request may keep going round in circles or end up at the issuer. Likewise, it assumes that a system's nxt never points to itself. We now do the work needed to make the argument rigorous.

16.3.1 Digraph LR

We start with the relationship between last pointers and request messages. Define LR to be the digraph over addresses formed by last edges and request edges. That is,

```
LR : [ADDR, bag([j,k]: [j,k] is a last edge or a request edge)]
```

We now establish that B_1 and B_2 below are invariant. B_1 ensures that j.1st never equals j, that [REQ,j] is never in transit to j, and that [j,k] is not a last edge and a request edge at the same time. B_2, which is directly implied by B_1, is stated for convenience.

B_1 :   LR has exactly one undirected path between every two nodes
B_2 :   forall(j: j.1st $\neq$ j)

Proof of Inv B_1 B_1 holds initially because there are no request edges and the last edges form an in-tree. B_1 is preserved by every rule given A_1, A_2, as follows. If a system starts or stops eating, LR is not affected. If a system issues a request, its outgoing last edge becomes a request edge, thus preserving B_1. When system k with non-nil 1st equal to p receives [REQ,j], request edge [j,k] and last edge [k,p] are replaced by last edge [k,j] and request edge [j,p]. Because the old LR satisfies B_1, it has no edge between j and p and the nodes j, k and p are distinct; hence B_1 is preserved. When system k with nil 1st receives [REQ,j], request edge [j,k] is replaced by last edge [k,j], hence preserving B_1.   □

Next we establish that the next pointers and request messages satisfy the following invariantly.

B_3 : forall j: *exactly one* of the following holds:
                        (j not hungry)
                        or ([REQ,j] in transit)
                        or forsome(k: k.nxt = j)
                        or ([OBJ] in transit to j)
                        or (j eating)
B_4 : forall(j: at most one [REQ,j] in transit)
B_5 : forall(j: j.nxt $\neq$ j and num(k: k.nxt = j) $\leq$ 1)

Proof of Inv B_3–B_5: B_3–B_5 holds initially and is preserved by each rule given the invariance of A_1–A_3 and B_1.   □

16.3.2 Digraph Pr

We now introduce a priority ordering among the systems that reflects how conflicts would be resolved. Given two hungry systems j and k, under what situations do we expect j to eat before k? One situation is if j.nxt equals k. Another situation is if k's request is in transit to j. What if k's request is in transit to j but j is thinking? This reduces to the previous situation if j becomes hungry before k's request arrives. Whereas if j becomes hungry after it receives k's request, then we expect j to eat after k. What if j and k are thinking and k.1st equals j? This reduces to the situation of k's request in transit to j if both systems become hungry.

With this motivation, define the digraph Pr (for "priority") consisting of request edges, next edges in reverse, and last edges from thinking nodes. Let [j,k] be a **pr-next** edge iff [k,j] is a next edge. Let [j,k] be a **pr-last** edge iff [j,k] is a last edge and j is thinking. Thus

PR :   [ADDR, bag([j,k]: [j,k] is a request edge, pr-next edge or pr-last edge)]

We will show that if there is path in PR from a node k to a hungry node j, then j will eat before k. We say that j is **pr-reachable from** k to mean there is a directed path in Pr from k to j. We say **lr-path** to mean an undirected path in LR. We establish that the following are invariant.

C_1 : (Pr is an in-tree)
  and (Pr's root is eating or object is in transit to it)
C_2 : (j pr-reachable from k)
  $\Rightarrow$ (j pr-reachable from every node on the lr-path between j and k)
C_3 : ((j not thinking) and (j.1st = k $\neq$ nil))
  $\Rightarrow$ ((j pr-reachable from k) and (k hungry))

Proof of Inv C_1–C_3: Initially Pr is the same as LR, hence C_1, C_2, C_3 hold. We show that C_1, C_2, C_3 are preserved by every rule given the invariants already established. We start with C_1. Let us first dispense with the easy cases. If a system starts eating, Pr is not affected. If a system issues a request, its outgoing pr-last edge becomes a request edge, thus preserving C_1.

Now for the less easy cases. Suppose system j stops eating. Let j.nxt be x and j.1st be w. Then pr-next edge [x,j] is replaced by pr-last edge [j,w]. The old Pr is an in-tree with j as its root. We need to show that the new Pr is an in-tree with x as its root. It suffices to show that x is pr-reachable from w in the old Pr. Suppose this was not the case. Then in the old Pr, the path from w to j went through some node y that was a parent of j other than x, i.e., either y.1st = j and y was thinking, or [REQ,y] was in transit to j. If y and w are the same, there is a cycle [y,j,y] in the old LR, which contradicts B_1. If y and w are different, the lr-path between y and w did not go via j (because the old Pr satisfies C_1 and C_2). Thus, this lr-path together with the lr-edges [y,j] and [j,w] formed an undirected cycle in LR, again contradicting B_1.

Suppose system j receives [REQ,k] when j is thinking. Then [j,w] and [k,j] are replaced by [k,w] and [j,k], and C_1 is preserved.

Suppose system j receives [REQ,k] when j is not thinking. If j.1st is nil, [k,j] changes from a request edge to a pr-next edge, and C_1 is preserved. If j.1st is non-nil, [k,j] is replaced by [k,w]. For the new Pr to be an in-tree, it suffices if k is not reachable from w in the old Pr. (In the old Pr, note that w is not equal to k by B_1, and j is pr-reachable from w by C_3.) Assume k was reachable from w. Then there was an lr-path between k and w that did not use the lr-edges [k,j] and [j,w] (because the old Pr satisfied C_1 and C_2). Thus, there was an undirected cycle in the old LR, contradicting B_1.

This establishes that C_1 holds after every rule execution assuming that C_1–C_3 holds prior to the rule execution and given the invariance of A_1–A_3 and B_1–B_5. It remains to show the same for C_2 and C_3. The details are straightforward and are left as an exercise. $\qquad\square$

16.4 Algorithm Analysis: Monotonic Progress Metric

Recall that Pr can have several next-edge paths. For every j, define the **head of j's next-queue**, denoted by hd(j), as follows: If j has no incoming next edge, then hd(j) is j. Otherwise, hd(j) is the node reached from j by going backwards on incoming next edges until there is no incoming next edge. (The latter exists because the next edges do not form cycles because Pr is an in-tree.)

We will come up with a function $F(j)$, for any hungry system j, such that $F(j)$ increases monotonically and has an upper bound at which point either hd(j) is eating or hd(j) has the object in transit to it and will eventually become eating. If hd(j) is j, we are done. Otherwise, hd(j) will finish eating and then send the object to the next node on the next path, getting one hop closer to j. Thus in either case, the object will eventually arrive at j.

Consider a hungry system j such that hd(j) is not eating nor is the object in transit to hd(j). Then hd(j) has a request in transit (from B_3). When this request is received, we want $F(j)$ to increase. One candidate for $F(j)$ is the number of nodes from which hd(j) is pr-reachable. Let $\alpha(j)$ denote the set of nodes from which hd(j) is pr-reachable. The following hold:

D_1 : $\alpha(j)$ increases when [REQ,hd(j)] is received by a system that is thinking or whose last pointer is nil

D_2 : $\alpha(j)$ does not decrease while j is hungry

Proof of D_1–D_2: Suppose [REQ,hd(j)] is received by a system k. Prior to the reception, k is not in $\alpha(j)$ because Pr is an in-tree and includes request edge [hd(j),k]. If k is thinking when the request arrives, then request edge [hd(j),k] is replaced by last edge [k,hd(j)] in Pr, which increases $\alpha(j)$ by at least k. If k is not thinking and k.1st is nil when the request arrives, then [hd(j),k] changes from a request edge to a pr-next edge, making k the new hd(j), and thus increasing $\alpha(j)$ by at least k. If k is not thinking and k.1st equals non-nil x when the request arrives, then request edge [hd(j),k] is replaced by request edge [hd(j),x] in Pr, and $\alpha(j)$ is unchanged.

What remains is to establish D_2 for steps other than reception of hd(j)'s request. If system z starts eating, Pr does not change, hence $\alpha(j)$ does not change. If system z issues a request, the outgoing last edge from z becomes a request edge, hence $\alpha(j)$ does not change. A rule executed by a system z not in $\alpha(j)$ does not decrease $\alpha(j)$. Suppose system z in $\alpha(j)$ sends the object. This happens only if z is both hd(j) and root in the old Pr. In the new Pr, the node to which the object is sent is both hd(j) and root in new Pr. So $\alpha(j)$ is unchanged (and contain all nodes). Suppose system z in $\alpha(j)$ receives [REQ,k] when 1st is non-nil. This replaces request edge [k,j] by request edge [k,x] where x is the old value of z.1st. Because x is pr-reachable from z (from C_3), this does not remove any node from $\alpha(j)$. What remains is the case of a system z in $\alpha(j)$ receives [REQ,k] when 1st is nil. This left as an exercise.   □

We now look for a function that

- Increases when hd(j)'s request arrives at a non-thinking system, say k, with non-nil 1st, and
- Decreases only if $\alpha(j)$ simultaneously increases.

Let $\beta(j)$ be the set of non-thinking systems whose 1st equals hd(j). $\beta(j)$ satisfies the first condition because when system k receives the request, node k gets added to $\beta(j)$. Node k is not in $\alpha(j)$ before the reception (because Pr is an in-tree and includes request edge [hd(j),k]), and no rule execution changes this as long as k is non-thinking. Thus $\alpha(j)$ and $\beta(j)$ have no node in common.

Does $\beta(j)$ satisfy the second condition? A node x leaves $\beta(j)$ in only two ways: it becomes thinking or its 1st changes. The former happens only if x stops eating; this introduces the pr-last edge [x,hd(j)], thus increasing $\alpha(j)$ with x. The latter happens only if x receives a request [REQ,k]; then x forwards the request to hd(j), thereby introducing the request edge [k,hd(j)], thus increasing $\alpha(j)$ with x (which was not in the old $\alpha(j)$ because Pr was an in-tree and included request edge [hd(j),x]). So $\alpha(j)$ increases whenever $\beta(j)$ decreases.

Thus the tuple $[\alpha(j).\text{size}, \beta(j).\text{size}]$ under lexicographic ordering is a suitable $F(j)$. It keeps increasing as long as j is hungry. It is upper bounded by $[N,N]$, where N is the number of nodes, at which point hd(j) is the root of Pr.

We are done with progress. Assertions D_3 and D_4 below have been established. D_3 says that if a system is hungry then the eating system is eventually informed of this (by having its nxt become non-nil). D_4 says that if an eating system stops eating when its nxt is non-nil, then every hungry system eventually eats.

D_3 : ((j eating) and (k hungry)) *leads-to* (j.nxt is non-nil)
D_4 : (((j eating) and (j.nxt is non-nil)) *leads-to* (j.nxt is nil))
  $\Rightarrow$ ((k hungry) *leads-to* (k eating))

We have also established the following, which will be used in the serializability analysis.

D_5 : ((j and k are hungry) and (j pr-reachable from k))
    unless ((j eating) and (k hungry))

16.5 Algorithm Analysis: Serializability

We show that any finite evolution *x* can be transformed by a sequence of commutations to a serial evolution *y* in which systems eat in the same order and undergo the same message sends and receives. Hence *x* and *y* have the same amortized message complexity, which, for serial evolutions, is $\log N + 1$,

Recall (from Fig. 16.2) the following labels for the steps of the algorithm:

- $H(p)$: system p becomes hungry.
- $E(p)$: system p becomes eating.

- $T(\mathsf{p})$: system p becomes thinking.
- $R(\mathsf{p},\mathsf{q})$: system p receives [REQ,q].

Consider the sequence of steps in evolution x. Let $e_2, e_3, \cdots, e_J$, where $J \geq 1$, be the sequence of (indices of) E steps in x. Let $t_1, t_2, \cdots, t_K$, where $K \geq 0$, be the sequence of (indices of) T steps in x. (Recall that initially one system is eating. The numbering in these sequences is such that t_1 precedes e_2 and, for all i, t_i ends the eating session started in e_i. K equals J if x ends with no eating system; otherwise K equals $J - 1$.)

Each e_i is the culmination of a sequence of steps, starting with the H step that issued the request satisfied in e_i, then the R steps that successively forwarded the request to a system with a nil last pointer, then the T step that sends the object to the system that eats in e_i, then e_i itself. Let v_i refer to this sequence of steps. Formally, if e_i is an E step of a system p, then v_i is the sequence of steps in x consisting of

- The last $H(\mathsf{p})$ step, say z, before e_i,
- The $R(.,\mathsf{p})$ steps between z and t_{i-1},
- And e_i.

Let w be the sequence of (indices of) steps in x that do not belong to any v_i. The steps in w are H steps, R steps, and possibly t_K (iff x ends with the object in transit).

Consider the list of sequences $v_1, \cdots, v_J, w$. Evolution x corresponds to a *merge* of these sequences. We now show that the serial evolution y we seek corresponds to the concatenation of these sequences, i.e., $v_1 \circ \cdots \circ v_J \circ w$.

Lemma 16.1. *Let f and g be two successive steps in x such that g belongs to v_i and f belongs either to v_j, $j > i$, or to w. Then f and g commute and the commutation preserves the number of messages sent and received.*   □

Evolution x can be transformed to evolution y by repeatedly applying the commutations allowed by the lemma. All that remains is to establish the lemma, which we do now.

Proof of Lemma 16.1. For each possible case of f and g in x, we show that f and g commute, i.e., they can be interchanged and their intermediate state modified such that the resulting sequence is an evolution. Furthermore, the commutation preserves the number of messages sent and received.

Case 1:   Let g be a H or R step of v_i. Let f be a H or R step of v_j. Let g involve [REQ,p] and f involve [REQ,q]. First, suppose f sends a message received by g. Then g would be a R step of v_j, contradicting the assumption $j > i$. Hence g does not receive a message from f. Second, suppose f and g are steps of the same system, say x. Then p would be pr-reachable from q just after f, and hence p would eat before q (from D_5), contradicting the assumption $j > i$. Hence f and g are not at the same system. In either case, f and g are not causally related. So f and g commute. The commutation preserves message sends and receptions.

Case 2:   Let g be a H or R step of v_i. Let f belong to w. The argument is exactly as in case 1.

Case 3: Let g be a E step of v_i. Let f be a H or R step of v_j or w. First, because g receives the object and f can only send a request, g does not receive a message sent by f. Second, if f and g are at the same system then the order of receptions can be interchanged, because the system responds to a request reception (f) in the same way whether it is hungry (f before g) or eating (f after g). In either case, f and g commute, and the commutation preserves messages sends and receptions.

Case 4: Let g be a T step of v_i, i.e., g is t_{i-1}. Let f be a H or R step of v_j or w. First, step g does not receive a message sent by f because g, being a T step, does not receive a message. Second, suppose f and g are at the same system, say x. Then f cannot be a H step (because then g cannot be a T step of the system). Thus f is a R step. Suppose x.1st was nil prior to f. Then g would send the object in response to f, which means that f belongs to v_i, contradicting the assumption that $j > i$. Thus x.1st was non-nil prior to f, in which case f and g commute (in both cases x forwards the request message to its old 1st and sets 1st to the issuer of the request message). So in all cases, f and g commute and and the commutation preserves messages sends and receptions. □

16.6 Distributed Program Implementing Object-Transfer Service

This section presents a distributed program that implements the object transfer service (in Chap. 15). The program, called ObjTrPathReversalDist, is given in Fig. 16.7. It has the same parameters as the object transfer service: ADDR, the set of addresses of the service; OID, the set of object ids; OVAL, the set of possible values

```
program ObjTrPathReversalDist(ADDR, OID, OVAL, initObjs) {
    ic {Set(ADDR,OID,OVAL) and Map<ADDR, Set<OID>>(initObjs)
        and min(ADDR.size, OID.size, OVAL.size) ≥ 1
        and ADDR.size = initObjs.size
        and disjoint(initObjs[i]: i in ADDR)
        and union(initObjs[i]: i in ADDR) = OID}

    Sid c ← startSystem(FifoChannel(ADDR));
    Map v ← map();
    for (j in ADDR)
        v[j] ← startSystem(ObjTrPathReversal(ADDR,j,c[j],OID,OVAL,initObjs));
    return v;
} // end ObjTrPathReversalDist
```

Fig. 16.7 Distributed program of object-transfer component systems and fifo channel

of an object; and initObjs, map where initObjs[j] is the set of ids of objects initially held by the user at v[j]. It starts a fifo channel with addresses ADDR, and then starts a component system at each address.

Each component system essentially executes a separate instance of the path-reversal program for each object of the service. The system is an instantiation of program ObjTrPathReversal, given in Figs. 16.8 and 16.9. The boxes are comments containing fragments of the object-transfer service inverse, each matching the code to its left.

The main code first defines message types. Request messages now have the form [REQ,j,oid]. Object-carrying messages now have the form [OBJ,oid,oval], where oval is the value of object oid. The main code then defines map variables lst and nxt, both indexed by object ids. Map lst has an entry for object oid iff the last pointer for oid is non-nil and lst[oid] is its value. Map nxt stores the non-nil next pointers in the same way.

The main code then defines a map variable objBuff, in which to buffer received object-value pairs awaiting delivery to the local user (in acq returns). The main code then defines a sequence variable reqBuff, in which to queue the object ids of received requests awaiting delivery to the local user (in rxReq returns). It is accessed as a fifo queue, to ensure that every entry eventually leaves if the user keeps removing entries.

For each object, we want the (effectively) atomic steps of the program to correspond to the rules in Fig. 16.2, so that the properties proved in Sects. 16.3, 16.4 and 16.5 can be assumed to hold here without further analysis. We will have the program update lst and nxt upon receiving a request message from the fifo channel (exactly as in the rules). This implies that a ObjTrPathReversal system is "eating" with respect to an object oid if object oid is with the user or in objBuff.

The program has three input functions, acq(oid), rxReq() and rel(oid,oval), and a function doRx executed by a local thread tRx. The "//**...**//" comments indicate the code chunks that match the rules in Fig. 16.2.

- Function acq(oid) sends message [REQ,aL,oid] to lst[oid], removes the oid entry from lst, and waits for an oid entry in objBuff. When the entry shows up, it returns objBuff[oid], the value of object oid.
- Function rxReq() waits for reqBuff to be non-empty and returns the object id at the head of reqBuff.
- Function rel(oid,oval) sends message [OBJ,oid,oval] to nxt[oid], removes the oid entry from nxt, and returns.
- Function doRx receives a message from the channel and does the following.

    - If a [OBJ,oid,oval] message: add [oid,oval] to objBuff.
    - If a [REQ,j,oid] message: if oid is in lst.keys, send the message to lst[oid] and set lst[oid] to j; otherwise, create and set lst[oid] to j, and append oid to reqBuff.

```
program ObjTrPathReversal(ADDR, aL, cL, OID, OVAL, initObjs) {
    // aL: local address.
    // cL: sid of local channel access system
    ia {true}

    // request/object
    REQ ← 1; OBJ ← 2;
    type ReqMsg = Tuple<REQ, ADDR, OID>;
    type ObjMsg = Tuple<OBJ, OID, OVAL>;
    Set objs ← initObjs[aL];
    Map objBuff ← map();
    // reqBuff accessed as fifo queue
    Seq reqBuff ← seq();
    Map 1st ← map([oid,j]: j in ADDR, j ≠ aL,
                            oid in initObjs[j]);
    Map nxt ← map();
    Tid tRx ← startThread(doRx());
    return mysid;


    //** become-hungry rule **//
    input OVAL mysid.acq(OID oid) {
        ia {(oid in 1st.keys)
            and 1st[oid] ≠ aL}
        await (true) {
            cL.tx(1st[oid], [REQ,aL,oid]);
            1st.remove(oid);
        }
        //** become-eating rule **//
        await (oid in objBuff.keys) {
            oval ← objBuff[oid];
            objBuff.remove(oid);
            return oval;
        }
    }

    input Seq mysid.rxReq() {
        ia {true}
        await (reqBuff.size > 0) {
            oid ← reqBuff.remove();
            return oid;
        }
    }

// continued
```

```
ObjTransferServiceInverse(
    ADDR, OID, OVAL, initObjs) {
ic {...}
objs ← initObjs;
reqs ← map([j,set()]: j in ADDR);
val ← map();
return mysid
```

```
ObjTransferServiceInverse
// doAcq(aL,oid)

oc {not ongoing(v[aL].acq(oid))
        and not (oid in objs[aL])}
rval ← v[aL].acq(oid);
ic {(oid in val.keys)
        and (rval = val[oid])}
val.remove(oid);
objs[aL].add(oid);
```

```
ObjTransferServiceInverse
// doRxReq(aL)

oc {not ongoing(v[aL].rxReq())}
oid ← v[aL].rxReq();
ic {((oid in objs[aL])
        or ongoing(v[aL].acq(oid)))
    and not (oid in reqs[aL])}
reqs[aL].add(oid);
```

Fig. 16.8 Part 1: Program ObjTrPathReversal. Boxes are comments containing matching parts from ObjTransferService inverse

```
// ObjTrPathReversal continued

  //** become-thinking rule **//
  input void mysid.rel(OID oid, OVAL oval) {       ObjTransferServiceInverse
    ia {(oid in nxt.keys)                          // doRel(aL,oid,oval)
        and nxt[oid] ≠ aL}
    await (true) {                                 oc {(oid in objs[aL])
      cL.tx(nxt[oid], [OBJ,oid,oval]);                 and (oid in reqs[aL])}
      nxt.remove(oid);                             objs[aL].remove(oid);
      objs.remove(oid);                            reqs[aL].remove(oid);
      return;                                      val[oid] ← oval;
    }                                              v[aL].rel(oid,oval);
  }                                                ic {true}


  function doRx() {       // executed by thread tRx
    while (true) {
    ● msg ← c.rx();
      ia {msg in union(ReqMsg,ObjMsg)}
      await (true) {
        if (msg[0] = OBJ) {        // msg = [OBJ,oid,oval]
          //** Receive object rule **//
          objBuff[msg[1]] ← msg[2];
          objs.add(msg[1]);
        }
        else
        //** Receive request rule **//
        if (msg[2] in lst.keys) {  // msg[0] = [REQ,j,oid], lst non-nil
          cL.tx(lst[msg[2]], msg);  // forward msg
          lst[msg[2]] ← msg[1];
        }
        else {                                // msg[0] = [REQ,j,oid], lst nil
          nxt[msg[2]] ← lst[msg[2]] ← msg[1];
          reqBuff.append(msg[2]);
          }
        }
      }
    }
  }

  atomicity assumption {awaits}

  progress assumption {weak fairness for threads}
} // end ObjTrPathReversal
```

Fig. 16.9 Program ObjTrPathReversal part 2

```
system Z(ADDR, OID, OVAL, initObjs) {
  ia [ObjTransferService.ic]
  inputs(); outputs();
  v ← startSystem(ObjTrPathReversalDist(ADDR,OID,OVAL,initObjs));
  oti ← startSystem(ObjTransferServiceInverse(ADDR,OID,OVAL,initObjs));
} // end Z
```

Fig. 16.10 Closed program of ObjTrPathReversalDist and ObjTransferServiceInverse

16.7 Proving the Implements Conditions

We now establish that ObjTrPathReversalDist(ADDR, OID, OVAL, initObjs) implements ObjTransferService(ADDR, OID, OVAL, initObjs) (in Figs. 15.2 and 15.3). Figure 16.10 shows the closed program Z of instantiation v of ObjTrPathReversalDist and instantiation oti of ObjTransferServiceInverse. The latter is available from the boxes in Figs. 16.8 and 16.9. Z.ia is the same as ObjTransferService.ic.

We have to establish that Z satisfies the assertions E_1–E_5 below. (We continue to use j.x to mean v[j].x.)

E_1 : Inv (thread at oti.doAcq(j,oid).ic)
                $\Rightarrow$ (oti.doAcq(j,oid).ic)   // v[j].acq return
E_2 : Inv (thread at oti.doRxReq(j).ic)
                $\Rightarrow$ (oti.doRxReq(j).ic)   // v[j].rxReq return
E_3 : ongoing(j.rel(oid,oval)) *leads-to* not ongoing(j.rel(oid,oval))
E_4 : (objs[j].size > 0 *leads-to* ongoing(j.rxReq))
                $\Rightarrow$ (((oid in oti.objs[j]) and ongoing(k.acq(oid)))
                        leads-to (oid in oti.reqs[j]))
E_5 : forall(j: (((oid in oti.objs[j]) and ongoing(k.acq(oid)))
                        leads-to (oid in oti.reqs[j]))
                and ((oid in oti.reqs[j]) *leads-to* not (oid in oti.reqs[j])))
        $\Rightarrow$ forall(k: ongoing(k.acq(oid)) *leads-to* not ongoing(k.acq(oid)))

We now restate (slightly stronger versions of) E_1 and E_2, accounting for Z's atomicity points. F_1 corresponds to E_1's predicate, and F_2 to E_2's predicate.

F_1 : (oid in j.objBuff.keys)
        $\Rightarrow$ (oid in oti.val.keys)
        and j.objBuff[oid] = oti.val[oid]   // v[j].acq return
F_2 : (oid in j.reqBuff.keys)
        $\Rightarrow$ ((oid in oti.objs[j]) or ongoing(j.acq(oid))
                and not (oid in oti.reqs[j]))   // v[j].rxReq return

Thus the implements safety condition holds if Inv (F_1–F_2) holds. For this to hold, we also have to prove the following: (1) when v[j].acq(oid) is called, j.1st[oid] exists and does not equal j; (2) when v[j].rel(oid,..) is called, j.nxt[oid] exists and does not equal j; (3) when a request message is received, j.last[oid] does not equal j; (4) at most one call of c[j].tx is ongoing at any time; and (5) at most one call of c[j].rx is ongoing at any time. These, along with F_1–F_2, would ensure that program Z is fault-free (including that Z uses the fifo channel c correctly). Condition 4 holds because every c[j].tx call is within an await. Condition 5 holds because c[j].rx is called by only one thread (j.tRx). Conditions 1–3 are implied by F_3–F_6 below.

F_3 : (not ongoing(j.acq(oid)) and not (oid in oti.objs[j]))
         $\Rightarrow$ (oid in j.1st.keys)
F_4 : (oid in oti.objs[j]) and (oid in oti.reqs[j])
         $\Rightarrow$ (oid in j.nxt.keys)
F_5 : (oid in j.1st.keys) $\Rightarrow$ j.1st[oid] $\neq$ j
F_6 : (oid in j.nxt.keys) $\Rightarrow$ j.nxt[oid] $\neq$ j

In sum, we have to prove that Z satisfies $Inv\,F_1$–F_6 and E_3–E_5. In this task, we can make use of the fruits of the analysis of the distributed path-reversal program.

16.7.1 Assertions from Path Reversal Analysis

Recall that program PathReversalDist (Fig. 16.1) consists of systems, each defined by the rules in Fig. 16.2, interacting over a fifo channel. Every atomic step of program Z at address j concerning object oid either corresponds to a rule in Fig. 16.2 or has no effect on the variables in Fig. 16.2, provided we treat "j eating" in Z as corresponding to object oid in oti.objs[j] or in j.objBuff. The systems in PathReversalDist interact over a fifo channel. The messages in Z concerning object oid also travel in fifo order, and every such message in transit to j is eventually received (because the ObjTrPathReversal system at j remains ready to receive incoming messages). Thus for every oid, program Z satisfies the assertions established in Sects. 16.3–16.5 provided we parameterize the assertions with oid and translate "j eating", "j hungry" and "j thinking" as follows.

        eating(j,oid):   (oid in oti.objs[j]) or (oid in j.objBuff.keys)
        hungry(j,oid):   ongoing(j.acq(oid)) and not (oid in j.objBuff.keys)
     thinking(j,oid):   not eating(j,oid) and not hungry(j,oid)

Here are A_1–A_3, B_2, (part of) B_5, D_3 and D_4 from the path reversal analysis, translated into the context of program Z. The same labels are used but a "'" is added, e.g., A_1 becomes A_1'. As explained earlier, Z satisfies $Inv\,(A_2'$–A_3' and B_2' and $B_5')$ and D_3'–D_4'.

A_1' : forone(j: either eating(j,oid) or ([OBJ,oid,..] in transit to j))
A_2' : (oid in j.nxt.keys) $\Rightarrow$ ((oid in j.1st.keys) and not thinking(j,oid))
A_3' : thinking(j,oid) $\Rightarrow$ (oid in j.1st.keys)
B_2' : (oid in j.1st.keys) $\Rightarrow$ j.1st[oid] $\neq$ j
B_5' : (oid in j.nxt.keys) $\Rightarrow$ j.nxt[oid] $\neq$ j

D'_3 : (eating(j,oid) and hungry(k,oid)) *leads-to* (oid in j.nxt.keys)
D'_4 : ((eating(j,oid) and (oid in j.nxt.keys))
$\quad\quad$ *leads-to* not (oid in j.nxt.keys))
$\quad\quad \Rightarrow$ (hungry(k,oid) *leads-to* eating(k,oid))

16.7.2 Assertions Concerning objBuff and reqBuff

We now state some obvious safety properties of Z. G_1 says that if [oid,oval] is in transit or in j.objBuff, then oval equals oti.val[oid]. G_2 says that if a request for object oid is in j.reqBuff or with j's user, then j.nxt[oid] exists. G_3 says that j.reqBuff and oti.reqs[j] are disjoint. G_4 says that j.objBuff and oti.objs[j] are disjoint. G_5 says that if oid is in j.objBuff then a j.acq(oid) call is ongoing. Z satisfies $Inv\,G_1$–G_5. (Proof is left as an exercise.)

G_1 : (([OBJ,oid,oval] in transit) or ([oid,oval] in j.objBuff))
$\quad\quad \Rightarrow$ ((oid in oti.val.keys) and oval = oti.val[oid])
G_2 : ((oid in j.reqBuff.keys) or (oid in oti.reqs[j]))
$\quad\quad \Rightarrow$ (oid in j.nxt.keys)
G_3 : disjoint(j.reqBuff.keys, oti.reqs[j])
G_4 : disjoint(j.objBuff.keys, oti.objs[j])
G_5 : (oid in j.objBuff.keys) $\Rightarrow$ ongoing(j.acq(oid))

Now for some obvious progress properties of Z. (Proof left as an exercise.)

H_1 : (oid in j.objBuff.keys) *leads-to* (oid in oti.objs[j])
H_2 : ((oid in oti.objs[j]) *leads-to* ongoing(j.rxReq))
$\quad\quad \Rightarrow$ ((oid in j.nxt.keys) *leads-to* (oid in oti.reqs[j]))

16.7.3 Proof of Inv F_1–F_6

$Inv\,F_1$–F_6 holds because F_1–F_6 is implied by A'_1–A'_3, B'_2, B'_5, and G_1–G_5. Details follow.

- F_1 is implied by G_1.
- F_2 is implied by G_2, A'_2 and G_3 as follows. F_2's lhs and G_2 imply oid is in j.nxt.keys, which implies not thinking(j,oid) (from A'_2), which implies eating(j,oid) or hungry(j,oid), which implies the first conjunct in F_2's rhs. F_2's lhs and G_3 implies oid is not in oti.reqs[j], which is the second conjunct in F_2's rhs.
- F_3 is implied by G_2 and A'_3 as follows. F_3's lhs and G_5 implies thinking(j,oid), which implies F_3's rhs (from A'_3).
- F_4 is implied by G_2.

- F_5 is implied by B_2.
- F_6 is implied by B_5.

16.7.4 Proof of E_3–E_5

E_3 holds because j.rel(.) is executed with weak fairness.

E_4 holds as follows. Assume E_4's rhs's lhs, i.e., the conjuncts (1) (oid in objs[j]), (2) not (oid in reqs[j]), and (3) forsome(k, k ≠ j: thread in k.acq(oid)). Conjunct 1 implies eating(j,oid). This and conjunct 3 imply hungry(k,oid). Because j is eating and k is hungry, oid enters j.nxt.keys (from D'_3). Hence oid enters oti.reqs[j] (from H_2 and E_4's lhs).

E_5 holds as follows. Assume E_4's rhs's lhs, i.e., ongoing(k.acq(oid)). If oid is in k.objBuff.keys, then E_5's rhs's rhs eventually holds (from H_1). Now assume oid is not in k.objBuff.keys. Then hungry(k,oid) holds and E_5's rhs reduces to

hungry(k,oid) *leads-to* eating(k,oid)

But this is D'_4's rhs. So it suffices to establish D_4's lhs, i.e.,

(eating(j,oid) and (oid in j.nxt.keys)) *leads-to* not (oid in j.nxt.keys)

Assume D'_4's lhs. Its first conjunct leads to oid in oti.objs[j] (from H_1), and its second conjunct leads to oid in oti.reqs[j] (from H_2 and E_5's lhs). Thus it suffices to establish

((oid in oti.objs[j]) and (oid in oti.reqs[j]))
    leads-to not (oid in v[j].nxt.keys)

The above follows from E_4's lhs (and the fact that oid leaves j.nxt.keys when it leaves oti.reqs[j]).

16.8 Concluding Remarks

This chapter first presented the distributed path-reversal program and established relevant properties (including serializability). It then used this program in constructing a program that implements the object transfer service.

The path-reversal algorithm finds many applications. Early ones include (sequential) set union algorithms [5], distributed mutual exclusion [6], and page sharing in distributed shared memory [3]. The analysis of concurrent evolutions was done in [1], and the safety and progress analyses (but not the serializability analysis) are taken from there. Prior analyses considered only serial evolutions.

Exercises

16.1. Implement the awaits in program ObjTrPathReversal (Figs. 16.8 and 16.9) using locks condition variables.

16.2. This problem proposes to augment the path-reversal algorithm so that it provides (in addition to object transfer) a message-passing service in which any user without the object can send a message that is delivered to the owner of the object at the time of delivery. Modify the rules of PathReversal to handle this.

(Hint. Introduce a new message of the form [OWNR,msg], where msg is a user message to be delivered to the owner of the object. System j can send a [OWNR,msg] message only if it is not eating. If j is hungry then the message is buffered at j (to be "received" when j starts eating). Otherwise the message is forwarded along the path of last pointers *without updating them* until it reaches a system k that is non-thinking or whose last pointer is nil. System k does the following. If it is eating, the message is delivered immediately. If k is hungry, the message is buffered at system k until system k becomes eating, at which point the message is delivered. If system k is eating, then its last pointer is nil and its user has the object; the message is delivered immediately.)

16.3. Incorporate your solution in Exercise 16.2 into program ObjTrPathReversal.

16.4. Obtain the amortized cost of a path reversal for in-tree of N nodes as follows [2]. Let the "size" $s(x)$ of a node x be the number of descendants of x, including x itself. Let the "potential" of the tree be $\Phi = (1/2)\sum_{x\in tree}\log s(x)$. Consider a path reversal of length k in nodes $x_0, x_1, \cdots, x_k$ as illustrated below (triangles denote subtrees).

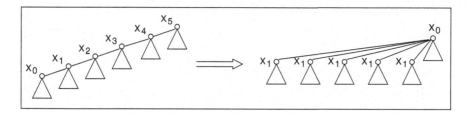

Define the "potential gain" of the reversal to be $k + \Phi_{new} - \Phi_{old}$, where Φ_{new} and Φ_{old} are the values of Φ before and after the reversal. Show that the potential gain is upper bounded by $\log N$. (Hint: use the inequality $1 + (1/2)\log(\alpha - 1) \le \log\alpha$ for all $\alpha > 1$.)

Next show that for any sequence of m path reversals, the sum of the costs is equal to the sum of the potential gains plus an offset which is at most $(N/2)\log N$. (Hint: $\Phi_0 \le (1/2)N\log N$ (because $s(x) \le N$ for any node x), and $\Phi_M \ge (1/2)\log N$ (smallest Φ achieved when the root has $N-1$ children).)

References

1. D. Ginat, A.U. Shankar, An assertional proof of correctness and serializability of a distributed mutual exclusion algorithm based on path reversal. Technical report, University of Maryland, Computer Science Department, 1988. CSTR-2104
2. D. Ginat, D.D. Sleator, R.E. Tarjan, A tight amortized bound for path reversal. Inf. Process. Lett. **31**(1), 3–5 (1989)
3. K. Li, P. Hudak, Memory coherence in shared virtual memory systems. ACM Trans. Comput. Syst. **7**(4), 321–359 (1989). doi: http://doi.acm.org/10.1145/75104.75105
4. M. Naimi, M. Trehel, A. Arnold, A log(n) distributed mutual exclusion algorithm based on path reversal. J. Parallel Distrib. Comput. **34**(1), 1–13 (1996)
5. R.E. Tarjan, J. van Leeuwen, Worst-case analysis of set union algorithms. J. ACM **31**(2), hbox245–281 (1984). doi:10.1145/62.2160. http://doi.acm.org/10.1145/62.2160
6. M. Trehel, M. Naimi, A distributed algorithm for mutual exclusion based on data structures and fault tolerance, in *6th Annual International Phoenix Conference on Computers and Communication*, Scottsdale, pp. 35–39 (1987)

Chapter 17
Distributed Shared Memory Service

17.1 Introduction

The component systems of a distributed system can interact by message passing
or by shared memory. In the former, their programs have send and receive calls.
In the latter their programs read and write shared memory locations. Component
systems that interact over a channel typically interact by message passing because
that is the natural way to use the channel. **Distributed shared memory** provides an
alternative [6, 8]. Here, a distributed system uses message passing to implement a
shared memory accessible to component systems on different computers (perhaps
on the same chip). The memory address space is divided into **pages**, and the
pages are allocated among the component systems. When a component system
attempts access a page that is not locally present, the distributed shared memory
implementation brings the page to the component system.

This chapter defines a distributed shared memory service, implementations of
which are given in later chapters. Figure 17.1 illustrates a distributed shared memory
service. Users access the service by issuing read and write calls to their local access
systems. A write call has two parameters, a page id and a value to be written; it
returns void. A read call has one parameter, a page id; it returns with a value of the
page. (In reality, reads and writes would have an additional parameter, the location
in a page that is to be read or written. We omit this for brevity.)

Ideally, we want distributed shared memory to be equivalent to traditional shared
memory. The standard assumption for the latter (implicit in all our analyses) is

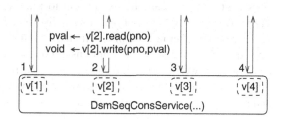

Fig. 17.1 A distributed
shared memory service
spanning addresses 1, 2, 3, 4,
with access system v[j] at
address j

A.U. Shankar, *Distributed Programming: Theory and Practice*,
DOI 10.1007/978-1-4614-4881-5__17,
© Springer Science+Business Media New York 2013

that reads and writes are atomic: a read or write call is immediately followed by its return, and a read of a memory location returns the value last written into that location. We refer to this shared memory as **sequential** shared memory.

We want distributed shared memory service to provide *effectively* atomic reads and writes (so that programs running on it can be analyzed in the same old way). That is, the read values returned by the service should be such that in any evolution, the sequence x of calls and returns of reads and writes can be reordered to a sequence y such that (1) y and x have the same sequence of calls and returns for each user and (2) y obeys the restrictions of sequential shared memory. Such a distributed shared memory is referred to as **sequentially-consistent** shared memory [4].

17.2   Service Program

The service program is given in Figs. 17.2 and 17.3. It has the following parameters: ADDR, set of addresses of the service; PNO, set of page ids, referred to as **page numbers**; and PVAL, the possible values of a page.

The main code defines variables α and v. Variable α is the sequence of write calls and read returns thus far. It has a [WCALL,j,pn,pv] entry for every v[j].write(pn,pv) call, and a [RRET,j,pn,pv] entry for every v[j].read(pn) return with value pv. Variable v is the usual sid map of the access systems.

There are three helper functions, used for expressing sequential consistency. In all of them, the parameter h is a sequence of write call and read return entries. Function lastWrite(h,pn) returns the last value written to pn. Function sequential(h) returns true if h is sequential. Function seqConsistent(h) returns true if h is sequentially consistent.

The service has two input functions at each address j: v[j].read and v[j].write. Each is called only if there is no ongoing call at j. Function v[j].read(pn) reads page pn. It returns a value pv of page pn and appends [RRET,j,pn,pv] to α, such that the updated α remains sequentially consistent. Function v[j].write(pn,pv) writes the value pv to page pn. It appends [WCALL,j,pn,pv] to α.

17.3   Concluding Remarks

This chapter defined a distributed shared memory service that is sequentially consistent, which means it's equivalent to traditional sequential shared memory. There are many implementations of such distributed shared memory, e.g., [1, 5, 6].

There are weaker notions of distributed shared memory consistency, e.g., [2, 3, 7]. The advantage of these weaker notions of consistency is that their implementations can achieve lower wait times for users, i.e., their reads and writes can return in less time. Their disadvantage is that they are not equivalent to sequential shared memory, and so programs executing on them can behave in non-traditional ways.

```
service DsmSeqConService(ADDR, PNO, PVAL) {
// Sequentially-consistent distributed shared memory
// ADDR: addresses of service. PNO: page numbers. PVAL: page values.
   ic {Set(ADDR, PNO, PVAL) and min(ADDR.size, PNO.size, PVAL.size) ≥ 1}

   // α: sequence of [WCALL,j,pn,pv] and [RRET,j,pn,pv] entries
   //      [WCALL,j,pn,pv] denotes a v[j].write(pn,pv) call
   //      [RRET,j,pn,pv] denotes a v[j].read(pn) return with value pv
   WCALL ← 1; RRET ← 2;                 // write-call/ read-return tags
   Seq α ← [];
   Map v ← map([j, sid()]: j in ADDR); // v[j]: sid of access system at j
   return v;

   // helper functions. h is a sequence of WCALL and RRET entries
   // last value written to page pn in h; undefined if no such write
   function PVAL lastWrite(Seq h, PNO pn) {
       Seq xh ← [s: s in h, s[0] = WCALL, s[2] = pn];
       return xh.last[3];
   }

   // true iff every read returns the value of the last write prior to it
   function boolean sequential(Seq h) {
       return forall(i in h.keys, h[i][0] = RRET:
                       h[i][3] = lastWrite(h[0..i-1], h[i][2]))
   }

   // true iff h sequentially consistent
   function boolean seqConsistent(Seq h) {
       return
         forsome(Seq xh: sequential(xh) and
                      forall(j in ADDR:
                            [s: s in xh, s[1]=j] = [r: r in h, r[1]=j]))
   }

   input PVAL v[ADDR j].read(PNO pn) {
       ic {not ongoing(v[j].read(.)) and not ongoing(v[j].write(.))}
       output (pv) {
           oc {seqConsistent(α∘ [[RRET,j,pn,pv]])}
           α.append([RRET,j,pn,pv]);
           return pv;
       }
   }
}

// continued
```

Fig. 17.2 Part 1: distributed shared memory service DsmSeqConService

```
// Program DsmSeqConService continued

input void v[ADDR j].write(PNO pn, PVAL pv) {
   ic {not ongoing(v[j].read(.)) and not ongoing(v[j].write(.))}
   α.append([WCALL,j,pn,pv]);
   oc {true}
   return;
}

atomicity assumption {input parts and output parts}

progress assumption {
   // every read call and write call returns
   ongoing(v[j].read(.))  leads-to  not ongoing(v[j].read(.));
   ongoing(v[j].write(.))  leads-to  not ongoing(v[j].write(.));
}
} // end DsmSeqConService
```

Fig. 17.3   Part 2: distributed shared memory service DsmSeqConService

There is also a notion of consistency, referred to as **coherent shared memory**, that is stronger than sequential consistency [5, 6]. Intuitively, coherent shared memory is traditional atomic shared memory that is located remotely; that is, every memory operation appears to occur atomically at some point between the call and its return. To clarify the relationship between sequential consistency and coherency, let the *read-write history* of a shared memory be the sequence of calls and returns of reads and writes, i.e., α augmented with read calls and write returns. The read-write history is sequentially consistent if it can be permuted to a sequential history in which each user's read-write history is preserved. For the read-write history to be coherent, there is an additional requirement: for every read or write return, the permutation must not move any part of the history after the return to before the return. This naturally captures the constraint that once a write operation w to a page returns, the remote sequential shared memory has been updated and so any future read of the same page cannot get a value prior to w. Reference [1] is an example of a distributed shared memory that is sequentially consistent but not coherent.

Exercises

17.1. Provide a value of α, i.e., a sequence of WCALL and RRET entries, that is sequentially consistent but not coherent.

17.2. Obtain the inverse program of DsmSeqConService.

17.3. Obtain a service program for coherent distributed shared memory.

References

1. Y. Afek, G. Brown, M. Merritt, Lazy caching. ACM Trans. Program. Lang. Syst. **15**(1), 182–205 (1993). doi:http://doi.acm.org/10.1145/151646.151651
2. M. Dubois, C. Scheurich, Retrospective: memory access buffering in multiprocessors, in *25 Years of the International Symposia on Computer Architecture (Selected Papers), ISCA '98* (ACM, New York, 1998), pp. 48–50. doi:10.1145/285930.285951. http://doi.acm.org/10.1145/285930.285951
3. M. Dubois, C. Scheurich, F. Briggs, Memory access buffering in multiprocessors, in *25 Years of the International Symposia on Computer Architecture (Selected Papers), ISCA '98* (ACM, New York, 1998), pp. 320–328. doi:10.1145/285930.285991. http://doi.acm.org/10.1145/285930.285991
4. L. Lamport, How to make a correct multiprocess program execute correctly on a multiprocessor. IEEE Trans. Comput. **46**(7), 779–782 (1997). doi:10.1109/12.599898. http://dx.doi.org/10.1109/12.599898
5. D. Lenoski, J. Laudon, K. Gharachorloo, W.D. Weber, A. Gupta, J. Hennessy, M. Horowitz, M.S. Lam, The Stanford Dash multiprocessor. Computer **25**(3), 63–79 (1992). doi:10.1109/2.121510. http://dx.doi.org/10.1109/2.121510
6. K. Li, P. Hudak, Memory coherence in shared virtual memory systems. ACM Trans. Comput. Syst. **7**(4), 321–359 (1989). doi:http://doi.acm.org/10.1145/75104.75105
7. D. Mosberger, Memory consistency models. SIGOPS Oper. Syst. Rev. **27**(1), 18–26 (1993). doi:10.1145/160551.160553. http://doi.acm.org/10.1145/160551.160553
8. J. Protic, M. Tomasevic, V. Milutinovic (eds.), *Distributed Shared Memory: Concepts and Systems*, 1st edn. (IEEE Computer Society Press, Los Alamitos, 1997)

Chapter 18
A Single-Copy Distributed Shared Memory

18.1 Introduction

This chapter presents a distributed system program that implements the sequentially-consistent distributed shared memory service (in Chap. 17). It employs a straightforward algorithm. Initially, the shared memory pages are arbitrarily distributed among the component systems of the implementation. When a user at a component system attempts to access a page that is not locally present, the page is moved to the component system, after which the access proceeds as usual. We refer to this as a "single-copy" implementation because at any time there is exactly one copy of each page in the distributed system. The component systems use the object-transfer service (Chap. 15) to move pages. (Any implementation of the object-transfer service can be used, e.g., the one in Chap. 16.)

Having only one copy of a page is unrealistic. It results in poor performance (high delay for page access) because it does not allow a page to be read by different component systems simultaneously. All practical implementations allow multiple copies of a page to exist, enforcing some protocol so that writes are propagated consistently to all copies (e.g., [1–3]). We will see such an implementation in the next chapter.

18.2 Distributed Program

The distributed program, called DsmSCopyDist, is given in Fig. 18.1. It has four parameters. The first three are as in the distributed shared memory service: ADDR, set of addresses of the service; PNO, set of page numbers; and PVAL, the possible values of a page. The fourth parameter, initPages, is a map over addresses, where initPages[j] is the set of pages initially located in the component system at address j.

Program DsmSCopyDist first starts the object-transfer service, an instantiation of program ObjTrService (Figs. 15.2 and 15.3) with parameters ADDR (for the addresses

A.U. Shankar, *Distributed Programming: Theory and Practice*,
DOI 10.1007/978-1-4614-4881-5__18,
© Springer Science+Business Media New York 2013

```
program DsmSCopyDist(ADDR, PNO, PVAL, initPages) {
    ic {Set(ADDR, PNO, PVAL)
        and min(ADDR.size, PNO.size, PVAL.size) ≥ 1
        and Map<ADDR, Set<PNO>>(initPages)
        and disjoint(initPages[i]: i in ADDR)
        and union(initPages[i]: i in ADDR) = PNO}
    Map w ← startSystem(ObjTransferService(ADDR, PNO, PVAL, initPages));
    Map v ← map();
    for (j in ADDR)
        v[j] ← startSystem(DsmSCopy(PNO, PVAL, initPages[j], w[j]));
    return v;
} // end DsmSCopyDist
```

Fig. 18.1 Distributed program of component systems and object-transfer service

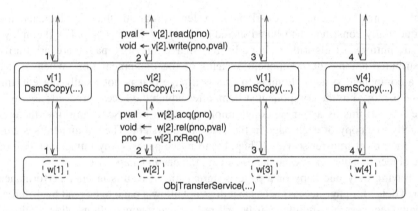

Fig. 18.2 A distributed shared memory implementation over addresses 1, · · ·, 4, with component systems v[1], · · ·, v[4], using an object-transfer service with access systems w[1], · · ·, w[4]

of the service), PNO (for OID, the set of object ids), PVAL (for OVAL, the set of values of an object), and initPages (for initObjs, the initial placement of objects). It saves the sid map of the object-transfer service in variable w. It then starts a component system at each address j, and returns the sid map of the component systems. The resulting configuration is illustrated in Fig. 18.2.

Each component system is an instantiation of program DsmSCopy, which is shown in Figs. 18.3 and 18.4. In addition to parameters PNO and PVAL, the program has the following parameters: initPagesL, the set of pages locally present initially; and wL, the sid of the local object-transfer access system. The boxes are comments containing fragments of the distributed shared memory service inverse, each matching the DsmSCopy code at the left. Ignore the statement labels b1–b5 for now.

The main code defines a map variable pgVal from page numbers to page values. Entry pgVal[pn] exists and equals the value of the page pn iff page pn is locally present. Initially, entry pgVal[pn] exists and equals an arbitrary initial value 0 for every pn in initPagesL.

The program has two input functions, read(pn) and write(pn,pv), and a function doRxReq, executed by local thread tRxReq.

Function read(pn) returns pgVal[pn] if the entry is already present in pgVal. Otherwise it gets the page value from the object-transfer service (via wL.acq(pn)), saves it in pgVal and returns it.

Function write(pn,pv) updates pgVal[pn] to value pv if the entry is already present in pgVal. Otherwise it gets the page value (via wL.acq(pn)), saves it in pgVal, and then updates it to pv. (It makes sense to save the received page before updating it because, in reality, the update pv would affect only a (small) part of the page.)

Function doRxReq, executed by local thread tRxReq, repeatedly does the following: calls wL.rxReq to receive the number of a page to release, waits if the page is not in pgVal, then removes the page from pgVal and releases it to the object-transfer service (via wL.rel). It would have to wait for the page to show up in pgVal if the wL.acq call to acquire the page has not yet returned or because the read or write call that issued the wL.acq call has not yet returned. In any case, the wait is temporary, hence atomicity breakpoints are not needed at these awaits.

18.3 Proving the Implements Conditions

The goal is to prove that DsmSCopyDist(ADDR,PNO,PVAL,initPages) implements DsmSeq-ConService(ADDR,PNO,PVAL). Figure 18.5 gives the closed program Z of instantiation v of DsmSCopyDist and instantiation si of the service inverse, DsmSeqConServiceInverse. (The latter is available from the boxes in Figs. 17.2 and 17.3, or from Exercise 17.2.) For ease of reference, program Z exposes the body of the DsmSCopyDist instantiation, explicitly showing the object-transfer service system w and the component systems v[j]. Z.ic does not constrain DsmSeqConService.ic. What remains is to prove that Z satisfies the following assertions. (Below, we use j, pn and pv to range over addresses, page numbers and page values, respectively. Also, the si prefix for α is omitted.)

A_1:   *Inv* (thread at si.doRead(j,pn).ic)
       $\Rightarrow$ seqConsistent($\alpha \circ$ [[RRET,j,pn,pv]])
A_2:   ongoing(v[j].read(.)) *leads-to* not ongoing(v[j].read(.))
A_3:   ongoing(v[j].write(.)) *leads-to* not ongoing(v[j].write(.))

```
program DsmSCopy(PNO, PVAL, initPagesL, wL) {
    // PNO: page numbers. PVAL: page values.
    // initPagesL: local page numbers initially
    // wL: local object-transfer access system
    ic {Set(PNO, PVAL)
        and Set<PNO>(initPagesL) and Sid(wL)}
    Map pgVal ← map([pn,0]): pn in initPagesL);
    Tid tRxReq ← startThread(doRxReq());
    return mysid;


    input PVAL mysid.read(PNO pn) {
        ic {true}
        await (true)
            if (pn in pgVal.keys)
b1:             return pgVal[pn]; // end await
    • tmpPval ← wL.acq(pn);
        await (true)
            pgVal[pn] ← tmpPval; // end await
b2:     return pgVal[pn];
    }


    input void mysid.write(PNO pn, PVAL pv) {
        ic {true}
        await (true)
            if (pn in pgVal.keys) {
                pgVal[pn] ← pv;
b3:             return;
            }                    // end await
b4: • tmpPval ← wL.acq(pn);
        await (true) {
            pgVal[pn] ← tmpPval;
            pgVal[pn] ← pv;
b5:         return;
        }
    }


// continued


} // end DsmSCopy
```

```
DsmSeqConServiceInverse
    (ADDR,PNO,PVAL,v)
// v[j]: access system at j
ic {...}
WCALL ← 1; RRET ← 2;
Seq α ← [];
return mysid;
```

```
DsmSeqConServiceInverse
// doRead(j,pn)
oc{not ongoing(v[j].read(.)
    and not ongoing(v[j].write(.)}
pv ← v[j].read(pn);
ic {seqConsistent(
        α ∘ [[RRET,j,pn,pv]])}
α.append([RRET,j,pn,pv]);
```

```
DsmSeqConServiceInverse
// doWrite(j,pn,pv)
oc{not ongoing(v[j].read(.)
    and not ongoing(v[j].write(.)}
α.append([WCALL,j,pn,pv]);
v[j].write(pn,pv);
ic {true}
```

Fig. 18.3 Part 1: program DsmSCopy. Boxes are comments containing matching parts from DsmSeq-ConService inverse

```
// DsmSCopy continued

    function doRxReq() {
        while (true) {
          • pn ← wL.rxReq();
            ic {pn in PNO}
            await (pn in pgVal.keys) { // NOTE no '•'
                wL.rel(pn, pgVal[pn]);
                pgVal.remove(pn);
            }
        }
    }

    atomicity assumption {mutex, condRxReq}

    progress assumption {weak fairness for all threads}

} // end DsmSCopy
```

Fig. 18.4 Part 2: program DsmSCopy

```
program Z(ADDR, PNO, PVAL, initPages) {
    ic {DsmSCopyDist.ic}
    inputs(); outputs();   // closed system
    atomic {
        Map w ← startSystem(ObjTransferService(ADDR,PNO,PVAL,initPages));
        for (j in ADDR)
            v[j] ← startSystem(DsmSCopy(PNO,PVAL,initPages[j]));
        Sid si ← startSystem(DsmSeqConServiceInverse(ADDR,PNO,PVAL,v));
        return mysid;
    }
} // end Z
```

Fig. 18.5 Closed program of DsmSCopyDist and DsmSeqConServiceInverse

18.3.1 Proving Safety: A_1

A_1 is equivalent to $Inv\,B_1$ (because appending a WCALL entry to α preserves its sequential consistency).

B_1 : seqConsistent(α)

We will prove B_1 by defining an auxiliary variable β in program Z such that Z satisfies $Inv\, B_2$–B_3 below. B_2 says that β and α have the same sequence of reads and writes at each address j. B_2 says that β is sequential. Together, they imply B_1. (Recall the definition of seqConsistent.)

B_2 : forall(j: [s: s in β, s[1]=j] = [s: s in α, s[1]=j])

B_3 : sequential(β)

To satisfy $Inv\, B_2$, β should be initially empty, and whenever an entry is appended to α the same entry should be inserted into β. The question is where to insert it so that β satisfies B_2 and B_3. It is convenient to view β as consisting of a "stable" prefix β_S, which changes only by appends, and a "transient" suffix β_T, which changes by appends and removals. When a [..,j,pn,pv] entry is appended to α, the entry is appended to β_S if pn is in v[j].pgVal.keys at that point; otherwise the entry is appended to β_T. Consequently β_T has only WCALL entries, one for each write call that is currently blocked. When the write call becomes unblocked (due to the page becoming locally available), the entry is moved to β_S.

The precise update rules for β_S and β_T and the definition of β are as follows. Below, b1, $\cdots$, b5 are the statement labels in program DsmSCopy and aL is the local address of the program.

- Immediately before b1 and b2, insert
    β_S.append([RRET,aL,pn,pgVal[pn]])
- Immediately before b3, insert
    β_S.append([WCALL,aL,pn,pv]).
- Immediately before b4, insert
    β_T.append([WCALL,aL,pn,pv]).
- Immediately before b5, insert
    $\beta_T\leftarrow$ [x: x in β_T, x[1]$\neq$aL);   // remove write entry for aL
    β_S.append([WCALL,aL,pn,pv])

In proving that program Z satisfies $Inv\, B_2$–B_3, one also has to prove that the object-transfer service w is used correctly. Its instantiation is correct because ADDR, PNO and PVAL are sets and initPages partitions PNO (from Z.ia). For it to be called correctly, Z should satisfy $Inv\, B_4$–B_6 below.

B_4 : (thread at w[j].acq(pn)) $\Rightarrow$ not ongoing(w[j].acq(pn))

B_5 : (thread at w[j].rel(pn,pn)) $\Rightarrow$ ((pn in w.objs[j]) and (pn in w.reqs[j]))

B_6 : (thread at w[j].rxReq()) $\Rightarrow$ not ongoing(w[j].rxReq())

Proving that Z satisfies $Inv\, B_2$–B_6 is left as an exercise. (Proving $Inv\, B_4$–B_6 is trivial.) Here are some predicates that may be invariant and helpful.

B_7 : forall(pn in PNO, exactly one of the following hold:
        (a) forone(j: pn in v[j].pgVal.keys)
        (b) forall(j: not (pn in v[j].pgVal.keys)) and (pn in w.val.keys)
)

B_8 : (pn in w.val.keys) $\Rightarrow$ (w.val[pn] = lastWrite(β_S,pn))

B_9 : (pn in v.pgVal.keys) $\Rightarrow$ (v.pgVal[pn] = lastWrite(β_S,pn))

18.3.2   Proving Progress: A_2–A_3

Consider a v[j].read(pn) or v[j].write(pn,pv) call. If pn is in v[j].pgVal.keys when the call is made, then the call is not blocked and hence returns. If pn is not in v[j].pgVal.keys when the call is made, then w[j].acq(pn) is called. So it suffices to show that the w[j].acq(pn) call returns.

At every address j, system v[j] has a thread tRxReq executing doRxReq and blocked at w[j].rxReq. The code chunk in doRxReq after w[j].rxReq returns removes [pn,pv] from v[j].pgVal and releases it (via w[j].rel(pn,pv)). This code chunk is effectively atomic. (Recall that any blocking at its await is temporary.) Thus the following hold:

P_1 : *Inv* ongoing(w[j].rxReq)
P_2 : (pn in w.reqs[j]) *leads-to* not (pn in w.reqs[j])

Here are the assertions in system w's progress assumption (from program ObjTransferService in Figs. 15.2 and 15.3). These hold because program Z uses system w correctly.

P_3 : ongoing(w[j].rel(pn,pv)) *leads-to* not ongoing(w[j].rel(pn,pv))
P_4 : (w.objs[j].size > 0 *leads-to* ongoing(w[j].rxReq))
     $\Rightarrow$ (((pn in w.objs[j]) and ongoing(w[k].acq(pn)))
        leads-to (pn in w.reqs[j]))
P_5 : forall(j: (((pn in w.objs[j]) and ongoing(w[k].acq(pn)))
         leads-to (pn in w.reqs[j]))
       and ((pn in w.reqs[j]) *leads-to* not (pn in w.reqs[j])))
     $\Rightarrow$ forall(j: ongoing(w[j].acq(pn)) *leads-to* not ongoing(w[j].acq(pn)))

P_1 implies P_4's lhs. Hence P_4's rhs holds. P_4's rhs and P_2 imply P_5's lhs. Hence P_5's rhs holds, which implies that every w[j].acq(pn) call eventually returns. We are done.

18.4   Concluding Remarks

The implementation presented here is conceptually simple: when a user issues a read or write on a page, if the page is not at its component system then the latter simply acquires the page and then performs the access. The resulting program is simple, as is its analysis, because the non-trivial task of acquiring pages is handled by the object-transfer service. The program can be efficient because one can use an efficient implementation of the object-transfer service, such as the one based on the path-reversal algorithm (in Chap. 16).

Exercises

18.1. In program DsmSCopy, the body of function read (and that of function write) consists of two awaits, with the wL.acq call coming between them. Suppose that the entire body of the function was a single await, e.g., as shown below.

```
input PVAL mysid.read(PNO pn) {
    ic {true}
    await (true)
        if (not (pn in pgVal.keys)) {
            tmpPval ← wL.acq(pn);
            pgVal[pn] ← tmpPval;
        }
        return pgVal[pn];
}
```

Would this work? If no, show an evolution that does not satisfy the shared memory service. If yes, prove that the program still satisfies the service.

18.2. Implement the awaits in program DsmSCopy using locks and condition variables. (Hint: At least one condition variable would be needed to implement the await in doRxReq.)

18.3. Program DsmSCopy starts thread tRxReq at instantiation and never terminates it, although it is not needed if the instantiation has no pages. Modify the program so that the thread exists only when needed. (Hint: Start the thread whenever the instantiation makes the transition from owning no pages to owning one page. Terminate the thread whenever the instantiation makes the transition in the opposite direction.)

18.4. Prove that program Z satisfies $Inv\,B_4-B_6$ (in Sect. 18.3).

18.5. Prove that program Z satisfies $Inv\,B_2-B_3$ assuming that it satisfies $Inv\,B_4-B_6$ (in Sect. 18.3).

References

1. D. Lenoski, J. Laudon, K. Gharachorloo, W.D. Weber, A. Gupta, J. Hennessy, M. Horowitz, M.S. Lam, The Stanford Dash multiprocessor. Computer **25**(3), 63–79 (1992). doi:10.1109/2.121510. http://dx.doi.org/10.1109/2.121510
2. K. Li, P. Hudak, Memory coherence in shared virtual memory systems. ACM Trans. Comput. Syst. **7**(4), 321–359 (1989). doi:http://doi.acm.org/10.1145/75104.75105
3. J. Protic, M. Tomasevic, V. Milutinovic (eds.), *Distributed Shared Memory: Concepts and Systems*, 1st edn. (IEEE Computer Society Press, Los Alamitos, 1997)

Chapter 19
A Multi-copy Distributed Shared Memory

19.1 Introduction

This chapter presents a "multi-copy" version of the single-copy distributed shared memory implementation given in Chap. 18. The multi-copy version maintains, for each page, one **write** copy and zero or more **read-only** copies. All the copies have the same value. Each copy is with a different component system. The write copy is accompanied by a so-called **copyset**, which is the set of addresses of component sytems that have read-only copies.

A component system can read from the write copy or a read-only copy. It can write to the write copy only, and that too only when there are no read-only copies anywhere. When a component system attempts to read or write a page that is not locally present, it acquires the write copy of the page, leaving a read copy at the previous location of the write copy. The component system can then read from the page. To write to the page, the component system informs all component systems in the page's copyset to "invalidate" (i.e., delete) their copies, after which it can update its (write) copy [1].

The implementation program uses an object-transfer service, to acquire pages and their copysets, and a fifo channel, to perform invalidation. Thus each component system interacts with a local user above and an object-transfer access system and fifo channel access system below, as illustrated in Fig. 19.1. If the object-transfer service is replaced by the path-reversal implementation (Chap. 16), the resulting program corresponds to a popular implementation by Li and Hudak (Algorithm 2 in [2]).

The multi-copy version performs better than the single-copy version in situations where the application using the distributed shared memory has many pages that are frequently read by many users and infrequently written. It allows users to read such pages in parallel, whereas the single-copy version would require these reads to be done serially.

A.U. Shankar, *Distributed Programming: Theory and Practice*,
DOI 10.1007/978-1-4614-4881-5__19,
© Springer Science+Business Media New York 2013

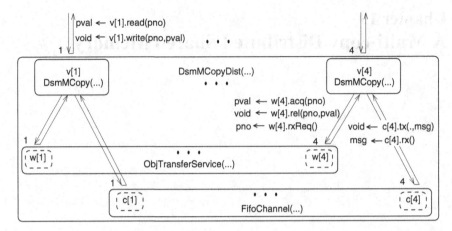

Fig. 19.1 A distributed shared memory implementation over addresses 1, · · · , 4, with component systems v[1], · · · , v[4], using an object-transfer service with access systems w[1], · · · , w[4]. and a fifo channel with access systems c[1], · · · , c[4]

```
program DsmMCopyDist(ADDR, PNO, PVAL, initPages) {
    ic {Set(ADDR,PNO,PVAL)
        and min(ADDR.size, PNO.size, PVAL.size) ≥ 1
        and Map<ADDR, Set<PNO>>(initPages)
        and disjoint(initPages[i]: i in ADDR)
        and union(initPages[i]: i in ADDR) = PNO}
    Map w ← startSystem(ObjTransferService(ADDR, PNO, PVAL, initPages));
    Map c ← startSystem(FifoChannel(ADDR));
    Map v ← map();
    for (j in ADDR)
        v[j] ← startSystem(DsmMCopy(PNO, PVAL, initPages[j], j, w[j], c[j]));
    return v;
} // end DsmMCopyDist
```

Fig. 19.2 Distributed program of component systems, object-transfer service and fifo channel

19.2   Distributed Program

The distributed program, called DsmMCopyDist, is given in Fig. 19.2. It has the same parameters as the single-copy implementation: ADDR, set of addresses of the service; PNO, set of page numbers; PVAL, the possible values of a page; and initPages, a map over addresses, where initPages[j] is the set of pages initially located in the component system at address j.

Program DsmMCopyDist first starts the object-transfer service, an instantiation of program ObjTrService (Figs. 15.2 and 15.3) with parameters ADDR (for the addresses of the service), PNO (for OID, the set of object ids), PVAL (for OVAL, the set of values of an object), and initPages (for initObjs, the initial placement of objects). It saves the sid map of the object-transfer service in variable w. The program then starts the fifo channel, an instantiation of program FifoChannel (Fig. 4.2) with parameter ADDR. It saves the sid map of the fifo channel in variable c. It then starts a component system at each address j, and returns the sid map of the component systems. Each component system is an instantiation of program DsmMCopy.

The object-transfer service w is used to transfer pages and copysets. System v[j] calls w[j].acq(pn) to acquire page pn and its copyset. The call returns with a two-tuple [pv,cpset], where pv is page pn 's value and cpset is its copyset. System v[j] calls w[j].rel(pn, [pv,cpset]) to release page pn and its copyset cpset. System v[j] calls w[j].rxReq() to receive page numbers of pages and copysets to be released.

The fifo channel c is used to transfer invalidation requests and acks. An invalidation request is a message of the form [IREQ,j,pn], where IREQ is a constant, j is the address of the sender, and pn is the number of the page to be invalidated. An invalidation ack is a message of the form [IACK,j,pn], where IACK is a constant, j is the address of the sender, and pn is the number of the page that has been invalidated.

Each component system is an instantiation of program DsmMCopy, which is given in Figs. 19.3–19.5. In addition to parameters PNO and PVAL, program DsmMCopy has the following parameters: initPagesL, the set of pages locally present initially; aL, its address; wL, the sid of the local object-transfer access system; and cL, the sid of the local channel access system. The program has a map variable, page, indexed by page number. Entry page[pn] exists iff a (write or read-only) copy of the page is present locally. The entry is a four-tuple with the following entries.

- page[pn][0] holds the value of the page.
- page[pn][1] is a boolean that is true iff a write copy.
- page[pn][2] is a boolean that is true iff the page is releasable (to the object-transfer service). It will be false iff the entry is a write copy and is being invalidated.
- page[pn][3] is the set of addresses whose component systems have read-only copies of this page. Valid only for a write copy (i.e., only if page[pn][1] is true).

Initially, for every pn in initPagesL, page has an entry equal to [0, true, true, set()], signifying a releasable write copy with value 0 and zero read-only copies.

Program DsmMCopy has two input functions: mysid.read(pn), to get the value of page pn; and mysid.write(pn,pv), to update the value of page pn to pv. The program has two functions executed by local threads: doReqInd, to receive requests for pages from object-transfer service w, and doRx, to receive invalidation messages from fifo channel c. (The first three functions are analogous to the corresponding functions in the single-copy version.) Each function is described in more detail below.

- Input function mysid.read(pn). If entry page[pn] exists when the function is called, it returns page[pn][0]. Otherwise, the function calls wL.acq(pn). When the call returns, the function creates a releasable write-copy entry page[pn] with the returned page value and copyset, and returns page[pn][0].

- Input function mysid.write(pn,pv). There are three possibilities when it is called.

  1. Entry page[pn] exists, is a write copy, and its copyset is empty. Then the function updates pgVal[pn][0] to pv and returns.
  2. Entry page[pn] exists and is a write copy, but its copyset is not empty. Then the function makes the entry unreleasable and sends out [IREQ,aL,pn] messages to every address in the copyset. It waits until the copyset is emptied (by thread tRx), and then updates pgVal[pn][0] to pv, makes it releasable, and returns.
  3. Entry page[pn] does not exist or is a read-only copy. Then the function calls wL.acq(pn). When the call returns, bringing the page value and copyset, the function creates an unreleasable write-copy entry page[pn], after which it proceeds as in case 2.

- Function doReqInd(), executed by local thread tRxReq, repeatedly does the following. It calls wL.rxReq(). When the call returns, bringing a page number pn, it waits for entry page[pn] to exist and be releasable. Then it adds the local address, aL, to page[pn]'s copyset, releases the entry's value and copyset (via wL.rel(pn,page[pn][0,3])), makes the entry read-only, and returns.
- Function doRx() is executed by local thread tRx. It repeatedly does the following. It calls aL.rx(). When the call returns, it brings an invalidation request or ack message. If a [IREQ,j,pn] message, the function removes the entry for pn from pgVal and sends an ack (via aL.tx(j,[IACK,aL,pn])). If a [IACK,j,pn] message, the function removes pn from page[pn]'s copyset entry.

19.3   Concluding Remarks

Establishing that program DsmMCopyDist implements DsmSeqConService is left as an exercise. The analysis would closely mirror that of the single-copy version. In fact, the auxiliary variable β defined there also works here. Various optimizations are possible, and some of these are covered in the exercises.

Exercises

19.1. Implement the awaits in program DsmMCopy (Figs. 19.3–19.5) with locks and condition variables.

19.2. Prove that DsmMCopyDist implements DsmSeqConService. The procedure is outlined below.

- Write down the closed program, say Z, of a DsmMCopyDist instantiation and a DsmSeqConService inverse instantiation.
- Write down the desired invariant and progress assertions to be satisfied by Z.

- Modify the assertions to account for effective atomicity and any other simplifications.
- Develop intermediate assertions such that (1) each intermediate assertion holds by a simple operational argument and (2) the intermediate assertions imply the desired assertions.

19.3. Program DsmMCopy starts thread tRxReq at instantiation and never terminates it, although it is not needed if the instantiation has no pages. Modify the program so that the thread exists only when needed.

19.4. In program DsmMCopy, thread tRxReq (executing function doRxReq) waits after receiving a request for a page if the requested page is undergoing validation. This wait can be quite long. During this time no thread is waiting on rxReq, and hence any further requests would not be processed until the ongoing invalidation is over, *even if the additional requests are for pages that can be immediately released.* Modify the program to fix this, i.e., start another thread to wait on rxReq.

19.5. In program DsmMCopy, a read entry is deleted when it is invalidated. Modify the program so that the read entry is restored with the updated value.

References

1. J. Archibald, J.L. Baer, Cache coherence protocols: evaluation using a multiprocessor simulation model. ACM Trans. Comput. Syst. **4**(4), 273–298 (1986). doi:10.1145/6513.6514. http://doi.acm.org/10.1145/6513.6514
2. K. Li, P. Hudak, Memory coherence in shared virtual memory systems. ACM Trans. Comput. Syst. **7**(4), 321–359 (1989). doi:http://doi.acm.org/10.1145/75104.75105

```
system DsmMCopy(PNO, PVAL, initPagesL, aL, wL, cL) {
   // PNO: page numbers. PVAL: page values.
   // initPagesL: local pages at start
   // aL: local address
   // wL: sid of object-transfer access system
   // cL: sid of fifo channel access system
   ia {Set(PNO,PVAL) and Set<PNO>(initPagesL)
       and ADDR(aL) and Sid(wL,cL)}

   // page[pn]: [value, write copy?, releasable?, copyset (if write copy)]
   Map page ← map([pn, [0,          // value
                        true,       // write copy?
                        true ,      // releasable?
                        set()]      // copyset
                    ]: pn in initPagseL);
   Tid tRxReq ← startThread(doRxReq());
   Tid tRx ← startThread(doRx());
   return mysid;

   input PVAL mysid.read(PNO pn) {
      ia {true}
      await (true) {
         if (pn in page.keys)
            return page[pn][0];
      }
      // acquire page and return value
 •    tmp ← wL.acq(pn);      // tmp = [pagevalue, copyset]
      await (true) {
         page[pn] ← [tmp[0],     // value
                     true,       // write copy?
                     true,       // releasable?
                     tmp[1]      // copyset
                    ];
         return page[pn][0];
      }    // end await
   }

   // continued
```

Fig. 19.3 Part 1: program DsmMCopy

```
// DsmMCopy continued

    input void mysid.write(PNO pn, PVAL pv) {
      ia {true}
      await (true) {
        acqPage ← false;
        // page[pn]: [value, write copy?, releasable?, copyset]
        if (not (pn in page.keys) or not page[pn][1])
            // do not have write copy
            acqPage ← true;
        else // have write copy but copyset not empty; make unreleasable
            pagne[pn][2] ← false;
        else if (page[pn][3].size = 0) {
            // have write copy with copyset empty: do write and return
            page[pn][0] ← pv;
            return;
        }
      }
      // acqPage true: no write copy
      // acqPage false: page[pn]: unreleasable write copy, nonempty copyset
      if (acqPage)
      ●  tmp ← wL.acq(pn);              // tmp = [pagevalue, copyset]
      await (true) {
        if (acqPage)
            // move tmp to page[pn], make unreleasable
            page[pn] ← [tmp[0],          // value
                        true,            // write copy?
                        false,           // releasable?
                        tmp[1] \ set(aL) // copyset
                       ];
        // page[pn] is unreleasable write copy with nonempty copyset
        // send invalidation requests to all in copyset
        for (j in page[pn][2])
            cL.tx(j, [IREQ,aL,pn]);
      }
      // wait for copyset to become empty, write, make releasable
      await (page[pn][2].size = 0) {
        page[pn][0] ← pv;                // write value
        page[pn][2] ← true;              // releasable?
        return;
      }
    }

// continued
```

Fig. 19.4 Part 2: program DsmMCopy

```
// DsmMCopy continued

    // receive pn from object-transfer service; release write copy of page[pn]
    // executed by local thread tRxReq
    function doRxReq() {
        while (true) {
        ● pn ← wL.rxReq();
            ia {pn in PNO}
            // wait for page[pn] to exist and be releasable
            await ((pn in page.keys) and page[pn][2]) {
                wL.rel(pn, [page[pn][0],                      // pagevalue
                            union(page[pn][3], set(aL))       // copyset
                          ]);
                page[pn][1] ← false;                          // write copy?
            }
        }
    }


    // receive invalidation request/ack for page pn from fifo channel
    // executed by local thread tRxReq
    function doRx() {
        while (true) {
        ● msg ← cL.rx();
            ia {msg in union(Tuple<IREQ,ADDR,PNO>, Tuple<IACK,ADDR,PNO>}
            if (msg[0] = IREQ)
                // msg = [IREQ, sender, pn]
                // page has or will soon have read-only entry for msg[2]
                // remove the entry and send ack
                await (msg[2] in page.keys) {
                    page.remove(msg[2]);
                    cL.tx(msg[1], [IACK, aL, msg[2]]);
                }
            else if (msg[0] = IACK)
                // msg = [IACK, sender, pn]
                // page has write copy for msg[2], undergoing invalidation
                // remove msg[1] from its copyset
                await (true)
                    page[pn][3].remove(msg[1]); // page[pn][3]: copyset
        }
    }

    atomicity assumption {awaits}
    progress assumption {weak fairness for all threads}

} // end DsmMCopy
```

Fig. 19.5 Part 3: program DsmMCopy

Chapter 20
Reliable Transport Service

20.1 Introduction

A simplistic connection-oriented channel was defined in Sect. 4.5. This
chapter defines a more realistic connection-oriented channel, one that is
implementable over an unreliable channel. (Such an implementation is presented
in Chap. 21.) The channel is similar to the reliable streaming service of Internet
sockets [2, 3, 10]; hence we refer to it as the **reliable transport service**.

Figure 20.1 illustrates an instantiation of the service program. A user accesses
the channel as a **client** or as a **server**. A server user at address j starts by calling
j.accept(), to indicate that it will accept any incoming connect request. (For readability, we abbreviate the sid prefix v[j] to j in informal discussion.) The call puts
address j in **server mode** if it was not already in that mode. The call returns a
remote address tuple, say [k], to indicate that it is connected to a client at k. If
no client is connecting, the call remains blocked. While in server mode, additional

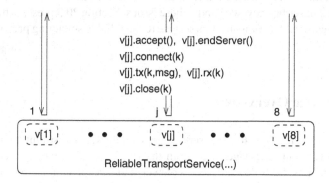

Fig. 20.1 Reliable transport service spanning addresses 1, ⋯, 8, with access system v[j] at
address j

A.U. Shankar, *Distributed Programming: Theory and Practice*,
DOI 10.1007/978-1-4614-4881-5__20,
© Springer Science+Business Media New York 2013

incoming connect requests may be buffered (to be handled by subsequent j.accept calls). The user calls j.endServer() to end server mode, cancel any ongoing j.accept, and delete all buffered connect requests. A canceled j.accept returns [].

A client user at j starts by calling j.connect(k), to request a connection to another address k. The call returns [k] to indicate that a connection is established. The connection is either to a server accepting at k or to a client at k simultaneously requesting to connect to j. The former results in a "client-server" connection, the latter in a "client-client" connection. The call returns [] to indicate that the connect attempt was rejected.

Once the users are connected to each other, they can exchange messages. The user at j calls j.tx(k,.) to send messages to k and j.rx(k) to receive messages from k. The corresponding calls at the other end are k.tx(j,.) and k.rx(j). The service requires that the message transfer be fifo. (The fifo requirement can be replaced by any other requirement, e.g., bounded loss and delay.)

The user at j calls j.close(k) to indicate that it has no further messages to send in this connection. The corresponding call at the other end is k.close(j). Call j.close(k) returns only after (1) the remote user has called k.close(j), and (2) the local user has received all messages sent by the remote user. Thus, depending on the user-user protocol, the local user may need to issue j.rx(k) calls while j.close(k) is ongoing. When the latter returns, it also ends any ongoing j.rx(k) call.

An address j can participate simultaneously in multiple connections, each with a different remote address. It is customary to identify each end of a connection by the *pair* of local and remote addresses, e.g., at j, a connection to k is identified by the pair [j,k]. These address pairs are referred to as **sockets**. (This corresponds to a socket in Internet sockets if each address in our service is a two-tuple of an IP address and a TCP port number.)

The above description omits several issues. For instance, how does the service ensure that a [j,k] socket receives only messages sent from the [k,j] socket to which it connected, and not, say, from the [k,j] socket instance of a previous connection between j and k. Under what conditions does a connect call establish a connection? Section 20.2 describes how we handle these issues. Section 20.3 presents the service program. Section 20.4 compares this service to the reliable streaming part of Internet sockets.

20.2 Service Overview

There are several ways for the service to capture the constraint that a [j,k] socket receives only messages sent from the [k,j] socket to which it connected. Our approach is as follows. Every connect and accept call is tagged with a unique number, referred to as its **call id**. Every socket is tagged with its local and remote call ids, where the former is the call id of the local (connect or accept) call whose return created the socket and the latter is the call id of the remote call to

Fig. 20.2 Client j and server k connect, talk, close

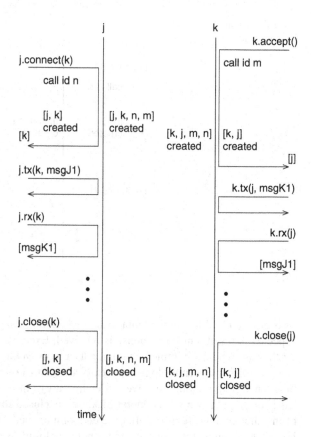

which the local call became connected. For example, if a j.connect(k) with call id n becomes connected to a k.accept with call id m, the [j,k] socket that is created at j is tagged by [n,m]. We refer to the four-tuple [j,k,n,m] as a **service endpoint**, or **endpoint** for short. The corresponding endpoint at k, if it is created, would be [k,j,m,n]. Then the desired constraint is that endpoint [j,k,n,m] can only receive messages sent at endpoint [k,j,m,n]. *Call ids are internal to the service* (and they introduce internal nondeterminism).

Figure 20.2 illustrates the life of a connection between a client at j and a server at k. A connect call with call id n at j connects to an accept call with call id m at k. The connect returns creating endpoint [j,k,n,m]. The accept returns creating endpoint [k,j,m,n]. Messages are sent at each endpoint and received in order at the other endpoint. Later, both client and server close their respective endpoints. Figure 20.3 illustrates the same thing except that at k the accept is replaced by a connect to j.

We next describe the functions of the service, including the conditions under which an endpoint is created and the conditions that hold when an endpoint is closed. The formulation below is tailored to be implementable by a transport protocol, specifically, a collection of systems communicating over an LRD channel.

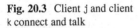

Fig. 20.3   Client j and client
k connect and talk

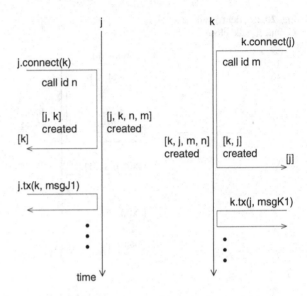

(It is also tailored for implementations in which a message for which a response is expected is resent until a response is received. Exercise 20.5 develops the service for the case where the implementation puts a limit on the number of resends.)

Now for some terminology. Two calls are said to **overlap** if there is a point in time when both are ongoing. We say endpoint [j,k,n,m] is **opened** to mean that it has been created. We say endpoint [j,k,n,m] is **closed** to mean that j.close(k) has been called and has returned after the endpoint opened. We say endpoint [j,k,n,m] is **open** to mean that it is opened and is not yet closed. We say endpoint [j,k,n,m] is **closing** to mean that it is open and j.close(k) is ongoing.

20.2.1   *Function* j.connect(k)

Function j.connect(k) requests to connect to remote address k. It is called only if j.connect(k) is not ongoing and a [j,k,...] endpoint is not open. The call is assigned a unique call id. It returns either [k], creating an endpoint, or [], not creating an endpoint.

A j.connect(k) with call id n returns creating endpoint [j,k,n,m] only if:

* The j.connect(k) call has overlapped a k.accept or k.connect(j) with call id m.
* A [j,k] socket does not exist. (This could only have been created by a concurrent j.accept call connecting to a k.connect(j) call.)
* If a remote endpoint [k,j,..,n] has opened, then m equals its remote call id (i.e., the remote endpoint is [k,j,m,n]).

Regarding progress, a j.connect(k) call eventually returns creating an endpoint if there is a **dedicated accept** call, by which we mean the following.

- When the connect call is issued, a k.accept call is ongoing and is not canceled, and there is no [k,j] socket.
- No other client attempts to connect to k.accept. (Otherwise the accept call may connect to one of them, and the j.connect(k) may be rejected.)
- A j.accept call is not ongoing when the j.connect(k) call is issued. (Otherwise, it may connect to a k.connect(j) call, creating a [j,k,.,.] endpoint, which would force the j.connect(k) call to return without creating an endpoint.)

Note that the presence of a dedicated k.accept call does not mean that the j.connect(k) call will connect to it. It may connect to a k.connect(j) call, if one happens to be ongoing. But if that does not happen, it will eventually connect to the dedicated k.accept call. We could account for more situations where j.connect(k) creates an endpoint, for example, an ongoing k.connect(j) call or the buffering of connect requests while k is in server mode. But we don't: these issues of "server availability" are best investigated in a (probabilistic) performance model.

A j.connect(k) call returns without creating an endpoint only if it has no dedicated k.accept call. This is the minimum possible requirement for the progress condition stated above to be realizable.

20.2.2 *Function* j.accept()

Function j.accept() starts accepting incoming connect requests at address j. It is called only if j.accept() is not ongoing. The call is assigned a unique call id. It returns either a remote address tuple [k], creating an endpoint [j,k,.,.], or [], creating no endpoint.

A j.accept with call id n returns creating endpoint [j,k,n,m] only if:

- The j.accept call overlapped a k.connect(j) with call id m.
- A [j,k] socket does not exist. (This could only have been created by concurrent j.connect(k) and k.accept calls.)
- If a remote endpoint [k,j,.,n] has opened, then m equals its remote call id (i.e., the remote endpoint is [k,j,m,n]).

Note that endpoint [j,k,n,m] can open before or after endpoint [k,j,m,n]. (Thus the service accommodates both standard TCP implementations, where the client opens first, as well as "transaction" TCP implementations, where the server opens first.)

Regarding progress, a j.accept call eventually returns with an endpoint if there is a **dedicated connect** call, by which we mean that the following holds for some k.

- While the accept call is ongoing, a k.connect(j) call is issued and there is no [j,k] socket.
- A j.connect(k) call is not issued after the k.connect(j) call is issued. (Otherwise, it may connect to the k.connect(j) call, forcing the j.accept to not connect.)
- The accept call is not canceled.

Note that the presence of a dedicated k.connect(j) call does not mean that the accept call will connect to it. It may connect to a connect call of another client. But if that does not happen, it will eventually connect to the k.connect(j) call.

Finally, j.accept returns without creating an endpoint only if it is canceled, by an ongoing j.endServer. If it is canceled, it will eventually return, with or without an endpoint.

20.2.3 *Functions* j.tx(k,msg) *and* j.rx(k)

Function j.tx(k,msg) is called only if j.tx(k,.) is not ongoing and an endpoint [j,k,n,m] is open and not closing. It sends message msg at endpoint [j,k,n,m]. Regarding progress, it returns unconditionally.

Function j.rx(k) is called only if j.rx(k) is not ongoing and an endpoint [j,k,n,m] is open. It returns [0,msg] iff msg is the next message to be received from endpoint [k,j,m,n]. It returns [-1] iff all messages from endpoint [k,j,m,n] have been received and endpoint [k,j,m,n] is closing or closed.

20.2.4 *Function* j.close(k)

Function j.close(k) is called only if j.close(k) is not ongoing and an endpoint [j,k,n,m] is open. Its call makes the endpoint closing (but still open). Its return closes the endpoint. It returns only when

- All messages sent on endpoint [k,j,m,n] have been received by the local user.
- Endpoint [k,j,m,n] is closing or closed.
- There is no ongoing j.rx(k) or j.tx(k,.).

Regarding progress, j.close(k) eventually returns if the local user maintains an ongoing j.rx(k) and the remote endpoint is closing or closed.

20.3 Service Program

The service program is given in Figs. 20.4–20.8. The program has the usual parameter: ADDR, the set of addresses of the service. The main code defines the following variables.

- srvr: boolean map over addresses. Entry srvr[j] is true iff address j is in server mode; initially false.
- cidGen: integer; initially zero. Call id generator.
- α: map indexed over addresses and address pairs; initially empty. Entry α[j] exists and equals n iff a j.accept with call id n is ongoing. Entry α[[j,k]] exists and equals n iff a j.connect(k) with call id n is ongoing.
- β: map indexed over addresses pairs; initially empty. Entry β[j,k] exists and equals [n,m] iff endpoint [j,k,n,m] is open.
- ψ: sequence; initially empty. History of accept/connect/close calls and returns. Entries are appended as follows, where ACPT, CONN, RET, NEP, EP and CLSD are constants.

  - [ACPT,j,n]: Call of j.accept with call id n.
  - [CONN,j,k,n]: Call of j.connect(k) with call id n.
  - [RET,n], [NEP,n]: Return of j.accept or j.connect(k) with call id n that does not create an endpoint. (Two entries are appended.)
  - [RET,n], [EP,j,k,n,m]: Return of j.accept or j.connect(k) with call id n that creates endpoint [j,k,n,m].
  - [CLSD,j,k]: Return of j.close(k).

- txh, rxh: maps indexed over call id pairs; initially empty. Each has an entry for [n,m] iff endpoint [.,.,n,m] has opened. Entry txh[[n,m]] equals the sequence of messages sent at that endpoint. Entry rxh[[n,m]] equals the sequence of messages received at that endpoint.
- v: map indexed over addresses. Entry v[j] is the sid of the access system at j.

The program then defines the following boolean helper functions, corresponding to the conventions developed in Sect. 20.2. These functions make use of the construct, x.keyOf(y), where x is a sequence. The construct returns x.size if y is not in x, and otherwise returns the first position of y in x.

- overlapped(j,k,n,m): true iff a j.connect(k) with call id n has overlapped a k.accept or k.connect(j) with call id m.
- opened(j,k,n,m): true iff endpoint [j,k,n,m] has been created.
- closed(j,k,n,m): endpoint [j,k,n,m] has been closed.
- openedTo(j,n): opened(k,j,m,n) holds for some k and m.
- dedicatedAccept(j,k,n): A k.accept call is dedicated to j.connect(k) with call id n.
- dedicatedConnect(k,m): A connect call is dedicated to k.accept with call id m.

The program then defines the input functions, v[j].accept(), v[j].endServer(), v[j].connect(k), v[j].tx(k,msg), v[j].rx(k), and v[j].close(k), exactly as described in Sect. 20.2. Note that v[j].accept's output part has an external parameter, the returned value rval, and two internal parameters, the remote address k and the remote call id m. Parameter k equals rval[0]; it is only for notational convenience and does not give rise to internal nondeterminism. Whereas parameter m does give rise to internal nondeterminism. Function v[j].connect(k)'s output part has an internal parameter, the remote call id m, which does give rise to internal nondeterminism. Function v[j].rx(k)'s output part has an internal parameter, msg, which is for notational convenience only.

The program then defines the progress assumption. The assertions state the following. An accept call eventually returns if it is canceled. An endServer call eventually returns unconditionally. If an endpoint has opened, then the corresponding remote endpoint is opened eventually. An accept call eventually returns if it has a dedicated connect. A connect call eventually returns with an endpoint if it has a dedicated accept. (Otherwise the call may never return.) A tx call eventually returns unconditionally. A rx call eventually returns if there are messages to be received. A rx call eventually returns if there is no more messages to be received and the remote endpoint is closing or closed. A close call eventually returns if the other end is closing or closed and a local rx is ongoing (to receive any incoming message).

The service inverse program is given in Figs. 20.9–20.12. We will refer to it in the next chapter. The underlined text in the program highlight the output calls of the output functions. Note that some of the output calls return internal parameters in addition to the visible return value rval. In function doAccept(j), the v[j].accept() call is expected to return values for rval, k and m, the last two being internal parameters. In function doConnect(j,k), the v[j].connect(k) call is expected to return values for rval and m, the last being an internal parameter. In function doRx(j,k), the v[j].rx(k) call is expected to return values for rval and msg, the last being an internal parameter.

20.4   Concluding Remarks

The service defined here is comparable to the reliable streaming service provided by Internet sockets [2, 3, 10]. Users access the service as clients and servers: the former issue connect requests and the latter accept them. Connected users can exchange data reliably and close the connection when it is no longer needed. Our service program uses local and remote call ids to distinguish between different instances of the same socket. Call ids are internal to the service, introducing internal nondeterminism; as always, they can be avoided (see Exercise 20.4).

An address in our service corresponds to a pair of IP address and TCP port. It's easy to constrain our addresses to reflect this. Simply treat each service address as a pair of IP address and TCP port, and collapse all access systems with the same IP address to one access system. (Formally, if IPADDR denotes the set of IP addresses and TCPPORT denotes the set of TCP ports, then let ADDR be Tuple<IPADDR, TCPPORT> and let v[[j1,p1]] equal v[[j2,p2]] iff j1 equals j2.)

Our service allows an address to be in server mode (with an ongoing accept call) and simultaneously have ongoing connect calls. Internet sockets, by default, allows an address (i.e., a pair of IP address and TCP port) to have an ongoing connect call only if the address has no open socket and is not in server mode. It is trivial to incorporate this restriction in our service program. Also, Internet sockets has options (e.g., socket reuse) that overcome this restriction.

Our service allows both client-server and client-client connections. It is the same in Internet sockets. However no application seems to use client-client connections, at least not intentionally. (To achieve a client-client connection in Internet sockets, simply have two clients on different computers simultaneously issue connect requests to each other. The connect requests need to be simultaneous, otherwise they will be rejected. One way to achieve this is to schedule each connect at the same time, assuming that the two computers have sufficiently accurate real-time clocks. An easier way is to have each client continuously repeat the request after a rejection; eventually, the two clients will issue simultaneous requests.)

In a client-server connection, the service allows either the client or the server to be the first to create an endpoint. Thus the service accommodates both standard TCP implementations (where the client opens first) as well as "Transaction" TCP implementations (where the server opens first) [1, 5, 6, 8, 9].)

The service program here is implementable over an LRD channel provided each system in the implementation resends a message for which a response is expected until the response is received. But it is not implementable if each system puts a limit on the number of resends, and aborts the attempt if a response is not received in that time. If aborts are allowed then it's possible, for example, that endpoint $[j,k,n,m]$ becomes open but endpoint $[k,j,m,n]$ never becomes open. Exercise 20.5 develops a service appropriate for this situation.

Reliable transport services were first defined in [4, 7]. The services there differed from the one here in two ways. First, the services were defined without the intervening sockets layer, i.e., what the users would experience if they were to interact directly with the transport protocol. Second, internal nondeterminism was avoided; in [4] by making call ids externally visible, and in [7] by resorting to the approach described in Exercise 20.4.

Exercises

20.1. Modify the transport service program (in Figs. 20.4 and 20.5) so that it disallows client-client connections. Does this significantly simplify the program?

20.2. Modify the transport service program so that it disallows client-server connections in which the server side becomes open first. Does this significantly simplify the program?

20.3. Modify the transport service program so that it has the restrictions of Exercises 20.1 and 20.2. Does this significantly simplify the program?

20.4. The call ids in the transport service program (in Figs 20.4 and 20.5) gives rise to internal nondeterminism, in particular, the internal parameter m in the output parts of v[j].accept() and v[j].connect(k). Obtain an equivalent transport service program without internal nondeterminism.

(Hint: The purpose of the call ids is to pair sockets [j,k] and [k,j] such that each receives data only from the other. How can this pairing be achieved without internal nondeterminism? Here is one approach [7]. Let cns([j,k]) be the set of local call ids of socket [j,k]. It suffices if there exists a 1-1 matching between cns[[j,k]] and cns[[k,j]] such that if x in cns[[j,k]] and y in cns[[k,j]] are matched then rxh[x] is a prefix of txh[y] and rxh[y] is a prefix of txh[x].)

20.5. Modify the service so that it is implementable over an LRD channel where systems give up resending a message if a response is not received within some number of resends. Thus the service has to accommodate the situation where the message or its response was not received; this means that a user call may return without its intended work being done, i.e., with an abort.

(Hint: Here are some evolutions that the modified service must allow.

- j.connect(k) returns without an endpoint even if it is not rejected, indeed, even if there is a dedicated k.accept.
- j.close(k) returns without ensuring that the remote endpoint is closing or that all data sent has been received.
- Endpoint [j,k,n,m] becomes open but endpoint [k,j,m,n] never becomes open; presumably the user at j eventually aborts endpoint [j,k,n,m]).

References

1. R. Braden, T/TCP – TCP extensions for transactions functional specification. Technical report, RFC 1644, Internet Engineering Task Force (1994). http://tools.ietf.org/html/rfc1644
2. D.E. Comer, D.L. Stevens, *Internetworking with TCP/IP*, 1st edn. Vol. 3: Client-Server Programming and Applications, Linux/Posix Sockets Version (Prentice Hall, Upper Saddle River, 2000)
3. M.J. Donahoo, K. Calvert, *TCP/IP Sockets in C, Practical Guide for Programmers*, 2nd edn. (Morgan Kaufmann, Burlington, 2009)
4. S.L. Murphy, A.U. Shankar, Connection management for the transport layer: service specification and protocol verification. IEEE Trans. Commun. **39**(12), 1762–1775 (1991). doi:10.1109/26.120163. Earlier version in Proceedings ACM SIGCOMM '87 Workshop, Stowe, Vermont, August, 1987
5. A.L. Oláh, Design and analysis of transport protocols for reliable high-speed communications. Ph.D. thesis, University of Twente, Enschede, 1997. http://doc.utwente.nl/13676/
6. A.L. Oláh, S.M. Heemstra de Groot, Comments on "minimum-latency transport protocols with modulo-n incarnation numbers". IEEE/ACM Trans. Netw. **4**(4), 660–666 (1996). doi:http://dx.doi.org/10.1109/90.532874
7. A. Shankar, Modular design principles for protocols with an application to the transport layer. Proc. IEEE **79**(12), 1687–1707 (1991). doi:10.1109/5.119547

8. A.U. Shankar, D. Lee, Minimum-latency transport protocols with modulo-n incarnation numbers. IEEE/ACM Trans. Netw. **3**(3), 255–268 (1995). doi:10.1109/90.392385. http://dx. doi.org/10.1109/90.392385

9. M. Stacey, I. Griffin, J. Nelson, T/TCP: TCP for transactions. Linux J. (70) (2000). http://www. linuxjournal.com/article/3075

10. W.R. Stevens, *UNIX Network Programming*, vol. 1. Second Edition: Networking APIs: Sockets and XTI. (Prentice-Hall, Upper Saddle River, 1998). Chapter 4, ISBN 0-13-490012-X

```
service ReliableTransportService(Set ADDR) {
  ic {ADDR.size ≥ 1}

  ACPT ← 1; CONN ← 2; RET ← 3;
  NEP ← 4; EP ← 5; CLSD ← 6;
  Map srvr ← map([j,false]: j in ADDR);   // server mode
  int cidGen ← 0;                         // call id generator
  Map α ← map();                          // ongoing connect/accept call ids
  Map β ← map();                          // open socket local-remote call ids
  Seq ψ ← [];                             // connect/accept/close history
  Map txh ← rxh ← map();                  // transmit/receive histories
  Map v ← map([j,sid()]: j in ADDR);      // access system sids
  return v;

  function boolean overlapped(j,k,n,m) {
    return forsome(i1,i2:
             ψ[i1] = [CONN,j,k,n]
             and (ψ[i2] = [ACPT,k,m] or ψ[i2] = [CONN,k,j,m])
             and (i1 < i2 < keyOf([RET,n]) or i2 < i1 < keyOf([RET,m])));
  }

  function opened(j,k,n,m) {
    return ([EP,j,k,n,m] in ψ);
  }

  function openedTo(j,n) {
    return forsome(k,m: opened(k,j,m,n));
  }

  function closed(j,k,n,m) {
    return forsome(i1,i2: ψ[i1] = [EP,j,k,n,m]
                          and ψ[i2] = [CLSD,j,k] and i2 > i1);
  }

  function dedicatedAccept(j,k,n) {
    return forsome(m:
             keyOf([CONN,j,k,n]) > keyOf([ACPT,k,m]) and not ([NEP,m] in ψ)
             and not ([k,j] in β.keys)
             and not forsome(j1,n1, j1 ≠ j: overlapped(j1,k,n1,m))
             and not forsome(i1,n2:
                       ψ[i1] = [ACPT,j,n2]
                       and i1 < keyOf([CONN,j,k,n]) < keyOf([RET,n2])));
  }

// continued
```

Fig. 20.4 Part 1: reliable transport service

```
// ReliableTransportService continued

   function dedicatedConnect(k,m) {
      return not ([NEP,m] in ψ)
              and forsome(j,n: keyOf([CONN,j,k,n]) > keyOf([ACPT,k,m]))
              and not ([k,j] in β.keys)
              and not forsome(m1: overlapped(k,j,m1,n));
   }

    input Seq v[ADDR j].accept() {
      ic {not (j in α.keys)}
      srvr[j] ← true;
      n ← cidGen; cidGen ← cidGen+1;          // local call id
      α[j] ← n;
      ψ.append([ACPT,j,n]);

      // return value, remote addr, remote call id
      output (Seq rval, ADDR k, int m) {
        oc {(rval = []                         // canceled
             and ongoing(v[j].endServer)
             and not openedTo(j,n))
           OR (rval = [k]                       // connected to [k,m]
               and overlapped(k,j,m,n)
               and not ([j,k] in β.keys)
               and (not openedTo(j,n) or opened(k,j,m,n)))
        }
        ψ.append([RET,n]);
        if (rval = []) {
           ψ.append([NEP,n]);
        }
        else {
           ψ.append([EP,j,k,n,m]);
           β[[j,k]] ← [n,m];
           txh[[n,m]] ← rxh[[n,m]] ← [];
        }
        α.remove(j);
        return rval;
     }
   }

// continued
```

Fig. 20.5 Part 2: reliable transport service

```
// ReliableTransportService continued

    input void v[ADDR j].endServer() {
        ic {not ongoing(v[j].endServer)}
        srvr ← false;
        oc {not ongoing(v[j].accept)}
        return;
    }

    input Seq v[ADDR j].connect(ADDR k) {
        ic {not ([j,k] in union(α.keys, β.keys))}
        n ← cidGen; cidGen ← cidGen+1;                    // local call id
        α[[j,k]] ← n;
        ψ.append([CONN,j,k,n]);

        // return value, remote call id
        output (Seq rval, int m) {
            oc {(rval = [])                               // no endpoint
                and not dedicatedAccept(j,k,n)
                and not openedTo(j,n))
                OR (rval = [k]                            // connected to [k,m]
                    and overlapped(j,k,n,m)
                    and not ([j,k] in β.keys)
                    and (not openedTo(j,n) or opened(k,j,m,n)))
            }
            ψ.append([RET,n]);
            if (rval = []) {
                ψ.append([NEP,n]);
            }
            else {
                ψ.append([EP,j,k,n,m]);
                β[[j,k]] ← [n,m];
                txh[[n,m]] ← rxh[[n,m]] ← [];
            }
            α.remove([j,k]);
            return rval;
        }
    }

// continued
```

Fig. 20.6 Part 3: reliable transport service

```
// ReliableTransportService continued

    input Seq v[ADDR j].tx(ADDR k, Seq msg) {
        ic {([j,k] in β.keys) and not ongoing(v[j].tx(k,.))
            and not ongoing(j.close(k))}
        txh[β[[j,k]]].append(msg);
        oc {true}
        return;
    }

    input Seq v[ADDR j].rx(k) {
        ic {([j,k] in β.keys) and not ongoing(v[j].rx(k))}
        output (Seq rval, Seq msg) {
            oc {(rval = [0,msg]                     // msg received
                and (rxh[β[[j,k]]] ◦ [msg]) prefixOf txh[β[[j,k]][1,0]])
                OR (rval = [-1]                     // nothing to receive
                    and (rxh[β[[j,k]]] = txh[β[[j,k]][1,0]])
                    and (ongoing(k.close(j))
                        or closed(k,j,β[[j,k]][1,0])))
            }
            if (rval[0] = 0)
                rxh[β[[j,k]]].append(msg);
            return rval;
        }
    }

    input void v[ADDR j].close(k) {
        ic {([j,k] in β.keys) and not ongoing(v[j].close(k))}
        oc {not (ongoing(v[j].tx(k,.)) or ongoing(v[j].rx(k)))
            and rxh[β[[j,k]]] = txh[β[[j,k]][1,0]]
            and ongoing(k.close(j))
                or closed(k,j,β[[j,k]][1],β[[j,k]][0]))
        }
        ψ.append([CLSD,j,k]);
        β.remove([j,k]);
        return;
    }

// continued
```

Fig. 20.7 Part 4: reliable transport service

```
// ReliableTransportService continued

    atomicity assumption {input parts and output parts}

    progress assumption {
        (ongoing(v[j].accept and ongoing(v[j].endServer)))
            leads-to  not ongoing(v[j].accept);

        ongoing(v[j].endServer)  leads-to  not ongoing(v[j].endServer);

        opened(j,k,n,m)  leads-to  opened(k,j,m,n);

        (ongoing(v[j].accept and dedicatedConnect(j,α[j])))
            leads-to  not ongoing(v[j].accept);

        (ongoing(v[j].connect(k)) and dedicatedAccept(j,k,α[[j,k]]))
            leads-to  opened(j,k,α[[j,k]],.)

        (ongoing(v[j].close(k)) and β[[j,k]] = [n,m]
         and (ongoing(k.close(j)) or closed(k,j,m,n)))
            leads-to  (not ongoing(v[j].close(k)) or not ongoing(v[j].rx(k)));

        ongoing(v[j].tx(k,.))  leads-to  not ongoing(v[j].tx(k,.));

        (ongoing(v[j].rx(k)) and β[[j,k]] = [n,m] and rxh[n,m] ≠ txh[m,n])
            leads-to  not ongoing(v[j].rx(k));

        (ongoing(v[j].rx(k)) and β[[j,k]] = [n,m] and rxh[n,m] = txh[m,n]
         and (ongoing(k.close(j)) or closed(k,j,m,n)))
            leads-to  not ongoing(v[j].rx(k))
    }
}  // ReliableTransportService
```

Fig. 20.8 Part 5: reliable transport service

```
service ReliableTransportServiceInverse(Set ADDR, Map<ADDR,Sid> v) {
    // v[j]: sid of service access system at addres j
    ic {ADDR.size ≥ 1}
    ACPT ← 1; CONN ← 2; RET ← 3;
    NEP ← 4; EP ← 5; CLSD ← 6;
    Map srvr ← map([j,false]: j in ADDR);  // server mode
    int cidGen ← 0;                         // call id generator
    Map α ← map();                          // ongoing connect/accept call ids
    Map β ← map();                          // open socket local-remote call ids
    Seq ψ ← [];                             // connect/accept/close history
    Map txh ← rxh ← map();                  // transmit/receive histories
    return mysid;

    function boolean overlapped(j,k,n,m) {...}

    function opened(j,k,n,m) {...}

    function openedTo(j,n) {...}

    function closed(j,k,n,m) {...}

    function dedicatedAccept(j,k,n) {...}

    function dedicatedConnect(k,m) {...}

// continued
```

Fig. 20.9 Part 1: reliable transport service inverse

```
// ReliableTransportServiceInverse continued

    output doAccept(ADDR j) {
        oc {not (j in α.keys)}
        srvr[j] ← true;
        n ← cidGen; cidGen ← cidGen+1;          // local call id
        α[j] ← n;
        ψ.append([ACPT,j,n]);

        // v[j].accept returns [rval, remote addr, remote call id]
        [rval, k, m] ← v[j].accept();

        ic {(rval = [])                          // canceled
            and ongoing(v[j].endServer)
            and not openedTo(j,n))
            OR (rval = [k]                        // connected to [k,m]
                and overlapped(k,j,m,n)
                and not ([j,k] in β.keys)
                and (not openedTo(j,n) or opened(k,j,m,n)))
        }
        ψ.append([RET,n]);
        if (rval = []) {
            ψ.append([NEP,n]);
        }
        else {
            ψ.append([EP,j,k,n,m]);
            β[[j,k]] ← [n,m];
            txh[[n,m]] ← rxh[[n,m]] ← [];
        }
        α.remove(j);
    }

// continued
```

Fig. 20.10 Part 2: reliable transport service inverse

```
// ReliableTransportServiceInverse continued

    output doEndServer(ADDR j) {
        oc {not ongoing(v[j].endServer)}

        v[j].endServer();

        ic {not ongoing(v[j].accept)}
        srvr ← false;
    }


    output doConnect(ADDR j, ADDR k) {
        oc {not ([j,k] in union(α.keys, β.keys))}
        n ← cidGen; cidGen ← cidGen+1;              // local call id
        α[[j,k]] ← n;
        ψ.append([CONN,j,k,n]);

        // v[j].connect(k) returns [rval, remote call id]
        [rval, m] ← v[j].connect(k);

        oc {(rval = [])                            // no endpoint
            and not dedicatedAccept(j,k,n)
            and not openedTo(j,n))
          OR (rval = [k]                           // connected to [k,m]
            and overlapped(j,k,n,m)
            and not ([j,k] in β.keys)
            and (not openedTo(j,n) or opened(k,j,m,n)))
        }
        ψ.append([RET,n]);
        if (rval = []) {
            ψ.append([NEP,n]);
        }
        else {
            ψ.append([EP,j,k,n,m]);
            β[[j,k]] ← [n,m];
            txh[[n,m]] ← rxh[[n,m]] ← [];
        }
        α.remove([j,k]);
    }


// continued
```

Fig. 20.11 Part 3: reliable transport service inverse

```
// ReliableTransportServiceInverse continued

    output doTx(ADDR j, ADDR k, Seq msg) {
        oc {([j,k] in β.keys) and not ongoing(v[j].tx(k,.))
            and not ongoing(j.close(k))}
        txh[β[[j,k]]].append(msg);

        v[j].tx(k,msg);

        oc {true}
    }

    output doRx(ADDR j, ADDR k) {
        oc {([j,k] in β.keys) and not ongoing(v[j].rx(k))}

        // v[j].rx(k) returns [rval, msg]
        [rval, msg] ← v[j].rx(k);

        ic {(rval = [0,msg]                         // msg received
            and (rxh[β[[j,k]]] ∘ [msg]) prefixOf txh[β[[j,k]][1,0]])
            OR (rval = [-1]                          // nothing to receive
                and (rxh[β[[j,k]]] = txh[β[[j,k]][1,0]])
                and (ongoing(k.close(j))
                    or closed(k,j,β[[j,k]][1,0])))
        }
        if (rval[0] = 0)
            rxh[β[[j,k]]].append(msg);
    }

    output doClose(ADDR j, ADDR k) {
        oc {([j,k] in β.keys) and not ongoing(v[j].close(k))}

        v[j].close(k);

        ic {not (ongoing(v[j].tx(k,.)) or ongoing(v[j].rx(k)))
            and rxh[β[[j,k]]] = txh[β[[j,k]][1,0]]
            and ongoing(k.close(j))
                or closed(k,j,β[[j,k]][1],β[[j,k]][0]))
        }
        ψ.append([CLSD,j,k]);
        β.remove([j,k]);
    }

    atomicity assumption {input parts and output parts}
    progress condition {...}

} // ReliableTransportServiceInverse
```

Fig. 20.12 Part 4: reliable transport service inverse

Chapter 21
Reliable Transport Protocol

21.1 Introduction

This chapter presents a distributed program that implements the reliable transport
service (Chap. 20) over an LRD (loss, reorder, duplication) channel, as illustrated
in Fig. 21.1. In computer networking, such a program is referred to as a **transport
protocol**. Following this terminology, we refer to the system at each address as a
"tp" system, where "tp" is short for transport protocol. We refer to the messages
exchanged between tp users as "data blocks", and reserve the term "messages" for
the messages exchanged between the tp systems; the former would be sent inside
the latter.

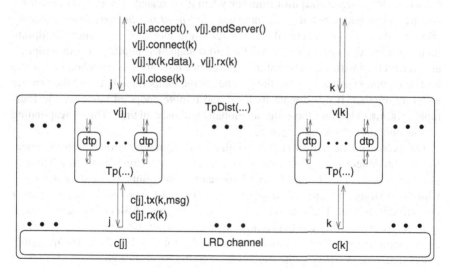

Fig. 21.1 Transport protocol configuration, with tp system v[j] attached to LRD channel access
system c[j] at address j. Each aggregate tp system contains a dtp system for each connection

A.U. Shankar, *Distributed Programming: Theory and Practice*,
DOI 10.1007/978-1-4614-4881-5_21,
© Springer Science+Business Media New York 2013

The tp system at address j has input functions corresponding to those of the service. A user at address j calls j.accept() to enter server mode and accept any incoming connect request. (In informal discussion, we abbreviate the sid prefix v[j] by its address j.) In server mode, arriving connect requests are buffered. The user calls j.endServer() to end server mode, cancel any ongoing j.accept call, and delete any buffered connect requests. A user at j calls j.connect(k) to connect to either an ongoing k.accept or k.connect(j) at address k. If neither is available, the j.connect(k) is rejected. While connected, the user at j calls j.tx(k,.) to send a data block, and j.rx(k) to receive a data block. When the user has no further messages to send, it calls j.close(k), which returns after the remote user has called k.close(j) and the local user has received all incoming data blocks.

Our transport protocol has similarities to TCP [2, 7, 10], the Internet transport protocol that implements the reliable streaming part of Internet sockets. Connection establishment between a j.connect(k) and a k.accept involves a three-way handshake: j.connect(k) sends a connect request, to which k.accept sends its own connect request, to which j.connect(k) sends an ack. The tp system at j maintains state about the tp system at k only when it is interacting with it. The state, referred to as a **protocol endpoint**, or **endpoint** for short, is created when j.connect(k) is called or when an ongoing j.accept receives a connect request from k. The endpoint is initially **active opening**, if it was started by connect, or **passive opening**, if it was started by accept. An endpoint goes from opening to **open** if it becomes connected. An open endpoint is **closing** (and still open) when j.close(k) is called. A closing endpoint becomes **closed** when j.close(k) returns, at which point it is deleted. An opening endpoint goes directly to closed if its connect request is rejected.

To distinguish different endpoints for the same remote address, each endpoint at j is assigned a unique **endpoint number** when it is created. The endpoint numbers for successive endpoints at j are increasing but *need not be consecutive*, thereby allowing them to be generated from a real-time clock or a counter. (Endpoint numbers play the same role as TCP's initial sequence numbers.) An endpoint at j interacting with an endpoint at k stores not only its own number, called the **local** endpoint number, but also the number of the endpoint at k, called the **remote** endpoint number. If n and m are its local and remote endpoint numbers, the four-tuple [j,k,n,m] identifies the endpoint globally and over all time. The corresponding remote endpoint would be [k,j,m,n].

Our protocol differs from TCP in that there is a clean separation between connection establishment and data transfer within a connection. Connection establishment provides a dedicated *virtual* channel between the endpoints, by tagging messages with the sending endpoint's four-tuple. Any data-transfer protocol can be run over this virtual channel. For concreteness, we use the **graceful-closing** data transfer protocol from Sect. 5.7. The tp system starts a dtp (data-transfer protocol) system for an endpoint when the latter becomes open, as illustrated in Fig. 21.1. The tp system relays data blocks between the dtp system and the local user above. It also relays dtp messages between the dtp system and the local channel access system below, encapsulating the dtp messages in tp messages. The dtp system executes its protocol with the remote dtp system to achieve data transfer and connection termination. The dtp program differs from the one in Sect. 5.7 in one way: it terminates itself at the end of connection termination. After this, the tp system itself responds to any FIN message from the remote dtp system.

Our protocol differs from TCP in another, subtle but important, way. In our protocol, a connect request message also indicates whether the sender is active opening or passive opening. TCP does not convey this extra bit of information, and as a result has a serious flaw: old messages in the channel can cause two *accepting* users to become connected to each other [3].

Section 21.2 summarizes the dtp protocol and its properties. Section 21.3 gives an overview of the transport protocol, describing its messages and typical handshakes. Section 21.4 presents the distributed program of the transport protocol, assuming unbounded endpoint numbers. Section 21.5 establishes that the protocol implements the reliable transport service. Section 21.6 refines the transport protocol to use modulo-N endpoint numbers. We obtain a lower bound on N that ensures correct operation assuming a minimum time interval between endpoint creations and upper bounds on the LRD channel message lifetime and the opening, open and closing durations of an endpoint. (The upper bound on the open duration of an endpoint can be dispensed with if one is willing to accept correctness with a high probability $(\approx 1 - (1/N^2))$ rather than with certainty.)

21.2 Graceful-Closing dtp Program

The dtp program used in the transport protocol is the graceful-closing dtp program from Sect. 5.7 with some minor changes. Below, we first summarize the graceful-closing dtp program, then we state its correctness properties, and finally we give the changes to the dtp program.

The graceful-closing dtp program (Sect. 5.7) has the following parameters: aL, local address; aR, remote address; x, sid of local channel access system; and sliding window parameters N, SW and RW. The program's messages are as follows: [DAT,cn,data] data messages, [ACK,cn] ack messages, [FIN] message, and [FINACK] message. The program makes only two kinds of output calls, x.tx(.) and x.rx(), to send and receive dtp messages, where x is the local channel access system. At any time, at most one call of each type is ongoing. The program has the following functions:

- Input function tx(aR,data) sends data block data. Called only while not closing or closed.
- Input function rx() receives a data block. Called only while not closed. Returns [0,data] iff data is the next incoming data block in order. Returns [-1] iff the local user has received all incoming data blocks and the remote dtp is closing or closed.

- Input function close() initiates closing. Returns only when (1) all outgoing data has been acked, (2) local user has received all incoming data, (3) the remote user is closing or closed.
- Function doTxDat, executed by a local thread, sends (and resends) data messages.
- Function doRxDatAck, executed by a local thread, receives messages and processes them, including sending ACK and FINACK responses. After the system is closed, this function's only activity is to send FINACK responses.

The distributed system of two graceful-closing dtp systems communicating over an LRD channel satisfies the following properties, where j and k identify the dtp systems, j.drxh is the sequence of data blocks received at j, and k.dtxh is the sequence of data blocks sent at k.

A_1 : if j.rx returns [0,data] then j.drxh ∘ [data] is a prefix of k.dtxh.

A_2 : if j.rx returns [-1] then j.drxh equals k.dtxh and k is closing or closed.

A_3 : if j is closed then neither j.tx and j.rx are ongoing, j.drxh equals k.dtxh, and k is closing or closed.

A_4 : if j.tx is ongoing then eventually j.tx returns.

A_5 : if j.rx is ongoing and j.drxh $\neq$ k.dtxh holds then eventually j.rx returns.

A_6 : if j.rx is ongoing and j.drxh = k.dtxh holds and k is closing or closed
then eventually j.rx returns.

A_7 : if j is closing and k is closing or closed
then eventually j becomes closed or j.rx is not ongoing.

The dtp program used in the transport protocol is referred to as program GcDtp. It is the above graceful-closing dtp program with the following changes.

1. In function close, insert endSystem() just before the return.
2. Rename the output calls x.tx(.) and x.rx() to x.dTx(.) and x.dRx(), respectively.

Regarding the first change, recall that the only work done by a closed dtp system is to send FINACK responses to any received FIN message. The tp system takes care of this when the dtp system no longer exists. Regarding the second change, recall that the dtp system's output calls are now directed to the tp system. The latter already has input functions tx and rx (from the transport service), hence the need for renaming.

21.3 Protocol Overview

The distributed program TpDist of the transport protocol is shown in Fig. 21.2. The program starts an LRD channel and then a tp system at each address of the channel. Each tp system is an instantiation of program Tp. The interactions between the tp systems are fairly involved because the transport service is not simple and because the underlying channel can lose, reorder, and duplicate messages. To get some insight into the protocol, we start by looking at some interactions between two tp systems *assuming* for now that the underlying LRD channel behaves as a fifo

```
program TpDist(ADDR) {
    ic {ADDR.size ≥ 1}
    Map c ← startSystem(LrdChannel(ADDR));
    Map v ← map();
    for (j in ADDR)
        v[j] ← startSystem(Tp(ADDR,j,c[j]));
    return v;
}
```

Fig. 21.2 Distributed program of transport protocol and LRD channel

channel. Figure 21.3 illustrates the typical life of a connection between a client at address j and a server at address k. There are three phases: connection establishment, data transfer, and connection termination. Each is expanded upon next.

Connection establishment. The j.connect(k) call gets an endpoint number, say n, creates an active-opening endpoint [j,k,n,-1], and sends message [CCR,j,k,n,-1], where CCR stands for "client connect request" and –1 denotes a "nil" value. Upon receiving the message, the k.accept call gets an endpoint number, say m, creates a passive-opening endpoint [k,j,m,n], and responds with message [SCR,k,j,m,n], where SCR stands for "server connect request". Upon receiving this, j.connect(k) updates the remote endpoint number to m, makes endpoint [j,k,n,m] open, starts a dtp system, say dtp1, responds with message [CRACK,j,k,n,m], where CRACK stands for "connect request ack", and returns. Upon receiving this, k.accept makes endpoint [k,j,m,n] open and starts a dtp system, say dtp2.

Data transfer. After the endpoints are open, dtp1 and dtp2 run their data transfer protocol to provide a fifo channel to the users of the connection. At j, when the user calls j.tx(k,data), the tp system converts it to a dtp1.tx(k,data) call. Similarly, a j.rx(k) call is converted to a dtp1.rx() call. When the dtp system sends a dtp message dtmsg (which would be a DAT or ACK message), the tp system encapsulates it in a [EDT,j,k,n,m,dtpmsg] message and sends it on the LRD channel; EDT stands for "encapsulated data transfer", When the tp system receives a [EDT,k,j,m,n,dtmsg] message, it passes dtmsg to dtp1. The interaction at k between the tp system and dtp2 system is similar.

Connection termination. When the user at j calls j.close(k), the tp system converts it to a dtp1.close call. The latter proceeds as in program GcDtp: wait for all outgoing data to be acked, send [FIN] (which the tp system encapsulates in a EDT message), receive [FINACK] from dtp2, wait to receive [FIN], send [FINACK], call endSystem (to end system dtp1), and return dtp1.close, which returns j.close(k). System dtp2 does the same.

Client-client connection establishment. Figure 21.4 illustrates connection establishment between two clients, one at address j and one at address k. Each side

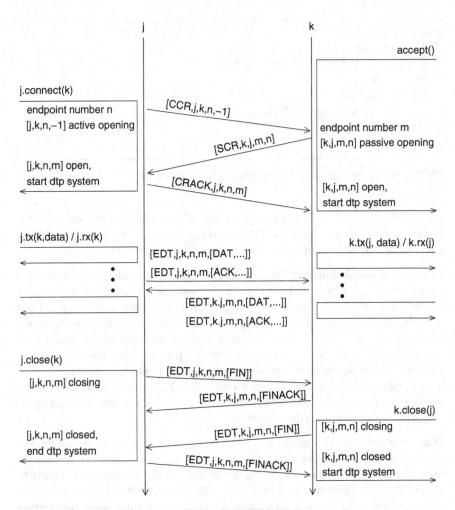

Fig. 21.3 Connection establishment, data transfer, and closing

becomes active opening and sends a CCR message. The other side responds with a CRACK message. Upon receiving it, the endpoint becomes open and starts a dtp system.

Connect request rejection. Figure 21.5 illustrates the rejection of a j.connect(k) request. As before, an active opening endpoint [j,k,n,-1] sends a [CCR,j,k,n,-1] message. But now address k is not in server mode and there is no k.connect(j) ongoing. So the tp system at k responds with a [REJ,k,j,-1,n] message, where REJ stands for "reject". Upon receiving this, the j.connect(k) closes endpoint [j,k,n,-1] and returns.

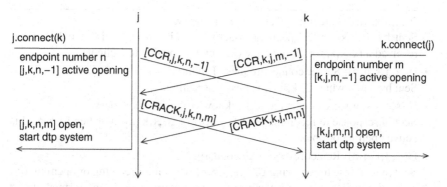

Fig. 21.4 Client j and client k connect

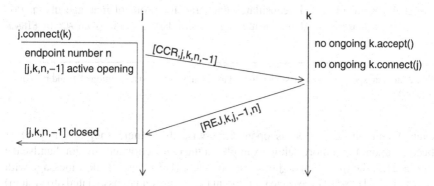

Fig. 21.5 Client j connection request rejected

21.3.1 Handling Message Losses

The above interactions assumed the underlying LRD channel behaved as a fifo channel. To handle message loss, we classify the messages into two types: primary and secondary. A **primary message** is one that is sent repeatedly until a response is received. A **secondary message** is one that is sent in response to a received message.

Figure 21.6 lists the messages exchanged between the tp systems, along with their primary or secondary status. CCR, SCR and FIN are primary. CRACK, REJ and FINACK are secondary. A EDT message is primary if it encapsulates a primary dtp message (DAT and FIN), and secondary if it encapsulates a secondary dtp message (ACK and FINACK).

The final message of a handshake is always secondary, otherwise the handshake would never end. Every non-final message is primary, otherwise a loss would stop the handshake prematurely. Note that the final message of a handshake must be sent each time the pre-final message is received, even though the handshake is over from the receiver's perspective. For example, in the connection establishment handshake in Fig. 21.3, the tp system at j must respond to a [SCR,k,j,m,n] message

- [CCR,j,k,n,m]: Client connect request. Primary.

  Sent by j to k while [j,k,n,m] is active opening. Entry m is -1 unless j has received a [CCR,k,j,m,.] message (i.e., client opening to a client).

- [SCR,j,k,n,m]: Server connect request. Primary.

  Sent by j to k while [j,k,n,m] is passive opening.

- [CRACK,j,k,n,m]: Connect request acknowledgment. Secondary.

  Sent in response to receiving [SCR,k,j,m,n] or [CCR,k,j,m,n] when [j,k,n,.] is active opening or open.

- [REJ,j,k,n,m]: Reject response. Secondary.

  Sent in response to receiving [CCR,k,j,m,n] when not accepting or opening to k, or receiving [SCR,k,j,m,n] when not active opening to k. In the former case, m can be -1.

- [EDT,j,k,n,m,dtmsg]: Encapsulates data transfer protocol message dtmsg. Primary if dtmsg is a DAT or FIN message. Secondary if dtmsg is an ACK or FINACK message.

Fig. 21.6 Transport protocol messages from j to k. Unless otherwise mentioned, m and n are non-negative

even if endpoint [j,k,n,m] is open. Otherwise the remote endpoint may never become open. For a more subtle example, in the connection termination handshake in Fig. 21.3, the tp system at j must respond to a [EDT,k,j,m,n,[FIN]] message with [EDT,k,j,m,n,[FINACK]] message if endpoint [j,k,n,m] (and its associated dtp system) no longer exists.

21.3.2   Handling Old Messages

Because the LRD channel can duplicate and reorder messages, a tp system can receive a message from an old connection that no longer exists. This may cause the tp system to initiate a handshake, which must then be terminated. For example, suppose an ongoing k.accept receives a [CCR,j,k,n,-1] message while j is not opening or open to k. The tp system at k chooses a new endpoint number, say m, and responds with [SCR,k,j,m,n]. The tp system at j responds with [REJ,j,k,m,n], whose reception ends the handshake.

The situation can be more twisted. When k.accept receives the old [CCR,j,k,n,-1] message, there may be an ongoing j.connect(k) with a more recent endpoint number, say n1. When the tp system at j receives [SCR,k,j,m,n], it ignores it because it is sending [CCR,j,k,n1,-1] and awaiting a response to that. When the tp system at k receives [CCR,j,k,n1,-1], it observes that n1 is higher than n and now sends [SCR,k,j,m,n1]. Note that this requires endpoint numbers issued by an address to be increasing.

21.3.3   Overlapping Handshakes

We have seen that the evolution of the transport protocol consists of a succession of
handshakes. The easiest evolutions to understand are those in which each handshake
between a pair of addresses runs to completion before the next handshake between
the same addresses begins. This happens when connect requests are spaced apart
sufficiently in time. But in general evolutions are more complex. One side can start
a new handshake while the other side has not yet completed the previous handshake.
In this case, when the other side receives a message of the new handshake, it would
treat the previous handshake as completed.

For example, in the client-server connection establishment in Fig. 21.3, suppose
the tp system at k is passive opening, awaiting a response to its [SCR,k,j,m,n]. If it
receives a [EDT,j,k,n,m,dtmsg] message, this means the other side has become open
and so it sets endpoint [k,j,m,n] to open.

For another example, suppose endpoint [k,j,m,n] is closing and the tp system at
k receives a [CCR,j,k,n1,-1] where n1 is greater than n. This means that endpoint
[j,k,n,m] has closed and a new endpoint [j,k,n1,-1] is active opening. This
happens only if the dtp system of endpoint [k,j,m,n] is closing and needs only
to receive a FINACK to become closed. Thus the tp system at k can make the dtp
system at [k,j,m,n] closed (e.g., by treating the [CCR,j,k,n1,-1] message as a
[EDT,j,k,n,m,[FINACK]] message).

21.3.4   Buffering Incoming CCR Messages in Server Mode

An address k in server mode maintains a map, ccrBuff, to buffer the remote address
and remote endpoint number of incoming client connect requests. A k.accept
chooses a request from this map to serve. The map is indexed by remote address.
When [CCR,j,k,n,.] is received, ccrBuff[j] is updated to n only if (1) endpoint
[k,j,.,.] does not exist, and (2) ccrBuff[j] does not exist or is less than n. One
would usually impose additional constraints on the map, such as a limit on the
number of entries and a queueing discipline (fifo, priority).

21.4   Program Tp with Unbounded Incarnation Numbers

Program Tp, which is executed by each tp system, is given in Figs. 21.10–21.16.
Treat the boxed text as comments and ignore them for now. The program uses
unbounded endpoint numbers in messages. It has three parameters: ADDR, the set
of addresses; aL, the local address, and cL, the sid of the local LRD channel access
system. The main code defines the following variables.

- srvr: boolean; initially false. True iff address aL is in server mode.
- acptng: boolean; initially false. True iff accept is ongoing.
- nGen: integer; initially non-negative. Endpoint number generator. Incremented by one after each endpoint creation. It can also be a real-time clock that ticks at least once between successive endpoint creations.
- st, ln, rn: maps indexed by address and initially empty. Each has an entry for address k iff an endpoint exists for k. Entry st[k] indicates whether the endpoint is active opening, passive opening, rejected or open. Entry ln[k] is the endpoint's local number. Entry rn[k] is the endpoint's remote number; it equals –1 if not known (possible only when active opening).
- ccrBuff: map from addresses to endpoint numbers. Empty if srvr is false. Otherwise, ccrBuff[k] exists and equals n only if (1) an endpoint for k does not exist, (2) at least one CCR message was received from k while there was no endpoint for k, and (3) n is the highest sender endpoint number in these CCR messages.
- dtp: map from addresses to sids. Entry dtp[k] is the sid of the dtp system associated with the endpoint for k; it exists iff the endpoint is open.
- dtpRxQ: map from addresses to sequences. Entry dtpRxQ[k] is the queue of received dtp messages awaiting delivery to dtp[k]; it exists iff the endpoint for k is open.

Program Tp has input functions for the transport service: accept(), endServer(), connect(k), tx(k,data), rx(k), and close(k), where parameter k is a remote address. They are called by users. The program also has input functions dTx(k,dtmsg) and dRx(k), called by the dtp system dtp[k]. The former encapsulates dtmsg in a EDT message and sends it on the LRD channel. The latter gets a dtp message from message queue dtpRxQ[k]. The program also has a function doRx executed by a local thread, which repeatedly receives a message from the LRD channel and processes it. The latter consists of sending any secondary message response, buffering connect requests in server mode, updating the state of an existing endpoint, and starting a dtp system and its receive message queue. Each function is described in more detail next.

- Input function accept() does the following.

  1. Set srvr and acptng to true.
  2. Wait for srvr to be false or ccrBuff to be not empty.
  3. If srvr is false then return [].
  4. If ccrBuff is not empty, do the following: remove the earliest entry [k,m] from ccrBuff; get an endpoint number n from nGen; set st[k], ln[k] and rn[k] to passive opening, n and m, respectively; repeatedly send [SCR,aL,k,n,rn[k]] to k until st[k] is open or rejected.
  5. If st[k] is open then return [k]; otherwise remove the entries for k from st, ln and rn and go to step 2.

- Input function endServer() does the following: set srvr to false, send REJ responses to every entry in ccrBuff, empty ccrBuff, wait for acptng to be false, and return.
- Input function connect(k) does the following:

  1. Get an endpoint number n from nGen; set st[k], ln[k] and rn[k] to active opening, n and –1, respectively; repeatedly send [CCR,aL,k,n,rn[k]] to k until st[k] is open or rejected.
  2. If st[k] is open then return [k]; otherwise remove the entries for k from st, ln and rn and return [].

- Input function tx(k,data) calls dtp[k].tx(k,data) and returns.
- Input function rx(k) calls dtp[k].rx() and returns the value returned (either [0,data] or [-1]).
- Input function close(k) does the following: call dtp[k].close(); remove the entry for k from dtp and dtpRxQ; return.
- Input function dTx(k,dtmsg) is called by system dtp[k]. It sends the message [EDT,aL,k,ln[k],rn[k],dtpmsg] to k.
- Input function dRx(k) is called by system dtp[k]. It waits for dtpRxQ[k] to be not empty, then removes the entry at the head of dtpRxQ[k] and returns it.
- Process a received message [CCR,k,aL,m,n] as follows.

  - If there is no endpoint for k: if srvr is true then merge [k,m] into ccrBuff else send [REJ,aL,k,n,m] to k.
  - If the endpoint for k is active opening and n equals ln[k], then send [CRACK,aL,k,n,m] to k, set st[k] to open, start a dtp system for k and store its sid in dtp[k], and set dtpRxQ to [].
  - If the endpoint for k is passive opening and m is greater than rn[k], then update rn[k] to m.
  - If the endpoint for k is open and [n,m] equals [ln[k],rn[k]], then send [CRACK,aL,n,m] to k.
  - If the endpoint for k is open and m is greater than rn[k], then send [REJ,aL,n,m] to k. Optionally, append [FINACK] to dtpRxQ[k] (because the endpoint is closing and awaiting a FINACK).

- Process a received [SCR,k,aL,m,n] message as follows.

  - If there is no endpoint for k, then send [REJ,aL,k,n,m] to k.
  - If the endpoint for k is active opening and n equals ln[k], then send [CRACK,aL,k,n,m] to k, set st[k] to open, start dtp system for k and store its sid in dtp[k], and set dtpRxQ to [].
  - If the endpoint for k is passive opening and m is greater than rn[k], then send [REJ,aL,k,n,m] to k.
  - If the endpoint for k is open and [n,m] equals [ln[k],rn[k]], then send [CRACK,aL,n,m] to k.
  - If the endpoint for k is open and m is greater than rn[k], then send [REJ,aL,n,m] to k and, optionally, append [FINACK] to dtpRxQ[k].

- Process a received [CRACK,k,aL,m,n] message as follows.

  - If the endpoint for k is active opening or passive opening and [n,m] equals [ln[k],rn[k]], then set st[k] to open, start dtp system for k and store its sid in dtp[k], and set dtpRxQ to [].

- Process a received [REJ,k,aL,m,n] message as follows.

  - If the endpoint for k is active opening or passive opening and [n,m] equals [ln[k],rn[k]], then set st[k] to rejected.

- Process a received [EDT,k,aL,m,n,dtmsg] message as follows.

  - If no endpoint for k exists: if dtmsg is [FIN] then send [EDT,aL,k,n,m,[FINACK]].
  - If the endpoint for k is active opening or passive opening and [n,m] equals [ln[k],rn[k]], then set st[k] to open, start dtp system for k and store its sid in dtp[k], set dtpRxQ to [], and append dtmsg to dtpRxQ[k].
  - If the endpoint for k is open and [n,m] equals [ln[k],rn[k]], then append dtmsg to dtpRxQ[k].

21.5   Establishing the Implements Condition

We now establish that TpDist(ADDR) implements RelTransportService(ADDR). Figure 21.7 shows the closed program Z of an instantiation v of TpDist and an instantiation tsi of the transport service inverse (available in Figs. 20.9 and 20.12). The map γ is an auxiliary variable that maps protocol endpoint numbers to service call ids. It is updated and accessed in the boxed parts of program Tp, which are now *not* treated as comments. Specifically, in every instantiation of program Tp in program Z, every boxed return replaces the preceding return, and every boxed update to γ is executed.

We have to establish that Z satisfies the input conditions and the progress condition of the service inverse. For readability, the analysis here will be less

```
system Z(Set ADDR) {
    ic {ADDR.size ≥ 1}
    Map γ ← map();        // auxiliary: call ids of endpoint numbers
    Map c ← startSystem(LrdChannel(ADDR));
    Map v ← map();
    for (j in ADDR)
        startSystem(Tp(ADDR,j,c[j]));
    Sid tsi ← startSystem(RelTransportServiceInverse(ADDR,v));
}
```

Fig. 21.7 Closed program of transport protocol and transport service inverse

detailed than usual. Assertions will be stated informally (but precisely). We say tp
j to mean the tp system at address j. We often omit the tsi prefix when there is no
ambiguity, e.g., with functions overlapped, opened, etc., and with variables α, β, ψ.

We use "hatted" names, e.g., $\hat{n}$, to refer to call ids. Also, if $\hat{n}$ appears in the context
of an endpoint number n, then $\hat{n}$ denotes the call id corresponding to n, i.e., $\gamma[[j,n]]$,
where n was generated at address j. Thus [j,k,n,m] refers to a *protocol endpoint*
whereas [j,k,$\hat{n}$,$\hat{m}$] refers to a *service endpoint*.

We say [j,k,n,m] is active opening (passive opening, etc.) to mean that j.ln[k]
equals n, j.ln[k] equals m, and j.st[k] is active opening (passive opening, etc.).
Similar terminology applies to service endpoints, e.g., "[j,k,$\hat{n}$,$\hat{m}$] is opened".

21.5.1 Assertions to Be Proved

We now list the assertions that Z must satisfy. Assertions B_1–B_8 are the invariant
assertions corresponding to the service inverse's input conditions, after accounting
for program Z's effective atomicity. For example, the requirement for doAccept(j)'s
input condition when j.accept returns [] is the invariant assertion:

- If a thread is at doAccept.ic and doAccept has call id $\hat{n}$ and rval equals []
  then j.endServer is ongoing and openedTo(j,$\hat{n}$) is false.

After accounting for effective atomicity of program Z, this is equivalent to assertion
B_1 below.

B_1 : If a thread is at j.accept.s1 with call id $\hat{n}$ and srvr is false,
    then j.endServer is ongoing and openedTo(j,$\hat{n}$) is false.

B_2 : If a thread is at j.accept.s2 with endpoint [j,k,n,m] open,
    then overlapped(k,j,$\hat{m}$,$\hat{n}$) is true and [j,k] is not in β.keys
        and either openedTo(j,$\hat{n}$) is false or opened(k,j,$\hat{m}$,$\hat{n}$) is true.

B_3 : If a thread is at j.endServer.s1 and acptng is false,
    then j.accept is not ongoing.

B_4 : If a thread is at j.connect(k).s1 with endpoint [j,k,n,.] rejected,
    then dedicatedAccept(j,k,$\hat{n}$) and openedTo(j,$\hat{n}$) are both false.

B_5 : If a thread is at j.connect(k).s1 with endpoint [j,k,n,m] open,
    then overlapped(j,k,$\hat{n}$,$\hat{m}$) is true and [j,k] is not in β.keys
        and either openedTo(j,$\hat{n}$) is false or opened(k,j,$\hat{m}$,$\hat{n}$) is true.

B_6 : If a thread is at j.rx(k).s1 with endpoint [j,k,n,m]
        and rval equals [0,data],
    then tsi.rxh[[$\hat{n}$,$\hat{m}$]]∘[data] is a prefix of tsi.txh[[$\hat{m}$,$\hat{n}$]].

B_7 : If a thread is at j.rx(k).s1 with endpoint [j,k,n,m]
        and rval equals [-1],
    then tsi.rxh[[$\hat{n}$,$\hat{m}$]] equals tsi.txh[[$\hat{m}$,$\hat{n}$]]
        and [k,j,$\hat{m}$,$\hat{n}$] is closing or closed.

B_8 : If a thread is at j.close(k).s1 with endpoint [j,k,n,m],
        then neither j.tx and j.rx are ongoing
            and tsi.rxh[[ñ,m̂]] equals tsi.txh[[m̂,ñ]]
            and [k,j,m̂,ñ] is closing or closed.

Assertions C_1–C_9 are progress assertions, corresponding to the service inverse's
progress condition.

C_1 : If j.accept is ongoing and j.endServer is ongoing,
        then eventually j.accept returns.

C_2 : If j.endServer is ongoing, then it eventually returns.

C_3 : If opened(j,k,ñ,m̂) holds, then eventually opened(k,j,m̂,ñ) holds.

C_4 : If j.accept is ongoing with call id ñ and dedicatedConnect(j,ñ) holds
        then eventually j.accept returns.

C_5 : If j.connect(k) is ongoing with call id ñ
            and dedicatedAccept(j,k,ñ) holds,
        then eventually opened(j,k,ñ,.) holds.

C_6 : If j.tx(k) is ongoing, then it eventually returns.

C_7 : If j.rx(k) is ongoing with endpoint [j,k,ñ,m̂]
            and tsi.rxh[[ñ,m̂]] is not equal to tsi.txh[[m̂,ñ]]
        then eventually j.rx(k) returns.

C_8 : If j.rx(k) is ongoing with endpoint [j,k,ñ,m̂]
            and tsi.rxh[[ñ,m̂]] equals tsi.txh[[m̂,ñ]]
            and [k,j,m̂,ñ] is closing or closed,
        then eventually j.rx(k) returns.

C_9 : If j.close(k) is ongoing with endpoint [j,k,ñ,m̂]
            and [k,j,m̂,ñ] is closing or closed,
        then eventually j.close(k) returns or j.rx(k) is not ongoing.

21.5.2 *Proof of B_1–B_5 and C_1–C_5*

We first establish that program Z satisfies the following.

D_1 : if [j,k,n,m] is passive opening then eventually [j,k,n,m] is opened or rejected.

D_2 : if [j,k,n,m] is opened then eventually [j,k,n,m] is opened.

D_3 : if [j,k,n,m] is active opening and dedicatedAccept(j,k,ñ) holds, then eventually [j,k,n,m] is opened.

Proof of D_1. A passive opening [j,k,n,m] repeatedly sends SCR, to which tp k always
responds with a CRACK or a REJ. Eventually a response is received, at which point
[j,k,n,m] becomes open or rejected, if that has not already happened (e.g., due to
receiving an EDT).   □

Proof of D_2. Suppose [j,k,n,m] opened from passive opening. Hence it received a
CRACK or EDT from [k,j,m,n], which means that [k,j,m,n] has already opened.

Suppose [j,k,n,m] opened from active opening. Hence it received a SCR, CCR, CRACK or EDT from [k,j,m,n]. If CRACK or EDT was received, then [k,j,m,n] has already opened.

Suppose [j,k,n,m] opened from active opening at time t_0 upon receiving SCR, which was sent at some time t_1 where $t_1 < t_0$ holds. At t_1, [k,j,m,n] was passive opening. Let it have become passive opening at t_2. (Note that [k,j,m,n1], for n1 less than n, may have become passive opening earlier; that doesn't matter.) Let [j,k,n,-1] have became active opening at t_3. We have $t_3 < t_2 \leq t_1 < t_0$. So tp j does not send a [REJ,j,k,n,m] while [k,j,m,n] is passive opening. Because [k,j,m,n] repeatedly sends SCR, it eventually gets a CRACK or EDT, at which point it becomes open.

Suppose [j,k,n,m] opened from active opening at time t_0 upon receiving CCR, which was sent at some time t_1 where $t_1 < t_0$ holds. At t_1, [k,j,m,n] was active opening. Let it have become active opening at t_2, and let [k,j,m,-1] have become active opening at t_3. Let [j,k,n,-1] have became active opening at t_4, We have $t_3 < t_2 < t_1$ and $t_4 < t_2$ holding (t_4 may be lower or higher than t_3). So tp j does not send a [REJ,j,k,n,m] while [k,j,m,n] is active opening. Because [k,j,m,n] repeatedly sends CCR, it eventually gets a CRACK or EDT, at which point it becomes open. (Note that if t_3 is less than t_4, it is possible that tp j responded with a [REJ,j,k,m,n1], for some n1 less than n. But tp k did not receive it before t_2, otherwise [k,j,m,n] would not have become active opening. It would be ignored if was received after t_2.)   □

Proof of D_3. Assume [j,k,n,-1] is active opening and k.accept with call id m̂ is dedicated to [j,k,n,-1]. (Recall that the latter means: (1) the k.accept is not canceled; (2) no other client attempts to connect to the k.accept; (3) when [j,k,n,-1] became active opening, the k.accept was ongoing, j.accept was not ongoing, and a [k,j] socket did not exist.)

Case 1. There is a [k,j,x,.] endpoint when the CCR sent by [j,k,n,-1] first arrives at k. Endpoint [k,j,x,.] has to be active or passive opening (because there was no [k,j,.,.] endpoint when [j,k,n,-1] became active opening). The CCR changes the remote number in endpoint [k,j,x,.] to n (because n is higher than whatever was there before). From this point onwards, endpoints [k,j,x,n] and [j,k,n,x] cannot be rejected. So eventually [j,k,n,x] becomes open.

Case 2. There is no [k,j,.,.] endpoint when the first CCR sent by [j,k,n,-1] arrives at k. Then k.ccrBuff[j] is set to n. If this is the earliest entry in ccrBuff, then k.accept creates a passive opening endpoint [k,j,x,n] for some x. Eventually [j,k,n,x] becomes open. If the entry for j is not the earliest one in ccrBuff, then k.accept gets the ccrBuff entry for some other address, say j1, and creates a passive opening endpoint [k,j1,.,.]. This is rejected eventually (because j1 is not attempting to connect to k), at which point k.accept repeats the process. Eventually it gets the entry for j, leading to [j,k,n,.] becoming open.   □

We now prove B_1–B_5 and C_1–C_5.

B_1 holds as follows. Assume B_1's lhs holds. Then j.endServer is ongoing. D_2 implies that openedTo(j,n̂) is false as follows. Suppose some [k,j,m̂,n̂] is opened to [j,n̂]. Then [k,j,q,p] has opened, for some q and p such that [q̂,p̂] equals [m̂,n̂]. Hence [j,k,p,q] eventually opens (by D_2), which means that [j,k,n̂,m̂] eventually opens, which means that j.accept cannot return without an endpoint.

B_2 holds as follows. Assume B_2's lhs holds. Condition overlapped(k,j,m̂,n̂) holds because [j,k,n,m] and [k,j,m,n] were opening simultaneously, in particular, when the latter responded to the former's connect request. Socket [j,k] is not in β.keys because that would mean that endpoint [j,k,p,q] has opened, for some q and p such that [q̂,p̂] equals [m̂,n̂]. In this case, j.accept with call id n̂ would not be ongoing. Condition not openedTo(j,n̂) or opened(k,j,m̂,n̂) holds because of D_2 (as in the proof of B_1).

B_3 holds because tsi.srvr[j] always equals j.srvr, and the latter is true whenever j.accept is ongoing.

B_4 holds as follows. Assume B_4's lhs holds. Condition dedicatedAccept(j,k,n̂) is false because if it were true then that would contradict D_3. Condition openedTo(j,n̂) is false because of D_2 (as in the proof of B_1).

B_5's proof is similar to that of B_2.

C_1 holds as follows. Assume C_1's lhs. Then j.endingSrvr is true. If j.accept is at s1, it will return. If j.accept is at s2, its passive opening endpoint will become open or rejected (by D_1). If open, j.accept returns. If rejected, j.accept goes to s1, which reduces to the previous case.

C_2 holds as follows. Assume C_2's lhs. Then endingSrvr is true. If an accept is ongoing, it will return setting j.accepting false (as in C_1's proof), after which j.endServer returns.

C_3 holds from D_2.

C_5 holds from D_3.

C_4's proof is similar to that of C_5.

21.5.3   Proof of B_6–B_8 and C_6–C_9

Properties B_6–B_8 and C_6–C_9 follow from the properties of the graceful-closing data transfer protocol that is run between connected endpoints. Below, we say "dtp [j,k,n,m]" to mean the dtp system associated with endpoint [j,k,n,m], i.e., system j.dtp[k] when endpoint [j,k,n,m] is open.

Suppose endpoint [j,k,n,m] becomes open. Consider the composite system of dtp [j,k,n,m] and dtp [k,j,m,n]. Any message received by dtp [j,k,n,m] is sent by dtp system [k,j,m,n], because (1) dtpRxQ[k] is empty when dtp [j,k,n,m] is started, (2) while dtp [j,k,n,m] exists, only dtp messages in received [EDT,k,j,m,n,.] messages are added to dtpRxQ[k], and (3) such dtp messages are sent only by dtp [k,j,m,n]. Thus the composite system of dtp [j,k,n,m] and dtp [k,j,m,n] interact with its environment in exactly the same way as if they were connected by a dedicated

LRD channel that is initially empty. Thus program Z satisfies the properties A_1–A_5 (in Sect. 21.2), with j.drxh renamed to tsi.rxh[[ñ,m̂]], and j.dtxh renamed to tsi.txh[[ñ,m̂]], and so on.

Let E_1–E_7 be the assertions A_1–A_7 renamed in this fashion. For concreteness, E_1 and E_4 are given below.

E_1 : if dtp [j,k,n,m]'s rx returns [0,data]
    then tsi.rxh[[ñ,m̂]] ∘ [data] is a prefix of tsi.txh[[m̂,ñ]].
E_4 : if dtp [j,k,n,m]'s tx is ongoing then eventually it returns.

Note that E_1 implies B_6; in fact, it is almost identical to B_6. Similarly, E_2 implies B_7 and E_3 implies B_8. The story is the same for the progress assertions. E_4 implies C_6. E_5 implies C_7. E_6 implies C_8. E_7 implies C_9. Thus Z satisfies B_6–B_8 and C_6–C_9. We are done.

21.6 Using Cyclic Incarnation Numbers

We now refine the transport protocol to use modulo-N endpoint numbers instead of unbounded endpoint numbers. We show that it suffices if

$$N \geq \frac{6L + 4W + 2C}{\delta}$$

where L is the maximum message lifetime of the LRD channel, δ is the minimum time interval between endpoint creations at an address (i.e., maximum rate at which nGen increases), W is the maximum opening duration of an endpoint, and C is the maximum open duration of an endpoint. The need for the L and δ constraints should be obvious based on our experience with the sliding window protocol (Chap. 5). It turns out that the W and C constraints are needed because a tp system maintains information about a remote tp system only while opening or open to it. The dependency on C can be dispensed with if one is willing to accept correctness with a high probability (order of $1 - (1/N^2)$) rather than with certainty. In this case, simply set C to zero in the above expression.

The crucial step in using cyclic endpoint numbers is to come up with bounds on the unbounded endpoint numbers in the LRD channel relative to values stored in the receiver (just as with the sliding window protocol). Consider a message [.,k,j,m,n] received by tp j. System tp j uses the endpoint numbers m and n in the following ways only: store m in j.ccrBuff[k]; compare m and n to j.rn[k] and j.ln[k]; and store m in j.rn[k]. The possible comparison tests in program Tp (all are in the message handler functions) are shown in Fig. 21.8.

Conventions. We use "|" to denote a range of values for a message field; e.g., [CCR|SCR,k,j,m,n] denotes a [CCR,k,j,m,n] or [SCR,k,j,m,n] message. We use "[X,k,j,m,n]" to denote a [.,k,j,m,n] message or a [EDT,k,j,m,n,.] message. When

Message	Receiving endpoint	Possible tests
[CCR|SCR,k,j,m,n]	[opening,$\tilde{n}$,$\tilde{m}$]	$n = \tilde{n}$; $m > \tilde{m}$; $m >$ ccrBuff[k]
[CCR|SCR,k,j,m,n]	[open,$\tilde{n}$,$\tilde{m}$]	$m = \tilde{m}$; $n = \tilde{n}$; $m > \tilde{m}$
[CRACK|REJ,k,j,m,n]	[opening,$\tilde{n}$,$\tilde{m}$]	$m = \tilde{m}$; $n = \tilde{n}$
[EDT,k,j,m,n,.]	[opening or open,$\tilde{n}$,$\tilde{m}$]	$m = \tilde{m}$; $n = \tilde{n}$

Fig. 21.8 Possible tests involving received endpoint numbers. "Opening" is short for "active or passive opening"

analyzing the reception of a [X,k,j,m,n] message, we use $\tilde{n}$ and $\tilde{m}$ to denote the local and remote numbers of tp j's endpoint for k (if it exists). Parameters $\tilde{n}$, $\tilde{m}$, m and n do not take a value of –1 unless stated otherwise explicitly. *End of conventions.*

To use modulo-N endpoint numbers, it suffices to find equivalent tests that can work with the modulo-N values rather than the unbounded values (other than –1). We can do this for the tests involving m if we can find a bound K such that m lies within K of $\tilde{m}$, i.e., $K \leq m - \tilde{m} \leq K$ is invariant. Let N be greater than $2K$. Then test $m = \tilde{m}$ is equivalent to $\text{mod}(m,N) = \text{mod}(\tilde{m},N)$, and test $m > \tilde{m}$ is equivalent to $1 \leq \text{mod}(m-\tilde{m},N) \leq K$. Similarly, for the tests involving n we would need n to lie within some K of $\tilde{n}$. We obtain these bounds by exploiting the fact that m and $\tilde{m}$ originate from k.nGen, and n and $\tilde{n}$ originate from j.nGen.

We start by establishing the invariance of predicates $F_1 - F_6$ below.

F_1 : ([j,k,$\tilde{n}$,$\tilde{m}$] exists) $\Rightarrow$ $\tilde{m} \leq$ k.nGen
F_2 : ([j,k,$\tilde{n}$,$\tilde{m}$] exists) and ([.,k,j,m,n] receivable) $\Rightarrow$ $m \leq$ k.nGen
F_3 : ([j,k,$\tilde{n}$,$\tilde{m}$] exists) $\Rightarrow$ $\tilde{n} \leq$ j.nGen
F_4 : ([j,k,$\tilde{n}$,$\tilde{m}$] exists) and ([.,k,j,m,n] receivable) $\Rightarrow$ $n \leq \tilde{n}$
F_5 : ([j,k,$\tilde{n}$,$\tilde{m}$] opening) $\Rightarrow$ k.nGen $\leq \tilde{m} + (L+2W)/\delta$
F_6 : ([j,k,$\tilde{n}$,$\tilde{m}$] open) $\Rightarrow$ k.nGen $\leq \tilde{m} + (C+L+2W)/\delta$

Proof of Inv. $F_1 - F_6$

Inv F_1 holds because $\tilde{m}$ is a past or current value of k.nGen and the latter is non-decreasing. Inv F_2 holds because m is a past or current value of k.nGen and the latter is non-decreasing.

Inv F_3 holds because $\tilde{n}$ is a past or current value of k.nGen and the latter is non-decreasing. Inv F_4 holds because n is a past or current value of k.nGen and $\tilde{n}$ is the highest value of k.nGen sent to k.

Inv F_5 holds as follows. Let the current time be t_0. Endpoint $\tilde{n}$ started after $t_0 - W$ (because an opening duration is at most W). So j received a [CCR,k,j,$\tilde{m}$,.] message after $t_0 - W$. That message was sent after $t_0 - W - L$ when endpoint $\tilde{m}$ was opening (because the message lifetime is at most L). So endpoint $\tilde{m}$ started after

$t_0 - W - L - W$, and $\widetilde{m}$ equaled $k.\text{nGen}$ then. So $\widetilde{m} \geq k.\text{nGen} - (W + L + W)/\delta$ (because $k.\text{nGen}$ increases at most once every δ). The latter is equivalent to F_5's rhs.

$Inv\,F_6$ holds as follows. Endpoint $\widetilde{n}$ changed from opening to open at some point t_1, where $t_1 > t_0 - C$ (because an open duration is at most C). Thus $\widetilde{m} \geq k.\text{nGen} - (L + 2W)/\delta$ held at t_1 (from F_5). Between t_1 and t_0, $k.\text{nGen}$ increases by at most C/δ, leading to F_6.   □

Next we establish the invariance of predicates G_1–G_8 below. The combination of message and endpoint status covered in G_3–G_8 correspond to those in Fig. 21.8.

G_1 : ([j,k,$\widetilde{n}$,$\widetilde{m}$] opening) and ([.,k,j,m,n] receivable)
$\qquad \Rightarrow \quad$ ($m = -1$ or $\widetilde{m} = -1$ or $m \leq \widetilde{m} + (L + 2W)/\delta$)

G_2 : ([j,k,$\widetilde{n}$,$\widetilde{m}$] open) and ([.,k,j,m,n] receivable)
$\qquad \Rightarrow \quad m \leq \widetilde{m} + (C + L + 2W)/\delta$

G_3 : ([j,k,$\widetilde{n}$,$\widetilde{m}$] opening or open) and ([CCR|SCR,k,j,m,n] receivable)
$\qquad \Rightarrow \quad m \geq \widetilde{m} - (L + W)/\delta$
$\qquad\qquad$ and $n \geq \widetilde{n} - (2L + 2W)/\delta$

G_5 : ([j,k,$\widetilde{n}$,$\widetilde{m}$] opening) and ([CRACK,k,j,m,n] receivable)
$\qquad \Rightarrow \quad m \geq \widetilde{m} - (2L + 2W)/\delta$
$\qquad\qquad$ and $n \geq \widetilde{n} - (2L + W)/\delta$

G_6 : ([j,k,$\widetilde{n}$,$\widetilde{m}$] opening) and ([REJ,k,j,m,n] receivable)
$\qquad \Rightarrow \quad m \geq \widetilde{m} - (3L + 2W)/\delta$
$\qquad\qquad$ and $n \geq \widetilde{n} - (2L + W)/\delta$

G_7 : ([j,k,$\widetilde{n}$,$\widetilde{m}$] opening or open) and ([EDT,k,j,m,n,.] receivable)
$\qquad \Rightarrow \quad m \geq \widetilde{m} - (L + C + W)/\delta$
$\qquad\qquad$ and $n \geq \widetilde{n} - (L + C + 2W)/\delta$

Proof of Inv. G_1–G_8

$Inv\,G_1$ holds because G_1 follows from F_2 and F_5. $Inv\,G_2$ holds because G_2 follows from F_2 and F_5.

$Inv\,G_3$ holds as follows. Let the current time be t_0. Message [CCR|SCR,k,j,m,n] was sent after $t_0 - L$ by opening endpoint [k,j,m,n]. So endpoint m started at t_1 where $t_1 > t_0 - L - W$, yielding $m \geq k.\text{nGen} - (L + W)/\delta$. This and $k.\text{nGen} \geq \widetilde{m}$ (from F_1) yield $m \geq \widetilde{m} - (L + W)/\delta$, which is G_3's bound on m. Assume $n \neq -1$. So k received message [CCR|SCR,j,k,n,.] after t_1 ($> t_0 - L - W$). So endpoint n started after $t_1 - L - W$, i.e., after $t_0 - L - W - L - W$, yielding $n \geq j.\text{nGen} - (2L + 2W)/\delta$. This and $j.\text{nGen} \geq \widetilde{n}$ (from F_2) yield $n \geq \widetilde{n} - (2L + 2W)/\delta$, which is G_3's bound on n.

$Inv\,G_5$ holds as follows. Let the current time be t_0. Message [CRACK,k,j,m,n] was sent after $t_0 - L$ by open endpoint [k,j,m,n], in response to a [CCR|SCR,j,k,n,m] message, which was sent after $t_0 - L - L$ by an opening endpoint [j,k,n,m]. So the latter endpoint started after $t_0 - L - L - W$, which yields $n \geq j.\text{nGen} - (2L + W)/\delta$. This and F_3 yield $n \geq \widetilde{n} - (2L + W)/\delta$, which is G_5's bound on n. Now for the bound on m. Because endpoint [j,k,n,m] started after $t_0 - L - L - W$, endpoint [k,j,m,n] became open after $t_0 - L - L - W$, and so m started after $t_0 - L - L - W - W$, yielding $m \geq k.\text{nGen} - (2L + 2W)/\delta$. This and $k.\text{nGen} \geq \widetilde{m}$ (from F_1) yields $m \geq \widetilde{m} - (2L + 2W)/\delta$, which is G_5's lower bound on m.

Old test	New test
m = rn[k]	no change
n = ln[k]	no change
m > ccrBuff[k]	$1 \leq \mathrm{mod}(m - \mathrm{ccrBuff[al]}) \leq N/2$
m > rn[k]	(rn[k] = -1 and m ≠ -1)
	or $1 \leq \mathrm{mod}(m - rn[k]) \leq N/2$

Fig. 21.9 Modulo-N versions of tests involving received endpoint numbers

Inv G_6 holds as follows. Let the current time be t_0. Message [REJ,k,j,m,n] was sent after $t_0 - L$ when k was not in server mode nor active opening to j, in response to [CCR|SCR,j,k,n,m]. So the latter message was sent after $t_0 - 2L$. So endpoint [j,k,n,.] was started after $t_0 - 2L - W$, which yields $n \geq j.\mathrm{nGen} - (2L + W)/\delta$. This and F_3 yield $n \geq \tilde{n} - (2L + W)/\delta$, which is G_6's bound on n. Now for the bound on m. Because endpoint [j,k,n,m] started after $t_0 - 2L - W$ and it learned of m through a CCR or SCR message, endpoint m was started after $L + W$ before that. i.e., after $t_0 - 3L - 2W$, yielding $m \geq k.\mathrm{nGen} - (3L + 2W)/\delta$. This and F_1 yield $m \geq \tilde{m} - (3L + 2W)/\delta$, which is G_6's bound on m.

Inv G_7 holds as follows. Let the current time be t_0. Message [EDT,k,j,m,n,.] was sent after $t_0 - L$ by open endpoint [k,j,m,n], so m started after $t_0 - L - C - W$, yielding $m \geq k.\mathrm{nGen} - (L + C + W)/\delta$. This and F_1 yield $m \geq \tilde{m} - (L + C + W)/\delta$, which is G_7's bound on m. Now for the bound on n. Because m started after $t_0 - L - C - W$, endpoint n started after $t_0 - L - C - W - W$, yielding $n \geq j.\mathrm{nGen} - (L + C + 2W)/\delta$, which is G_7's bound on n. □

From the above invariants we get the following bounds in the context of endpoint [j,k,$\tilde{n}$,$\tilde{m}$] and receivable [.,k,j,m,n], assuming that no $\tilde{m}$, m and n equals −1.

$H_1 : \quad m \leq \tilde{m} + (C + L + 2W)/\delta$ (from G_1, G_2)

$H_2 : \quad m \geq \tilde{m} - \max(3L + 2W, L + C + W)/\delta$ (from G_3–G_7)

$H_3 : \quad n \leq \tilde{n}$ (from F_4)

$H_4 : \quad n \geq \tilde{n} - \max(2L + 2W, L + C + 2W)/\delta$ (from G_3–G_7)

$H_5 : \quad -\max(3L + 2W, L + C + W)/\delta \leq m - \tilde{m} \leq (C + L + 2W)/\delta$ (from H_1, H_2)

$H_6 : \quad -\max(2L + 2W, L + C + 2W)/\delta \leq n - \tilde{n} \leq \tilde{n}$ (from H_3, H_4)

$H_7 : \quad K \leq m - \tilde{m}, n - \tilde{n} \leq K$, where $K = (3L + 2W + C)/\delta$ (from H_5, H_6)

21.6.1   Program Tp with Modulo-N Endpoint Numbers

Modify program Tp (in Figs. 21.10–21.16) as follows.

- Let N be any integer higher than $(6L + 4W + 2C)/\delta$ (twice K in H_7).

- Endpoint numbers in messages and in variables (i.e., 1n and rn) now take values from -1..N-1.
- *Optional*: Variable nGen now takes values from 0..N-1, with increments done modulo-N.
- The tests involving these values are changed as shown in Fig. 21.9.

21.7 Conclusion

We have presented a protocol that implements the reliable transport service of Chap. 20. Like TCP, our protocol executes a three-way handshake for client-server connection establishment, and two 2-way handshakes for client-client connection establishment and for connection termination. It stores information of a remote tp only while opening or open to it (Fig. 21.9).

Unlike TCP, our protocol's connect request message also indicates whether the sender is active opening or passive opening; TCP does not convey this extra bit of information and as a result has a serious flaw: old messages in the channel can cause two *accepting* users to become connected to each other [3].

Also unlike TCP, our protocol has a clean separation between connection establishment and data transfer. TCP uses a single 32-bit cyclic sequence number space to identify both endpoints and data blocks. When an endpoint is created, it is assigned an **initial sequence number**. Successive new primary messages sent by the endpoint, whether of connection-management or data-transfer, occupy increasing sequence numbers starting from this initial sequence number. In particular, if an endpoint sends a primary connection-management message (that has no data), the message is assigned sequence number $n + 1$, where n is the highest sequence number sent thus far by the endpoint.

A preliminary version of this protocol, one using unbounded endpoint numbers, was specified and verified in [3]. The service considered there was different from the one here in that endpoint numbers were visible to the users and returns were modeled as output functions.

The three-way handshake for connection establishment is necessary because a tp system maintains information about a remote tp system only while it is opening or open to it. A two-way handshake would suffice if a tp system retains information about remote clients even when it is not connected to them. To illustrate, suppose server tp system x remembers the endpoint number, say m_1, that a remote client y had used when it was previously open to x. Now if x receives a connect request from y with endpoint number m_1, it can become immediately open to m_1 if m_1 is higher than n_1. A server cannot be expected to indefinitely remember the last endpoint number of every client to which it was connected, due to the enormous number of clients in a typical network. However, a caching scheme is feasible and has been proposed as a TCP extension [1,9]. Transport protocols with such cacheing schemes (and using cyclic endpoint numbers) have been specified and verified in [4–6, 8].

Exercises

21.1. Modify program Tp so that it disallows client–client connections. Does this significantly simplify the program?

21.2. Modify program Tp so that it informs a user when its endpoint has been aborted.

21.3. Extend program Tp with aborts. Specifically, a tp system should abort an endpoint if a response is not received to a primary message after K retransmissions.

(Hint: Have the returns of your functions distinguish between closing (or rejection) and abort. Use the abortable dtp program and service developed in Exercises 5.12 and 5.11.)

21.4. Refine your solution to Exercise 21.3 to use modulo-N endpoint numbers.

References

1. R. Braden, T/TCP–TCP extensions for transactions functional specification. Technical Report, RFC 1644, Internet Engineering Task Force, 1994. http://tools.ietf.org/html/rfc1644
2. D. Comer, *Principles, Protocols, and Architectures*. Internetworking with TCP/IP, vol. 1, 4th edn. (Prentice-Hall, Englewood Cliffs, 2000)
3. S.L. Murphy, A.U. Shankar, Connection management for the transport layer: service specification and protocol verification. IEEE Trans. Commun. **39**(12), 1762–1775 (1991). doi:10.1109/26.120163. Earlier version in *Proceedings ACM SIGCOMM '87 Workshop*, Stowe, Vermont, August, 1987
4. A.L. Oláh, Design and analysis of transport protocols for reliable high-speed communications. Ph.D. thesis, University of Twente, Enschede, 1997. http://doc.utwente.nl/13676/
5. A.L. Oláh, S.M. Heemstra de Groot, Comments on "minimum-latency transport protocols with modulo-n incarnation numbers". IEEE/ACM Trans. Netw. **4**(4), 660–666 (1996). doi:http://dx.doi.org/10.1109/90.532874
6. A.L. Oláh, S.M.H.d. Groot, Assertional verification of a connection management protocol, in *Proceedings of the IFIP TC6 Eighth International Conference on Formal Description Techniques VIII* (Chapman & Hall, Ltd., London, 1996), pp. 401–416. http://dl.acm.org/citation.cfm?id=646214.681518
7. J. Postel, Transmission control protocol: protocol specification. Technical Report, RFC 793, Internet Engineering Task Force, 1981. http://www.ietf.org/rfc/rfc793.txt
8. A.U. Shankar, D. Lee, Minimum-latency transport protocols with modulo-n incarnation numbers. IEEE/ACM Trans. Netw. **3**(3), 255–268 (1995). doi:10.1109/90.392385. http://dx.doi.org/10.1109/90.392385
9. M. Stacey, I. Griffin, J. Nelson, T/TCP: TCP for transactions. Linux J. **70**, (2000). http://www.linuxjournal.com/article/3075
10. W.R. Stevens, *Networking APIs: Sockets and XTI*. UNIX Network Programming, vol. 1, 2nd edn. (Prentice-Hall, Upper Saddle River, 1998). Chapter 4, ISBN 0-13-490012-X

```
program Tp(Set ADDR, ADDR aL, Sid cL) {
   ic {ADDR.size ≥ 1}

   // message types
   CCR = 1; SCR = 2; CRACK = 3; REJ = 4;
   EDT = 5; FIN = 6; FINACK = 7;
   // active opening, passive opening, rejected, open
   AOPN = 1; POPN = 2; RJCT = 3; OPEN = 4;

   boolean srvr ← false;           // server mode
   boolean acptng ← false;         // accept ongoing
   int nGen ← 0;                   // endpoint number generator
   Map ccrBuff ← map();            // ccrBuff[k] is SCR endpoint number
                                   //    (in server mode)
   Map st ← map();                 // endpoint status
   Map ln ← map();                 // endpoint local number
   Map rn ← map();                 // endpoint remote number
   Map dtp ← map();                // dtp[k]: sid of dtp system for k
   Map dtpRxQ ← map();             // dtpRxQ[k]: msg rx queue for dtp[k]
   Tid tRx ← startThread(doRx());
   return mysid;

// continued
```

Fig. 21.10 Program Tp: part 1

```
// Tp continued

    input Seq mysid.accept() {
        ia {not ongoing(mysid.accept)}
        srvr ← true;                            // enter/stay in server mode
        acptng ← true;
        while (true) {                          // exit loop via return
  s1:   • await (not srvr or ccrBuff.size > 0) {
                if (not srvr) {
                    acptng ← false;
                    return [];
                    return [[],0,0];  // replaces above return in program Z
                }
                k ← ccrBuff.earliestKey();    // get key of earliest ccrBuff entry
                st[k] ← POPN;                 // create passive-opening endpoint
                ln[k] ← nGen; nGen ← nGen+1;
                rn[k] ← ccrBuff[k];
                ccrBuff.remove(k);
                // executed in program Z
                γ[[aL,ln[k]]] ← tsi.doAccept(aL).n; // accept call id
            }
            while (true)                        // exit loop via return or break
  s2:       • await (true)                      // Note: • is required
                if (st[k] = POPN)
                    cL.tx(k, [SCR,aL,k,n,rn[k]]);
                else if (st[k] = OPEN) {
                    acptng ← false;
                    return [k];
                    return [[k],k,γ[[k,rn[k]]]];   // replaces above return in Z
                } else { // st[k] = RJCT
                    st.remove(k); ln.remove(k); ln.remove(k);
                    acptng ← false;
                    break;
                }
    }

// continued
```

Fig. 21.11 Program Tp: part 2

```
// Tp continued

    input void mysid.endServer() {
       ia {srvr}
       await (true)
          srvr ← false;
          for (k in ccrBuff.keys)                    // reject buffered requests
             cL.tx(k, [REJ,aL,k,ccrBuff[k]],-1);
          ccrBuff ← [];                              // empty buffer
s1: • await (not acptng)
          return;
    }

    input Seq mysid.connect(ADDR k) {
       ia {not (k in st.keys)}
       await (true) {
          st[k] ← AOPN;                              // create active-opening endpoint
          ln[k] ← nGen; nGen ← nGen+1;
          rn[k] ← -1;
          ┌─────────────────────────────────────────────────────────────────┐
          │ // executed in program Z                                         │
          │ γ[[aL,ln[k]]] ← tsi.doConnect(aL,k).n; // connect call id        │
          └─────────────────────────────────────────────────────────────────┘
       }
       while (true)                             // exit loop via return
 s1:   • await (true)                           // Note: • is required
             if (st[k] = AOPN)
                cL.tx(k, [CCR,aL,k,n,rn[k]]);
             else if (st[k] = OPEN)
                return [k];
                ┌────────────────────────────────────────────────────────────┐
                │ return [[k],γ[[k,rn[k]]]]; // replaces above return in Z     │
                └────────────────────────────────────────────────────────────┘
             else { // st[k] = RJCT
                st.remove(k); ln.remove(k); ln.remove(k);
                return [];
                ┌──────────────────────────────────────────────────────┐
                │ return [[],0,0]; // replaces above return in Z        │
                └──────────────────────────────────────────────────────┘
          }
    }

    input void mysid.tx(ADDR k, Seq data) {
       ia {(k in st.keys) and st[k] = OPEN}
       dtp[k].tx(k,data);
       return;
    }

// continued
```

Fig. 21.12 Program Tp: part 3

```
// Tp continued

  input Seq mysid.rx(ADDR k) {
     ia {(k in st.keys) and st[k] = OPEN}
  • Seq rval ← dtp[k].rx();
s1: return rval;                          // rval: [0,data] or [-1]
  }


  input void mysid.close(ADDR k) {
     ia {(k in st.keys) and st[k] = OPEN}
  • dtp[k].close();
s1: dtp.remove(k);
     dtpRxQ.remove(k);
     return;
  }


  input void mysid.dTx(ADDR k, Seq dtmsg) { // called by system dtp[k]
     ia {(k in st.keys) and st[k] = OPEN}
     await (true)
        cL.tx(k, [EDT,aL,k,ln[k],rn[k],dtmsg]);
     return;
  }


  input Seq mysid.dRx(ADDR k) {            // called by system dtp[k]
     ia {(k in st.keys) and st[k] = OPEN}
  • await (dtpRxQ[k].size > 0) {
        Seq dtmsg ← dtpRxQ[k][0];
        dtpRxQ[k].remove(0);
        return dtmsg;
     }
  }


//continued
```

Fig. 21.13 Program Tp: part 4

// Tp continued

```
function void doRx() {  // executed by local thread tRx
   while (true) {
   • Seq msg ← cL.rx();
      ic {(msg in Tuple<set(CCR,SCR,CRACK,REJ),ADDR,ADDR,int,int>)
            or (msg in Tuple<EDT,ADDR,ADDR,int,int,Seq>)}
      // k, m, n: sender addr, sender number, rcvr number
      Val [k,m,n] ← msg[1,3,4];
      await (true)
         if (msg[0] = CCR)
            handleCCR(k,m,n);
         else if (msg[0] = SCR)
            handleSCR(k,m,n);
         else if (msg[0] = CRACK)
            handleCRACK(k,m,n);
         else if (msg[0] = REJ)
            handleREJ(k,m,n);
         else if (msg[0] = EDT)
            handleEDT(k,m,n,msg[5]);
   }
}


// helper function: start dtp system and dtp rx queue for k
function void startDtp(ADDR k) {
   dtp[k] ← startSystem(GcDtp(aL,k,mysid,...));
   dtpRxQ[k] ← [];
}
```

//continued

Fig. 21.14 Program Tp: part 5

```
// Tp continued

    // helper function: handle received [CCR,k,aL,m,n]
    function void handleCCR(k, m, n) {
        if (not (k in st.keys)) {
            if (not srvr)
                cL.tx(k, [REJ,aL,k,n,m]);
            else if (not (k in ccrBuff.keys) or ccrBuff[k] < m)
                ccrBuff[k] ← m;
        }
        else if (st[k] = AOPN and n = ln[k]) {
            st[k] ← OPEN; rn[k] ← m;
            startDtp(k);
            cL.tx(k, [CRACK,aL,k,n,m]);
        }
        else if (st[k] = POPN and m > rn[k])
            rn[j] ← m;
        else if (st[k] = OPEN)
            if ([m,n] = [rn[k],ln[k]])
                cL.tx(k, [CRACK,aL,k,n,m]);
            else if (m > rn[j])
                cL.tx(k, [REJ,aL,k,n,m]);
                // optional: dtpRxQ[k].append([FINACK]);
    }

    // helper function: handle received [SCR,k,aL,m,n]
    function void handleSCR(k, m, n) {
        if (not (k in st.keys))
            cL.tx(k, [REJ,aL,k,n,m]);
        else if (st[k] = AOPN and n = ln[k]) {
            st[k] ← OPEN; rn[k] ← m;
            startDtp(k);
            cL.tx(k, [CRACK,aL,k,n,m]);
        }
        else if (st[k] = POPN and m > rn[k])
            cL.tx(k, [REJ,aL,k,n,m]);
        else if (st[k] = OPEN)
            if ([m,n] = [rn[k],ln[k]])
                cL.tx(k, [CRACK,aL,k,n,m]);
            else if (m > rn[k])
                cL.tx(k, [REJ,aL,k,n,m]);
                // optional: dtpRxQ[k].append([FINACK]);
    }

// continued
```

Fig. 21.15 Program Tp: part 6

```
// Tp continued

    // helper function: handle received [CRACK,k,aL,m,n]
    function void handleCRACK(k, m, n) {
        if ((k in st.keys) and [n,m] = [ln[k],rn[k]]
            and (st[k] = AOPN or st[k] = POPN))
            st[k] ← OPEN;
            startDtp(k);
    }


    // helper function: handle received [REJ,k,aL,m,n]
    function void handleREJ(j, k, n, m) {
        if ((k in st.keys) and [n,m] = [ln[k],rn[k]]
            and (st[k] = AOPN or st[k] = POPN))
            st[k] ← RJCT;
    }


    // helper function: handle received [EDT,k,aL,m,n,dtmsg]
    function void handleEDT(k, m, n, dtmsg) {
        if (not (k in st.keys)) {
            if (dtmsg = [FIN])
                cL.tx(k, [EDT,aL,k,n,m,[FINACK]]);
        }
        else if ((st[k] = AOPN or st[k] = POPN)
                and [n,m] = [ln[k],rn[k]]) {
            st[k] ← OPEN;
            startDtp(k);
            dtpRxQ[k].append(dtmsg);
        }
        else if ([n,m] = [ln[k],rn[k]] and st[k] = OPEN)
            dtpRxQ[k].append(dtmsg);
    }


    atomicity assumption {await}

    progress assumption {weak fairness of all threads}
} // Tp
```

Fig. 21.16 Program Tp: part 7

Appendix A
Conventions

A.1 Predicates and Assertions

Predicates A predicate is a boolean-valued expression constructed from

- Boolean-valued terms (typically involving program quantities).
- Propositional operators (in order of decreasing binding strength):
  not, and, or, $\Rightarrow$ (implies), $\Leftrightarrow$ (iff), OR (non-short-circuited or).
- Quantifiers: forall, forsome, forone.

Short-circuiting The propositional operators and, or and $\Rightarrow$ are "short-circuit" evaluated from left to right; e.g., when evaluating "A and B", first A is evaluated and then B is evaluated iff A is true.

Lhs and rhs For predicates of the form $A \Rightarrow B$ and $A \Leftrightarrow B$ and assertions of the form A *leads-to* B, we refer to A as the "lhs" (left-hand side) and to B as the "rhs" (right-hand side). (In particular, we do not use "antecedent" and "consequent" for predicates of the form $A \Rightarrow B$.)

Quantified predicates The quantified predicates are as follows, where x is a parameter, D is the type or set of values over which x ranges, and Q is a predicate (usually involving x).

- forall(x in D: Q): true iff every value of x in D satisfies Q. Evaluates to true if D is empty.
- forsome(x in D: Q): true iff at least one value of x in D satisfies Q. Evaluates to false if D is empty.
- forone(x in D: Q): true iff exactly one value of x in D satisfies Q. Evaluates to false if D is empty.

Don't-care value "." We use "." as a "don't-care" value to abbreviate the writing of predicates. Let predicate P contain a "." and let R denote the smallest predicate in P containing the ".". Then P is equivalent to P with with R replaced by forsome(x:R). For example,

A.U. Shankar, *Distributed Programming: Theory and Practice*,
DOI 10.1007/978-1-4614-4881-5,
© Springer Science+Business Media New York 2013

- ([1,.] in S) is equivalent to forsome(x: [1,x] in S).
- (thread in f(a,.)), where f(.,.) is a function with two parameters, is equivalent to forsome(x: thread in f(a,x)).
- (not ([1,.] in S)) is equivalent to (not forsome(x: [1,x] in S)).
  (It is not equivalent to forsome(x: not [1,x] in S), because quantification is over the minimal predicate enclosing the ".".)

A.2   Referencing System Quantities

We use s.x to refer to a quantity x of a system whose instantiation returned the value s, i.e., the instantiated program's main code returned s. This uniquely identifies the system because s is required to contain an sid generated in the main code.

If x is a quantity specific to a thread t in the system, e.g., a local variable of a function, then use s.t.x to refer to the quantity.

A.3   Types

Types as sets The construct "X y", where X is a type (e.g., Seq<int>), defines y to be a new variable of type X. Types can be treated as sets for membership predicates. Thus "y in X", where X is a type and y is a variable, parameter or expression, is a predicate that is true iff y's value is of type X. This can also be stated as X(y).

Containers as types Sets, bags and sequences can be treated as types for defining variables and for denoting the allowed values of pre-defined variables. Let X be a set or bag or sequence. Then "X y" defines y to be a new variable that takes values from X. The predicate "y in X" can also be written as X(y).

A.4   Sids

The type Sid denotes sids (system ids); they are pointers to systems. Every system has a unique (non-null) sid. Every (non-null) sid z has an attribute z.alive that is true iff system z (i.e., a system with sid z) has been created and not yet terminated.

- Sid x: defines variable x with the value null, and constrains it to take an sid value or null.
- startSystem(P(.)), where P is a program: instantiates P(.) and returns its (unique non-null) sid.
- sid(): returns an sid that is non-null and not alive (i.e., not pointing to a system).
- sid(z), where z is an integer or character string: returns a non-null not-alive sid with value z if it is not currently allocated; otherwise it returns null.

For notational convenience, we assume that the state of a system z is available for writing assertions even after z has been terminated; this allows us, for example, to shorten "z.alive and (thread in z.f)" to "thread in z.f".

A.5   Tids

The type Tid denotes tids (thread ids); they are pointers to threads. Every thread has a unique (non-null) tid. Every (non-null) tid z has an attribute z.alive that is true iff thread z (i.e., a thread with sid z) has been created and not yet terminated.

- Tid x: defines variable x with the value null, and constrains it to take a tid value or null.
- startThread(f(.)), where f is a function: creates a thread, starts it executing f(.), and returns its (unique non-null) tid.
- tid(): returns a non-null not-alive tid.
- tid(z), where z is an integer or character string: returns a non-null not-alive tid with value z if it is not currently allocated; otherwise it returns null.

Predicates in threads   In the following constructs, t is a non-null alive tid and S is a statement or code chunk.

- thread t in S: true iff thread t is inside S.
- thread in S: true iff some thread is inside S.
- not (thread in S): true iff no thread is in S.

In these constructs, "in" can be replaced by "at" to denote that the thread is at the start of S, and by "on" to denote that the thread is at or in S. We also have the following abbreviation.

- ongoing(S): same as (thread in S).

A.6   Sets

The type Set denotes sets. A set is a collection of values where duplicates are not distinguished. The type Set<U> denotes sets whose entries are of type U. For a set x:

- x.size is the number of entries in x.
- x.add(m) adds m to x.
- x.remove(m) removes m from x if m is in x and otherwise has no affect on x.

Set constructor set(...)   The construct set($e_1, \cdots, e_n$: x in Z; P), where

Z is a type or set or bag or sequence,
x is a parameter,

P is a predicate which can involve x, and

each e_i is an expression which can involve x,

denotes the set of values of $e_1, \cdots, e_n$ for x ranging over the entries of Z such that P holds. If P is missing, it is taken as true. For example,

- set() is the empty set.
- set(0,4,2) is the set {0,4,2}.
- set(0,4,4,2,0) is the set {0,4,2}.
- set(2*i: i in 0..4; mod(i,2) = 0) is the set {0,4,8}.
- set(2*i, 3: i in 0..4; mod(i,2) = 0) is the set {0,3,4,8}.

Operators on sets

- A\B, where A and B are sets, returns A minus B, i.e., set(x: x in A, not x in B).
- union(...) takes a list of sets as its argument and returns their union.
- disjoint(...) takes a list of sets as its argument and returns true iff the sets are disjoint.

A.7 Bags

The type Bag denotes bags. A bag is like a set except that duplicates are distinguished. The type Bag<U> denotes bags whose entries are of type U. For a bag x,

- x.size is the number of entries in x.
- x.add(m) adds m to x.
- x.remove(m) removes one instance of m from x if m is in x and otherwise has no affect on x.

The construct bag($e_1, \cdots, e_n$: x in Z; P) is analogous to set($e_1, \cdots, e_n$: x in Z; P). For example,

- bag(2*i, 3: i in 0..4; mod(i,2) = 0) is the bag {0,3,4,3,8,3}.

The construct "A\B" denotes bag A minus bag B, i.e., for each instance of an entry x in B, an instance, if present, of x in A is removed. For example,

- bag(1,1,1,1,2,3)\bag(1,1,3) equals bag(1,1,2).

A.8 Sequences

The type Seq denotes sequences. A sequence is a list of entries. The type Seq<U> denotes sequences whose elements are of type U. For a sequence x:

- x.size is the number of items in x.
- x[j] is the jth entry in x, with x[0] being the head.

- x.last is the last entry in the sequence, i.e., x[x.size-1].
- x.keys is the sequence of indices of x, i.e., the sequence 0, $\cdots$, x.size-1.
- x.append(m) appends m to the tail of x.
- x.remove() removes the entry at the head of x; it has no effect if x is empty.
- x.remove(k) removes the entry x[k]; it has no effect if k is not in x.keys. (Thus x.remove(0) is the same as x.remove().)
- x.keyOf(y) returns x.size if y is not in x, and otherwise returns the first position of y in x.

The construct $[e_1, \cdots, e_n$: x in Z; P] is analogous to bag($e_1, \cdots, e_n$: x in Z; P) except that Z must be a sequence. The order of the constructed sequence is defined by the order of Z and the order of the expressions $e_1, \cdots, e_n$. For example,

- [] is the empty sequence.
- [2,3,1] is the sequence with 2 at the head and 1 at the tail.
- [2*i: i in 0..4; mod(i,2) = 0] equals [0,4,8].
- [2*i, 3: i in 0..4; mod(i,2) = 0] equals [0,3,4,3,8,3].

The construct j..k, where j and k are integers, is the sequence of integers j,j+1, $\cdots$, k; it is empty if j exceeds k. Thus x.keys and 0..x.size-1 are the same, for a sequence x.

Given a sequence x, the following yield subsequences of x.

- x[j..k]: the sequence [x[i]: i in x.keys, i in j..k].
  Note that x[j..j], for j in x.keys, is [x[j]] and not x[j].
- x[$j_1, j_2, \cdots, j_n$], for n $\geq$ 2: the sequence [x[i]: i in x.keys, i in [$j_1, j_2, \cdots, j_n$]].

Given sequences x and y,

- x$\circ$y is the concatenation of x and y. So [a]$\circ$[b,c] equals [a,b,c], as does [a,b]$\circ$[c] and [a,b,c]$\circ$[].
- x prefixOf y: true iff x is a prefix of y.
- x suffixOf y: true iff x is a suffix of y.
- x subsequenceOf y: true iff x is a subsequence of y.
- x substringOf y: true iff x is a substring (i.e., contiguous subsequence) of y.

The construct mergeOf(S), where S is a set or bag of sequences, is the set of all merges of the sequences in S.

The integer type, int, also denotes the sequence of increasing integers, i.e., [$\cdots$, -2, -1, 0, +1, +2, $\cdots$].

Sorted sequences and inserts A sequence x is **sorted** if its entries are comparable by "<" and are in non-decreasing order. Given a sorted sequence x, the construct x.insertSorted(p) inserts p in x so that x remains sorted.

A.9   Maps

The type Map denotes maps. A map is a set of two-tuples where the first element is a key and the second is a value, the keys are distinct, and map entries can be indexed by the key. The type Map<U,V> denotes maps with keys from U and values from V. For a map x:

- x.size is the number of entries in the map.
- x.keys is the bag of its keys, i.e., bag(y[0]: y in x).
- x.vals is the bag of its values, i.e., bag(y[1]: y in x).
- x[j], for j in x.keys, refers to the value associated with j, i.e., x has the tuple [j,x[j]].
- x.add(j,v) removes any tuple with key j and adds the tuple [j,v] to x.
- x[j] ← v: same as x.add(j,v).
- x.remove(j) removes the tuple with key j; it has no effect if j is not in x.keys.

The construct $map(e_1, \cdots, e_n: x \text{ in } Z; P)$ is analogous to $set(e_1, \cdots, e_n: x \text{ in } Z; P)$ except that each expression e_i must return a two-tuple. For example,

- map() is the empty map.
- map([2,100], [3,200]) is the map with entries [2,100] and [3,200].
- map([2*i,10*i]: i in 0..4; mod(i,2) = 0) equals map([0,0], [4,20], [8,40]).

A.10   Channels

For a connection-less channel with an address j and a message msg, the predicate "msg receivable at j" is true iff the channel in its current state can deliver the message at j. Formally (below k ranges over addresses of the channel),

(msg receivable at j)

$$= \begin{cases} \text{forsome}(k: \text{rxh}[[k,j]] \circ [msg]) \text{ prefixOf txh}[[k,j]] & \text{if fifo channel} \\ \text{forsome}(k: \text{rxh}[[k,j]] \circ [msg]) \text{ subsequenceOf txh}[[k,j]] & \text{if lossy channel} \\ (msg \text{ in txh}[j]) & \text{if LRD channel} \end{cases}$$

If address j is fixed by the context, "msg receivable at j" is shortened to "msg receivable".

Let chan be an instantiation of service FifoChannel, let j and k be addresses of chan, and let msg be a message. Then the following constructs are available.

- chan.transit(j,k): sequence of messages in transit in chan from j to k.
  = [chan.txh[[j,k]][i]: i in chan.txh[[j,k]].keys, i ≥ chan.rxh[[j,k]].size]
- chan.numTransit(msg,j,k): number of msg instances in transit in chan from j to k.
  = num(i: i in chan.transit(j,k).keys, chan.transit(j,k)[i] = msg)

- chan.numTransit(msg): number of msg instances in transit in chan (between any two addresses).
    = sum(numTransit(msg,j,k): [j,k])

A.11 Graphs

A directed graph, or a digraph, G is a two-tuple, where the first entry is a set of nodes and the second entry is a bag of directed edges on the nodes, with each edge being a two-tuple of nodes. Because the edges are specified by a *bag*, there can be one or more edges from a node to itself or to another node (so our digraphs are multi-graphs). The digraph [set(1,2,3,4), bag([1,1], [1,2], [1,2], [2,4], [4,2], [4,1])] is illustrated below.

Let G be a digraph. A directed (undirected) path in G is a sequence of (at least two) nodes such that for every two successive nodes u and v in the sequence, [u,v] is an edge ([u,v] or [v,u] is an edge). A directed (undirected) cycle is a directed (undirected) path whose starting and ending nodes are the same.

An out-tree is a digraph that has no undirected cycles and has a node u that has a directed path to every other node. Node u is referred to as the root node of the out-tree.

An in-tree is a digraph that has no undirected cycles and has a node u such that there is a directed path from every other node to u. Node u is referred to as the root node of the out-tree.

The following constructs are available for a digraph G. Note that some of them can be used with more than one kind of parameter, e.g., dPath(p,G) and dPath(u,v,G). All the constructs can be formally defined, and this is illustrated for some of them.

- diGraph(G): true iff G is a digraph.
    = Tuple<.,.>(G) and Set(G[0]) and Tuple<G[0],G[0]>(G[1])
- dPath(p,G): true iff p is a directed path in digraph G.
    = Seq<G[0]>(p) and p.size ≥ 2
        and forall(i in [0..p.size-2]: [p[i],p[i+1]] in G[1])
- dPath(u,v,G): true iff there is a directed path from node u to node v in digraph G.
    = forsome(Seq<G[0]>(p):
            p.size ≥ 2 and p[0] = u and p.last = v and dPath(p,G))
- dCycle(G): true iff there is a directed cycle in digraph G
    = forsome(Seq<G[0]>(p):
            p.size ≥ 2 and p[0] = p.last and dPath(p,G))

- uPath(p,G): true iff p is a undirected path in digraph G.
  = Seq<G[0]>(p) and p.size ≥ 2
      and forall(i in [0..p.size-2]:
                      ([p[i],p[i+1]] in G[1]) or ([p[i+1],p[i]] in G[1]))
- uPath(u,v,G): true iff there is an undirected path from node u to node v in digraph G.
- uCycle(G): true iff there is an undirected cycle in digraph G
- outTree(G): true iff digraph G is an out-tree.
  = diGraph(G) and not isUCycle(G)
      and forsome(u in G[0]: forall(v in G[0] \ set(u): isDPath(u,v,G)))
- inTree(G): true iff digraph G is an in-tree.
- root(G): the root of out-tree G.
  = [u: u in G[0], diGraph(G), not isUCycle(G),
          and forall(v in G[0] \ set(u): isDPath(u,v,G))][0]
- root(G): the root of in-tree G.

A.12 Miscellaneous

Assignment is denoted by "←" and equality by "=".

The construct mod(j,N) stands for j modulo-N, i.e., the non-negative remainder of j divided by N.

The construct num(...) stands for bag(...).size.

The construct sum(...) takes a bag of numbers as its argument and returns their sum.

Below, each construct takes a list of scalars, sets, sequences and/or maps as its argument. The term "bagified argument" refers to the bag of all the scalars, set entries, sequence entries, and map values in the argument.

- distinct(...): true iff the bagified argument has no duplicate entries.
- nonNull(...): true iff the bagified argument has no null entries, i.e., any pointers in it are non-null.
- notAlive(...): true iff the bagified argument has no alive sid or tid entries, i.e., z.alive is false for every sid or tid entry z.
- distinctNonNull(...): conjunction of distinct(...) and nonNull(...).
- distinctNonNullNotAlive(...): conjunction of distinct(...), nonNull(...) and notAlive(...).

Given an atomic step e and predicates P and Q:

- "e unconditionally establishes Q from P": Means Q holds after an execution of e assuming *only* that P and any input assumption of e hold prior to the execution.
- "e unconditionally establishes Q": Same as "e unconditionally establishes Q from true".
- "e unconditionally preserves P": Same as "e unconditionally establishes P from P".

Index